D1573179

modern
world architecture

THIS IS A CARLTON BOOK

Design copyright © 2006, 2011
   Carlton Books Limited

Text copyright © 1998, 2006, 2011
   Jonathan Glancey

Published in 2011 by
Carlton Books Limited
20 Mortimer Street
London
W1T 3JW

A catalogue record for this book is
available from the British Library.

ISBN: 978 1 84732 729 1

Executive Editors: Sarah Larter,
   Stella Caldwell and Alice Payne
Project Art Direction: Zoë Maggs
   and Zoë Dissell
Jacket Design: Alison Tutton
Designers: Simon Mercer,
   Andrew Grove and James Pople
Picture Research: Alex Pepper,
   Steve Behan and Ben White
Production: Janette Burgin

Printed and bound in China

CARLTON
BOOKS

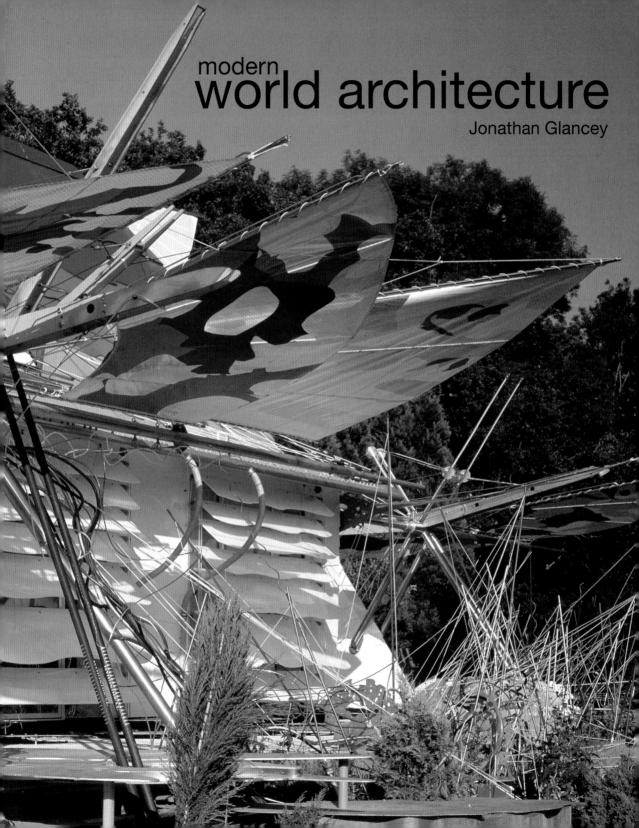

modern
world architecture

Jonathan Glancey

CONTENTS

FOREWORD

STEIN HOUSE, p.289
SETH STEIN, 1995

This is a vast subject and no book can realistically cover the entire history of twentieth and twenty-first century architecture. If it could, it would either be too heavy to carry or else be set in such tiny type that it would be unreadable. This book is meant as an introduction or guide to the riches and sheer diversity of buildings from 1900 onwards, a period that has witnessed mind-boggling change and has seen human society rise to peaks of civilization and troughs of savagery and destruction. Human life at the beginnings of the twenty-first century is still very much a fight for living space, a space that architects shape and frame. Many of the best architects of the past century have been practical dreamers who have tried to push their art and society to new and civilized heights. They have set their compasses and T-squares (computers, too) on the face of the world and tried to create beautiful buildings in perfect towns and cities. People, however, are never as perfect as they are in architectural drawings and, all too often, the architect's dream has been diffused or shattered by irrational human behaviour. War has been the one great destroyer. Greed, narrow-mindedness and the architect's own inability to communicate ambitious ideas have been others. In fact, architects – Le Corbusier first among them – have been accused of trying to destroy civilization with designs for towers of concrete and steel and ambitions that have witnessed the unprecedented demolition of historic buildings, streets and squares. This is unfair, although the architect has, on the whole, been a willing collaborator of governments, property developers and the moving spirit of the times. Architects, as Philip Johnson, a very clever US architect said, "are whores": as members of one of the world's oldest professions, they get paid for doing what other people want. And that means the design of banal office blocks and brainless shopping malls as well as beautiful private houses and churches that have the power to reduce the noisiest citizen to silence.

Perhaps the problem for modern architects is that their talent has been spread thinly. They have been asked to design an ever increasing number and range of buildings across the world on an ever decreasing share of national and global income. Up until the Industrial Revolution, buildings were one of the greatest expenses most societies faced. They were expensive partly because they took a long time to build and required a great deal of skilled manual labour to do so and partly because they were the most visible means society had of expressing its confidence, power and culture. As the twentieth century drew on, there were so many other things for society to spend its money on: sophisticated weaponry, health, education, clothes, food, cars, holidays. Society might have wanted more buildings than it had in the past – and especially housing – and it certainly wanted a far greater range of buildings too – swimming pools, superstores, motorway service stations, airports, bowling alleys, corporate headquarters – but it wanted much more for much less.

Increasingly sophisticated technology and new materials enabled modern societies to build with ever increasing speed. The results could be dire, and the architect was, plinth by cornice, reduced to the role of decorating highly-serviced boxes that might be office blocks, apartment blocks, factories or out-of-town shopping malls. During the twentieth century, a century that saw the rise (and fall) of more buildings than ever before, the role of the architect was inexorably marginalized. Architects themselves do not see, or do not like to see, the world this way. And yet, increasingly, their role has been limited and powers curtailed. Again, this has been all but inevitable in a world in which the speed, scale and complexity of so much building construction means that the architect is simply a part of a team led increasingly by engineers and contractors. To preserve their role, architects have had to become "imagineers", shaping and guiding the look of buildings and the way they relate to their settings.

This is a quantum leap from the architect's role at the beginning of the twentieth century. Yet the writing was already on the wall. The new century required a new type of building, highly serviced machines for making and processing money, sophisticated junction boxes that were a world away from churches and country houses. The sharpest architectural minds could see what was happening, and struggled to interpret and express a new machine age in buildings that were intended to break with the past, but never could. For architecture is an art that seems never to have escaped its roots. Perhaps this is because in the cultures of East, West, North and South, the earliest architecture was also some of the very best. Over the last hundred years, as this book shows, Western architects have harked back to ancient Greece where architecture reached a state of near perfection in the fifth century BC. The Parthenon, even in its ruined state (blown apart accidentally by Turkish gunpowder stored there in the seventeenth century) stands as judge of all the architecture that has been built in the cast of its long shadow.

Again, this should not be surprising: architects try in their different ways to create order and would-be perfection from an imperfect world. Each new building by a good architect is a fresh attempt to create a model of perfection. A truly great architect, as you can see in these pages, can get close, but none has ever bettered the Parthenon. In one sense, it is also impossible to do so in an age that demands so much from its buildings and expects them to be machines for performing specific functions rather than as icons that express the core values, worth, technology and ideals of a society. The Parthenon did all these things. In those sun-bleached, pollutant-etched stones, the patient observer can read the story of Athenian society.

Twentieth and twenty-first century societies, for the most part, have been more complex (if not better) than that of fifth-century Athens and no single building is able to tell such a comprehensive

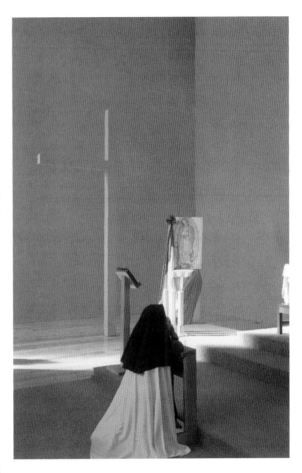

CAPUCHINAS CHAPEL, p.216
LUIS BARRAGÁN, 1955

NEUE STAATSGALERIE, p.331
STIRLING–WILFORD, 1995

tale as the Parthenon does. Our architecture is kaleidoscopic, its message fragmented and inconclusive. From the end of World War One to perhaps as late as the early 1970s, there was some sort of collective attempt by architects to create a new and comprehensive order: the Modern Movement. This cannot be readily defined, but, without doubt, there did appear to be a more or less collective desire among architects around the world to invent a language of design that the equivalent of Latin was in medieval Europe or English is today. If there really was such a thing as the Modern Movement, it was doomed to failure. Architecture moves with society (although architects like to believe that it is the other way around) and social change ensured that there could be no one style of architecture that would ever be capable of freeze-framing the world.

To help make sense of the many moods and styles of architecture that have emerged over the past hundred years, I have divided the buildings illustrated in this book into broad sections. These are not meant to be a perfect fit, but rather compounds in which buildings that would probably get on with each other pretty well if they could meet are herded. It is probably true to say that in the twentieth century, architectural ideas were exported and imported with great speed and so you will find many visual cross-references from one style of building to another. All art, said Picasso, is copying and architects, with rare exceptions, have learned from one another and quoted from one another in their designs with pride as well as abandon. In fact, in architecture it is a sign of great sophistication to ensure that your peer group knows that you are making knowing references to past masters. Masters rather than mistresses, of course, for nearly every building shown in this book was designed and built by men.

Because this is an introduction to modern architecture and because it can only be so big, this book relies almost entirely on photographs of buildings to represent them. To fully understand a building, it is necessary to get behind its façade and to study the way it is built up from a plan. Modern Movement architects saw the plan as a kind of moral as well as practical and aesthetic guideline. A building must be raised up from an "honest" (ie. functional) plan and its final shape should reveal the workings of that plan. In fact even the greatest Modernists cheated – thank goodness – and very many buildings shown in the following pages are not nearly as rational as their designers claimed them to be. Architecture is as much about emotion as function. Even so, it would have been nice to have had the space to show plans and other drawings. In the event, it is probably better to look at the buildings, to long to see them and to find out more about them. There are thousands of books on various aspects of modern architects and architecture that will explain in detail most of the buildings shown here . And many monographs devoted to single designs. What I think this book can offer you is the big picture and the chance to make some sort of sense of an immense and inexhaustable story. If it makes you want to find out more, then it has done its job. If it encourages you to want to be an architect, good luck.

I have visited very many of the buildings shown in the book and have included a number of those I find beautiful, moving or fascinating that have been excluded from previous "pantechnicons" of this kind. There are, however, many buildings that no writer would dare or dream of excluding. Why? Because there are buildings that define a moment, generate a mood, first make use of a new technology that cannot be ignored, not only because they are fascinating in themselves but because they were so influential.

You will find prejudices in the writing. I think this is fair. How can anyone look at every building they meet objectively? I really do not have the stomach for most of the buildings listed in the section labelled "Less is a Bore". I find what passed for Postmodernism in architecture, with honourable exceptions, ugly and crass. I do not think that architecture is a particularly funny subject and jokes writ on the scale of a building are embarrassing and even pitiful some years down the line. Buildings, except where land is very scarce and property values exceptionally high as in Tokyo or Hong Kong, tend to have long lives. There are very few jokes from the nineteenth century that we still find funny. But the Parthenon, Le Corbusier's chapel at Ronchamp and the Farnsworth House by Mies van der Rohe remain things of great and ineffable beauty. They are not remotely funny.

I hope the book, and especially because we have tried to source really good photographs, will also help you see that a beautiful building might well be made from tough modern materials that most people associate with ugliness and even inhumanity. Look again and then go and see how a genius like Le Corbusier or Louis Kahn uses concrete, or of how the play of sunlight on steel beams or weather-boarded concrete transforms what you had imagined to be a brute of a building into an unexpected beauty. As you turn through these pages and begin to visit some of these buildings, I hope you will feel some of the same excitement I felt as a teenager as I began to discover the architecture of my own century after childhood years spent heaving open the doors of old parish churches and padding the corridors of crumbling country houses. If I was ill or when I was sneaking off "games", I would lie on the floor and pore through old picture books on architecture dreaming of what the buildings were really like and wondering who designed them. This is a rainy day book although unfamiliar architecture is generally best experienced when the sun is shining.

It has been fun to put together – faster than any building – and I just hope it makes you want to discover more: the architectural interpretation of history is, after all, as valid as any other.

Jonathan Glancey

PARC DE LA VILLETTE, p.341
BERNARD TSCHUMI, 1989

ARTS AND CRAFTS

THE SEARCH FOR EARTHLY PARADISE

The Industrial Revolution was a brutalizing experience. For anyone with half a conscience there was something very wrong with the manner in which the wretched of the earth poured into towns and cities looking for work and with the ways they were subsequently treated. For anyone with an eye, the brutal new architecture, if it could be called that, the intrusion of railways, of steam and smoke and choking smogs was nothing but horror piled upon horror. For high-minded aesthetes there was something rotten in the way that the new machine age could mass-produce goods and architectural details and undermine the work of the skilled craftsmen whose ancestors had once given shape and breathed life into great cathedrals, market crosses and cloth halls.

The Industrial Revolution also meant that ideas could be transported rapidly by train from county to county and country to country so that vernacular traditions were increasingly in danger of being elbowed out from their ancient homes. Artists, writers and architects began, bit by bit, to revolt against these perceived horrors and excesses. John Ruskin (1819–1900), the Brotherhood of the Pre-Raphaelites, and William Morris (1834–96) were key figures in the rise of what was to become the Arts and Crafts movement. It began in England and spread its gospel far and wide in the early part of the twentieth century. Its traditions took firm root in Britain and, throughout the radical investigations of the Modern Movement, to which it offered its creed of honest construction and functional plans, and the game-playing of the Postmodern era, the spirit of Ruskin and Morris continued to haunt new architecture, from schools to county halls.

The Arts and Crafts movement was both an aesthetic and a moral crusade. It was part and parcel of a peculiarly English sentiment in which a primitive form of socialism, nostalgia for a medieval world of knights in shining armour and damsels in distress, fear of new technology, love of hand-made objects and a sense of decency and fair play combined to create a recognizable yet informal style of architecture that acted as a rustic stick with which to beat formal artistic decadence.

At first it was more a form of escape from the industrial world than a challenge to it. Followers of Morris founded what they hoped would be idyllic rural communities of fellow craft workers and architects. A younger generation, however, such as the fine young architects of the London County Council (created in 1889) took Arts and Crafts ideals into the heart of the city and used them as a basis for improving the lot of those who delved and span for a pittance and lived in squalor. The Boundary Estate in London's Shoreditch (p.14) remains a model of civilized urban housing inspired by Arts and Crafts principles.

Elsewhere in Europe, Arts and Crafts ideas were blended with those of Art Nouveau (or Jugendstijl) with high art colluding with the highest standards of craftsmanship. As well as an idea and a set of ideals, the movement was also, in the hands of many architects, simply another style and one well suited for a new wave of country houses for the newly rich who wished to escape the grubby roots of their wealth by living in romantic "honest" splendour.

The freedom that the Arts and Crafts movement offered architects ensured rich and varied buildings. What they have most in common is their free and "honest" plans and superb standards of construction. At best they are thoughtful and life-enhancing buildings; at worst, they seem gratuitous and ride headlong into the buffers of kitsch.

THE ORCHARD

C. F. A. VOYSEY, 1900 CHORLEYWOOD, HERTFORDSHIRE, ENGLAND

Charles Francis Annesley Voysey (1857–1941) was the tiny, bird-like son of a Yorkshire parson who was expelled from the Church of England for denying the existence of Hell. As an architect, Voysey worked tirelessly from 1882 in his own idiosyncratic idiom trying, perhaps, to create a vision of earthly paradise influenced by the socialist Arts and Crafts thinker and designer William Morris and the fiery Gothic Revivalist A. W. N. Pugin.

Voysey's paradise was to be as clean as a new pin: aside from furniture and wallpapers, he designed his own bright blue suits without cuffs or lapels as these gathered unacceptable dust. He lived in a house of his own design, The Orchard, the finest of a group of suburban houses on the northwest fringe of London. Although The Orchard, like

many Voysey designs, appears superficially to draw on a mythical Olde-English past, its interior is free-flowing and if not Modern, as has been claimed by Modern Movement apologists, it has a freedom of plan and clarity of design that made it quietly revolutionary. The house's features – doors, window ledges – are scaled down to Voysey's own miniature scale.

Although The Orchard was to influence the look of England's cosy (and cloying) suburban homes over the next 100 years, it remains at heart – and there are heart motifs to be found throughout its loving detailing – the expression of an architect who wished to create a quiet and ordered domestic heaven on earth under steep roofs and within immaculate white walls.

HÔTEL TASSEL

VICTOR HORTA, 1900 BRUSSELS, BELGIUM

Victor Horta (1861–1947)
studied at the Académie des
Beaux-Arts in Brussels after
which he began working with
Alphonse Balat, a reputable
Neoclassical architect. Horta,
however, was much taken with
the writings of Viollet-le-Duc,
the French Gothic revivalist
who made great play with the
latest industrial materials. The
result, when Horta set up on his
own, was an exotic flowering
of extraordinary houses that
manage to combine Baroque
and Classical elements with
free-flowing plans, serpentine
ironwork, tapestries of richly
coloured glass and sensuality
with common sense. Fitted out
in lavish detail by the architect,
Hôtel Tassel is probably the
most mature of the many
houses Horta designed and the
one that most fully expresses
the ideals of Art Nouveau.
The revolutionary aspect of
this house, however, lies less
in its gorgeous decorated
structure and more in its plan
and section: these allow rooms
to be reached at different
levels, in some ways heralding
the free use of interior space
made by Modern Movement
architects after World War One.
Yet, what the visitor really feels
here is a sense of being inside
a three-dimensional illustration
by Walter Crane or Aubrey
Beardsley.

Horta went on to become
a professor at the Académie
des Beaux-Arts. He later
abandoned curves and
decorative sensation for the
rigours of straight lines and
plain concrete construction.

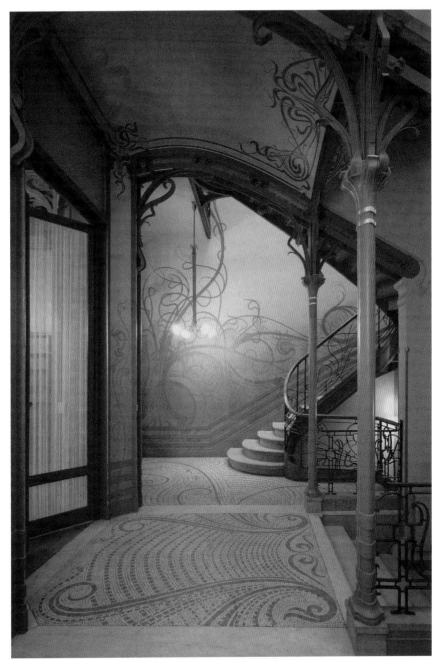

BOUNDARY STREET ESTATE

LONDON COUNTY COUNCIL ARCHITECT'S DEPARTMENT, 1900 SHOREDITCH, LONDON, ENGLAND

Under the direction of Owen Fleming, the young architects of the London County Council's (LCC) Housing of the Working Class Branch (set up in 1893) designed this, the first and best of several major slum clearance housing projects. Fired by the theories of John Ruskin, William Morris and Karl Marx, the LCC architects created what might truly be called "palaces for the people", bringing art into the life of the artless and downtrodden. More than 5,500 people were housed in the magnificent red and yellow brick Arts and Crafts blocks that form the Boundary Estate. These radiate from Arnold Circus in which an elevated central garden boasts a once fashionable bandstand that lends a festive air to what had long been – and remains in many ways – a grim, down-at-heel quarter of east London.

Many of the details are clearly derived from older masters of the Arts and Crafts movement, and it is easy to spot the guiding hands of Norman Shaw and, more particularly, of Philip Webb, who built a much-copied house for William Morris in Bexley Heath in south London in 1859. Social housing in Britain and continental Europe was rarely to rise to this noble and popular standard again. In the 1990s, the Estate was renovated. It remains a testimony to intelligent city government administration, proving that mass housing can fit elegantly and seamlessly into city centres.

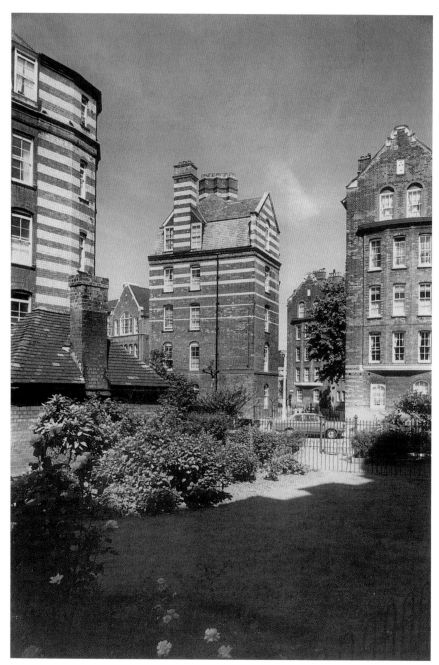

DEANERY GARDEN

EDWIN LUTYENS, 1901 SONNING, BERKSHIRE, ENGLAND

Sir Edwin Landseer Lutyens (1869–1944) was one of the greatest architects of his generation. Described by his biographer, Christopher Hussey, as "a perfect architectural sonnet", Deanery Garden is the best known of his early English country houses.

The house was radical in its use of space, yet its appearance was a clever contrivance of old English materials and formulas: timber, great windows laced with mullions and transoms and beautifully made, handsomely laid bricks. The house was built for Edward Hudson, the proprietor of *Country Life* magazine and Lutyens' champion. An Edwardian countryside "bachelor pad", it was within easy reach of London via the Great Western Railway. The

garden, landscaped by Lutyens and Gertrude Jekyll, is all of a piece with the house as was, when this masterpiece was photographed for a 1903 edition of *Country Life*, the oak furniture and simple decor. The conceit of the house was to create an idyllic domestic setting for the quintessential Edwardian gentleman, a man of great restraint, understated elegance and with a deep attachment to a very English take on history.

The house has worn well over the century, demonstrating the advantage of Lutyens' training in builders' yards: like many of the century's greats, he was not a qualified architect. He built with intuition and love, virtues that can be felt in the construction of this impeccable, inventive English house.

ALL SAINTS' CHURCH

W. R. LETHABY, 1902 BROCKHAMPTON, HEREFORDSHIRE, ENGLAND

William Lethaby (1857–1931) is best known, perhaps, as a teacher and theorist. He was the first director of the Central School of Arts and Crafts, London, which was, in many ways, the precursor of the Bauhaus. Lethaby also designed some striking and curious buildings, attempts to bring together Arts and Crafts sensibilities with the use of modern materials.

The church Lethaby built in a backwater of rural Herefordshire is a fascinating attempt to marry ancient and modern technologies and styles. At first glance, All Saints' Church appears to be truly ancient, rooted close to the ground, its muscular stone walls protected by a roof of straw. Inside, it gives up the pretence and we know we

have entered not just a very English parish church, but the twentieth century. The roof is made, quite unashamedly, of concrete and its structure is determinedly like no medieval or Victorian Gothic Revival design. Idiosyncratic window details add to the sense of the strangely new and different.

All Saints' Church is not simply a curiosity – and beautiful, too, in its odd way – but an expression of the tug and tussle so many British architects had, and were to have, with the possibilities and expression of new materials and technologies and with the idea of what exactly constituted the "vernacular" in building design throughout the twentieth century.

STOCK EXCHANGE

H. P. BERLAGE, 1903 AMSTERDAM, THE NETHERLANDS

Massive, Romanesque in spirit, a modern castle in a city centre, the new Stock Exchange was the greatest work of Hendrik Petrus Berlage (1856–1934). The building's great unbroken brick walls and semi-circular arches recall the work of the Dutch architect's American contemporaries, H. H. Richardson and Frank Lloyd Wright, whose buildings he had known of, yet not seen until a visit to the United States in 1911. Berlage considered himself to be a highly "moral" architect, which appears to imply that the construction of a building should be clearly exposed; so much so that the rooms of the severe houses he designed, such as the Henny House, The Hague (1898), were not allowed plaster over

the brickwork. And, as for wallpaper ...

Berlage was reacting against the eclectic free-style architecture of the last two decades of the nineteenth century. In doing so, he helped pave the way for a school or feel for architecture that was to have considerable influence on such later Dutch masters as Willem Marinus Dudok (p.180), who brought together a passion for crafted brickwork and rigorous, Modern elevations.

The Stock Exchange, situated on Amsterdam's busy Damrak, continues to dominate this part of the city and has been beautifully maintained. Its solid, if not entirely austere, exterior conceals a procession of remodelled exhibition halls within.

HILL HOUSE

CHARLES RENNIE MACKINTOSH, 1903 HELENSBURGH, SCOTLAND

Hill House is the largest and most ambitious of five poetic homes Charles Rennie Mackintosh (1868–1928) designed in and around Glasgow. It was commissioned by the publisher W. W. Blackie and caught the imagination of European observers even though his English contemporaries thought his designs decadent. Mackintosh's furniture designs, shown at the Arts and Crafts Exhibition of 1896 in London were widely criticized for their poor construction and the Scot was never invited to show again. Oddly enough, having designed some of the most beautiful of all British buildings – all in Scotland – Mackintosh left Glasgow for London in 1913 and took up painting full-time instead.

Hill House is a modern interpretation of an old Scottish tower house, its austere walls covered, like them, in harl (roughcast), and yet inside itis all whiteness, delicacy and light. So exquisite is the wilfully artistic interior that the contemporary German writer, Herman Muthesius, author of the hugely influential *Das Englische Haus*, 1904, thought it "refined to such a degree which the lives of even the artistically educated are still a long way from matching ... Even a book in an unsuitable binding would disturb the atmosphere simply by lying on the table." In 1982 the house was taken into care by the National Trust for Scotland.

HOME PLACE

E. S. PRIOR, 1905 HOLT, NORFOLK, ENGLAND

"Perhaps there is something in the Norfolk air", wrote the historian Gavin Stamp in *The English House*, 1986, "which accounts for this strange architecture." Home Place is a glorious, wilful Arts and Crafts house designed for the Reverend Percy R. Lloyd by Edward Schroeder Prior (1852–1932).

In essence the house consists of a central range flanked by a pair of "butterfly" wings that flap off at angles of 60 degrees. These are wildly designed with all manner of picturesque detail and, as the architect Roderick Gradidge has observed, Home Place looks "as if it is covered with a very old Fairisle pullover that has been knitted by an imbecile child. Quaintness can be carried no further."

This rather eccentric product of stupendously wealthy Edwardian England became a convalescent home in the 1930s. It still is, although whether the architecture is restful is debatable. Prior designed some of the most extreme Arts and Crafts buildings in Britain, exaggerating the use of "found" and local materials. He liked, as one of his colleagues said, "to be in a minority of one". He built for the rich, he was an Old Harrovian and a Cambridge graduate, and was pretty much able to do what he wanted. His parish church at Roker in Sunderland (1907), however, was a model of restraint and one of the finest ecclesiastical buildings of its time.

POST OFFICE SAVINGS BANK

OTTO WAGNER, 1906 VIENNA, AUSTRIA

This is Otto Wagner's (1841–1918) most famous and brilliant building. The monumental main façade conceals an ingenious banking hall at the heart of the trapezoidal-shaped block. This features a glass floor, bringing daylight into the basement, and an extensively glazed arched roof. This in turn is protected by a glass roof at the top of the bank's six-storey lightwell. The whiteness and brightness of this space, together with its brilliant use of glass, means that it has never seemed anything other than up to date at any moment in the twentieth century. In Wagner's competition entry for the building, the roof of the banking hall was to have been even more radical: a canopy of glass suspended on cables held by steel masts. Such detailing might have been common in the 1980s, but was almost unheard of outside the world of structural engineering in 1904 when the building was commissioned.

The face the bank presents to central Vienna is no less daring: the anchorage points of the marble panels that form the main façade are not only exposed, but the chunky aluminium heads of their rivets are polished. These proudly ostentatious rivets take the place of conventional historic decoration. This highly distinctive form of construction was to be much copied by architects, notably in Japan, much later in the century.

SCOTLAND STREET SCHOOL

CHARLES RENNIE MACKINTOSH, 1906 EDINBURGH, SCOTLAND

Not all Mackintosh's buildings were as delicate and self-consciously "artistic" as Hill House (p.18). Scotland Street School is a substantial building that has stood the test of time. Its plan is very simple: two floors of classrooms divided by a central corridor behind massive stone walls. What is special here is the use of light. Not only are the castle-like windows vast, but daylight also floods into the school through the twin entrance and stair towers. The building points to a style of civic and commercial architecture that could well have been developed into a convincing alternative to the slipshod architecture that, under the misleading banner "Modern", was to pockmark so many British city centres in the course of the century.

Mackintosh was, in his lifetime, much more appreciated in Europe. He exhibited designs for furniture and buildings at Munich in 1898 and the annual exhibition of the Secession in Vienna in 1900. Mackintosh's design for an "Art Lover's House" was entered in a 1901 competition organized by the German magazine *Zeitschrift für Innerndekoration*. It was built, strangely enlarged as if the designs had been placed under a magnifying glass, in Glasgow in the 1990s. Mackintosh lived out his last years painting sublime watercolours of the landscape at Port-Vendres in the south of France, a long way in every sense from the rigours of Scotland Street School and Glasgow.

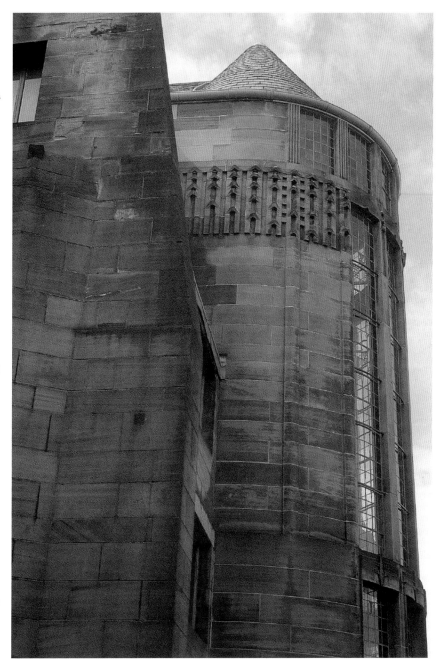

HAMPSTEAD GARDEN SUBURB

RAYMOND UNWIN, ET AL, 1907 LONDON, ENGLAND

The first garden suburb, Hampstead embodied the Garden City concept devised by the planner Ebeneezer Howard in the 1890s and put into practice by Raymond Unwin (1863–1940) at Letchworth (p.426).

Unwin was a Fabian socialist, which meant he looked to change society through steady reform rather than radical upheavals. Where and how people lived played a key part in this school of socialist thinking, much of which was rooted in the work of William Morris, father figure of the Arts and Crafts movement. The Arts and Crafts influence showed clearly not just in the architecture of Hampstead Garden Suburb but also in the way of life it was designed to engender: arty-crafty. The suburb was designed around a central square, influenced by

Lutyens who designed the three highly distinctive buildings that define the spirit of this leafy city annexe: St Jude's Church with its massive roofs and striking spire; the Free Church – an essay in Lutyens's "Wrenaissance" Baroque; and the Institute, the focal point of life in the new suburb. Around the square Lutyens and others filled in Unwin's plan with large Queen Anne and Neo-Georgian houses. Beyond this grand statement of intent, Unwin's plan unrolls in a sequence of avenues, never less than 12 metres (40 ft) wide that roll with the contours of the land and are lined with smaller Neo-Georgian and Voysey-inspired houses. The effect is neat and green, but more than 90 years on, the suburb still feels remote from the rest of the world; but perhaps that was the idea.

TEMPERE CATHEDRAL

LARS SONCK, 1907 TEMPERE, FINLAND

This apparently rough hewn romantic pile represented a significant moment in the history of Finnish architecture. It was at once an expression of the National Romantic movement in Finnish art and culture and at the same time a reaching out from what might have become a culturally isolated era to the world for inspiration. National Romanticism was a reaction, to a large extent, to Finland's fear of being swallowed by Russian imperialism in the late nineteenth century. Artists, musicians and architects sought inspiration in the Karelian heartland of old Finland and a spate of new wooden churches and houses were built in a Karelian revivalist style. Tempere Cathedral sprang from this movement and yet Lars Sonck (1870–1956) was also clearly influenced by the Neo-Romanesque designs of the Chicago architect, H. H. Richardson. The same influence can be seen at work in Sonck's Telephone Company building in Helsinki (1905), although he was also clearly influenced by the English Arts and Crafts movement; this shows in his Eira hospital in Helsinki (1905).

At the time of the building of Tempere Cathedral, Sonck was generally considered to be Finland's leading architect. Like many buildings that were influenced by Arts and Crafts thinking, a busy, picturesque exterior conceals a rational plan.

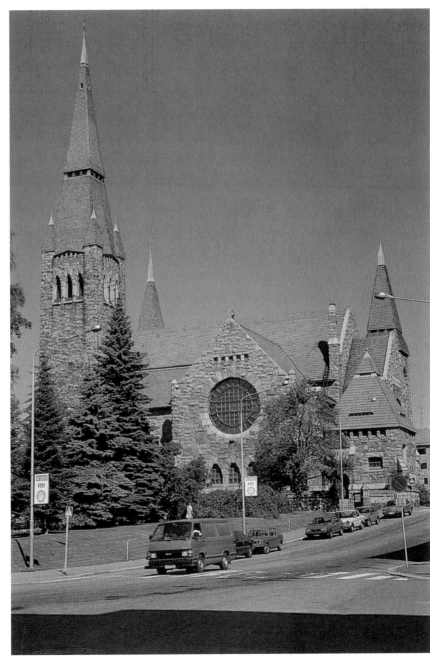

ST LEOPOLD'S CHURCH

OTTO WAGNER, 1907 STEINHOF, VIENNA, AUSTRIA

Stripped, in the mind's eye, of its pregnant dome and exquisite and haunting decoration – grave, beautiful angels and laurel wreaths outside; gold-leaf, mosaics and byzantine panels inside – the church of St Leopold could be an early twentieth-century railway station or exhibition pavilion. This might be an odd way of looking at one of the most memorable of modern churches, yet Wagner's design is fundamentally a secular building with just enough symbolic detail to give it a sacred air. The earliest Christian churches were developed from Roman basilicas and this handsome church is, perhaps, an update of this ancient theme. That it should have a secular character is not surprising.

From 1894, Wagner was Vienna's City Planner. He had already been commissioned to redevelop the heart of the Austrian Empire and was soon busy with the design not just of grand civic buildings, but also with that of Vienna's Stadtbahn – by 1901 he had supervised the design of 31 stations as well as bridges and viaducts – and the re-routing of the River Danube. Wagner had started designing in a grand Classical manner, but became increasingly radical in his approach. He joined the Vienna Secession group of artists in 1899. His later buildings are characterized by the clarity of their plan and organization and by the gorgeousness of their decoration. The church at Steinhof is no exception.

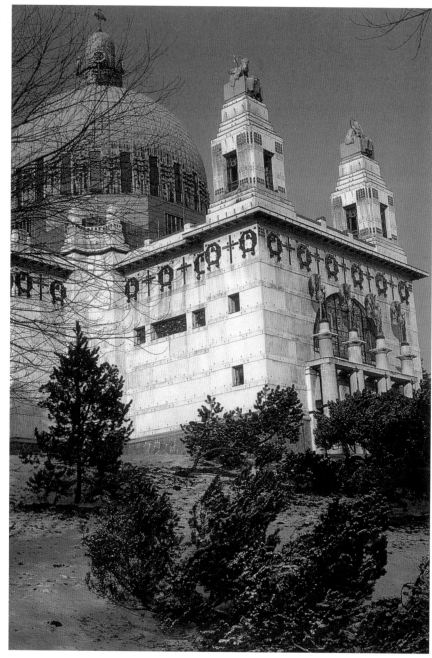

GLASGOW SCHOOL OF ART

CHARLES RENNIE MACKINTOSH, 1909 GLASGOW, SCOTLAND

This is a building in two parts, both by Mackintosh. The first wing, was built between 1897 and 1899. It is the western extension of 1907–9 that brings those who love architecture to Glasgow School of Art. The library wing soars from a steep hillside site, its sheer cliff-like walls interrupted on the west front by windows rising in three dramatic tiers. The trio lighting the library are 8 metres (25 ft) tall. The library is a glorious space, its galleries and ceiling supported by a grid of horizontal beams and rectangular pillars that, seen from certain angles, criss-cross in delightfully complex ways. Glasgow School of Art is Mackintosh's masterpiece. It demonstrates how references to history – there are Scottish castles and hill-houses in the mix – can be translated into a modern architecture that takes on a powerful life of its own. Mackintosh, an original talent, did not know how to copy, nor did he need to.

PALAIS STOCLET

JOSEF HOFFMANN, 1911 BRUSSELS, BELGIUM

Like some lavish ocean liner berthed far from its home port, Palais Stoclet is a Viennese house built in Brussels. The client was Adolphe Stoclet, a banker, and the architect Josef Hoffmann (1870–1956). This late-flowering Art Nouveau jewel comes as a surprise still, its white marble walls edged with bronze long since turned vivid green, in striking contrast to the subdued palette of Brussels. Owing something to Mackintosh and lavishly decorated throughout by, among other artists, Gustav Klimt, Adolphe Stoclet's palace is almost too exquisite to bear.

Hoffmann studied under Otto Wagner (p.20) in Vienna where he was one of the founders, in 1897, of the Secession group of artists. Six years later he founded the Wiener Werkstätte (Vienna Workshop), for which he designed much furniture. His interests in art, design andarchitecture were brought together as a kind of *tour de force* in the Palais Stoclet. Because of its informal plan and pristine whiteness, the house has often been described as being "based on Modern theories"; in fact, rather than looking to the future, it marked the end of an era. Although the European bourgeoisie would continue to demand lavish homes in the 1920s and 1930s, the avant-garde turned to a more rigorous and less overtly opulent style. That was the Modern Movement: Palais Stoclet was *fin de siècle* Vienna in prewar Brussels.

STORER HOUSE

FRANK LLOYD WRIGHT, 1912 LOS ANGELES, CALIFORNIA, USA

Frank Lloyd Wright (1869–1959) was a prolific and inspired architect who, perhaps more than anyone else, introduced the idea of the open-plan house. Away with conventional rooms; in with wide open interior spaces, one linking naturally with the rest. The result, especially in the luxurious houses Wright built in California,are homes that refuse to age and are considerably more modern even at the end of the twentieth century than anything offered for sale by conventional house builders. The Storer House also employed exposed concrete construction, although Wright's use of concrete blocks here is highly decorative and designed to give the building an exotic Mexican flavour. Wright was never slave to one material or style: he was eclectic in terms of form, yet his buildings tended to be inspired by and closely rooted to their surroundings: no matter how inventive, they seem to belong. Wright was one of the century's most influential architects and his concerns – to do with closeness to Nature, the passage of the sun, openness and a sense of freedom – are very much the concerns of many architects as they enter the twenty-first century after two decades of wilful Postmodernism and the wacky free-form design of the late 1990s.

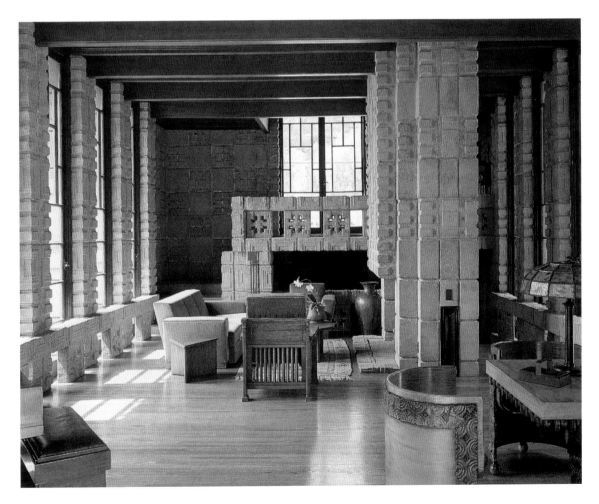

EIGEN HAARD HOUSING

MICHEL DE KLERK, 1921 AMSTERDAM, THE NETHERLANDS

This wonderfully idiosyncratic housing block is known locally as "*Het Scheep*" (The Ship) for the shape of its plan, the prow of which ploughs into the Zanstraat district of Amsterdam and the stern of which is marked by a tall tower or mast. Commissioned by the Eigen Haard ("Own Stove") company, Michel de Klerk (1884–1923) conjured a courtyard block from an apparently random collage of brick elements – towers, turrets, gables – each highly pronounced and demonstrating the art of peerless Dutch brickwork. Although personal in style, the decoration – which follows the principle of Pugin, father of the English Gothic Revival and a major influence on Arts and

Crafts architects – is never gratuitous, instead it enlivens the bold structure of this building.

De Klerk was a leading light of the Amsterdam School, a group of Expressionists whose work occupied an opposite pole to that of the De Stijl movement, with its belief in formal geometry and universal solutions. The "Eigen Haard" housing was beautifully built and, with its steep, tiled roofs and projecting eaves and gables, well proofed against wind and rain. Eigen Haard continues to surprise those who imagine all twentieth-century Dutch architecture to be austere and "rational". It is as pragmatic as it is romantic: a ship worth sailing on.

STOCKHOLM CITY HALL

RAGNAR ÖSTBERG, 1923 STOCKHOLM, SWEDEN

A beautiful building on a beautiful site, Stockholm City Hall shows how a skilled twentieth-century architect could raid history without getting confused on the way back to the drawing board or resorting to pastiche or kitsch. Here, Ragnar Östberg (1866–1945) has added to the romantic, nautical skyline of Stockholm, introducing a new family of copper-capped towers, spires and cupolas. What is intriguing here is the seamless way that östberg brings together a diversity of styles – medieval, Classical and a current National Romanticism – and makes them sit seamlessly and happily together.

The design, which dates from a competition of 1903–4, was to prove widely influential not just in Sweden, but also in Holland, Britain and the United States. Östberg's tower and use of brick can be seen reworked in buildings as diverse as Art Deco factories and metro stations. As an essay in how to learn from history it merits an "alpha" grade. Perhaps because so many architects proved to be unable to reinterpret history convincingly to serve their own times, a clean Modern break seemed, increasingly, to be the logical option. The plan of Stockholm City Hall, behind its highly crafted and thick skin of brick and stone, is essentially Classical in form, order and spirit. Yet, there is no contradiction here: the design feels seamless.

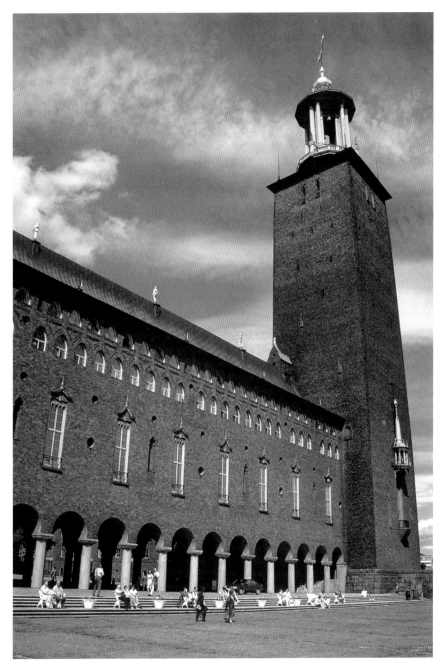

KARL MARX HOF

KARL EHN, 1930 VIENNA, AUSTRIA

A courageous example of socialist housing, Karl Marx Hof is one of the architectural sights of Vienna. Its powerful Expressionist entrance towers are rendered red and suggest the appearance of heroic industrial workers marching, muscular arms linked, through the city centre. This giant estate was designed under the guiding hand of Karl Ehn (1884–1957), the City Architect who, born in Vienna, had trained under Otto Wagner. The Karl Marx Hof was one of a series of large estates designed for the city by Ehn. He was highly influenced by the work of the socialist architects at the London County Council (LCC) who, at the turn of the century, had produced some of the most urbane and humane slum-replacement housing yet seen.

The ideas of the LCC architects were disseminated across Europe. The principal difference between the London and Vienna estates is the sheer sculptural power of the latter. Where the LCC estates were rooted in the ideals and aesthetics of the Arts and Crafts movement, Ehn's blocks, in purely aesthetic terms, owed much to Expressionist ideas. Although some of the flats are rather dim and pokey, they remain a remarkable example of the way in which mass housing can have a formal beauty of its own. Standing in landscaped gardens, the Karl Marx Hof has been remarkably well maintained.

From 1934 onwards Ehn received little work as Austria moved towards unity with Nazi Germany.

GRUNTVIG CHURCH

PETER VILHELM JENSEN-KLINT, 1940 COPENHAGEN, DENMARK

Designed in the guise of a gigantic organ, Gruntvig Church is a phenomenal work, an unlikely brick masterpiece that can be called neither beautiful nor ugly. Instead, the church has a fairy-tale quality and might illustrate the tales of the Brothers Grimm. The vast brick structure stands at the end of a street of Arts and Crafts almshouses in a Copenhagen suburb; here the world is a quiet place, save for music pealing from the church that Peter Vilhelm Jensen-Klint (1853–1930) built.

Jensen trained as an engineer, before becoming a painter and architect in his mid-forties. Construction of Gruntvig Church began in 1913, and took 27 years and a number of fits and stops to complete. In the design of the church, Jensen married a number of his enthusiasms, which at that time were brick architecture of northern Europe, German Expressionism and an exploration of the structural possibilities and limits of brick construction. The church pushes brick technology if not to its limits, then somewhere near them. The Expressionist quality of the building lies in its attempt to represent the notion, sound and force of ecclesiastical music in its outward appearance. The result – a church in the guise of a musical instrument – is unique, memorable and ultimately rather daunting. Jensen-Klint did not live to see his church in all its glory: it was completed by his son ten years after his death.

CLASSICISM

OBEYING ORDERS

Classical architecture is the cradle of Western culture. Other cultures talk of classical traditions too, yet Classicism is a style or approach to architecture most closely associated with ancient Greece and Rome. The greatest of the Greek temples was the Parthenon, which has never been bettered and which has inspired architects for the last 2,500 years. In the twentieth century it was an inspiration for the most radical Modern Movement architects – notably Le Corbusier – as well as those who sought either to look at Classicism anew (Gunnar Asplund, Charles Holden) or else to reproduce the Classical architecture of previous centuries in one form or another (Albert Speer, Ricardo Bofill), but always harking back through the Renaissance and Rome to Greece and the Parthenon.

The Classical architecture of the last hundred years has been rich and varied and has proved, in the right hands, to have adapted well to modern needs. Peter Behren's AEG factory in Berlin (p.34) is a Classical temple as factory; Pennsylvania Station in New York (p.36) is the Baths of Caracalla transformed into a railroad terminus; Les Arcades-du-lac in Paris (p.62) by Ricardo Bofill's Taller de Arquitectura takes the elements of Classical architecture, and transforms them through factory mass-production methods and concrete into mass suburban housing.

At its very best, the Classical tradition has been explored and reinvented by architects of the calibre of Edwin Lutyens and Gunnar Asplund who have shown how the design language of Greece and Rome has been far from dead. At its worst, Classical architecture has been used as a sop to the conceits of stuffed shirts – mostly newly rich business people – who think that a veneer of Classical details on a brick box is their passport to high society and culture. Or, as in the case of Albert Speer and Nazi Germany, it has been employed as a very obvious symbol of political and social order. In Nazi Germany, architecture obeyed the orders of Classicism as the German *volk* obeyed those of its dictatorial government.

It was often argued by proponents of Modernism and by libertarians of various aesthetic persuasions that Classicism was inherently anti-democratic. This was clearly untrue: Classicism was as much the language of Hitler's Germany and Mussolini's Italy as it was of Roosevelt's United States, the London Passenger Transport Board (p.46) and the city of Stockholm (p.45). Perhaps it was the trappings of Classical architecture that upset so many of those who adopted a moral view of architecture in the twentieth century. Not only did columns and pediments seem irrelevant to life in an industrial society, but the "dishonesty" of Classical façades, which hide the workings of a given building and do little to express its workaday purpose, seemed somehow wrong.

The Nazis certainly gave Classicism a bad name, but so did those who, most embarrassingly in Britain, sought to revive the outward form of Classical architecture in the 1980s as a reaction to the perceived excesses of Modernism. The results were pitiful and made a mockery of the attempts by an earlier generation of architects who had attempted to revive the spirit of Greece and Rome and not simply their most obvious forms. Classicism may have fallen into many of the wrong hands in the course of the last century, yet the Stockholm City Library stands as a testament to what it could be in the right hands.

AEG TURBINE FACTORY

PETER BEHRENS, 1909 BERLIN, GERMANY

Peter Behrens (1868–1940) has a special place in the history of twentieth-century architecture and design. Not only did he design the first modern factory – seen here – and train such future talents as Le Corbusier, Walter Gropius and Ludwig Mies van der Rohe, but he was perhaps the first designer to give a major, modern industrial company – AEG, the German General Electric Company – a convincing corporate image.

Behrens began his career as a painter before turning to architecture and industrial design. From 1907 he worked for AEG, turning his hand and eye to the appearance of cookers, radiators, and lamps as well as the company's packaging, catalogues, posters, letterheads, showrooms and shops. In 1909 he completed his first factory for AEG. It was and remains a masterpiece, a temple to modern industrial technology and production. The temple-like appearance of the turbine hall, however, is a cleverly realized and subtly expressed illusion. What looks at first to be rusticated stonework is, in fact, lightweight concrete serving to fill the gaps in the lightweight steel frame behind. The slim joints in the four corner pylons and the fine metal framing of what passes for a Greek tympanum are highlighted in a way that expresses their artificiality. The Turbine Factory was a brilliant attempt to reconcile Classical culture and history with the new reality of industrial commerce and production.

ADMIRALTY ARCH

ASTON WEBB, 1909 TRAFALGAR SQUARE, LONDON, ENGLAND

The sun was still shining over the British Empire when Aston Webb (1849–1930), the most successful and prolific British architect of the time, was commissioned to reface Buckingham Palace in a chaste Classical manner, to re-address The Mall, the one truly grand avenue in London, and to design Admiralty Arch as a gateway to the processional avenue and palace. Admiralty Arch is a handsome enough gateway, yet engagingly English in the way that in any other country it would be a grandiose monument.

Admiralty Arch was originally crowded with offices for use by the Royal Navy, which at the time was the world's most powerful. In 1997, the Navy offered to convert these into temporary accommodation for the many thousands of young people who sleep in the streets of a London stripped of Empire, ambition and the idea of social welfare. Webb was the right man for the original job because he never seemed to mind artistic compromise: he simply built what his clients wanted. And yet, as Admiralty Arch proves, it is perfectly possible to add to the experience of walking through a city while designing what in formal terms is a flawed work of art. Much derided in the past, Admiralty Arch has become a much liked gateway to a vision of Britain that is now more real in tourists' brochures than in the minds of its people.

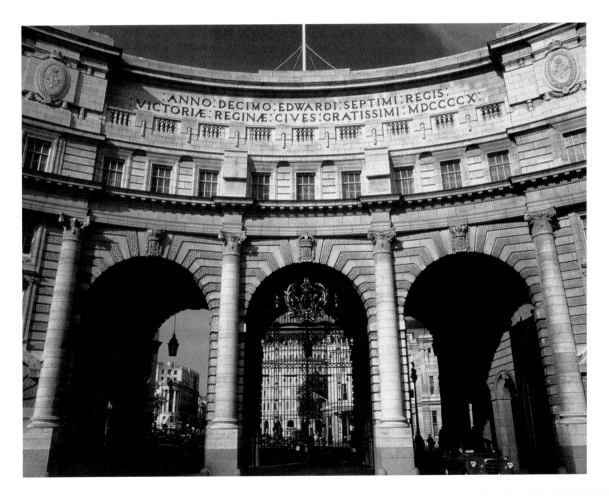

PENNSYLVANIA STATION

MCKIM, MEADE AND WHITE, 1910 NEW YORK CITY, USA

First there were the imperial baths of Ancient Rome. Then there were the railways. And then Paxton's Crystal Palace (London, 1851), Baltard and Hallet's Central Market Hall (Paris, 1866) and Dutert's Hall of Machines (Exposition Universelle, Paris, 1889). Put these together and the result was Pennsylvania Station, New York, perhaps the most majestic, romantic and thrilling of all railway stations. And, like the famous Euston Arch in London, wilfully demolished. Today a shabby hole-in-the-ground serves as the entrance to the terminus. What McKim, Meade & White had built was a palace of iron, steel and glass that matched the ambition and scale of US railroading at its zenith in the first four decades of the twentieth century.

McKim Meade & White was one of the best architectural practices of its time, its work ranging from superb country houses in the Shingle Style to grand civic monuments like Pennsylvania Station, Columbia University (1902) and the Brooklyn Museum (1915). The skills of the three architects coaslesced perfectly. Charles McKim (1847–1909) was gifted at monumental design; Stanford White (1853–1906) was decorative and painterly in style; William Rutherford Meade (1846–1928) made it all possible. Drawing its formal langauage from the great baths of Caracalla, Pennsylvania Station was a fitting temple to the mighty age of North American steam power.

GOVERNMENT OFFICES

JOHN BRYDON, 1912 PARLIAMENT SQUARE, LONDON, ENGLAND

This was the look of the British Empire as it went to war in 1914: pompous, stuffy, civil, correct, yet somehow deeply unsure of itself. These grandiloquent, yet handsome, government offices were the work of John Brydon (1840–1901), a Scot who believed that the one true style was the English Baroque of Christopher Wren, John Vanbrugh and Nicholas Hawksmoor. This style, he said in a talk at the Architectural Association, London, in 1889, was "in some respects superior to even the Italian Renaissance".

The revived Baroque style lasted well into the 1920s even though nominally superseded by the Beaux-Arts French Classicism of architects like Reginald Blomfield, who rebuilt John Nash's Regent Street, and the very talented Mewes and Davis, best known for the delicious Palm Court in London's Ritz Hotel. As for Brydon in Parliament Square, his government offices, although neatly composed and thoroughly well built, are more Palladian in spirit than Baroque. The only real evidence of Baroque design is in the decorative detail such as the twin towers, clearly inspired by Wren, that mark the entrance to the central courtyard. The building has none of the grace of Wren, the dark intelligence of Hawksmoor or the theatricality of Vanbrugh. British Classicism had a long way, however, to descend from this decent and gentlemanly effort.

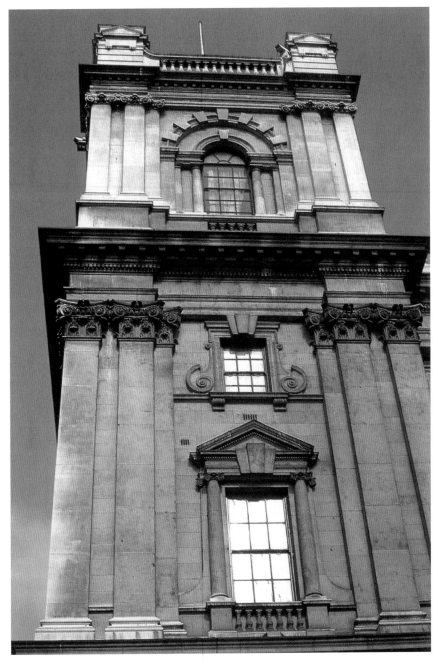

GRAND CENTRAL STATION

WARREN AND WETMORE, REED AND STERN, 1913 NEW YORK CITY, USA

The famous concourse of Grand Central Station is one of the greatest meeting places in the world. Not only is it lofty and ennobling, but it works supremely well. In a celebrated judgement in 1978, the US Supreme Court declared this greatest of all railway stations a historic landmark and thus saved it from the fate of Penn Station (p.36). The station was planned from 1902 after a serious accident in the old station caused by trapped smoke from steam locomotives. In future all trains in and out of Grand Central were to be electric. Because these could run safely underground, the platforms of the new station were dug under the streets and on two superimposed levels. Altogether there were more than 100 platforms.

The engineering work was by Colonel William John Wilgus (1865–1949). The architecture was initially by the Minnesota railroad specialists Reed & Stern, but the Beaux Arts-trained Warren and Wetmore took over in 1911 and transformed the building into a twentieth-century Roman basilica. The spectacular main concourse measures 36.5 metres (120 ft) by 125.5 metres (375 ft) by 38 metres (125 ft) high. Light pours in from decorated lunettes on high and the eyes of passengers not in too much of a rush are drawn up to Paul Hellau's flamboyant ceiling painting depicting the heavens.

UNION BUILDINGS

HERBERT BAKER, 1913 PRETORIA, SOUTH AFRICA

After the Boer Wars, South Africa was united under British hegemony. A parliamentary building followed, although it was some time before it arrived, in Pretoria. It was the design of Herbert Baker (1868–1942) an English architect who had come to Cape Town in 1903. Baker had been trained in the Arts and Crafts tradition, but once in the Cape he fell in love with Cape Dutch colonial architecture. When Cecil Rhodes appointed him to design the Union Buildings in 1909, he had arrived at a style that fused Cape Dutch, English Arts and Crafts, and the Baroque style of Wren and Hawksmoor.

Baker sited the Union Buildings in a steep hillside above Pretoria, a great garden tumbling down in terraces from the parliamentary complex to the city below. This elegant building comprises two stone-faced blocks capped with Wren-like domed towers, punctuated by courtyards, linked together by a Baroque arcade. Some commentators have found the central arcade a weakness in Baker's design. Yet Baker's elegant reticence speaks of a quietly confident system of government. The fact that South Africa had to wait 80 years for anything like a decent system of government is another story. Baker worked and fell out with Lutyens (p.47) in India before returning to England. Among other things, he designed South Africa House in Trafalgar Square.

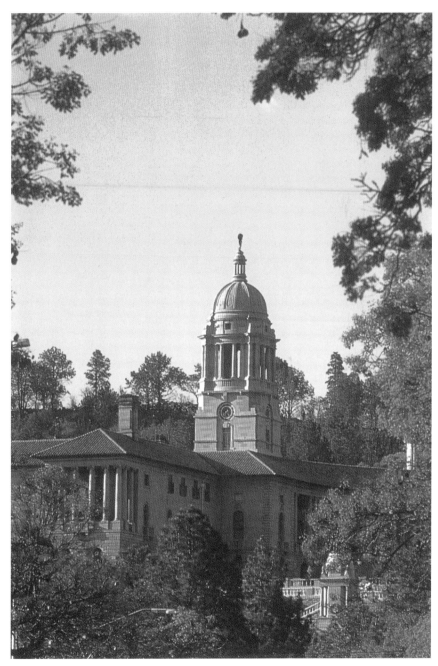

KING EDWARD VII GALLERIES

JOHN BURNET, 1914 BRITISH MUSEUM, LONDON, ENGLAND

John Burnet (1857–1938) was a Glaswegian who, after a training at the Ecole des Beaux Arts in Paris, designed many civic and commercial buildings in heroic styles – Greek, Egyptian, Chicago – in London over a period of nearly thirty years. If his most advanced was the Chicago-influenced Kodak Building in Kingsway (with Thomas Tait, 1911), his grandest is the extension he designed at the back of Robert Smirke's Neo-Greek British Museum. Burnet's long building is a steel-frame cloaked with a great screen of Ionic columns, separated by two tiers of decidedly modern commercial steel-framed windows. This long facade is interrupted just once with a small entrance, leading to a grand stair, guarded by a pair of imperious granite lions. Burnet's elevation, although Grecian, is very different in spirit from Smirke's entrance block, designed in the 1820s. Where Smirke aimed to be archeologically correct, Burnet's essay in modern Greek owes much to his Beaux-Arts training and would be at home in Washington or Paris. As it is, this was the architecture that saw Britain enter the blood and carnage of the Great War.

Burnet's later work includes Adelaide House (1925), the Neo-Egyptian pile flanking the north-east approach to London Bridge and the Classical sweep of Unilever House (1932), overlooking Blackfriars Bridge.

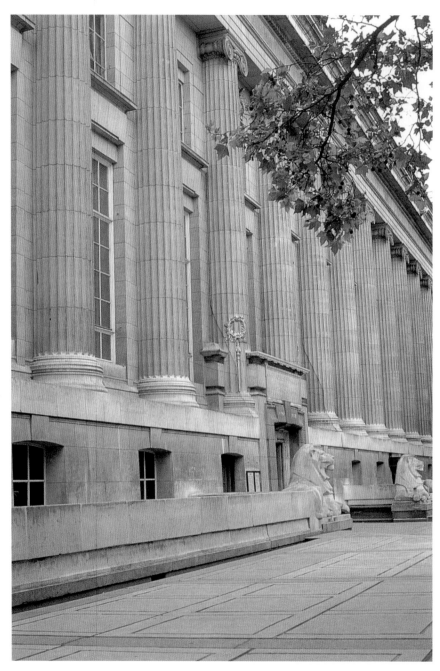

COUNTY COURT

GUNNAR ASPLUND, 1921 SOLVESBORG, SWEDEN

Gunnar Asplund (1885–1940) was one of the century's greats. At once Modern and as ancient as the temples of Greece, his buildings approached the elusive goal of timelessness more closely, perhaps, than those of any other twentieth-century architect. Without exception, his buildings are based on clear, symmetrical and deeply satisfying plans that have an elemental appeal.

The plan of the County Court in Solvesborg is that of a circle embedded in a rectangle. The circle is the court room, the focus of this romantic building. Asplund's hand is in evidence throughout the courthouse and includes most of the furniture and the handsome long-case clock that still marks the hours in this

remarkably humane seat of justice. From the outside this civic building is in the guise of a traditional Swedish farmhouse; inside it is light, warm and logical. Its sense of authority is simple, yet assured.

At the time of its construction, Sweden was still a predominantly rural country with a population of barely five million. The change in scale and ambition of Asplund's later work reflects the suddenness with which Sweden entered the industrial world. His lively and influential Modern design for the Stockholm Exhibition of 1930 was a clear pointer in the direction Swedish design and architecture would follow as the twentieth century progressed.

MIDLAND BANK

EDWIN LUTYENS, 1922 PICCADILLY, LONDON, ENGLAND

If anyone could keep alive the Classical tradition in the twentieth century in its original dress it was Lutyens. Just look at this branch of the Midland Bank next door to Christopher Wren's church of St James's, Piccadilly. A refugee from Hampton Court Palace, perhaps, it is a delightful, freestanding brick and dressed-stone garden pavilion writ large, punctuated by grand windows, entered by seemingly overscaled portals and capped with a handsome pitched roof. The quality of the brickwork is superb and the whole building simply feels good.

Lutyens knew instinctively that the Classical canon of architecture existed to be plundered and reinterpreted as well as respected, and because he knew this he was able to show that Classicism was far from dead in the age of the burgeoning Modern Movement. Perhaps because he refused to act seriously in public – architects tend to be very serious folk – Lutyens was all too readily dismissed by mid-twentieth century historians. Tackling a dreary plate of fish while seated next to King George V at a banquet, Lutyens leant over and said "This is the piece of Cod that passeth all understanding". At the opening of the Viceroy's House in New Delhi, he was introduced to a clergyman named Western. "Any relation to the Great Western?" asked Lutyens. Silly jokes, wonderful architect, even when put to designing a small city bank.

LINCOLN MEMORIAL

HENRY BACON, 1922 WASHINGTON D.C., USA

Untouched by the horror and ravages of the First World War, and by the philosophical and design currents nurtured in its wake, the USA was fairly isolated from Modern Movement ideas until what, from a European perspective, seemed like quite late in the day. The predominant styles of architecture right up until the Second World War were various forms of romantic vernacular and Hollywood-induced Art Deco, together with a grand, Beaux-Arts Classical tradition, nurtured in such influential offices as those of McKim, Meade and White.

Henry Bacon (1866–1942) was one of McKim, Meade and White's many successful graduates. While Erich Mendelsohn was at work on the design of the Einstein Tower, Potsdam, Bacon was at work on the grandiose Lincoln Memorial in Washington DC. Although this massive, white Doric monument might have seemed outmoded from a radical European perspective, in the States it represented the celebration and continuance of a democratic tradition and an architectural expression of that tradition rooted in the ideals of the Founding Fathers who themselves were steeped in the ways of ancient Greece and Rome. Far from representing the power of the state, the Lincoln Memorial was a celebration of the strength of US liberty and democracy. If nothing else, this helps to show that architecture can never be "read" in a simplistic way: one style can have several meanings.

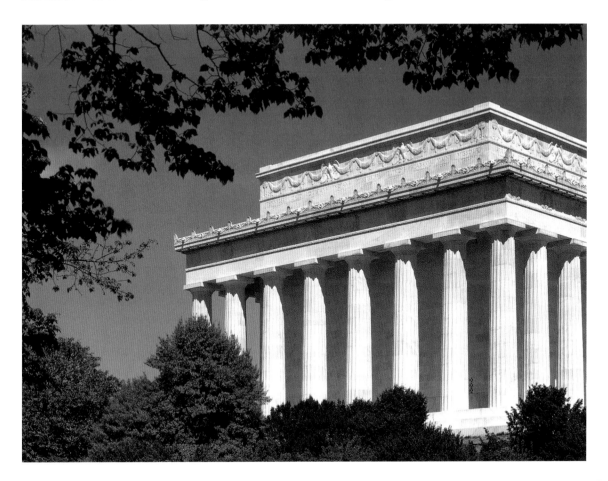

SELFRIDGES

DANIEL BURNHAM, 1926 LONDON, ENGLAND

This grand twentieth-century Roman basilica is one of London's most famous and grandest retail department stores. It was founded by Gordon Selfridge, a US retailer who had worked for Marshall Field, the famous Chicago department store, before he exported the same idea to London under his own name in 1908. Selfridges was revolutionary in several ways: so much so, that the London building regulations that had kept architecture within certain bounds and bonds for decades were changed to allow the store to rise on the site of what had been blocks of Georgian houses along the north side of Oxford Street.

It was one of the first, and certainly the largest, steel-framed building in Britain. It boasted a dramatic open-plan interior, quite unlike anything seen in Britain before. It was as much a palace of pleasure as it was a shop: there were smoking rooms and places to eat and drink. There were no floorwalkers to begin with: shoppers were encouraged to explore the galaxy of goods on display in their own time and under their own steam.

Although radical in plan and purpose, the store's steel frame was dressed in a grandiloquent Roman toga. The giant Classical order and decoration were the work of Francis Swales, although the plan, structure and overall concept were the work of Daniel Burnham (p.358), who designed Marshall Field. A great central tower was never realized.

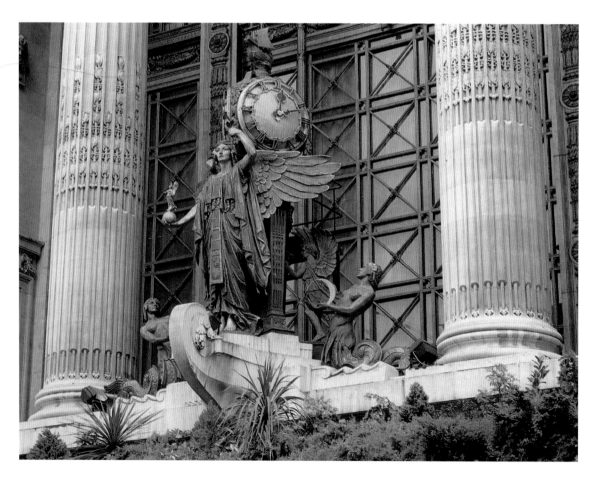

STOCKHOLM CITY LIBRARY

GUNNAR ASPLUND, 1928 STOCKHOLM, SWEDEN

This is one of the great buildings of the twentieth century. It cannot be called timeless, because no building can be, yet it gets close. It combines the essential elements of Classical architecture, Platonic in their archetypal purity – the cylinder, the cube, the square – bringing them together in a grand, sensual, profound manner. So much depends here on the richness of materials used throughout the building. This, and the quality of light that enters the superior drum and falls in studied shafts across desks and down stairs and corridors. The Library has a terrific sense of being hand-crafted and yet the enveloping architecture is severe. Asplund was only 43 when the Library opened and his most brilliant work was yet to come as he worked towards finding a resolution between the aesthetic and functional demands of twentieth-century architecture and the guiding spirit of Classicsm, reaching back 3,000 years.

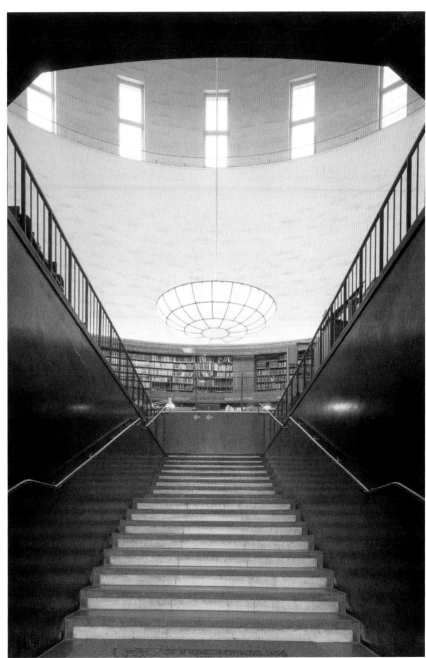

55 BROADWAY

CHARLES HOLDEN, 1929 LONDON, ENGLAND

Charles Holden (1875–1960) was a Quaker who twice refused a knighthood and, although much underrated, was one of Britain's finest architects. He began his career designing in an Arts and Crafts idiom, but this changed when he began to work closely with Frank Pick (1878–1941), the brilliant chief executive of the London Underground in the 1920s. For Pick's new headquarters near Westminster Abbey, Holden designed this unusual steel-framed, stone-clad office. The design is cruciform, so that every office is bathed in sunlight. These offices are raised above the booking hall and platforms of St James's Park station and crowned with a classical tower.

Stepped back from street level, 55 Broadway has a highly distinct profile, and yet this friendly giant, occupying an entire city block, is almost invisible until you get close to it. Its stone flanks have sculptures, representing the spirits of the winds, carved by such well-known sculptors as Henry Moore, Jacob Epstein and Eric Gill. These were deeply controversial at the time as architects debated whether buildings should be vehicles for Art and, equally, whether they should be considered artworks in their unadorned state. Holden went on to design a sequence of superb stations for London Underground and the Senate House tower for London University.

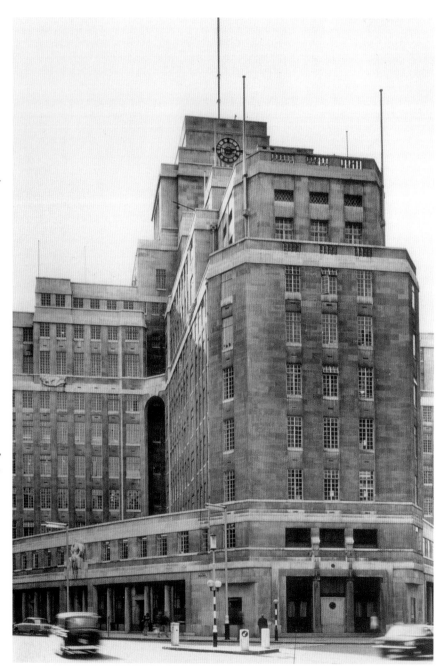

VICEROY'S HOUSE

EDWIN LUTYENS, 1931 NEW DELHI, INDIA

Before India gained its independence in 1947, British architectural styles were imposed on the country. Until the 1870s, the style of British Indian buildings reflected fads and fashions in Britain itself. During the Victorian "Battle of the Styles", Bombay became home to Gothic and Calcutta to the Classical. There was a move from the 1870s to mix indigenous styles with those of Britain, leading to a picturesque "Indo-Saracenic" style for official buildings. Although it was quaint, few architects were able to fuse the disparate Indian and European styles. The most successful attempt came late in the day as the sun was setting over the British Empire. It came in the form of Lutyen's imperious and utterly convincing Viceroy's House (now the Rashtrapati Bhavan), the jewel in the crown that is New Delhi. Even Le Corbusier was impressed.

The success of this great domed palace, built in beautiful red, ochre and sandy stone lies in its successful marriage between English Classicism – Lutyens's "Wrenaisance" Baroque under dazzling light – and Indian detailing. It also lies in its almost impossibly grand setting at the end of one of the heroic tree-lined avenues Lutyens and his rival Sir Herbert Baker (p.39) laid out in their creation of New Delhi between 1912 and 1931.

The marble-lined corridors of the Viceroy's residence are wonderfully cool in the Delhi heat; there is at least one room with cornices but no ceiling (to allow the heat out and the stars in) and a garden that just oozes oriental fantasy. The building has always been faultlessly maintained.

ARNOS GROVE TUBE STATION

CHARLES HOLDEN, 1932 LONDON, ENGLAND

This exquisite building brings together the needs of a modern railway station, the Classical architecture of ancient Rome, the modern architecture of Holland and northern Germany, gentlemanly English restraint and bricky British craftsmanship. A heavily corniced brick and glass drum atop a symmetrical glass and brick base, it is a delight to look at and to use. Most of all it is a credit to the vision of Frank Pick (1878–1941), the chief executive of the London Passenger Transport Board, who wanted London to have the world's finest integrated urban public transport system; because of his efforts, for many years it did. Pick teamed up with Holden in 1923. Holden had recently designed some memorable war memorials for the Imperial War Graves Commission (he had served as a Lieutenant in the Royal Engineers during the First World War) and something of their design rubbed off in the first sequence of stations Holden designed from 1925 for London Undeground's Northern Line. Arnos Grove was the finest of the stations built for the Piccadilly Line in the early 1930s. Before its design, Pick and Holden made a tour of the latest Dutch and German architecture; they were particularly impressed by the work of Dudok (p.183) and his influence was clearly at work on Holden, though Arnos Grove station also echoes the design of Asplund's Stockholm City Library (p.45).

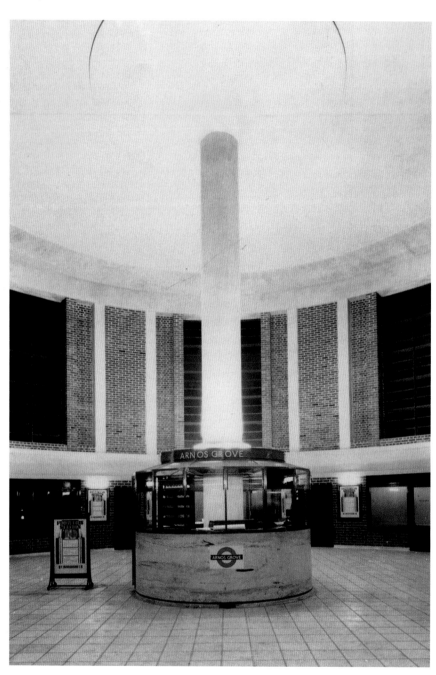

SABAUDIA NEW TOWN

LUIGI PICCINATO, GINO CANCELOTTI, EUGENIO MARTUORI, ALFREDO SCALPELLI, 1933 ITALY

Nearly seventy years on from its foundation, the Fascist new town of Sabaudia retains its powerful and, given the Roman climate, rather chilling aspect. Designed as an exercise in Rational architecture and urban planning, it was like a De Chirico painting come to life. And yet it is a compelling place, a small town on the Pontine marshes that has a scale and dignity very different from the New Town experience in, for example, Britain, where suburban values tended to hold sway.

Sabaudia was one of four new towns commissioned by Mussolini's government on the infamous, mosquito-infested Pontine marshes. By draining the marshes, Mussolini eradicated malaria. The design of the town was a conscious reaction to the "vernacular" style adopted elsewhere in the Roman new

towns. Piccinato (1899-1983) and his colleagues had shown what they intended to do here and elsewhere at the First Exhibition of Rational Architecture held in Rome in 1928. Clear lines, no decoration, a monumental sensibility. The architecture, especially the church at the centre of Sabaudia, is funereal and silent, yet to watch crisp shadows fall across its severe facade and to see the shadow of its tower etched into the piazza below is to be aware of architecture of a high and disciplined order.

The town was planned on an offset grid, its formal rigour softened by the park that opens up to the Lago di Paola at the southern end of its central axis. It was an important achievement and was to inform the work of a later generation of Italian Rationalists centred around Aldo Rossi (p.330).

OLYMPIC STADIUM

WERNER MARCH, 1936 BERLIN, GERMANY

The stirring backdrop for Leni Riefenstahl's powerful *Olympiad* documentaries, this imposing stadium is a building that reminds us how effective architecture can be as a symbol of political willpower. Architecture has been used as a political tool most effectively by Adolf Hitler's regime. When the Führer saw the first design for the 120,000 seat Olympic Stadium, he was critical of March's (1894-1976) use of exposed steel. March wanted to create a Modern monument: Hitler wanted to recreate the glories of ancient Rome. The upshot was that Hitler's favourite architect, Albert Speer (p.53) intervened. Speer had the structure clad in heroic masonry – granite and limestone – and ringed around with a grand colonnade. The entrance is breath-taking, for although the stadium seems quite big enough from the outside, its perceived height gives no inkling of what is to come. The running track and playing field are set low down, well below the line of the structure as seen from the seemingly interminable avenue that leads visitors here.

Scale aside, this is a remarkably civilized sports building: a ring of restaurants, restrooms and changing rooms is broken only to offer visionary views of the sports fields behind it. The stadium is still very much in use and will no doubt last a thousand years, unlike Hitler's regime which missed this target by 988 years.

HOTEL MOSKVA

ALEXEI SHCHUSEV, ET AL, 1936 MOSCOW, RUSSIA

The old joke about this monumental hotel is that when Alexei Shchusev (1873–1949) presented Stalin with the plans, he showed him two designs on the same sheet of paper. Stalin nodded, signed the document and that was that: the hotel had to be two designs in one. No one was going to argue with Comrade Stalin's signature. In fact, the Hotel Moskva, one of the first undiluted "Stalinist" designs, looks as if it might contain many more than two buildings. What really happened, and why the building is such a Borzoi's breakfast, is that Shchusev, a distinguished architect who proved able to design in any number of styles, was brought in to tart up a very Modern design by the young architects Savalev and Stapran who appeared

to be unaware of the fact that revolutionary Constructivist buildings were no longer acceptable in the Soviet Union.

Shchusev smothered the 17-storey design in lashings of granite, marble, bronze and monumental details. It looked hideous, but fitted the bill and was to be the benchmark for the often pretentious buildings of the Stalin era. The courtyard building is elephantine and was not finally completed until the 1970s when, after a brief "liberal" fling under Nikita Khruschev, the USSR was eeking out its dotage under the ponderous rule of Leonid Brezhnev. The rooms were handsomely appointed and the showy top-floor restaurant was, for many years, the best the comrades had to offer.

METRO MAYAKOVSKAYA

ALEKSEI DUSHKIN, 1938 MOSCOW, RUSSIA

The Moscow Metro opened in 1935 and from then on its tentacles spread inexorably across the Russian capital. By 2000, there were ten lines with nearly 150 stations.

The older stations are really extraordinary, lavishly decked out in the richest materials in the guise of palatial Baroque grottoes or underground cathedrals. There were essentially two types: the blisteringly Baroque and the balletic. Metro Mayakovskaya falls into the second category and is one of the most convincing of the early stations. It was designed by Aleksei Dushkin (1904–77), a talented designer and party favourite who won the coveted Stalin Prize three times and managed never to fall out of official favour. The underground concourse of the station

is covered with 36 oval cupolas lit by bronze torches and decorated with Soviet stars and hammers and sickles. The cupolas are supported by an impressively turned-out regiment of arches of light and dark marble inset with stainless steel reveals. The platforms are vaulted and lit with Neo-classical lamps. A model of the station was exhibited at the 1938 New York World Fair and won the Grand Prix. Its finest hour came, however, in November 1941 when the German "panzers" of General Guderian were at the gates of Moscow and the city had been partially evacuated. In this glittering concourse deep under the city, Stalin addressed the entire Politburo and effectively began the fight back for Moscow.

VOLKSHALLE

ALBERT SPEER, 1938 BERLIN, GERMANY

Had it been built, the Grosse Halle would have been nearly 300 metres (1,000 ft) tall, seated 180,000 of the Nazi party faithful, and would have been so voluminous that, packed to the gunwhales with a capacity audience, clouds would have formed inside and rain may even have fallen: a suitably Wagnerian environment for the rantings of the Führer. The Grosse Halle was intended to have stood on the site of the Reichstag, which was badly damaged by fire in 1933 and rebuilt by Sir Norman Foster (p.299). It marked the top end of the proposed north–south processional avenue that, lined with Nazi palaces, offices, hotels and cinemas, would have led to a new south Berlin railway terminus and to Tempelhof airport, one of the few surviving buildings of the Nazi era, built by Ernst Sagebiel, 1941.

The architect of the Dome was Hitler's pet Albert Speer (1905–81), who based the design on Hitler's sketches: it was essentially the Pantheon in Rome revisited, but five times taller and with a volume sixteen times greater. Speer rose via the design of Nuremberg Stadium (1937) to become Generalbauinspektor (head of architectural works) of the new Berlin. This was to be called Germania and the intention was to build it in 1948 after German victory. During the war, Speer rose again to become Minister for Mobilization and War Production. Tried at Nuremberg in 1946, he was imprisoned for 25 years. His memoirs were to become world-famous. He died in a hotel bedroom with his mistress in London while filming with the BBC.

REICH CHANCELLERY

ALBERT SPEER, 1939 BERLIN, GERMANY

The Reich Chancellery was built in a great hurry between 1938 and 1939, using labour and building materials from across Germany. The idea was that this Neoclassical palace, based essentially on the designs of the great nineteenth-century Prussian architect Karl Friedrick Schinkel, represented the spirit and substance of the new Germany under Hitler. Speer's organizational abilities were phenomenal: using a combination of new and tried and tested techniques and materials, the Chancellery was ready for the Führer to move into just before he invaded Poland in September 1939. Hitler's vast study was reached along an attentuated hall of mirrors that had been adapted

by Speer from Versailles. The infamous bunker in which Hitler sat out the last four months of the Second World War were below Speer's palace.

At the end of the century, the ruins of the Führerbunker were all that was left of a building that once occupied an entire city block. The building was bombed heavily and demolished by Allied troops after the fall of Berlin in May 1945. As an example of a kind of hi-tech Classicism it had been a fascinating exercise. As a symbol of a cold-hearted regime that was planned to last 1,000 years and, in the event, missed its target by 988 years, it was a fitting monument to the folly of political ambition.

SUPREME COURT

F. DORRINGTON WARD, 1939 SINGAPORE

This was one of the last flings of an Imperial style and owed its inspiration to the work of Sir Edwin Lutyens and Sir Herbert Baker in India and South Africa, who, in turn, owed a well-acknowledged debt to the English Baroque of Sir Christopher Wren (1632–1723). Many buildings for the judiciary were built in this style, notably the Old Bailey in London (Edward Mountford, 1906). Singapore's Supreme Court owes a clear debt to Mountford's precedent. British architects took this "Wrenaissance" style, as Lutyens dubbed it, to all four corners of the British Empire.

By the time Lutyens completed his imperial masterpiece –the Viceroy's House, New Delhi, India (p.47) – the sun was already setting on the world's most expansive empire. And by the time Dorrington Ward completed the Supreme Court, the empire was about to be overrun – the Japanese seized Singapore in 1940. The building survived the occupation and is still very much in use: it was clearly built to last for hundreds of years. Although it seems curious to see such overtly British buildings fanned by swaying palm trees and sweating under tropical skies, the substantial structure of the Supreme Court means that the interiors are cool, while vast corridors and lofty chambers allow air to circulate without the tyranny of air-conditioning. The Supreme Court has its place in Singapore.

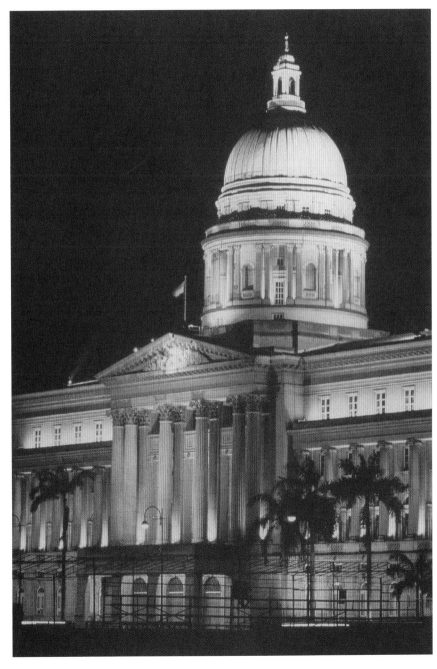

FOREST CREMATORIUM

GUNNAR ASPLUND, 1940 EMSKEDE, STOCKHOLM, SWEDEN

A work of genius. Standing mournfully, yet beautifully, on a gently sloping wooded hillside, Gunnar Asplund's crematorium is an ancient Greek acropolis for the dead seen through the eyes of a twentieth-century Classicist turned Modernist. The hillside complex at Emskede comprises three chapels, a columbarium (the vault containing funerary urns) and the crematorium itself. The generous entrance is designed for mourners to gather in all weathers. The gas lamps attached to the silent columns holding up the umbrella roof here are dimmed as urns are committed to the vault.

This is a place of great beauty and symbolism that ultimately transcends place and architecture. It is marked by a vast and simple wooden cross and has an elemental simplicity and a power to move that belongs to the very greatest buildings from the pyramids of ancient Egypt onwards. It was also Asplund's swan song. The Swedish architect's genius was to have found a way of bringing the architectural spirit of classical ages into the mid-twentieth century, to demonstrate that there was a way of being Modern that did not deny the past, that architecture was a continuum rather than a stacatto salvo of bombastic and radical styles and forms. While the rest of Europe was preparing for war, Asplund had the opportunity to design this *memento mori* that symbolizes eternal rest. He did not fail.

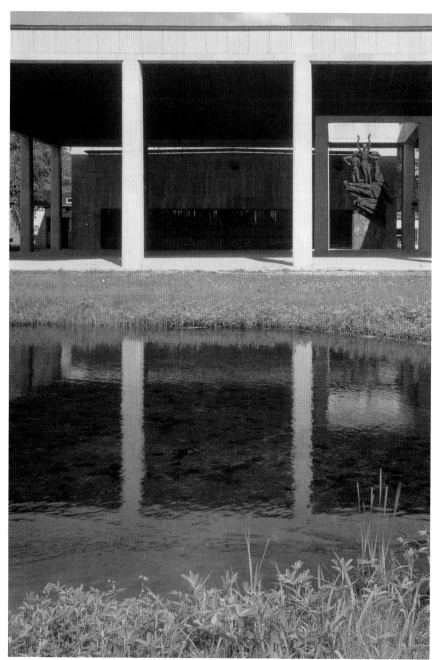

NATIONAL GALLERY OF ART

JOHN RUSSELL POPE, 1940 WASHINGTON D.C., USA

One way or another, the Classical tradition survived into the twentieth century, notably so in the United States. Perhaps this is because Classicism – a certain pure white Classicism – was associated with the democratic values of the ancient Greeks and with the architectural style in vogue immediately after the American War of Independence. Unlike in Germany, Italy or the Soviet Union, Classicism in America has not been linked or confused with authoritarian or fascist dogma and social straight-jacketing. John Russell Pope's (1874-1937) National Gallery of Art is a chaste exercise in Palladian design, yet although far more correct in a scholarly sense than Troost's near-contemporary Munich Art Gallery, it is equally cold, a building to respect grudgingly rather than to admire and certainly not to love.

The inspirations behind the building, from Thomas Jefferson to Karl Friedrick Schinkel, are clear enough, yet the museum took Classicism nowhere new. To outsiders it seems odd that such a gung-ho society as the United States should have aimed to embody its cultural values in such cold-hearted and stiff-shouldered architectural gestures; yet a part of the story of the taming of America is the quest for old-fashioned culture and respectability. Pope's National Gallery remains a very respectable, if lifeless, monument to the United States' cultural ambitions at a time when the country's emigré nuclear scientists were at work developing the atomic bomb.

LENIN LIBRARY

VLADIMIR SHCHUKO AND VLADIMIR GEL'FREIKH, 1941 MOSCOW, RUSSIA

The vast Lenin Library was built as a result of a competition for its design held in 1928–29. It was completed as the German army moved within sight of the walls of Moscow in 1941. The library is a stripped Classical design around two courtyards and entered through a dramatic and even aggressive colonnade: the columns are tall, square, largely bereft of decoration. This severity gives way to lavish lobbies, staircases and reading rooms (18 of them) designed for 2,300 readers who have access to more than 36 million volumes stacked away in this early Stalinist shrine. The vast building also contains exhibition halls, lecture rooms, concert halls, offices, and an entrance to the Moscow Metro.

At once stark and lavishly equipped and fitted, the Lenin Library symbolizes the ambitions of Stalin's mighty Soviet Union, a state which, far from withering into a Communist utopia, was a massively controlling and often frightening construct designed to keep the people firmly in their place; part of the weight that held them down was the sheer scale of official architecture. In Stalinism's early days, as in the Lenin Library, the style was heavy-handed yet crisp; in the years following the Soviet Union's triumph in the Great Patriotic War (1941–45), it became heavy-handed and flamboyant.

PALACE OF ITALIAN CIVILIZATION

GUERRINI, LAPADULA AND ROMANO, 1942 ROME, ITALY

The Palace of Italian Civilization was designed as the architectural showpiece of the Expositione Universale Roma (EUR), which was to have opened in 1942. World War Two intervened and the exhibition never happened. Instead, the EUR site became a new focal point for office, sport and leisure buildings after the war; thus the fascist architecture built for the exhibition was not wasted. The Palace is a powerful monument, chaste, formal and a little frightening. It is a simple building walled around with glistening travertine, each floor effectively arcaded and its interiors mysteriously hidden from view. It seems an empty building, a vacuous monument to a fundamentally flawed regime. It is also impressive and memorable: its simplicity, almost banal, is its formal strength.

The idea appears to have been to create an office building from the design of the Colosseum. The resulting effect of power and monumentality is strongly emphasized by the building's prominent position and by the muscular sculpture that surrounds it. The palace is one of a number of austere and apparently lifeless buildings at EUR. A Pantheon-inspired church and the Museum of Italian Civilization march alongside the palace, yet they too seem dead from the pavement upwards: acres of marble and big, bold proportions can only do so much to create enduring and endearing architecture. To make Classical buildings appear cold in the sensuous warmth of the Roman sun was quite some achievement.

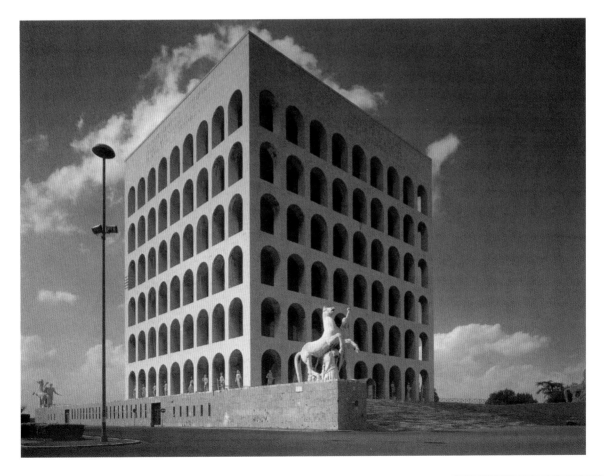

LOMONOSOV STATE UNIVERSITY

LEV RUDNEV, ET AL, 1953 MOSCOW, RUSSIA

Stalin died as this astonishing building neared completion. It had his enthusiastic endorsement and is widely cited as the symbol of the Communist dictator's unprecedented reign of civil terror. Even so, no one can be unimpressed by this towering wedding cake of Soviet brick and steel. Megalomaniacal it might be: it is also magnificent. Standing on a hilltop 70 metres (230 ft) above the River Moskva, the University dominates many views of the Russian capital. The main building is approached along a great avenue through a stupendous landscaped garden. The 26-storey central tower is topped with an exotic spire that cradles, at its peak, the Red Star symbol of the former Soviet Union. It contains a galaxy of offices, auditoria, club rooms, cafeterias, lecture rooms, offices and laboratories. Virtually every room is kitted out in lavish marbles and mosaics; the standard of finish is impeccable.

The tower is flanked by 18-storey wings (accommodation for students) and the wings by 12-storey blocks (flats for teaching staff). The whole complex is lavishly decorated and peppered with elaborate towers. Behind the main building are two gigantic low-rise blocks; these are the faculties of chemistry and physics. The design of this academic empire was led by Lev Rudnev (1885–1956) who, before the Great Patriotic War of 1941–45, had designed the equally daunting Frunze Military Academy, Moscow (1937) to symbolize the might of the Red Army.

GREAT HALL OF THE PEOPLE

ZHAO DONG-RI AND ZHANG BO, 1959 BEIJING, CHINA

The Chinese Revolution abounded in contradictions. Was it for the people or against them? Were Mao Zedong's "Great Leap Forward" of the 1950s and Cultural Revolution of the 1960s well meaning, if disastrous attempts, to make life better or to keep a billion, hard-working people under savage control, whether by starvation or brutal "justice"? It is hard to say. What we know is that architects were certainly confused. Should they represent the new Peoples' Republic in the guise of a revolutionary style adopted, perhaps, from Soviet or European inspiration; should they rework traditional Chinese motifs, or should they invent a wholly new way forward? They did none of these. Instead, mass housing was built along the grimmest and most brutally functional lines, while government buildings tended to be big, characterless boxes topped with token Chinese roofs and a nod, here and there, to the ancient principles of *feng-shui* – although this was meant to be anathema in Communist China, a land in which all religion and superstition were officially banned.

The Great Hall of the People is an example of the overscaled and dreary architecture of Communist China built during the disastrous years of the "Great Leap Forward", when the economy took a great leap back and millions starved to death. This decidely reactionary building was designed, among other state purposes, for multi-coursed official banquets.

LES ARCADES DU LAC

TALLER DE ARQUITECTURA, 1981 ST QUENTIN-EN-YVELINES, PARIS, FRANCE

The idea seemed to be a good one. Build Versailles for the people. Call in Ricardo Bofill's Taller de Arquitectura and have them run up blocks of flats around a lake in Neoclassical style. Very impressive. Have to make do with prefabricated, pre-dyed panels though. The result is grim indeed.

At the beginning of the 1980s, the Taller de Arquitectura was a cause célèbre throughout Europe. No one could quite believe what they had been commissioned to do: design and build huge sections of the new Paris suburbs in a grandiose Classical idiom. The drawings looked fascinating on the drawing boards in sunny Barcelona,

Spain, but the actual buildings were overpoweringly dreary. Many of the flats that were shoehorned into these highly stylized concrete containers were dark and cramped. Behind the facades, Classical proportion and harmony went by the board. Worse still, the policy of Jacques Chirac, then Mayor of Paris, to decant the poor and wretched into the biggest suburban developments – well away from the chic bourgeois glory of central Paris – ensured that what was meant to be a Renaissance heaven soon became a punky hell. If proof was ever needed that style alone does not make for attractive or desirable architecture, then this was it.

MARNE-LA-VALLÉE

TALLER DE ARQUITECTURA, 1982 PARIS, FRANCE

In this development of the pre-fabricated concrete classicism of St Quentin-en-Yvelines, the Taller de Arquitectura's idea of a Versailles for the people was taken to an even further extreme. Given the formless nature of the new Parisian suburbs – most are truly hideous and make one almost long for the Mock-Tudor and Neo-Georgian delights of Kingsbury or East Cheam – Bofill's idea of creating a powerful architecture and a sense of place made a certain sense. The problem, though, was largely one of scale. Proportion and light too. And this was just the beginning. The vast central block was kitted out with dreary flats and some of these featured slit-like kitchen windows facing out into Piranesian service routes coursing the depths of the weighty concrete pile above. Not much fun. It seemed as if the architect's efforts had gone into the layout of the development and its chunky facades, and not into individual flats.

In later schemes, notably in Montpelier in the Côte d'Azur, Bofill's classical extravaganzas became notably lighter in spirit and more humane. Classical proportions and a certain amount of detailing were even brought indoors. Perhaps the tragedy of this grandiose approach to suburban housing is that so many of us secretly hoped that it might really work.

NATIONAL MUSEUM OF ROMAN ART

RAFAEL MONEO, 1984 MERIDA, SPAIN

A fiercely distinguished building, this one of the best of the wave of new museums that washed over European cities in the 1980s. Here in Merida, Moneo (born 1937) has created a fitting home for a display of Roman art and archaeology, evoking the spirit of Roman architecture without recourse to imitation or pastiche. At first, the museum looks rather like a grand railway terminus of the 1930s, or, from other angles, a particularly impressive factory or power station. Close up, its intention is clear: the entrance pavilion draws visitors in through a muscular brick arch with the legend MUSEO carved in the style of Trajan's Column in a slab of veined white marble. From this pavilion, the visitor is guided across a courtyard and so into the unmitigated splendour of the museum proper. A

magnificent brick nave, based on the idea of what a Roman basilica might have felt like inside, runs the length of this cool, calm and collected space. The arches, all built in Roman brick, act as natural divisions between displays, so that the structure of the building does the job that screens do in other museums: Moneo has provided a sense of permanence appropriate to this museum's impressive collection. Beneath the arches is a crypt which houses a major archaeological site. Back upstairs, the brilliance of the design becomes apparent as one realizes that, instead of just the one commanding axis set by the basilica-like nave, there are many axes, criss-crossing the building at an angle, and set askew to the simple rectangular geometry of the building.

RICHMOND RIVERSIDE

QUINLAN TERRY, 1988 RICHMOND-UPON-THAMES, SURREY, ENGLAND

As reactionary as it could be revolutionary, the British architecture profession made a number of curious and fanciful diversions in the 1980s that seemed potty at the time, quaint within five years and all but forgotten within a decade. Quinlan Terry (born 1937), the son of very Modern parents, worked for James Stirling (p.331), before setting up a country practice in Dedham, Essex with a God-given mission, or so he himself believed, to convert Britain at least to the strictures of Classicism. A number of villas that resembled dolls' houses was the result and then Richmond Riverside, an annoying confection of pseudo-Georgian offices and shops built alongside the River Thames some 20 km (12 miles) south-west of central London. Annoying, because despite Terry's protestations, Richmond Riverside was a fake in the worst sense. It might have looked Georgian, but some of the buildings were no more than open-plan offices dressed in wannabe Georgian frock-coats and featured suspended ceilings rather than handsome wooden panelling. Chimneys proved to be air-extractors and, detail by detail, the whole picturesque affair began to stick in one's craw.

For a short while Terry and fellow Classical revivalists enjoyed a brief spell of fame and fortune as the Prince of Wales and his fawning acolytes championed their cause. It soon fizzled out.

TERRY'S ASSORTED VILLAS

QUINLAN TERRY, 1988 REGENT'S PARK, LONDON, ENGLAND

When John Nash and his pupils built their wonderful, picturesque villas and terraces around London's new Regent's Park in the 1820s and 1830s, they built rapidly, as if constructing in pen and ink, with cheap brick covered in weatherproof white stucco. The buildings were realized on a heroic scale and the details painted with a broad brush. They were, and thankfully remain, magnificent, urban stage scenery at its very best. Terry's assorted villas – this little one is Gothick, this little one is Venetian – built in the late 1980s alongside the Regent's Canal are quite the opposite. Each is detached, prissy and almost overwhelmed with coy period detail. They seem quite out of character with the park and with the work of Nash. Why? Because they are too self-conscious. They are nervy where Nash was confident, fussy where Terry's predecessor was supremely relaxed. Doubtless, Terry's villas are better made than Nash's: certainly, if you ever peep into one of the basements here, you will be amazed by how much "hi-tech" heating and cooling equipment a pseudo-Georgian house can have when compared to its clean-cut contemporaries.

The problem with such "period" architecture is always much the same; the real talent of any given period is always as the leading edge of design, as Nash was in his day. The best look back to learn, but not to copy.

PATERNOSTER SQUARE

JOHN SIMPSON, THOMAS BEEBY ET AL, 1990 LONDON, ENGLAND

This proposal came at a very peculiar moment in British architectural history – the peak of the Prince of Wales's influence which was also, by definition, a key moment for the would-be revival of Classical architecture. That it failed was perhaps inevitable. The proposal was for a new range of offices and shops, on a vast scale, flanking the north side of St Paul's Cathedral. These were to have replaced an existing group of dreary Portland-stone clad office blocks erected in the late 1950s and early 1960s on the site of what had once been Paternoster Row, a famous street of booksellers and printers, destroyed by the Luftwaffe during the Blitz. To mitigate their bulk and to

please Prince Charles, a would-be pantheon of Classical revivalist architects was brought in to dress the mighty air-conditioned offices and basement-level shops proposed here in antique fancy dress. Critical studies quickly proved that the proposed buildings would be a threat to the integrity of St Paul's Cathedral. The scheme was scaled down and then all but abandoned in the mid-1990s. A new scheme was masterminded by the veteran architect William Whitfield and was eventually announced in 1998. The idea seemed to be to keep the new scheme as quiet as possible in the hope that no one would notice how dull it was. Poor St Paul's.

POUNDBURY VILLAGE

LEON KRIER, ET AL, 1996 DORCHESTER, DORSET, ENGLAND

Only in Britain could such a thing happen. For some years an excited coterie of tweedy architects sporting bird's nest haircuts and ancient polished brogues sat at the dainty feet of the Prince of Wales discussing a grand new extension of Dorchester, the old county town of Dorset in south-west England. The discussions were dominated by the fiery Leon Krier (born 1946), a lucid theorist who had worked in the 1970s on a number of unbuilt, classically-inspired building and urban design projects with James Stirling. Poundbury – for that was it's name – was intended to be the forerunner of an entirely new way of living, a kind of idyllic "urbs-in-rure" in which houses and shops

newly built to look old-fashioned would doff their cornices to renaissance style piazzas. There would be no crime, no nods to fashion and no working-class types. Krier drew up handsome and ambitious plans. The architectural profession bridled. But the Poundbury bubble burst. The reality of planning bye-laws and regulations helped to scupper the plan, so did a general lack of interest.

In the end a few deferential architects turned out some cottages and Dorchester fell asleep again. Clough Williams-Ellis and Francois Spoerry (p.311) had done much better with their holiday villages in Wales and France (Portmeirion and Port Grimaud) years before.

QUEEN'S GALLERY

JOHN SIMPSON, 2002 LONDON, ENGLAND

On November 25, 1914, three days after the close of the first battle of Ypres, which had claimed the lives of 50,000 British soldiers, King George V devoted his time to the purchase for £18 of an agate and diamond Fabergé aardvark from the London branch of the famous Russian fancy-goods maker. Soldiers in the trenches must have been thrilled. The aardvark is now on display in the greatly enlarged Queen's Gallery at Buckingham Palace. This is an extraordinary place, a gathering of 500 years' worth of high art and crawling kitsch reflecting the tastes of monarchs from Henry VIII to Elizabeth II. These are housed in a rich range of new galleries designed in the styles of John Nash and John Soane, as reinvented by John Simpson, with more than a dash of Alexander "Greek" Thomson, the imaginative Scottish classicist, added to the mix. John Simpson might stand accused of trying to cram too many pet ideas into one project, yet his rich, playful, clever Neoclassical building is probably exactly the right frame for this cabinet of royal curiosities. Simpson is a classicist through and through, but not a stick-in-the-stucco history man. The Queen's Gallery is a nimble blend of Portland stone and air-conditioning, of Bath oak, marble, alabaster and hi-tech gadgetry. The building is eminently practical and suited to its royal purpose. It will age well, and is a box of architectural tricks that will delight those who wish architectural development had all but stopped in the 1830s.

ORGANIC

"THE STRAIGHT LINE BELONGS TO MAN, THE CURVE TO GOD." (GAUDÍ)

At the beginning of the twenty-first century, the word "organic" has been bandied about with incontinent imprecision. Organic vegetables, organic bread, organic toothpaste ... the word has been used as a kind of talisman to ward off the evils of consumer societies in which so many things, from what people eat to the homes they live in, has become mass-produced, unsettling and even unhealthy. Organic architecture is an equally loose term, yet it conveys at least an idea of buildings designed to grow naturally from the ground they stand on. It conjures too the idea of buildings that are made of natural materials, that seem somehow to belong in a way that Classical temples or white Modern Movement machines-for-living never do. It also gets over the idea of buildings that make a play on natural forms and employ geometries that have little to do with Euclid and mathematical perfection. And it suggests buildings that are designed to be wide open to the elements.

In extreme cases, as with the work of Antoni Gaudi (pp.75, 80, 81), buildings really do seem to be plants or animals growing naturally out of the ground rather than being projected unnaturally into the sky. Gaudí created a form of architecture made up of what appear to be bones and sinews, or tendrils and shoots. Architects like Bruce Goff (p.96) and Herb Greene (p.105) shaped a shaggy architecture that might be home for animals and insects as well as human beings. Frank Lloyd Wright, one of the century's most influential architects, left a legacy of Organic buildings that fit into the depths of rural America as they do into the grid-iron of Manhattan (p.102). Imre Makovecz, who founded an entire school of Organic architects and craftworkers in Hungary in the last quarter of the century described his designs as "building beings", and indeed at their strange and haunting best, such as the Mortuary

Chapel in Budapest (p.112) or the Catholic church at Paks (p.119), they really do feel as if they are alive and breathing.

There was always, however, a tight-rope to be walked in this tradition between inspiration and kitsch and some of the buildings shown here, although intriguing, were always in danger of falling from artistic grace.

What all the buildings in this section have in common is the sense of being close to nature, either in terms of location or materials used in their construction. This is why you will find such strange bedfellows as Tadao Ando, Antoni Gaudí and Hugo Häring here. Each of the buildings is highly individualistic, wilful even. obey conventional rules and none is held back by precedent or convention. They are all in their own way highly emotional buildings, but unlike the architectural expression of Postmodernism, none is cynical, clever-clever or too knowing. Quite the reverse: most have an innocence about them, each an attempt to take architecture into unknown waters.

This is not to say they lack power or gumption. You can see the energy expressed in the design of the Chilehaus in Hamburg (p.85) and feel the muscle of Stuttgart station (p.87). As for Arthur Shoosmith's garrison church in New Delhi (p.89) well there is all the might and mystic power of a Mayan temple or Babylonian ziggurat.

Veering between the eccentric and the proudly magnificent, this loose fraternity of buildings includes some of the twentieth century's most likeable as well as curious. By the start of the twenty-first century and with increasing concern for ecological issues and the natural world, it seems likely that Organic architecture in one or other of its many forms will blossom rather than wilt.

WESTMINSTER CATHEDRAL

JOHN FRANCIS BENTLEY, 1903 LONDON, ENGLAND

This magnificent building with its sky-piercing campanile and solemn, cavernous interior was utterly untypical of the work of John Francis Bentley (1839–1902). Born in Doncaster, Bentley trained as a mechanical engineer before working for a firm of builders, converting to Catholicism and launching a successful career as a church architect designing in a robust Gothic style. The unexpected move at Westminster into a Byzantine style came about when Bentley's client, Cardinal Vaughan, decided that it was closer in spirit to the founding fathers of the Catholic Church than either Gothic or Classical style. The cathedral is decidedly modern; a vast structure infused with the light of religion. Inside, the great arched space is capped with four immense concrete saucer domes.

Until the late 1970s, the cathedral was hidden at street level by the grim buildings of Victoria Street: a piazza has since been created that allows Bentley's masterpiece to take pride of place along this dreary thoroughfare.

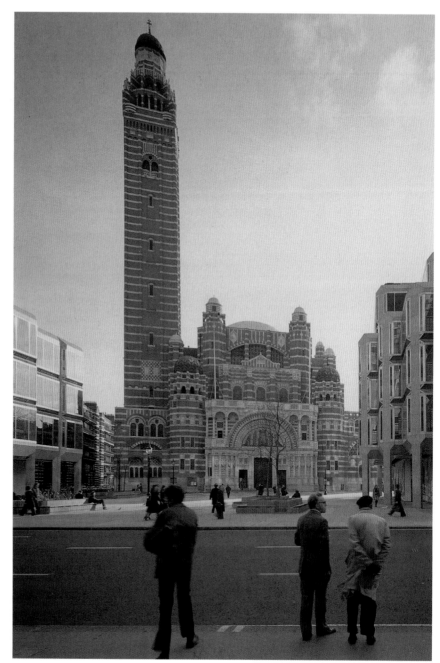

CASA BATLLÓ

ANTONI GAUDÍ, 1907 BARCELONA, SPAIN

Like some mythical beast – a dragon, perhaps, from a medieval fresco – the Casa Batlló still has the power to shock and surprise. Designed for the textile manufacturer Josep Battló I Casanova, this fantastic apartment block animates the imposing avenue, Paseo de Gracia, that forms the spine of central Barcelona. The waywardness of the exterior – prognathous lower floors in the guise of a gaping jaw, a roof like an armadillo's back and a coating of colourful broken tiles – is carried through into the individual apartments. To stay here is like being Jonah inside the belly of the whale, although the bellies of few whales feature such beautifully finished furniture and fittings. The architect, Antoni Gaudí I Cornet (1852–1926), was one of the most extraordinary architects ever. A devout Catholic, he lived the life of an aesthetic and ascetic monk and was taken for a tramp when admitted to hospital having been fatally knocked down by a tram while pondering on the construction of his unfinished masterwork, the Expiatiory Temple of the Holy Family. In his youth Gaudí was influenced by the "Renaixença", a cultural and political movement that sought to restore Catalonian pride and independence from Spain through the rediscovery of local language and history. Gaudí gave Barcelona an architecture very much of its own.

ROBIE HOUSE

FRANK LLOYD WRIGHT, 1910 CHICAGO, ILLINOIS, USA

The Robie House introduces us to a revolution in domestic design instigated by one of the century's greatest and most controversial talents, Frank Lloyd Wright. Wright's bombast and egomania was cleverly captured in *The Fountainhead* (both the rip-roaring novel by Ayn Rand and the Hollywood movie starring Gary Cooper as the misunderstood architect hero). Although sited in Chicago, the house Wright built for Frederick C. Robie was in spirit the last and finest of the long series of "Prairie" houses he designed from 1894 in the Illinois countryside. Described by Wright himself in a 1900 issue of *Ladies' Home Journal*, the Prairie House was characterized by its wide, deep-eaved roof, its emphasis on the horizontal and a free plan turned around a central hearth. The houses were

elegant, well built and as liberating as they were practical.

The Robie House was one of the very first houses anywhere to feature a built-in garage, and in this sense heralded a new era. Striking today, although overshadowed by clumsy later buildings, the house reveals itself as a low-lying intersection of dramatically elongated planes. The exaggerated overhang of the roof, recalling some ancient Japanese temple mirrored through the lens of early twentieth-century Chicago, is supported by four 30 metre (100 ft) steel beams; although finished throughout in a kind of free-flowing and almost streamlined Arts and Crafts manner, the Robie House is also an expression of the new technologies industrial Chicago had to offer by 1910.

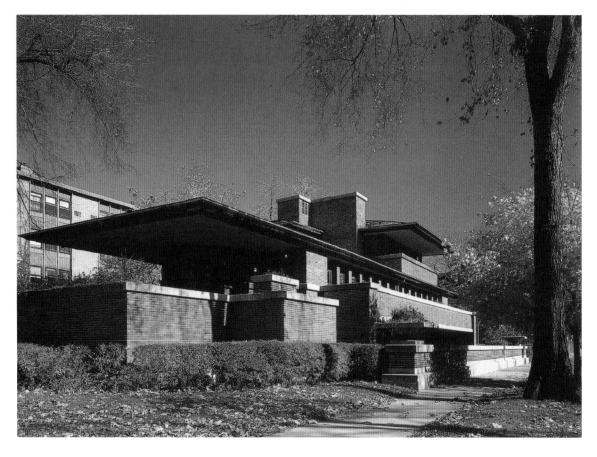

CASA MILÀ

ANTONI GAUDÍ, 1910 BARCELONA, SPAIN

"The straight line belongs to Man. The curved line belongs to God." Gaudí practised what he preached: finding a straight line inside or outside the Casa Milà, a Surrealist apartment block in the centre of Barcelona, is harder than watching a camel trying to pass through the eye of a needle. This truly strange building is known locally as *la Pedrera* (the quarry). Yet, far from being a heap of stones, it is a brilliantly resolved stone palazzo into which Gaudí has poured sinuous apartments that are like nothing else you will find on Earth.

The seven-storey building is grouped around two courtyards so that each flat, large or small, is well lit. Outside, the block appears to stand on the legs of stone elephants, while balconies and window mouldings jut out like strange lips or eyebrows of giants you would expect to meet in the grotesque gardens of Baroque Italy. Adding to the confusion, the balconies are girdled with bizarre garlands of encrusted ironwork. To cap it all, the roof garden is like a Dali painting come to life. Casa Milà has been used by many film makers. It remains utterly surreal and yet this is no gimcrack design. The building is thought through as all of a piece. Even then, if it chose to walk off by itself one night to live in another city, it would have to come back: only in Barcelona has architecture of this topsy-turvy character made sense.

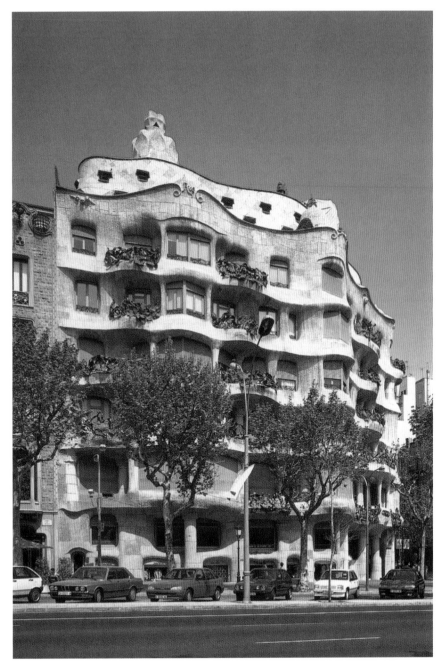

MICHELIN BUILDING

F. ESPINASSE, 1911 LONDON, ENGLAND

A comic-book building that pops up in London's snooty Fulham Road like a Jack-in-a-box. A florid Art Nouveau design by the French architect F. Espinasse (1880-1925), the Michelin Building was a kind of strident and witty advertisement for the French tyre company. The exuberant façades are decorated with colourful glazed bricks, white faïence tiles, a pot-pourri of flowery Classical references and, inevitably, representations of pneumatic rubber tyres. The corners are capped with the bulbous stacks of tyres that form the torso of the Michelin Man (add a head, legs and arms in your mind's eye).

The building was bought by the retailer, publisher and restaurateur Terence Conran in 1984 and has since been lovingly transformed into an oyster bar, restaurant, shop and offices for a publisher. The one jarring note is the extension behind and alongside which has none of the grace or humour of the original building. What makes the building special, aside from the fact that it is genuinely funny – a rarity in architecture, much though architects like to talk about "wit" in their designs – is its luminous quality; it glows in sunshine and shines in the rain, proving the durability and surprisingly good urban manners of its fancy dress.

GOETHEANUM I

RUDOLF STEINER, 1913 DORNACH, BASEL, SWITZERLAND

Rudolf Steiner (1861–1925) was the founder of Anthroposophy, which, aside from being hard to say, was a part educational and part religious movement aimed at "developing the faculty of cognition and the realization of spiritual reality." The movement led eventually to the construction of an increasing number of highly expressive and idiosyncratic schools across Europe, rated highly for their notably humane methods of education. The Goetheanum was the first headquarters, or meeting hall, of Steiner's movement. It was to have been built in Munich, but Steiner was refused permission. In 1913 the bulbous, exotic domes of the Goetheanum rose in the hills above Basel. The style of the building can be described, loosely, as Organic. Or, it can be labelled under the heading

Expressionist. The truth, however, is that for buildings designed by mavericks, no ready label is particularly helpful. The plan of the building, and to an extent its form, have, however, echoed down the century and found new roots in the work of architects such as Reima Pietilä (born 1923) in Finland and Imre Makovecz (p.112) in Hungary.

In effect, the plan of the Goetheanum was like a cross-section of the human womb, and the female form of the covering architecture supports this. The idea behind this was one of warmth and shelter. The building was short-lived: it burned down in 1922 and was replaced by an equally unusual design, by Steiner with Herman Ranzenberger, this time in concrete. It is still there.

CENTENNIAL HALL

MAX BERG, 1913 BRESLAU, GERMANY

A mind-blowing building realized on a truly heroic scale by
Max Berg (1870–1947), the city architect of Breslau. Built to
commemorate the centenary of the local uprising against
Napoleon, the Jahrhunderthalle was, in 1913, the most
ambitious concrete building yet attempted. So stupendous was
the achievement that Berg's decision to leave the concrete
exposed went all but unchallenged. The reinforced concrete
structure is in the form of a 65-metre (213-ft) dome made
up of 32 ribs stretching up from four giant arches to a central
lantern. The spaces behind the arches form four apses that can
be closed off from the central space. As contemporary glass

technology was not up to creating curved walls of glass over the
ribs of the concrete dome, Berg designed a sequence of four
concrete rings around it and fixed the biggest windows he could
into them.

There were few precedents for Berg's hall and in its day it
was looked on as a kind of twentieth-century Hagia Sophia.
Nevertheless, the structure had to be much heavier and more
substantial than Berg might have liked as the properties of
reinforced concrete on such a scale were, as yet, largely
unknown. The building survived World War Two and remains
almost exactly as it was built and still serving its original purpose.

HELSINKI STATION

ELIEL SAARINEN, 1914 HELSINKI, FINLAND

Eliel Saarinen (1873–1950) was a bridge between the architectural concerns of the nineteenth and twentieth centuries, between art and architecture and between the Old and New Worlds. Born in Rantasalmi, Finland, he trained as a painter and architect at the same time, flitting between Helsinki's University and Polytechnic. In 1904, he won the competition for the design of Helsinki Station. This imposing and theatrical monument represented Saarinen's breakaway from the National Romantic movement he had been a part of, in company with Jean Sibelius, the composer, the artist Akseli Gallen-Kallela and the architects he initially teamed up with, Herman Gesellius and Armas Lindgren. The station, famous for the sculpted granite giants that bear the great lamps to light the main entrance, was a rational, logical design, wrapped in a cloak of monumental, sculpted granite. The profile of the clocktower is almost streamlined and its influence was soon to be seen in railway and other civic buildings in America, the country to which Saarinen emigrated in 1923. Working with his son, Eero, Saarinen went on to design some of the most trendsetting mid-century Modern buildings, including the General Motors Technical Center, Warren, Michigan (p.214). He had journeyed a long way from Finnish National Romanticism and Helsinki Station.

PARC GÜELL

ANTONI GAUDÍ, 1914 BARCELONA, SPAIN

One of the most loved of all city parks was laid out on a steep hillside at the edge of Barcelona between 1900 and 1914 by Antoni Gaudí for the industrialist Eusebi Güell I Bacigalupi. Güell had originally planned a model new town on the site but this fell through. The park, however, remains. Its glory is a hall or cavern of massive fluted Doric columns supporting a serpentine balcony on which the stone benches, coated in a brilliant mosaic of broken tiles and glass fragments, are an integral part of the parapet. This is a wonderful place to sit, not just to meet people, but to look out across one of the world's most charismatic and idiosyncratic city centres.

Elsewhere in the park, sinuous paths lead through grotto-like tunnels supported by rough-cut columns that slope at what seem like wayward angles, yet, in truth, express the natural forces at work. Gaudí lived for many years in a small house of his own design at the bottom of the park. It has long been a Catalonian shrine. The architect's narrow cot is a moving sign of his monastic way of life; his, however, was a monasticism that in no way denied beauty or sensuality, as the magical design of Parc Güell proves. Although clever in concept and colourful in execution, the design of Parc Güell shows how clearly Gaudí felt for and understood the order of Nature to be found beneath its gorgeous skin.

SANTA COLOMA DE CERVELLÓ, COLONIA GÜELL

ANTONI GAUDÍ, 1914 BARCELONA, SPAIN

This is one of the most idiosyncratic buildings of the twentieth century, a chapel designed by Gaudí to be the spiritual heart of the ideal industrial community commissioned by his great patron Eusebi Güell I Bacigalupi. Strange enough seen from the outside with its vulva-like windows and mysterious porch, the crypt is absolutely extraordinary. Four massive columns, leaning at improbable – yet, from the point of view of natural physics, entirely rational – angles support a nave ribbed with determinedly hand-made bricks. Two of the columns are made of rudely cut stone, their counterparts of brick only partly covered in a cement render. Worshippers sit on or kneel at wooden benches that appear to have been designed by an insect or with insects in mind. Even so, the crypt has a wonderfully calm atmosphere and the logic of its construction grows clear.

Gaudí's was a highly individual attempt to reconcile Architecture to Nature. If God was in his details, it was the God who created birds, plants, insects and fish. The truly remarkable thing about Gaudí's work is that it is always logical in its own wilful manner; he may have looked at the world in a way very different from the majority of twentieth-century architects, yet he is never gratuitous, and although he steers close, never sinks into kitsch. So demanding is the alternative logic of Gaudí's sense of structure that it is obvious why he left no real followers. Or, at least, no one competent enough to take the risks he did.

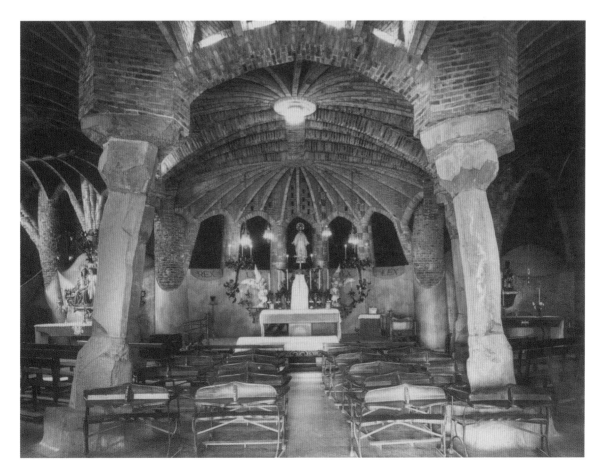

GROSSES SCHAUSPIELHAUS

HANS POELZIG, 1919 BERLIN, GERMANY

The buildings of Hans Poelzig's later years were designed in a monumental, stripped Classical style, an idiom that found much favour in Nazi Germany. Just after World War One, he indulged in a number of remarkable Expressionist projects, one of which – the Grosses Schauspielhaus – was actually built. Sadly, only fragments of this fantasy, designed for the flamboyant theatre director, Max Reinhardt, exist today in what is now the Friedrichpalast, Berlin. This cavern of Expressionist stalactites was a conversion of the old Schumann Circus building, housed in a steel-framed market hall. Poelzig (1869–1936) refaced the exterior in an imposing arcaded Roman style, but saved his best for the braggadocio interior. An Egyptian-style foyer led into the 5,000 seat auditorium which, to heighten the sense of exoticism and mystery, was painted blood red. The Nazis altered this haunting interior, which was later all but destroyed in the Allied assault on Berlin. The Grosses Schauspielhaus remains, in photographs, one of the most heightened examples of Expressionist architecture, a loose-knit philosophy of design that emerged in Germany in the lead up to World War One; there were no hard and fast rules, though it seems as if the Expressionists were seeking to break away from the formal, geometric bounds of architecture and the restraints imposed by all too solid building materials.

EINSTEIN TOWER

ERICH MENDELSOHN, 1921 POTSDAM, GERMANY

This curious boot-like building was designed to test Albert Einstein's theory of relativity. It was instigated by Einstein's assistant, Erwin Finlay-Freundlich and went into operation in 1924. A telescope in the observatory caught cosmic rays that were reflected by mirrors to the "spectographic" equipment housed in the basement laboratories. Erich Mendelsohn (1887–1953), recently returned from fighting on the Russian front, was the architect.

Before and during World War One, Mendelsohn, who was fascinated by the cosmos, drew superb sketches of fantastic buildings – streamlined designs that appeared to owe nothing to conventional architectural logic or to the constraints imposed by existing materials. He was certainly the right architect for the Einstein project, although it could not be built as he had hoped of a single material with highly plastic properties: the material didn't really exist and an exhausted German construction industry was hardly in a position to help. The result is a building made of crude brick and concrete, rendered to look as streamlined and otherworldy as possible. Although much smaller in reality than it appears to be in photographs, the Einstein Tower remains a captivating architectural experience and a pointer to a direction in which mainstream twentieth-century architecture might have gone.

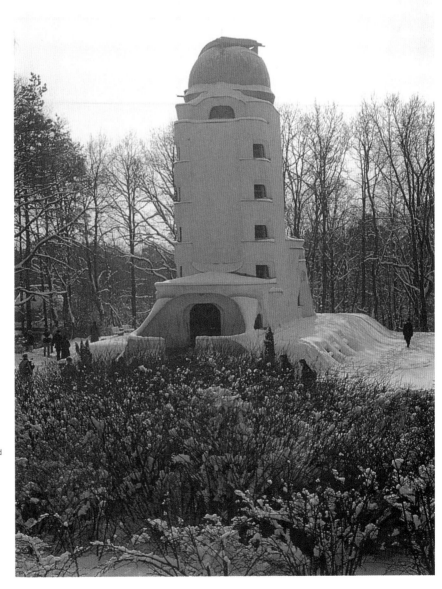

CHURCH OF THE SACRED HEART

ALBERT VON HUFFELL, 1922 BRUSSELS, BELGIUM

This vast domed basilica rises alongside the busy tramlines in central Brussels, dominates most views of the city and yet, as though everyone were ashamed of it, is barely ever mentioned in architectural histories. Perhaps this is because what was designed as a National Memorial or a kind of sacred pantheon to the glories of Belgium, was not completed until 1970, by which time its curious architectural style – National Romanticism of the 1880s meets Art Deco on a trip via Christopher Wren's St Paul's Cathedral – was as old-fashioned as it was unconvincing. And, yet the presence of the building and its idiosyncrasy make it unforgettable. The sheer scale of the basilica is impressive, yet its interior – awash with daylight – feels cold and unengaging: there is no sense of mystery or piety.

Although Albert von Huffell's design appears to have lead him up a stylistic cul-de-sac, the idea of a great domed building dominating a city centre was far from dead. It was to be revived soon afterwards by Edwin Lutyens in his unbuilt design for a Catholic cathedral in Liverpool and by Albert Speer in his design for a giant assembly hall in Berlin (the Red Army put paid to that). What von Huffell's design lacks, however, is the sense of awe or womb-like enclosure that Lutyens and Speer promised in their remarkable, if overbearing, designs.

CHILEHAUS

FRITZ HÖGER, 1923 HAMBURG, GERMANY

Fritz Höger (1877–1949) was born in Holstein and made his name in Hamburg from 1907 with the design of a number of small houses in an Arts and Crafts style rooted in the work of Herman Muthesius who imported many of his designs from England. The Chilehaus is his masterpiece, a magnificent Expressionist office block anchored in the city centre like a giant, barnacle-encrusted liner. It was commissioned by Henry Brarens Sloman who had made his fortune exporting saltpetre from Chile. Designed around two courtyards, the building forms a complete city block. Shops are incorporated into the Chilehaus at street level. Above, the offices follow the curve of a wave-like plan, that climaxes at the eastern tip or "prow". Offices step back from the street line above the sixth storey, and the windows gain arched tops.

A Wagnerian (Richard rather than Otto) *tour de force*, the Chilehaus is proof that the twentieth-century office block was able to develop in several directions and the Miesian model was far from being the only one. Höger's brilliance was to design a highly original and truly memorable city building that is urbane and well mannered from the perspective of those walking by. In Hamburg, pedestrians walk alongside Höger's rhythmic arcade: the age of walking past extractor fans and service entrances had yet to come.

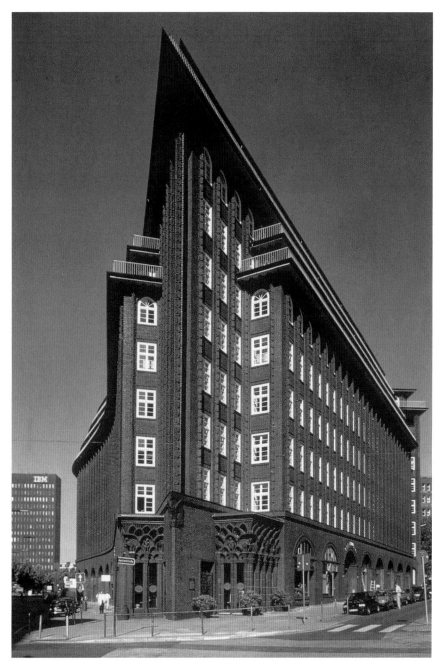

COW SHED

HUGO HÄRING, 1924 GUT GARKAU, NEAR LÜBECK, GERMANY

The Modern Movement was essentially an urban phenomenon. Hugo Häring (1882–1958), however, took it not just to the countryside but to the farmyard itself. This Expressionist cow shed is a wonderful oddity. The brick substructure conceals a uterine arrangement of concrete portal frames; the spaces between house 40 cows waiting to be serviced by a bull who is restrained in his own pen. The weather-boarded superstructure houses the haylofts. It all works very well and the cow shed has been in constant use since it was built. Of course it is a little scuffed, but one can only pray that in the age of artificial insemination it retains its seminal purpose and is not converted in to an art gallery

or architecture centre. The year the cow shed was finished, Häring became one of the founder members of Der Ring, a group of architects including Erich Mendelsohn (p.83) and Ludwig Mies van der Rohe (p.167), dedicated to fighting the stuffy attitudes of the planning authorities in Berlin. The group was disbanded by the Nazis when they were elected into power in 1933. Häring remained in Germany teaching at a private art school until 1943 and then retiring to Biberach where he was born. It seems curious to remember him for the design of a cow shed, yet at Gut Garkau he showed how local needs, local materials and even animals could benefit from a radical rethink of their treatment.

STUTTGART STATION

PAUL BONATZ, 1927 STUTTGART, GERMANY

To drink a coffee in the arcade of this great railway station is to enjoy German city making at its best. Catching a train from here is a delight too. Although clearly derived from Saarinen's terminus at Helsinki, this station has a memorable presence, its style a kind of stripped classicism shot through with a late-flowering National Romanticism. It has a wonderful "trains run on time" feel about it. It was designed by Paul Bonatz (1877–1956) in partnership with Friedrich Eugen Scholer. Bonatz was born in Lorraine, but studied in Munich, becoming a professor at Stuttgart's Technische Hochschule in 1908. Later, he worked with Fritz Todt on the design of the Nazi autobahn network, and continued to work throughout and beyond the Hitler era. He designed traditional houses and severe modern factories, yet it was in the monumental form and presence of Stuttgart Station, that like other architects of the interwar period, he found his voice. Work on the building began in 1911 in Imperial Germany, but was not completed until 1927, six years before the collapse of the Weimar Republic. With its great clock tower, severe colonnade and grand structural simplicity, it offered a distinctive vision of the way more twentieth-century architecture might have progressed had Classicism not become associated all too directly with Nazism in the 1930s.

FRIELINGSDORF CHURCH

DOMINIKUS BÖHM, 1927 COLOGNE, GERMANY

This magnificent church was an attempt by the Bavarian architect Dominikus Böhm (1880–1955) to reinvent the plan of the traditional Catholic church. His approach was prescient, although it was many more years before the deliberations of Vatican II dictated that congregation and priest be brought close together in the manner Böhm's church provided for. The Frielingsdorf church is essentially one large, dramatic space inside, Böhm doing away with the conventional hierarchy of spaces – nave, aisles, choir – that once characterized Catholic churches. The concrete vaults soar from floor to roof as if wings of angels enfolding the faithful. The pronounced spring of energy in these vaults creates the sense of a space devoted to prayer rising to Heaven. The clarity of the vaults and the

great expanse of window create a sublime, if ascetic interior that must rank as one of the finest of its type.

Böhm was born in Jettingen, Bavaria and like Paul Donatz who designed Stuttgart Station (p.87), which was completed the same year as the church, studied under Theodor Fischer in Stuttgart. In later years, although he continued to specialize in church design, his approach became less individual, as he gave up his Expressionist tendencies and came to adopt a more rigorous and less emotional Modern Movement approach. German church design, however, saw some of the very best architects following in Böhm's footsteps, including his son, Gottfried, who took this specialist branch of architecture to new heights in the 1950s and 1960s.

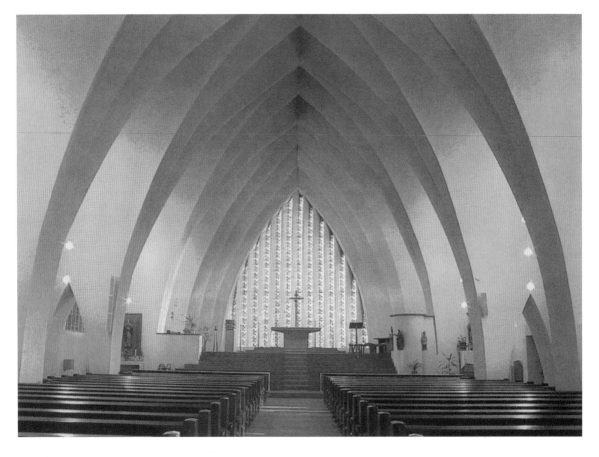

ST MARTIN'S CHURCH

ARTHUR GORDON SHOOSMITH, 1930 NEW DELHI, INDIA

For many historians and architectural critics, this is one of the finest British buildings of the century. Shoosmith (1888-1974) was an assistant of Edwin Lutyens. As Lutyens was extremely busy elsewhere in New Delhi, Shoosmith was allowed a free hand with the design of St Martin's. Partly to keep the heat and rain at bay, and partly because the material was cheap and easy for a largely unskilled labour force to utilize, he shaped his church from bricks, creating what amounts to a monumental and virtually impermeable brick sculpture. Although the form of the building is taken from Lutyens (the Cenotaph war memorial in London's Whitehall springs to mind), Shoosmith's masterpiece is free from all decoration. It somehow manages to combine the new industrial aesthetic of the 1920s with Classical geometry and the plan of a traditional English parish church: no mean achievement, although an odd one. The roof is made up of a series of concrete vaults. The interior is simple, lofty and deeply atmospheric. On sweltering summer days, it provides a cool, calm refuge from the city. The church was built for the military, which is why it has something of the look of a fortress. Today, it serves the Northern Diocese of the Church of India. Through the help of readers of the *Independent* newspaper in London, it was restored in the mid-1990s.

CHURCH OF THE HOLIEST HEART OF OUR LORD

JOSIP PLEČNIK, 1932 PRAGUE, CZECH REPUBLIC

Josip Plečnik (1872–1957) was one of the most distinctive of all central European architects working in the twentieth century and yet for many years his contribution was all but ignored. Even in what was once Czechoslovakia it was all but impossible to find anything written about him, much less to see his buildings listed and described in guide-books. There must have been many visitors to Prague who stumbled across this extraordinary church, rising from the gardens of George of Podebrady Square. The Church of the Holiest Heart clearly straddles two centuries of design. On the one hand it appears to date from the time of mid-nineteenth century Classicism, and yet the large, Surrealist clock punched through its shibbolethic

tower suggests it must be from the 1920s or 1930s, which, of course, it is.

Plečnik owed no loyalty to any school or style: he was very much his own designer, and the curious form of this unforgettable church was an attempt to evoke the power and spirit of the very first Christian basilicas in a contemporary manner. The body of the church measures 26 by 38 metres (85 by 125 ft) and is 13 metres (43 ft) high. The lower two-thirds of its walls are faced with vitrified bricks punctuated by cubic stone protrusions. The upper third is finished in snow white plaster. Above the pedimented hall, or nave, rises a mostly curious clocktower, the whole caboodle adorned with pylons and obelisks. All very curious and almost a precursor of Postmodernism.

SANTA MARIA NOVELLA RAILWAY STATION

GIOVANNI MICHELUCCI, 1936 FLORENCE, ITALY

Giovanni Michelucci (1891–1991) lived long enough to see his masterpiece – Santa Maria Novella Station – go in and out of fashion and back again. The building is a marvel, one of the finest of the Italian Rationalist buildings of the period. It cannot be crudely described as Fascist because it was commissioned and built during Mussolini's regime; it is much too fine a building for that.

Still a busy railway station, Santa Maria Novella is also an urban landmark and a public meeting place that has been looked after with great care and sensitivity by the Ferrovia Statale (FS) and the city of Florence.

In essence, the station is a Roman basilica shorn of decoration, but clad in marble and looking as noble as any imperial courthouse. Its massive walls act as thermal barriers in the hot Florentine summer: it is always cool here, a perfect place to sit and drink coffee and watch the world hurry by whether on its way to Sicily or Salzburg. Of all the sights in Florence, the Santa Maria Novella station ranks among the finest, and yet tourists rush out in search of Brunelleschi and Michelangelo as if Michelucci meant nothing.

Later on in his long career, Michelucci designed far freer and more overtly expressive buildings – notably the Church of San Giovanni Battista (1963) alongside the Autostrada del Sole near Florence, but these seemed forced and restless in comparison to his peerless railway station.

ST ANDREW'S HOUSE

THOMAS TAIT, 1936 EDINBURGH, SCOTLAND

St Andrew's House is the home of the Scottish Office, the government bureaucracy that will change its spots as Scotland gains its own political assembly at the end of the century. Positioned on a magnificent site between the heights and Classical follies of Calton Hill and the historic grandeur of Holyrood House and Edinburgh's Royal Mile, St Andrew's House is an impressive office block that demonstrates how large buildings of its type can contribute positively to a historic and sensitive cityscape. Thomas Tait's (1882–1952) genius was to incorporate new ideas arising from the Modern Movement in a building that was not only clad head to foot in local stone, but which had a formal air that suited the grand

city below it. In many ways, St Andrew's House shows how later generations of Scottish architects might have gone about renewing and adding to Edinburgh; instead of large, featureless concrete shoeboxes – Edinburgh boasts some of the blandest and ugliest British buildings of the 1960s and 1970s – these might have been realized imaginatively in stone and glass. It took until the 1990s before new buildings in Edinburgh gained anything of the urban grace and good manners of St Andrew's House. This is not a great building, yet its intelligence shines through its formal reticence and even stiffness in much the same way as, say, Charles Holden's Senate House in London.

CASA MALAPARTE

CURZIO MALAPARTE AND ADALBERTO LIBERA, 1942 CAPRI, ITALY

The fascist writer and adventurer Curzio Malaparte (1898–1957) entertained Field Marshall Erwin Rommell, commander of the Afrika Corps, at his new house on the edge of Capri, shortly before the Battle of El Alamein in 1942. The Field Marshall asked if Malaparte had designed the exquisitely beautiful house himself. No, lied the writer, he had found the house as it was, but had designed the landscape. That landscape, or seascape, remains one of the world's most desirable. Malaparte, with an initial helping hand from Aldalberto Libera (1903–63), chose the site for his house with infinite care. It sits on a rock jutting into the sea and was designed to represent the mind and body of Malaparte himself. In this sense, the Casa Malaparte is an intensely personal design and owes precious little to contemporary architectural currents.

A leading light of the Italian Fascist movement, although he was also imprisoned by it, Malaparte was later to become a Communist and on his deathbed a Catholic. Malaparte was a writer and journalist of great imagination. The house was as much a mausoleum as it was a seduction pad and writer's retreat, an image Malaparte said "of my own nostalgia." The plan of the house is certainly distinctly unusual: the Acropolis-like stair leads on to the roof of the house – for sunbathing and views – rather than to the entrance which is all but hidden below. The bedrooms resemble cells, while the living room is vast and washed in the shimmering light of the sea. The building is now the property of the Casa Malaparte Association and no one else has lived here since Malaparte's death.

CHURCH OF ST FRANCIS OF ASSISI

OSCAR NIEMEYER, 1946 PAMPÚLHLA, BRAZIL

The exuberant swoop of the roof of the Church of St Francis of Assisi echoes the waves crashing on the nearby Brazilian coast. It is a wonderful conceit and must have been a challenge to the concrete technology of the mid-1940s. Oscar Niemeyer's engineer, Cardozo, was clearly up to the job and the complex sequence of parabolic arches seems as inevitable as it is easy and assured. The result is a poetic and Organic building that uses its roof like a great umbrella to keep the sun at bay. What light there is in the church filters through vertical louvres set above the entrance and the main altar. The campanile and entrance porch are freestanding: the wave of the roofs is completely uninterrupted. The rear wall of the church is covered in blue and white tiles by the artist Portinari.

The overall effect is of a sea-shell washed up on a beach and a wave washing over it.

Niemeyer's quest, unlike that of his European contemporaries, was not to create a rational, functional architecture with precise rules and hard edges, rather he sought a form of poetry that an imaginative use of concrete made possible. Perhaps buildings like the Church of St Francis can be seen as the architectural equivalent of the poems of Pablo Neruda, or the novels of Gabriel García Márquez: they set out to be lyrical and to stretch our sensibilities. To be Modern, Niemeyer (born 1907) seems to say in the design of this voluptuous seaside church, is not the same thing as being austere and passionless.

GOURNA VILLAGE

HASSAN FATHY, 1947 LUXOR, EGYPT

Hassan Fathy (1900–89) tried harder than almost any other twentieth-century architect to reconcile Modern and traditional worlds and to create an architecture that was as ecologically correct as it was a delight for those it served. Not that he was always successful. Fathy's attempt to create a new village, or small town, on the edge of Luxor from the late 1940s was beset by petty local politics and even pettier local rows. Nevertheless, at Gourna, he managed to give shape to houses and other buildings that were rational in plan and built entirely of hand-baked mud bricks. The idea was partly to prove that housing in poor parts of the world could be built without expensive imported materials and without structures and techniques that would either overstretch or be beyond local skills.

Fathy was born in Alexandria; he later moved to Cairo where he was to become the genial head of architecture at the city's university. Fathy's mission was never less than a struggle; even as he was encouraging and developing a low-cost, environmentally aware architecture, the cities of north Africa and the Middle East were prey to banal, sub-Modern design that appeared in the guise of flamboyant, air-conditioned offices, hotels and, ultimately, shopping malls that required huge amounts of power to run, ignoring the power of the Sun, and which are a part of a system of latter-day imperialism that makes poor countries more and more, rather than less and less dependent on the rich. Fathy's struggle continues after his death.

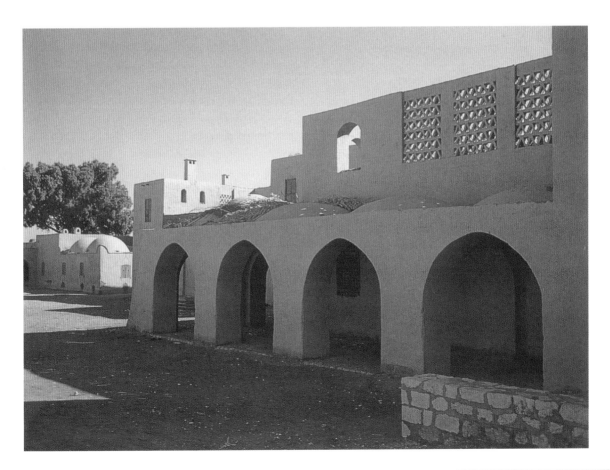

SAMUEL FORD HOUSE

BRUCE GOFF, 1949 AURORA, ILLINOIS, USA

Bruce Goff (1904–82) built houses that looked as if they were designed for fairy-tale animals rather than refrigerator-age Americans; yet, despite their pronounced eccentricity – Goff was a pupil of Frank Lloyd Wright – houses like the Samuel Ford residence in Aurora, Illinois were rational, intelligent and likeable homes.

The Ford house comprises a large 50.5-metre (166-ft) diameter dome made of steel and covered in shingles. A central lantern supported by an almost Gothic latticework of steel beams brings daylight into the very heart of the house, which boasts a spectacular galleried interior.

Goff can be counted among the most expressive of North American Organic architects and, far from being

a philosophical cul-de-sac, his ideas were to be echoed in the pioneering and experimental houses built by many Americans from the 1960s onwards. They were searching for a way of life that was ecologically sound and which represented, in twentieth-century guise, the pioneering spirit of early settlers.

Goff was born in Kansas and began working in Chicago. He later moved to Oklahoma where he became professor of the School of Architecture at the University of Oklahoma at Norman between 1947 and 1955. Most of his designs were for houses; he was fortunate to find clients willing to take the necessary leap of faith and imagination that enabled them to break away from conventional homes.

JOHNSON WAX BUILDING

FRANK LLOYD WRIGHT, 1950 RACINE, WISCONSIN, USA

An office like no other, the Johnson Wax Building was developed in two phases between 1936 and 1950. The exterior of the complex – a streamlined flow of bricks – is apparently impenetrable; it is impossible to imagine the nature of the idiosyncratic, Martian interior that flowers inside. The extensive offices are divided by a bizarre forest of lofty and unlikely mushroom-topped concrete columns that reach the polished linoleum floors as if standing on tip-toe. Around and between them, Johnson clerks toil from desks designed by Wright. They have no view out; daylight reaches them from the roof supported by the mushroom columns and from a near continuous 34-kilometre (21-mile) strip of Pyrex glass tubing that snakes around the tops of the walls. The inward-looking character of the building is pronounced. Between 1944 and 1950 Wright was asked to add a research laboratory and this he did in the form of a rounded, 15-storey brick and glass tower rising above the mushroom offices. Even here, Wright was unable to do the conventional thing. Each alternate floor is a circular mezzanine. All floors are cantilevered from a hollow, reinforced concrete core, housing the lifts and stairs. The result is a very special office tower that offers those who work here more light and space than offered in conventional high-rise buildings, designed for the most part like giant filing cabinets, in which each floor is a self-contained world and the others might as well not exist.

BREDA PAVILION

LUCIANO BALDESSARI, 1951 MILAN, ITALY

The "economic miracle" that saw Italy get back on its feet in the 1950s, after a shameful and destructive war fighting on the side of Nazi Germany, was founded to a large extent on the brilliance of the country's designers. Italian manufacturers put their trust in the talents of architects and designers to a degree unprecedented outside the United States. One of Italy's biggest and most dynamic manufacturers was Breda, famous for its railway locomotives and transport equipment. For the 1951 Milan trade fair, Breda commissioned Luciano Baldessari (1896–1982) to design its stand. Treating concrete as a sculptor might, Baldessari produced a sensational pavilion – great folds of white concrete through which visitors could walk on elevated gangways meeting the latest Breda designs on the way. By making the stand an adventure in itself, Baldessari created something that far from being worthy was much like a fun-fair ride.

Baldessari, a Milanese architect, had cut his teeth working with Expressionist designers in the theatre and cinema in the early 1920s: he worked on the fantastic sets of *The Cabinet of Dr Caligari* (p.437) before making a name for himself as an exhibition, furniture and lighting designer. He lived just long enough to see his playful and adventurous approach to form return to favour. Compare the Breda Pavilion with the Guggenheim Museum, Bilbao (p.347).

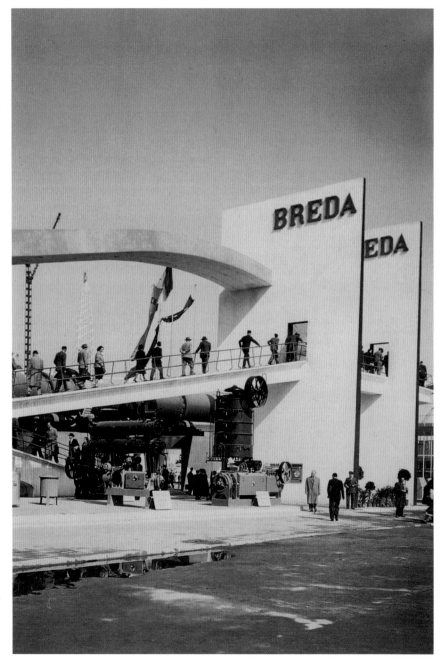

DOME HOUSE

PAOLO SOLERI, 1952 CAVE CREEK, ARIZONA, USA

Paolo Soleri (born 1919) was born, brought up and studied in Turin, but left Italy in 1947 to work with Frank Lloyd Wright at the master's studio at Taliesin West. He began working on the design of the Dome House with Mark Mills in 1949. It remains a truly radical habitation. The main body of the house is dug like a cave into a hillside and lined with masonry walls. The rooms are warm in winter, cool in the blazing Arizona summer. Daylight and air feed down into this man-made cave from a glass dome. Mounted on rails, this reacts to heat and light, opening up to the elements whenever it makes sense to do so. This makes the Dome House one of the first constructions to be truly concerned with notions of low energy and

sustainability. It has been copied in many different ways since by hippies, New Age settlers and others looking for an escape from irresponsible energy gobbling and city life.

Soleri went back to Italy between 1950 and 1955, returning to the USA in 1956 to set up the Cosanti Foundation in Scottsdale, Arizona, dedicated to the pursuit of new forms of urban living. These included a series of what Soleri called "Arcologies" (Noah's Arks for an age concerned with the ecology), which were megastructures in the desert capable of housing up to six million people. In 1970 he began the long process of building a trial "Arcology" for 150,000 people, in the Arizona desert.

CHURCH OF THE MIRACULOUS VIRGIN

FELIX CANDELA, 1955 MEXICO CITY, MEXICO

Soon after completing his studies at the Escuela Superior de Arquitectura and the Academia de Bellas Artes de San Fernando in Madrid, Felix Candela (born 1910) was fighting Franco, the future Spanish dictator, as a soldier in the Republican Army. He survived to reach Mexico via the refugee camps of the French Pyrenees in 1939 where he teamed up with his brother, Antonio, to work as builders and jobbing architects. Candela's study of concrete shell structures during this time stood him in good stead. Not only was concrete a cheap material – Mexico was, and remains, a poor country – but it could be used to create original and even flamboyant forms without over-taxing the skill of local labour. Candela proved the point with the design, assisted by Enrique de la

Mora, of this spectacular church. The double curved concrete vaults (hyperbolic paraboloids) could be formed, odd though it sounds, with the use of straight boards, making its apparently difficult construction remarkably easy.

Candela acted as his own engineer on the project and, typically, said the design and construction of the vaults was all down to intuition; it certainly was not – Candela is a fine and imaginative engineer. The exterior of the church is essentially a simple concrete rectangle; the interior comes as a mesmerising surprise. In a country in which Baroque architecture, brought here by the Jesuits, has long been appreciated, Candela has offered a new way of designing and building with passion and drama.

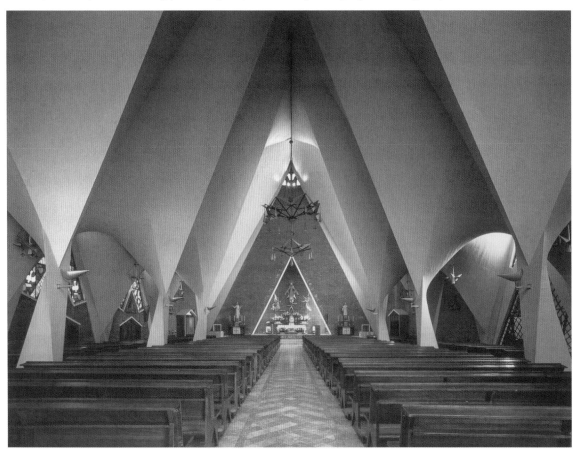

CHAPEL OF NOTRE DAME-DU-HAUT

LE CORBUSIER, 1955 RONCHAMP, FRANCE

Concrete poetry. Le Corbusier's pilgrimage chapel at Ronchamp stands on a site of ancient worship high on a hill in the Vosges. The chapel was a radical and, for many architects and critics at the time, shocking departure from the apparently rational Corbusier of the past 30 years. Yet, Ronchamp has its own logic. It is a deeply spiritual building and one that has most people praying, in whatever fashion, as they step inside its haunting interior. Before going inside, however, visitors need to understand that this is a church that works, from a ritual point of view, inside and out. The thick, white, roughcast concrete walls are a frame for outdoor masses and worship; the great overhanging shell-like roof acts as a sounding board for hymns sung, prayers said and sermons given outside the walls.

The extraordinary form of the chapel, said Le Corbusier (1887–1965), was inspired by a shell he picked up on a beach. The interior, protected by thick walls, is lit through an apparently random placing of tiny windows – some filled with coloured glass, others with plain glass – and by a ring of daylight that shines through the glazed gap between walls and roof. This device comes as something of a shock when thought about. What supports the roof? The answer is slim steel columns set into the thickness of the concrete walls; the roof itself, despite its apparent bulk, is a hollow shell and so very light. Ronchamp is unique and very special, an escape from the machine age into the realm of the spiritual.

SOLOMON R. GUGGENHEIM MUSEUM

FRANK LLOYD WRIGHT, 1959 NEW YORK CITY, USA

The Guggenheim museum is quite simply one of the world's most famous buildings. Wright's winding, gyrating, twisting Martian snail of a gallery is wonderfully mad, endearingly potty. There are many people who still find it a bad joke: a spiralling ramp that requires gallery-goers to peer at pictures while standing at an angle that makes one leg feel shorter than the other. One imagines the Surrealists must have loved it. So too must most New Yorkers and visitors to the Big Apple.

Although low for a Manhattan building, the Solomon R. Guggenheim Museum cannot be missed: its pillbox-like profile juts out into Fifth Avenue and ropes visitors into its spectacular interior. This consists of little more than a giant drum, tapering outwards as it rises, around which a ramp spirals. The roof is covered in a shallow glass dome. Visitors are encouraged to take the lift to the top of the museum and to walk slowly back down. Most spend a good long while leaning over the balustrades and watching other visitors as they wind round and round this artful climbing frame.

Wright had been toying with spiral designs from the mid-1920s, and began work on the Guggenheim as early as 1943. Various delays, not least World War Two, held progress back. His crowning and most popular achievement, the museum finally opened in the year Wright died. It has since been extended, yet the purity of the original experience – and what an odd one it is – remains.

JOSÉ MARTI MEMORIAL

VARIOUS ARCHITECTS, 1959 HAVANA, CUBA

Havana at the end of the 1950s and immediately before the Cuban Revolution led by Fidel Castro, Raul Castro and Che Guevara, was a sweltering hotbed of decadence and corruption. The Caribbean island was under the heel of the posturing dictator Fulgencio Batista, a former army sergeant, and its coffers were filled with ill-gotten revenue from prostitution, gambling, extortion, illegal trade of all sorts, as well as from rum, sugar and tobacco. This was a sad state of affairs for an island that had won its independence from Spain the hard way some 60 years earlier. Cuba's national hero, José Marti, died fighting the Spanish troops in the Cuban War of Independence. This bizarre memorial was finally erected to his memory in a new and highly planned government district of Havana in 1958. Its distinctive profile was adapted from a design taken from a contemporary whiskey advertisement, a rum thing to do given the reverence in which Marti is held in Havana.

The monument protrudes from the heart of the vast Plaza de la Revolucion where Fidel Castro has made many of his famous speeches. The limestone-clad tower rises from a star-shaped base and narrows to viewing platforms reached by a lift 80 metres (250 ft) above the tropical Havana skyscape. Today the monument is open to the public and is a kitsch shrine to both Marti and the Cuban revolution.

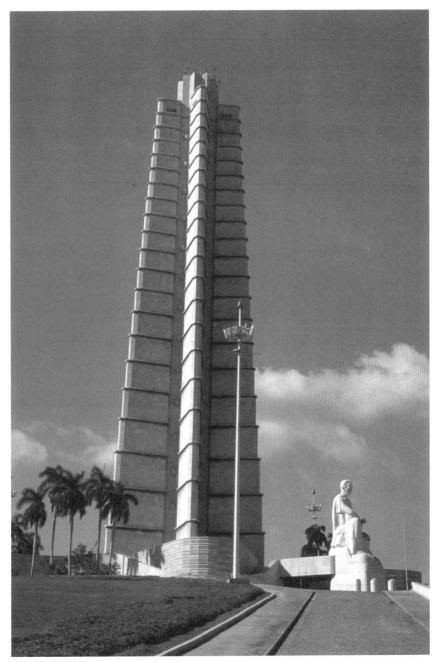

TWA TERMINAL

EERO SAARINEN, 1961 IDLEWILD (NOW JFK) AIRPORT, NEW YORK CITY, USA

You would have to be a miserable sort not to get a kick out of this effortlessly entertaining, stylish and decidedly upbeat airport building, and not least because so many buildings associated with air travel are so mind-numbingly dull. The TWA terminal really looks as if it might fly; its theatrical structure is made up from four intersecting concrete vaults, or wings, each supported by swooping Y-shaped buttresses. The gaps between are glazed, meaning that, unlike the vast majority of airport buildings, it is beautifully lit night and day. The interior lives up to expectations. The roofs soar up, and a gallery is gained by a suitably rousing stair. Every last detail was shaped for visual pleasure. You can't help feeling that the architect and his client had a lot of fun here, although the

structure must have been demanding to get set out and to get right. The TWA Terminal, at what is now New York's "JFK" airport, demonstrated how what had become a long tradition of showy, advertising-induced US buildings could happily meet new ways of buildings and some of the latest ideas in avant-garde architecture.

The TWA Terminal was a glorious match for US airliners and luxury automobiles of the time: it pleads for a Lockheed Super Constellation to land alongside and for passengers in pencil-skirts and mohair suits to be picked up in '59 Cadillac El Dorados. A more ambitious Saarinen design at Dulles Airport, Texas, partially collapsed in 1980. It has since been rebuilt.

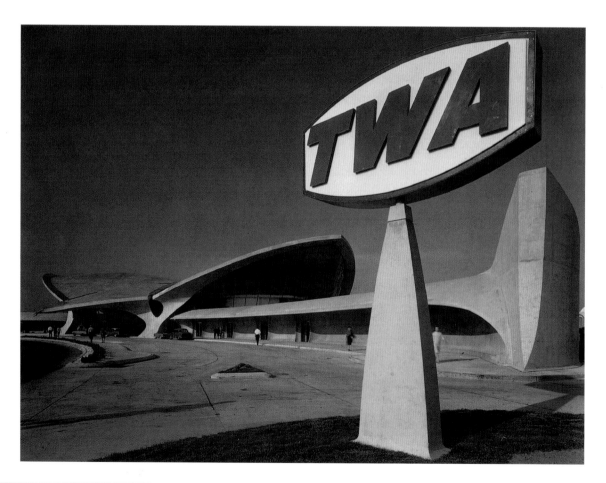

GREENE HOUSE

HERB GREENE, 1961 NORMAN, OKLAHOMA, USA

Is it a bird? Is it a buffalo? Can it be a house standing out there on the lonesome Oklahoma prairie? Who knows. Even Herb Greene (born 1929) is unsure. This curious shingle house, standing alone in the middle of nowhere, is meant to evoke any number of responses. It is, of course, a home, although a very peculiar one, and it does look at first like a buffalo the US Cavalry forgot to slaughter, grazing mournfully on the great mid-western plains. Close up, its shingles hang like the feathers of a bird of prey, a vulture perhaps. Even closer up – inside, for instance – the puzzle goes on. The interior is much like the outside, hung wall-to-wall with cedar shingles, lit from unaccustomed angles and explored by wooden ladders.

Herb Greene was clearly influenced by Bruce Goff (p.96) who in turn was a disciple of Frank Lloyd Wright (p.102). In the latest turn of events, Greene had a considerable influence on the school of Organic architects who grew up around Imre Makovecz (p.112) in Hungary.

A "natural' or "Organic" approach to architecture has always been an alternative to the rigours and rules of formal design. All too often the results are awkward and rather embarrassing: a building is not a living creature and cannot satisfactorily represent a bird of prey or a buffalo. It can, however, evoke the spirit of a natural, rural way of life, refuting the certainties of civil architecture. In these ways, the Greene House is an unexpected and breath-stealing jab in the ribs.

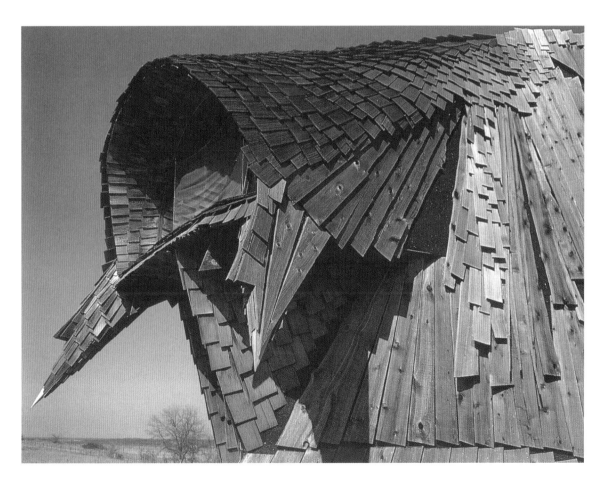

NATIONAL SCHOOL OF ART

RICARDO PORRO, ET AL, 1965 HAVANA, CUBA

The Cuban Revolution spawned little in the way of new architecture. This was not for want or lack of ideas, but because the island's economy was never able to take off after Washington imposed a petulant and spiteful economic embargo on what it regarded as an American colony after US-backed armed forces lost to Cuban troops at the Bay of Pigs in 1961. This failed attempt at counter-revolution was a moral triumph for Cuba but led, via the Cuban Missile Crisis of the following year, to economic pain despite financial support from the Soviet Union. This was hardly a climate in which architecture was likely to thrive.

The distinctive and sophisticated National School of Art, set in urban parkland at Miramar, a western suburb of Havana, was the glorious exception. The five buildings housed the faculties of Fine Arts, shown here, by Ricardo Porro (born 1925), a Cuban architect; the Music and Ballet Schools, by Vincent Garatti and the School of Scenic Arts, by Roberto Gotardi. Each architect brought their individual style to the complex, while maintaining the formal similarities – the connected series of bricked domes and the links with Nature – that result in a campus that is at once Organic and Modern.

THE SHRINE OF THE BOOK

FREDERICK KIESLER AND ARMAND P. BARTOS, 1965 JERUSALEM, ISRAEL

The Dead Sea Scrolls and other precious Biblical manuscripts are housed in this striking Israeli monument. What Kiesler (1890–1965) created here was a form of inhabitable sculpture. Certainly, it comes as a surprise to be able to walk into what appears, at first, to be a silent and solid monument in the guise of a shallow white brick dome rising from the depths of one of the world's most ancient and intriguing cities. The bulk of the building – museum and archives – is, in fact, below ground: the dome is very much the tip of an architectural iceberg. The space beneath the dome is contemplative and haunting: it's hard not to think of Jonah trapped in the belly of the Biblical whale.

Kiesler considered his work to be sculpture. He was born in Vienna and after working briefly for Adolf Loos (p.149) made his name principally as a stage designer; he went to New York in 1926 where he became Director of Stage Design at the Juilliard School of Music. He later taught at Colombia University before setting up an architectural office with Armand Bartos at the age of 67. Their work was mostly concerned with the theatre. The Shrine of the Book was Kiesler's last major work.

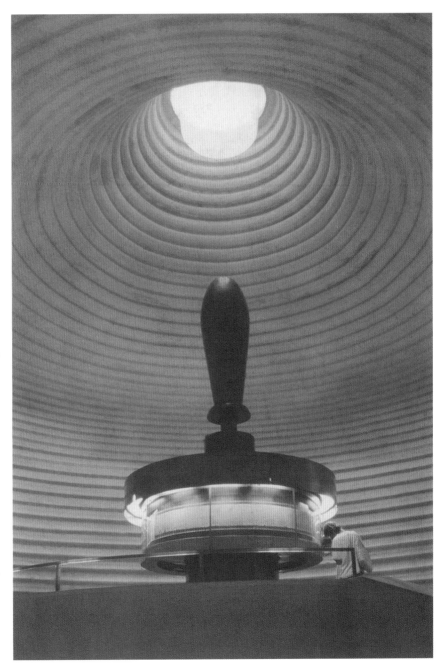

PILGRIMAGE CHURCH

GOTTFRIED BÖHM, 1968 NEVIGES, GERMANY

The pilgrimage church is a building type that has been pursued with remarkable vigour in Catholic countries during the twentieth century. The pilgrim movement has given us such gems as Le Corbusier's peerless chapel at Ronchamp (p.101). Also in the top league is this astonishing church in Neviges, Germany, which rises above a new settlement for pilgrims designed by Gottfried Böhm (born 1920). A stepped walkway winds up and around a snaking twist of pilgrims' hostels up to Böhm's imposing church. This is a triumphant mountain, or more accurately a giant crystal,represented in concrete. Not only is the building very moving, as well as

surprising – much like the Baroque and Rococo churches of eighteenth-century Germany which are far more spiritual in feel than photographs depict – but it demonstrates the possibilities of concrete as a building material. Symbolically, Böhm's masterpiece, appears to be the mountain pilgrims have to climb to reach the Celestial City and to meet God face to face. Even if you are not a believer, it has great power and a haunting majesty without once giving way to the conventional decorative trappings of lesser or more flamboyant Roman Catholic churches. This is very much an overlooked treasure.

BRASÍLIA CATHEDRAL

OSCAR NIEMEYER, 1970 BRASÍLIA, BRAZIL

Designed before Frederick Gibberd's Liverpool Cathedral (p.241) the cathedral at Brasília represents Modern architecture as uncompromised sculpture. It is all of a piece and if you don't like it there are no pretty details or nooks or corners for you to explore to take your eye off the main feast. The reason for this is that the cathedral is designed as much as a place of worship as an Organic and florid counterpart to the daunting geometrical abstraction of the Congress and ministry buildings Niemeyer had completed here previously. The cathedral represents the Crown of Thorns placed on Christ's head before his crucifixion. It is composed of swooping concrete buttresses that rise almost sensually from the ground and are held together almost invisibly at their apex by a ring of steel and concrete. The spaces in between are entirely glazed. The drama of the cathedral is enhanced by the fact that the church is entered from ground level, from a narrow defile or passageway that descends before it climbs in near darkness up into the light of the Crown of Thorns. It is a breathtaking experience. Inside, the cathedral appears to be much bigger than it is from outside. This is because the circular floor is set below ground level and because furniture and worshippers offer a sense of scale that is almost impossible to grasp when walking among the heroic civic monuments of central Brasília.

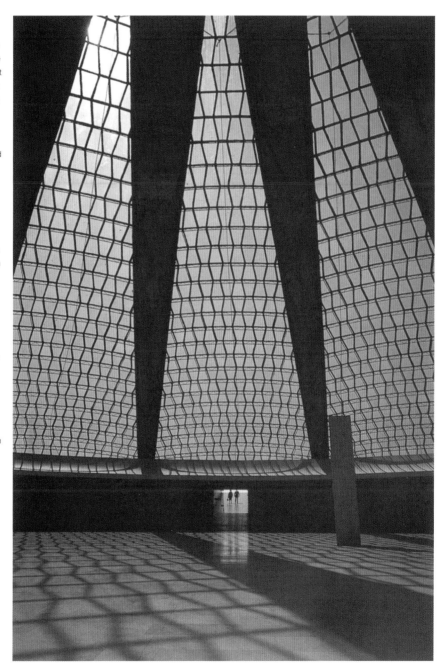

BRION CEMETERY

CARLO SCARPA, 1972 SAN VITO D'ALTIVOLE, TREVISO, ITALY

Carlo Scarpa (1906–78) worked very much in his own personal idiom, and his designs, if never self-effacing, were often a reworking of existing buildings such as the Accademia in Venice (1952), an annexe to the glorious Gipsoteca Canoviana in Treviso (1957) and the influential remodelling of the Castelvecchio at Verona (1964) into a museum (p.233).

Brion Cemetery is one of Carlo Scarpa's finest designs and here, for once, he was given a free hand. Cemetery design in Italy has long been a fine art and Scarpa added to a legacy of proud architecture for those who have moved on – hopefully – to the City of God blissfully free of shopping malls and Postmodernism.

Brion Cemetery has been described as a celebration of death. In actual fact it is difficult to define or categorize. Scarpa has grouped together what appear to be fragments of buildings belonging to no era and yet to all eras. These fragments, like the ruins of ancient Rome as they would have been when first rediscovered by the artists and architects of the Renaissance, are overgrown with rich foliage. The cemetery is alive with birds, insects and creeping things.

Brion Cemetery is a curious place and its is not a little unsettling, however, it is moving all the same. Scarpa built his architecture from fragments and these are curiously – and even mysteriously – often as powerful and as telling as entire buildings.

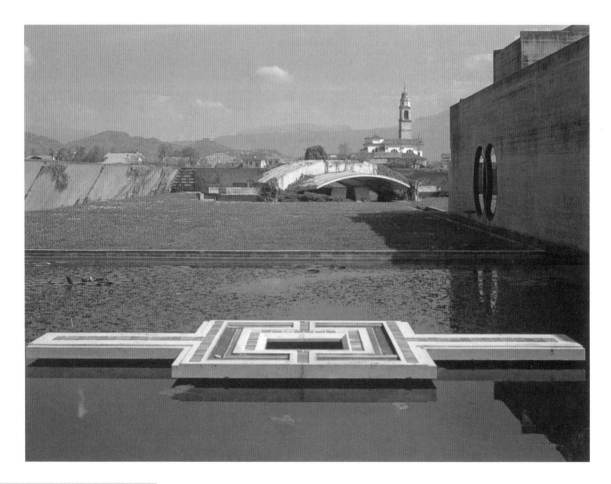

SYDNEY OPERA HOUSE

JØRN UTZON, 1973 SYDNEY, AUSTRALIA

It's fair to say that this highly memorable building put Sydney fairly, if not squarely, on the international map in a way that it never had been before. In truth, the Sydney Opera House is both brilliant and frustrating at one and the same time. No one can doubt the thrill of its roofline – whether you see in those remarkable roofshells the beaks of seagulls, shark fins, waves or wimples – and the fascinating story there is to be had of its construction. The latter was left largely to Peter Rice, a very young Irish structural engineer, working for Ove Arup, who was to be awarded the Royal Gold Medal for Architecture before he died in 1992. The interiors of the building, though, are rather pedestrian: the thrill of the

exterior fails to survive the long haul through the lobbies to the auditorium itself. This is probably because Jørn Utzon (born 1918), the Danish architect, resigned – or was pushed off the project – in 1966 and the building was completed without his special, if wayward, genius.

Rather like Gaudí, Utzon continued to work on the design of his buildings as he went along, so that we do not know quite how he would have finished his most ambitious work. His other buildings, mostly in his native Denmark, are all inventive and combine an intriguing marriage of experimentation with new materials and technologies with Organic forms.

FARKASRÉT MORTUARY CHAPEL

IMRE MAKOVECZ, 1977 BUDAPEST, HUNGARY

The extraordinary and moving interior of this building is a representation of the human rib cage. Coffins are placed where the heart would be and mourners sit on either side in carved wooden stalls that themselves resemble mourners: the chapel is never empty. Dug into the side of a hill in the extensive Farkasrét cemetery in the Buda hills, a winding tram ride from the centre of Budapest, the chapel was the first work of Imre Makovecz (born 1935) to gain international attention. Makovecz is the undisputed leader of an ever-growing band of architects who, like Robin Hood and his Merry Men, were all but outlaws during the Communist era, but since 1989 have been national heroes. Not everyone, of course, appreciates the Organic architecture Makovecz

has nurtured since the early 1970s, yet in the 1980s it became a symbol and rallying point for dissent in Hungary; it was significant that Makovecz was chosen to design the memorable Hungarian pavilion for Expo '92 in Seville.

The son of a carpenter, Makovecz trained as an architect in Budapest. Arrested and tried during the Hungarian uprising of 1956, he was often in trouble with the authorities and was only able to find work designing for the forestry commission and in some of Hungary's remoter villages. With limited materials he developed a style of architecture drawn from the ideas of Frank Lloyd Wright, Bruce Goff and Rudolf Steiner which, at the time, he was able to see only in prohibited books.

STATE LIBRARY

HANS SCHAROUN, 1978 BERLIN, GERMANY

It is hard to get turned on by this lumbering great library designed by Hans Scharoun (1893–1972) and completed by his one-time partner Edgar Wisniewski. The building straddles what was once Potsdammer Strasse and appears to be all over the place with no guiding strategy or form. The interior, though, is a revelation and in parts more than exceedingly good. The main reading room is a wonderful space in which to while away a rainy afternoon, and was used to great effect by Wim Wenders, the German film director, in his poetic film *Wings of Desire*.

The library is one part of a trio of cultural buildings – the other two are the Philharmonic Hall (1963) and the Chamber Music Hall (1987) – all designed by Scharoun who lived long enough only to see the first completed. All share the same wibbly-wobbly look and do not, from the outside anyway, feel like city buildings. Scharoun, however, was the director of building and housing in Berlin after World War Two and perhaps his Organic style was a deliberate reaction against the militaristic Neoclassicism, so beloved by the Nazis and the Prussian kings and emperors before them. His Berlin interiors, however, are a triumph as were the fine villas he built in Germany in the 1930s.

LIVERPOOL CATHEDRAL

GILES GILBERT SCOTT, 1978 LIVERPOOL, ENGLAND

This ecclesiastical Everest was 75 years in the making. It is one of the biggest buildings in the world and a gloriously disdainful design that makes anyone who dares to enter it feel utterly insignificant. The cathedral is 100 metres (330 ft) high, but seems much taller because of its magnificent, if weather-beaten, site on a hill commanding the city stretched out along the River Mersey below.

Giles Gilbert Scott (1880–1960) was just 21 years old when he won the competition to design the cathedral. The building committee insisted he work with an older architect, George Frederick Bodley (1827–1907), which is why the first part of the cathedral to be completed, the Lady Chapel in 1910, is so much fussier and, frankly, Victorian than the red sandstone grandeur that came afterwards.

After Bodley's death, Scott let rip, redesigning the main body of his great masterpiece several times. His genius was to create a vast space beneath the principal crossing quite unlike that of a medieval English cathedral. The sense of space here is daunting. Throughout, the building is masterful and proof that the Gothic tradition was far from exhausted. Construction continued throughout World War Two, during which time the cathedral was bombed.

The west front was finally completed by Frederick Thomas in 1978 with more than a little assistance from tons of concrete and the use of other modern materials. These have been carefully hidden.

NATIONAL ASSEMBLY BUILDING

LOUIS KAHN, 1983 DHAKA, BANGLADESH

Louis Kahn (1901–74) worked on the design of this highly original building – a cluster of covered spaces linked together – for the last 11 years of his life, and in the event it took 20 years to complete. A remarkable fusion of the religious and political spheres, it is first and foremost a superb meeting place. The programme is complex with assembly chamber, mosque and offices appearing to wrap around and even circle one another as one walks its watery perimeter. The essential architectural components are the cube and the sphere, worked and reworked until the repertoire is all but exhausted. The red brick walls are lined inside with concrete and marble

and, as one would expect of Kahn, washed, dappled and adorned with beautiful shafts and beams of daylight playing from slits and chutes, arches and skylights. Interior and exterior play complementary games and the whole complex can be experienced as a thrilling architectural puzzle. The construction is well able to hold back the wall of heat that leans against Dhaka much of the year.

The Assembly Building is located on the edge of the Bangladeshi capital in a city extension known as Sher-e-Bangla Nagur or "the city of the Bengal Tiger". Kahn's powerful design ensures it lives up to its formidable name.

LOWENGASSE AND
KEGELGASSE HOUSING

FRIEDENSREICH HUNDERTWASSER, 1985 VIENNA, AUSTRIA

Social housing like no other. Artist and architect Friedensreich
Hundertwasser (born 1928) broke away entirely from the constraints
of conventional city apartment blocks with this madcap design.
Future residents were engaged in a dialogue with the architect who
interpreted their needs and desires in a wilfully loose-fit manner. The
end result is a building that looks like a big bit of knitting or weaving
that has gone askew and in which every last colour of wool or thread
in the basket has been used up to get the job finished. These houses
might not be to everyone's taste and it does help to look at them
when wearing sunglasses, yet Hundertwasser's popularity should
not be in doubt. He has listened to people and, in a very literal way,

brought colour into the lives of those who previously have had little say
in where and how they live. But, is this a real improvement on, say,
Vienna's Karl Marx Hof (p.30)?

The 1980s were a time in which some of the big questions relating
to social housing were addressed. In Britain, the solution was to stop
building altogether. The French got Ricardo Bofill and the Taller de
Arquitectura (pp.62–3), the Genovese Renzo Piano (p.277) and the
Viennese Hundertwasser. Many mistakes were made during this
decade, but architects were being forced to learn how to discuss their
work and to engage with those who had to live in their designs. If
they didn't want to listen, then the likes of Hundertwasser would.

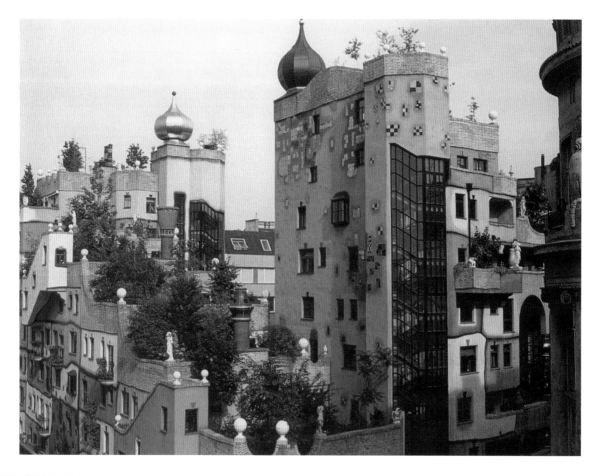

CHURCH OF THE LIGHT

TADAO ANDO, 1989 IBARAKI, OSAKA, JAPAN

Set in a built-up district of Osaka, Ando's Church of the Light transforms the congregation of the Ibaraki Kasugaoka Church (a branch of the United Church of Christ in Japan) into an otherworldly realm. The building is simple: a rectangle of concrete panels is cut through with a freestanding wall to create an opening sense of drama. The interior is immensely powerful. Behind the altar the wall is a cross of light. Ando (born 1941) wanted this to be unglazed so that the congregation would feel the spirit of God move upon them. But as this would have been more like the spirit of Azrael, the angel of death, in the cold winter months, he thought better of this. The light from the cruciform opening reflects on the concrete roof: the symbol of the cross feels omnipresent and there is no need for any religious art to reinforce this bold message. The blackened cedar floor slopes down to the altar, the Church believing that as Christ moved among his people, the priest should do the same.

This building is another reminder of how architecture can be free of decoration, yet rich in symbolism and even spiritual power. Much of this, as Ando knows better than perhaps any architect at the end of the twentieth century, is to do with the manipulation of light and shadow. The twentieth century was one that tried to banish the shadow and thus one of the key expressions of the realm of the spirit.

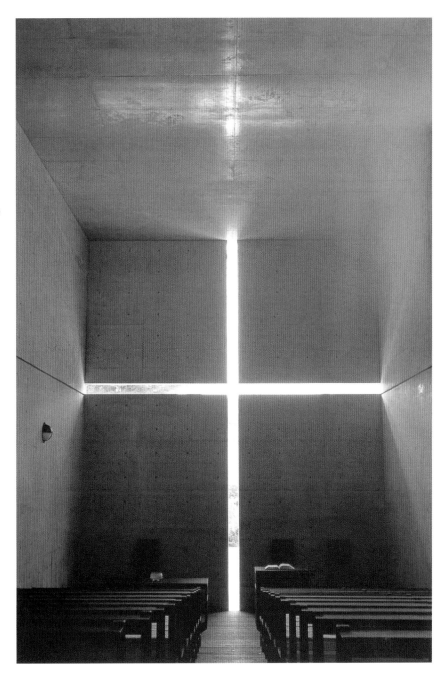

PHOENIX LIBRARY

WILL BRUDER, 1992 PHOENIX, ARIZONA, USA

Will Bruder (born 1946) trained as a sculptor, but as an architect he was self taught. A modern disciple of Frank Lloyd Wright, he is part of a US tradition that generates local colour and form while adapting to and taking up with new materials and building technologies. The result, as can be seen in this impressive library, is an architecture that seems relaxed and informal despite its monumental scale and strong sculptural form. On its sunny side, the library presents a tall and solid wall faced in local stone, coloured concrete and corrugated steel. On its shady side it presents an almost sheer wall of glass to the world, although this is tempered by a grille of steel mullions and transoms. The effect is dramatic, particularly so at night when the building casts strong shadows. The interior

on several levels is ultra-modern in a laid-back version of "Hi Tech". The lofty steel roof of the topmost reading room is held up by tapering masts that sprout struts like branches from a machine-made tree.

In effect, Bruder's library is rather like a modern barn. This is a reasonable comparison, not least because it was built cheaply and has none of the pretensions, delays and precious aesthetic foibles of the Bibliothèque Nationale (p.344) or the British Library (p.292). The library incorporates an abundance of new computer technology and is living proof that the rise of the home computer and the Internet is not a reason to suppose that the big public library will be disappearing anytime soon.

CHURCH OF THE HOLY SPIRIT

IMRE MAKOVECZ, 1992 PAKS, HUNGARY

Paks, a small town on the Danube south of Budapest, is famous for two modern buildings: Hungary's only nuclear power station and, this, the Church of the Holy Spirit, designed by Imre Makovecz. Local children call it the "devil's church" because of its rather Transylvanian look. It is one of Makovecz's most distinguished buildings. The womb-like body of the church is contrasted with the detached bell tower and its three spires. These are capped with symbols representing the sun, moon and crucifixion. The church – a superb example of the skill of Makovecz's roving band of carpenters – is meant to be a representation of the opposites of dark and light, earth and sky, male and female, sun and moon. Its symbolism is pagan and Catholic at one and the same time, and is all the more realistic and powerful for being so. The interior is lit from the top by a stained glass ceiling shaped like an ancient Celtic symbol, often used in jewellery, representing eternity. Daylight filters down into a nave and chancel that flow naturally into one another and are realized throughout in timber. Makovecz says that his mission is to reconcile Heaven with Earth and in his highly personal and moving buildings he gets a long way in recreating what must have been the sentiments and aesthetic expression of the early church at a time when the pagan tribes of the Hungarian plains took to Christianity.

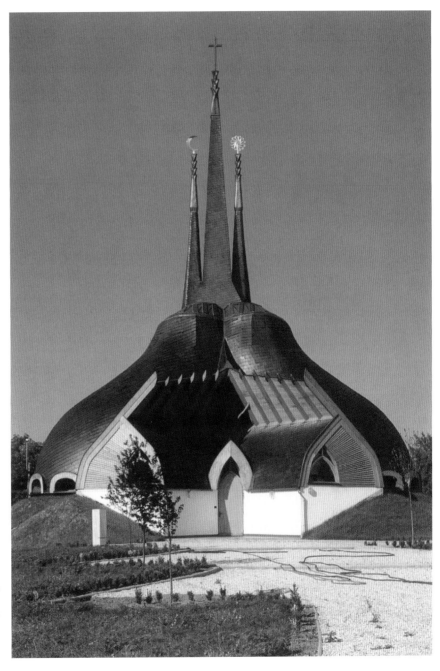

AMERICAN HERITAGE CENTER

ANTOINE PREDROCK, 1993 LARAMIE, WYOMING, USA

Antoine Predrock (born 1936) is keen on UFOs, which makes sense when you come across the American Heritage Center: it looks as if it might have landed from outer space and be full of "greys". Stuck out in a deserted landscape, it can certainly come across as rather sinister. This museum and heritage centre is one of those buildings visitors enjoy attaching labels to: it's a flying saucer; no, it's an Indian tepee. and so on. In fact, the architect seemed to enjoy this game too – while pointing out that it was also intended to reflect the nearby Medicine Bow mountains. Its location is a fascinating landscape of mountain, forest, desert, hot springs and the graveyards of dinosaurs:

these natural riches and historical depths are reflected in the building.

Predrock is a master of the dramatic architectural image and it is not a surprise to learn that he was also one of the architects of EuroDisney. The patinated copper dome of the main body of the Heritage Center rises from a podium along which are ranged a variety of stone-clad outbuildings that, although blocky and more strictly geometrical than the dome, are as equally enigmatic. Like the buildings of Frank Lloyd Wright, the Heritage Center creates a man-made drama out of a big landscape that would swamp a neat little something by a city architect.

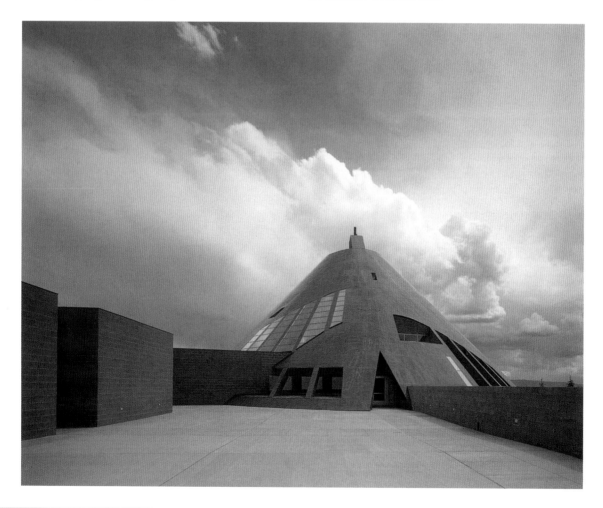

TRUSS-WALL HOUSE

EISAKU USHIDA AND KATHRYN FINDLAY, 1997 TOKYO, JAPAN

Throughout the 1990s, young architects began to rediscover the Modernism that had been buried under layers of Postmodern and other stylistic conceits in the previous twenty years. For many, this meant the pursuit of a soft Modern style that was more concerned with pure appearance or style, rather than the concerns that the first Moderns had with plan and purpose. The upshot was a creamy smooth and polite white architecture, beloved by fashion magazines, that could travel anywhere and be accepted everywhere. There were exceptions to this rule such as this clever and endearing house in Tokyo by Eisaku Ushida and Kathryn Findlay. Its soft, flowing, Organic style mirrors an intelligent plan that allows for a relaxed way of living in one of the worlds most intense cities. Delightfully, for a collaboration between a British and a Japanese architect, it makes no play on national traditions but has a character entirely of its own. The sweeping forms adopted by Ushida and Findlay were part of a move in the mid-1990s to more Organic forms in interiors, fashion and furniture. If there was a bit of the Space Agein the design mix, then this reflected the optimism of the architects who clearly believed that Postmodern irony (or defeatist decadence) was dead and that the Modern house was still a worthy subject for research and celebration.

HINDU TEMPLE

VARIOUS MASONS, 1997 NEASDEN, LONDON, ENGLAND

One of the most charming new buildings in London at the end of the twentieth century is this Hindu temple on the North Circular Road in Neasden, a suburb best known as a standing joke in the satirical fortnightly *Private Eye*, but here reinvented as a larger-than-life slice of life in India. Unlike previous Hindu architecture in Britain – which since the mid-eighteenth century had been used as a style for follies, rococo interior decoration, the Royal Pavilion in Brighton and the odd romantic country house like Sezincote – this is the real thing. The Hindu population in Britain has grown as thousands of Indian people previously settled in various parts of the world, notably East Africa, have come to Britain in search of security, education and freedom of religious expression. In Neasden, this freedom is expressed in a gloriously frothy white marble architecture that was cut and shaped, carved and decorated almost entirely in India with the numbered pieces being shipped over as and when needed. In this sense, this is certainly no fake and is part of a religious tradition that sees no need to reinvent the fundamentals and certainly not the details of the design of its temples. Rising in a wave of exuberant domes and filigree details above the red-tiled roofs of Mock Tudor Neasden, it is truly a sight to behold, a welcome addition to a hit-and-miss townscape.

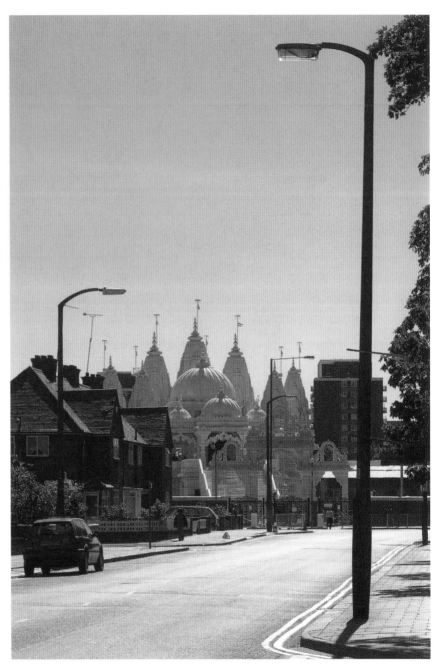

THERMAL BATH

PETER ZUMTHOR, 1997 VALS, SWITZERLAND

Peter Zumthor (born 1943) won international acclaim for this unexpected and beautiful thermal bath in southern Switzerland. Part of an old hotel that had run to seed and was in need of new life, the bath is reached by a tunnel. The ascent, through the various changing rooms, steam rooms and plunge pools, is thrilling and relaxing at one and the same time. At the top, a steaming pool opens up into the mountainscape where in winter the mix of snow, steam, hot water and icy air is intoxicating. The quality, invention and touch of Zumthor's architecture lifts the experience into that of the sublime. Every material that a hand or foot touches is a pleasure, whether it is stone, terrazzo, timber or leather. The bath is a feast for the senses and not least the eye.

The building itself is dug into a hillside leaving one handsome flank exposed and the rest a secret well worth discovering. Zumthor is a craftsman as well as an architect and this shows clearly throughout the building in which every join has been treated with a Zen-like care. Because of this and the fact that he worked with own building team, Zumthor's output is small and largely confined to a corner of his native Switzerland. To find an architect of such quality and originality working within such a tight confine is unusual at the end of a century of hurriedly consumed images.

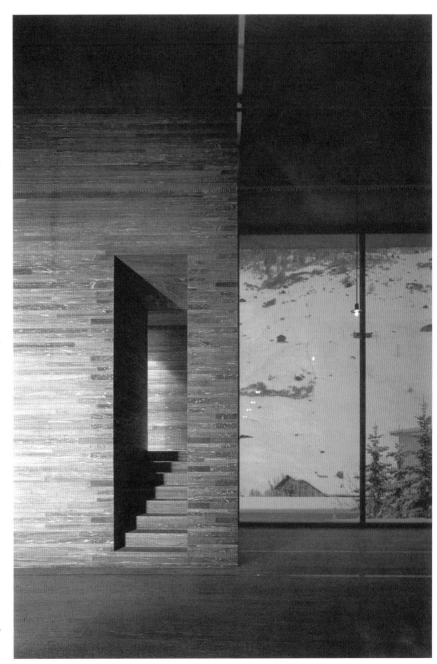

DRUK WHITE LOTUS SCHOOL

ARUP ASSOCIATES, 2001 LADAKH, INDIA

This magnificent Himalayan school is the result of years of inspirational work by the Ladakhi Buddhist community, the Drupka Trust, the engineers Arup and architects Arup Associates. Its patron is the Dalai Lama. Designed for 800 local children of all religious backgrounds, the school, due for completion in 2009, is like a small town comprising, to date, classrooms, dining hall, kitchen, clinic, a teachers' home and children's dormitories.

Each building faces either a tree-lined avenue or a garden, or small stone-paved streets or squares. In summer, classes are held outdoors whenever possible. The children, many of whom tend goats high in the mountains, are not kept cooped up in classrooms, no matter how graciously these have been designed. From necessity and common sense, the remotely located school is self-sufficient in both food and, thanks to solar power, energy.

"What everyone wanted," says Jonathan Rose, project architect, "is a design that is both traditional and modern, as timeless as possible. Local building skills are of a very high order, and we have been learning from them. In recent years, modern concrete construction has been slowly invading Ladakh. This is unsuitable because of the severe climate and frequent earth tremors. We agreed on granite walls inset with a mud core.

These are stable, well-insulated and blend in naturally with the mountain setting. When you see how well the surrounding monasteries have survived – up to a thousand years – in such hostile conditions, you learn to respect what has gone before."

STEPHENAEUM

IMRE MAKOVECZ, 2002 PILISCSABA, HUNGARY

The most sensational of Imre Makovecz's many sensational "organic" buildings is unquestionably the Stephenaeum, an auditorium and the cultural heart of the Pázmány Péter Catholic University of the Sacred Heart's faculty of humanities at Piliscsaba, some 20 kilometres (12 miles) north of Budapest. The Makovecz design – and, yes, it is real – takes the form of two circular buildings, one adopted from the form of a traditional Magyar *jurta* (yurt), the other a Renaissance tempietto, crashing into one other. Here, it appears, are two opposite worlds, urban and rural, rational and romantic, national and international, trying to match and marry.

In recent years, Piliscsaba has become a green-belt commuter town. Two thousand years ago, the Romans knew the site of the university campus as "ad lucum felicem" (happy meadow). It was also the home of the Hapsburg-era military, and, from 1957 to 1990, a no-go base for the occupying Red Army. Now a nature reserve, the campus has been developed peacefully. New pavilion-style buildings, no more than four stories high, jostle quietly for attention among trees, plants and Makovecz's bombast. The smaller, classical dome houses a proscenium stage, while the bigger, folkloric dome curves around stepped rows of auditorium seats. It is hard to know whether the twin domes are meant to be rising or falling, stretching up to the skies or sinking into the earth. The building complex, with its theatre, chapel, dining and meeting rooms, is, if extraordinary in almost every way, practical.

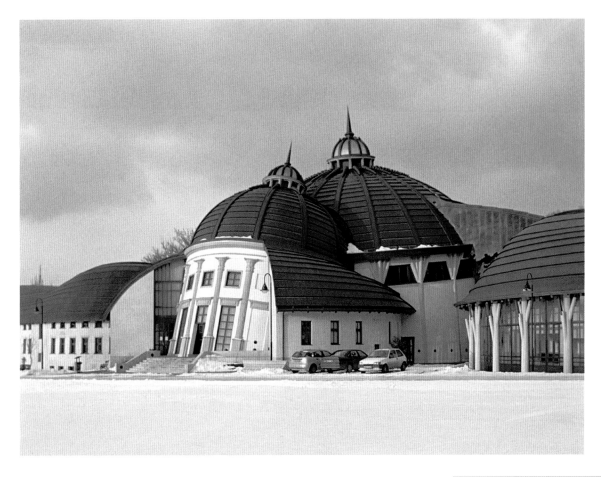

AN TURAS SHELTER

CHARLIE SUTHERLAND AND CHARLIE HUSSEY, 2003 TIREE, INNER HEBRIDES, SCOTLAND

The An Turas ferry shelter in Tiree, designed by a collaboration of Scottish architects and artists – Sandra Kennedy, Glen Onwin and Donald Urquhart – is one of the most beautiful new buildings in rural Britain. This haunting and elemental structure seems set to take its place alongside the island's Iron Age standing stones as a thing not of fleeting fashion but of a timeless history.

Warm and exceptionally sunny for much of the year, Tiree is battered by an angry Atlantic in winter. The shelter is where, when the winds are strong, passengers can wait for one of Cal-Mac's ferries as it struggles, not always successfully, to tie up alongside. The shelter, meanwhile, is an extension of the Hebridean landscape, although not slave to it. It frames spine-tingling views of sea, ships and sky. Its designers had tramped Tiree in search of visual inspiration. From the outset, this was to be no ordinary waiting room or windbreak. The clues they found included white walls, clean lines, minimalist character, ideal proportions, intimate spaces, light and shadow, panoramic views, vast sea, vast sky, black rock, white sand, green landscape, intense sun, driving rain. They observed how Tiree, flat and treeless, is like a low, level band stretching across the ocean. In between undulating ground and massive sky, the shelter presents a horizon of white render, black stained timber, glass and steel against a backdrop of clouds, hills, sea, patrolling swans and incoming ferries. It appears to be a self-evident part of its beautiful setting.

BIRD SANCTUARY

VAN HEYNINGEN AND HAWARD ARCHITECTS, 2004 RAINHAM, ESSEX, ENGLAND

The Thames Gateway was the name used by politicians and developers to describe tracts of Essex marshland east of London along the Thames, together with the corresponding north Kent coast, scheduled to be buried under new housing estates defined as "sustainable communities" between 2000 and 2020. Here, local wildlife was threatened, and architecture all but a lost cause.

Yet in the summer of 2000, the Royal Society for the Protection of Birds (RSPB) bought a redundant Ministry of Defence firing range on the Rainham Marshes. The wildlife charity commissioned Van Heyningen and Haward Architects to design a building that truly reflected the life and character of this delicate and hauntingly beautiful landscape. The new RSPB sanctuary promised to be a truly modern, yet all but timeless, cross between a barn and a boat,

anchored gracefully on the banks of the Thames. Clapboard-clad, naturally ventilated, relying on solar power and recycled rainwater, it was to work gently in a sensitive environment. Because this is a crime-ridden area, the building was designed to be reached over isolating drainage ditches by hydraulically powered drawbridges. Birkin Haward previously worked with Norman Foster and was thoroughly grounded in the design of lightweight structures and materials. Joanna van Heyningen was previously with Neylan and Ungless, architects with roots in the English vernacular tradition. As a result, what was proposed for RSPB Rainham was a light and carefully considered structure designed to belong here as eighteenth-century clapboard sea captains' houses do, and as most new architectural intrusions refuse to.

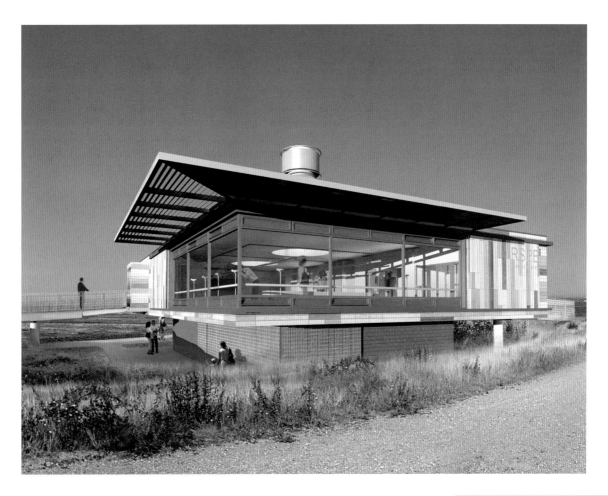

SCOTTISH PARLIAMENT

EMBT-RMJM, 2004 EDINBURGH, SCOTLAND

Monumentally over budget, this joyous building for Scottish MPs was the object of much mean-minded vilification in Scotland when it was completed, by which time its Catalan architect, Enric Miralles, commissioned in 1998, was dead and buried. In parsimonious Edinburgh, it seemed as if members of the local press had been issued with microscopes, hydrometers and micrometer screw-gauges to examine and measure the tiniest flaw in the completed design. A single drop of water issuing from pipe, gutter or glass-roof valley was to be the stuff of braying headlines and fist-waving leaders. It is, however, a building of great richness and complexity, and one that will both outlast fashion and concerns over its costs.

The complexity of Miralles's fairy-tale, walk-in-the-woods design is such that it is hard to talk of this as a single building. It is, instead, a cluster of boats, a sweeping of leaves, a collection of seaside shells, a Pandora's box of architectural motifs laced together ingeniously, this side of pandemonium. The structure stretches beyond its immediate setting at one end of the city's famous Royal Mile and out, as if organically, into the stirring hillsides beyond. Miralles might have woven this magical building through with unfathomable spaces, complex structures and arcane symbolism, yet whatever all this was ever meant to mean, it matters less than the feeling that the building's costly, splintered richness evokes the spirit of a confident, relaxed, inventive and even a generous democracy.

BUTTERFLY HOUSE

LAURIE CHETWOOD, 2004 GODALMING, SURREY, ENGLAND

If a caterpillar awoke one morning from uneasy dreams to find it had metamorphosed into a detached house in leafiest Surrey, it might look like this. The Butterfly House is a mutation of a 1930s timber-framed home. With its bright winged canopies, serpentine pathways and a garden that twists through its science-fiction interiors, it must surely be one of the most surreal homes ever to have been built. This is not the brainchild of some Mad Hatter-turned-housebuilder, however, but of a successful commercial architect. The Butterfly House is Laurie Chetwood's plaything: a building, part mechanical, part organic, that grew, as if by itself – at once artwork, laboratory for architectural experimentation, part-time family home, design studio and a richly planted attraction for bright clouds of butterflies.

Constructed of timber, Kevlar sails, steel, copper and plastic ducts, two kilometres (2,187 yards) of bungee rope, over 100 metres (328 ft) of fibre-optic cables and 50 interwoven carbon-fibre fishing rods, the house is inseparable from its garden, a tangle of natural and artificial plants. It is hard to tell where nature ends and architecture begins. Owing something to the imaginations of Lewis Carroll, Franz Kafka and Jules Verne, the house is also imbued with references to pop art designers such as Roger Dean, and to films by, among others, Terry Gilliam, or Jean-Pierre Jeunet and Marc Caro. The former's *Brazil* comes to mind, and the latter's *The City of Lost Children*. The result is a house that is unprecedented.

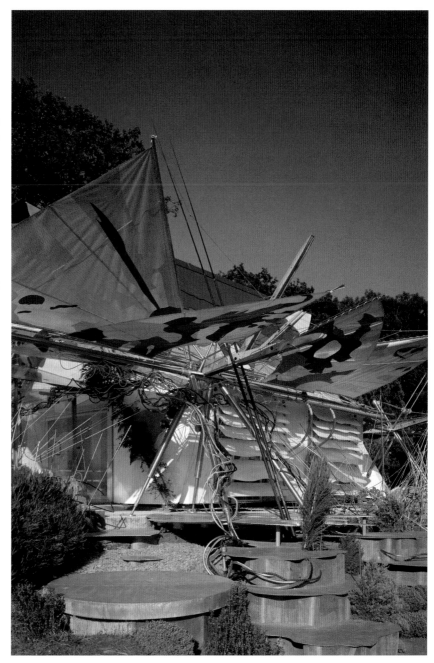

SANTA CATERINA MARKET

EMBT, 2005 BARCELONA, SPAIN

Seven years in the making, the renovated Santa Caterina market in central Barcelona is a retail food emporium utterly unlike a morgue-like global superstore, glistening with fresh fish and seafood, bloody with skinned rabbits and poultry, gleaming with fruit and vegetables, all set under a highly theatrical roof. The hundred or so market stalls housed in this three-level structure are covered with a great, wave-like magic carpet of 325,000 colourful ceramic tiles lifted on writhing, and intertwining, steel columns.

Inevitably, the market was the subject of much scrutiny in Edinburgh, where EMBT were also responsible for the new Scottish Parliament (p.128). The big question, rehearsed in the pages of the *Scotsman*, was whether or not the sinfully expensive Scottish Parliament building was merely a rehash of the much cheaper Santa Caterina market. But, as Bernadette Tagliabue of EMBT told the paper, "a series of buildings that one architect designs is like children from the same family. To the parents they are all different but to outsiders there are lots of similarities. I don't see any direct similarities between the Scottish Parliament and the Caterina Market, but they do have in common the aim to break boundaries. Both buildings are trying to influence their surroundings, which are both old parts of cities. They are both more than buildings, but a piece of the city. It is natural that there will be similarities, as architects are not infinite." Construction in Barcelona took so very long not because of political wrangling and rows over cash, but because of a complex brief and an archaeological dig.

ACCORDION HOUSE

24H ARCHITECTURE, 2005 GLAKOGEN NATURE RESERVE, SWEDEN

A house that pokes its horned and scaly head out of its red shingly shell deep in a forest, as if foraging for food, sounds like the stuff of Hobbity nightmares: it seems to be alive. If you stop and listen hard, you can almost hear it breathing. The cabin is, in fact, a summer escape for Maartje Lammers and Boris Zeisser, principals of the Rotterdam-based practice 24H Architecture, and their daughter. They bought an eighteenth-century fisherman's cottage in the Arjangs Commun, Varmland, four years ago, and set about transforming it.

There was, though, one small problem: local bylaws meant they could only extend the cabin by 30 square metres (36 square yards), to prevent over-development in a sensitive area invaded by Dutch and German families in the summer. To gain the extra space needed to make the cabin a decent size, and to take full advantage of the view over the adjacent stream, Lammers and Zeisser hit on the idea of an extending house. The original cabin is now the bedroom, while the turtle-like 30-square-metre (36-square-yard) extension is attached to pulleys and a retracting steel frame mounted on roller-bearings. In this way, it can be projected over the stream without breaking building laws. The family can open the windows of the cabin's head wide and sit above the meandering stream. When they return south in the winter, they pull the head back in, and the cabin is, once again, no bigger than is allowed.

SHEEP STABLE

70F ARCHITECTS 2008 ALMERE, NETHERLANDS

Because of their rugged simplicity, farm buildings are often some of the most satisfying and beautiful of all to look at. In an era when all too many architects and clients are trying all too hard to create exciting buildings for over-stimulated human beings, some farm animals appear to have a less stressful life. Here, in Holland, 70F have designed a truly special "sheep stable" for the City of Almere which has its own resident popuation of about 80 sheep. Designed to receive human visitors as well as to house sheep, the stable is a gently curved, steel-framed building clad in timber. On the first floor, there is a small office and a room for the city's shepherd. What is notable here is the humane way in which the animals have been provided shelter and, although people – especially schoolchildren – come to see them, the wellbeing of the animals takes first place; this is not a theme park. The form of the building is a happy one, curving in to the ground and with an organic feel that makes it exactly right for its purpose. Inside, the space is warm and generous, while outside the timber cladding is varied and crafted. It is a sobering thought to consider that not only do many new homes in European suburbs lack this quality of design and construction (Holland is often an exception), but all too many people worldwide live in homes Almere's sheep would turn their noses up at.

BRUDER KLAUS FIELD CHAPEL

PETER ZUMTHOR 2007 MECHERNICH, GERMANY

Rising from prosperous, vine-growing farmland at Mechernich, a village some 30 miles (48km) south-west of Cologne, the Bruder Klaus Field Chapel is a small, intensely spiritual shrine commissioned and built by a local farmer, Hermann Josef Scheidtweiler, in honour of "Brother Klaus", the religious mystic also known as Nicholas of Flue: a fifteenth-century hermit who is also the patron saint of Switzerland. The Zumthor chapel is a contemporary take on the hermit's chapel and cell. It takes the form of what appears to be a simple, handmade, concrete tower, rising 12 metres (39 ft) in 24 tiers above the surrounding hills. The form derives from one of the hermit's visions in which he looked up through a tunnel to the stars. The concrete of the tower was poured by Herr Scheidtweiler, family and friends over a wigwam-like timber frame. Once the concrete had set, this frame was set on fire, creating walls inside the chapel that are strangely blackened and haunted with the ghosts of the charred timbers that once supported them. The floor is a frozen pool of molten lead, while the roof is open to the sky and, by night, the field of stars above. Zumthor's chapel is numinously dark inside, but when you look up, the oculus itself resembles the flare of a star – a reference to a vision of Brother Klaus. Being here alone in a building that has no worldly purpose is close to feeling, if not understanding, the faith that sustained the Swiss hermit.

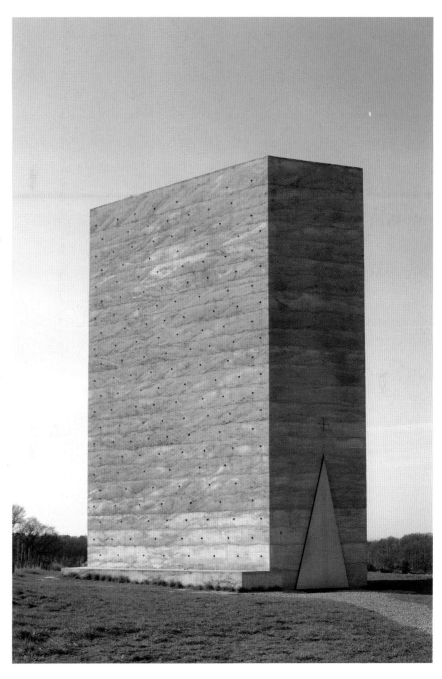

OSLO OPERA HOUSE

SNOHETTA 2008 OSLO, NORWAY

Like an iceberg that has floated into the city centre, Oslo's new opera house is an astonishing and delightful sight. Its surface gleams white. Its walls slope and disappear into the water. When covered with snow, young people snowboard down them. When the short summer comes to Oslo, people strip off and sunbathe against all this unexpected whiteness. And, yet, inside this architectural iceberg, all is seasoned Baltic oak, traditional boatyard craftsmanship and suitably hushed acoustics. What a complex and contradictory building. What a special place. Here is a public building – "a social democratic monument," say its designers – that captures something of the spirit of Norway's snow-smothered mountains and icebergs, with its white marble and clear glass

exterior. The roof, along with the aluminium-clad fly tower, is very much the dominant feature. In fact, from the waterside, the roof is the building. This vast undulating plane, or sequence of planes, comprising 36,000 individually cut slabs of Carrara marble, slopes down from the heights of the fly tower, covers the auditorium and ends up, very deliberately, under water. Although apparently isolated when first opened, the opera house is, in fact, only the anchor of a major new redevelopment of the docklands in this part of Oslo. Inside, it is like a city of its own, bustling with round-the-clock activity, while its auditorium is a superb and cosseting place, in which to experience opera. Here is a cultural mountain everyone who comes to Oslo will want to climb.

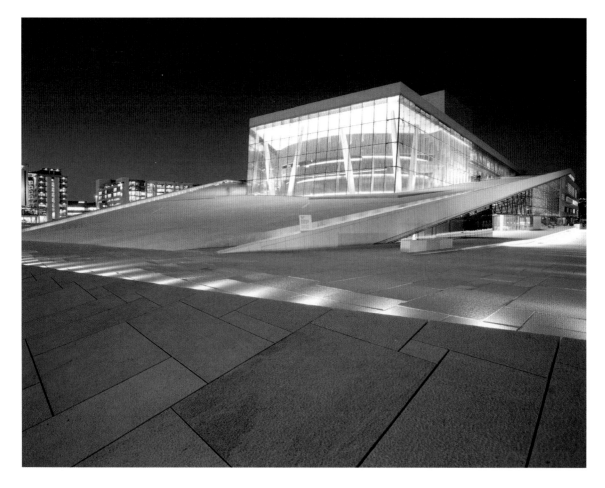

KIELDER OBSERVATORY

CHARLES BARCLAY 2008 NORTHUMBERLAND, ENGLAND

The Kielder Forest enjoys the lowest levels of light pollution in England, making it a perfect place to watch stars. Here, Charles Barclay has designed a gloriously inventive, yet low-key observatory. It is a place where amateur stargazers and professional astronomers can share telescopes, viewing platforms, ideas and knowledge, beneath one of the most wonderful sights the country has to offer, as the sun sets on clear days and eyes adjust to the seemingly infinite expanse of stars above. Set on concrete stilts, the observatory has two hand-cranked, rotating, telescope turrets; between them sits an open-air terrace where amateur stargazers can unfold their telescopes and a timber retreat called the "warm room". This is where professional astronomers can operate the smaller telescope remotely, by computer. The room is equipped with a stove, and there's a compost lavatory next door. All the energy the observatory needs is generated by a 2.5-kw wind turbine and by solar power. This special building touches down on the Kielder landscape as gently as a long-legged fly on the nearby reservoir. Barclay's observatory is a happy balance between what appears to be little more than a simple, almost cartoon-like, timber gangway with some sheds on top and some fine technology inside, with the cranks and cogs needed for the telescope turrets sitting delightfully within the simple wooden walls, floors and ceilings. It is rather like being in an early Victorian steamship, especially in the dark, when the red lamps glow and the brightest light is that of the stars.

HAFOD ERYRI

RAY HOLE 2008 SNOWDONIA, WALES

Hafod Eryri, the new Snowdon Mountain railway terminus and visitor centre on top of the Welsh peak replaced what the Prince of Wales had described as "the highest slum in Wales". This was the concrete café that tourists pouring from the steam mountain railway trains made a bee-line for, especially in the kind of weather that can make Snowdon a very ferocious place indeed. The new station and café set 1,069 metres (3,507 ft) above sea level is Britain's second highest inhabited building (the highest, at 1,097 metres [3,600 ft] – is the Ptarmigan station restaurant on Cairn Gorm in the Scottish Highlands); it is also a fine design. The curved stone- and slate-faced building is somehow both modern and ancient; it is elemental, and now

a piece of the Snowdon landscape, hunkering down into the rocks. Construction work took place in what were often appalling conditions. The workforce made their way up to the site, along with all the materials, by train. In winter, trains had to be dug out of the snow and, in the worst instances, builders had to trek back down the mountainside after a hard day's work. With its high roof and huge picture windows, this is a fine place to watch the elements. And, yet, not even this tough building is wholly immune to the weather. When the summer ends, it closes. Windows are closed and shuttered. As the snows fall, it becomes little more than a picturesque rock pile. This, truly, is architecture in extremis.

KNUT HAMSUN CENTRE

STEVEN HOLL 2009 PRESTEID, NORWAY

The Hamsun Centre at Presteid, a hamlet of Hamarøy, a village in Norway's Nordland district, some 200 miles (322 km) north of the Arctic Circle, commemorates Norway's most famous novelist, Knut Hamsun, a Nobel prize-winner and, for many writers, the father of the modern novel. Opened in time to celebrate the 150th anniversary of the writer's birth, the Hamsun Centre is an intriguing and special building by the American architect Steven Holl. A skewed tower rising from the site of the old parsonage where Hamsun grew up, the black, timber-clad building has been designed as the architectural personification of the novelist. Brilliant. Awkward. Difficult. Controversial. However brilliant he was, Hamsun supported Hitler. Jewish organizations have been relentless in their attack on the very idea of a centre ostensibly celebrating the life and work of this controversial writer. The Hamsun Centre, however, is very definitely not a hagiography written in concrete and timber. Holl and his clients set out from the beginning somehow to portray as well as explain Hamsun's complex and sometimes contradictory life, so the building is as challenging as it is haunting. Inside the building, whose spine is an exposed, brass-encased lift shaft, floors slope, daylight shines from unexpected angles and sudden balconies project over precipitous drops and stunning views. One of the unexpected windows here is in the shape of an open book, offering pages illuminated with mesmerising, real life views of Nordland. All this is slightly unsettling – as, of course, was Hamsun himself, his life and books.

NEUES MUSEUM

DAVID CHIPPERFIELD 2009 BERLIN, GERMANY

Neglected and unloved, the nineteenth-century Neues Museum (Friedrich August Stuler, 1855) had been no more than a dilapidated hulk since the end of the Second World War. Allied bombing had turned it into a charred ruin. An entire wing had gone. Spectacular spaces such as the Egyptian courtyard had been blasted to smithereens. The museum's collection – including the prized 3,300-year-old bust of Queen Nefertiti, found in Egypt in 1912 – had long been dispersed for safe-keeping. After the fall of the Berlin Wall, its fortunes looked up. In 1997, David Chipperfield won a competition that, over many painstaking years, has returned the Neues Museum to more than its former glory.

Chipperfield reconstructed and renewed the building, while Julian Harrap painstakingly restored murals, frescoes, mosaics, long-lost colour schemes and fine detailing. Where there was nothing left to restore, Chipperfield designed bold new spaces – notably the magnificent central stairwell. And he has cleverly tucked away modern lighting, heating and security essentials into hidden spaces so that Stüler's great promenade of rooms is entirely uninterrupted. This, despite great damage to the building during the Second World War, is a magical experience. While, from the outside, the museum appears to be the most severe pantechnicon, inside it abounds in architectural adventure and sorcery. The Neues Museum greatly extended the scope of Chipperfield's work. It showed that an unapologetic modernist could take a major historic building and bring fresh life to it without losing the old fabric, its charm and its ghosts.

ROLEX LEARNING CENTRE

SANAA 2010 LAUSANNE, SWITZERLAND

Here is a building resembling a giant donut that seems to have dropped on a university campus with a backdrop of a Swiss lake and the Alps. It seems a little unreal. It is also utterly fascinating and almost wholly original. This is a research centre designed by the Japanese architects, Sanaa (led by Kazuyo Sejima and Ryue Nishizawa), for the Ecole Polytechnique Federale de Lausanne. Here, many remarkable scientific, computing and engineering developments are nurtured, but, until the arrival of this new "Learning Centre" there was no one place on the campus that students and teachers from across the various disciplines could meet easily and exchange ideas. The big idea here is that new ideas might emerge from meetings of minds. So, the

building itself has been designed like some free form, and all but transparent brain. Here, as far as possible, barriers to movement (and thinking) have been removed; so, there are few doors or stairs: spaces flow freely one into the other. The building which is largely raised from the ground, rises and falls in a smooth and seamless sequence of glazed curves, winding their way around courtyard gardens. Although it houses libraries and places for quiet study, it is primarily one big meeting place, one extraordinary room, to encourage intellectual enquiry. It is also the building that put Sanaa firmly on the sky map of star architects; here is a dream of an ethereal, lightweight, floating architecture freed of conventional rooms and plans, made day-dreamingly real.

MARTELLO TOWER

PIERCY CONNER 2010 BAWDSEY, SUFFOLK, ENGLAND

Made of 750,000 bricks with walls 4 metres (13 ft) thick, this Martello tower was one of 103 built along the English coast at the time of the Napoleonic Wars when the threat of a French invasion seemed all too real. It was never meant for comfort. Duncan Jackson, an industrial designer who bought the tower in 2000 worked closely on the design with Stuart Piercy; the two had worked together at Nicholas Grimshaw and Partners. It was the new, undulating, plywood roof, swooping over three-quarters of the battlements, that did most to turn the tower into a modern home. This elegant parasol not only provides a dramatic ceiling for the top floor living space, kitchen and dining area, it also allows mesmerising 360-degree views of the Suffolk coast. Only

the two spiral staircases beckoning from the sides suggest that, below decks, there's another dimension: a cavernous, circular brick chamber, with oak floors set around a vast central brick column. Here, lit by windows set into those deep walls, is another ravishing living space. This circular living room boasts a large fireplace and sitting area, as well as a cloakroom, a storeroom and a lobby leading to the front door – set some 6 metres (20 ft) up from the ground and reached by a straight new steel stairway. Directly below that thrilling space, there are cosy bedrooms, the main ones ingeniously lit by lightwells cut through the brick at steep angles. These bring daylight into what would otherwise be dark storerooms better suited to housing cannonballs.

POMPIDOU METZ

SHIGERU BAN 2010 METZ, FRANCE

It's the roof of this curious building that draws attention to it. A complex structure, made of no fewer than 10 miles (16 km) of laminated spruce and larch, it appears to droop randomly over the concrete, steel and glass core of the building below as if a passing bird had dropped a giant floppy hat on its head. In fact, the roof is very much the defining element of this regional outpost of the Centre Georges Pompidou, Paris (p.388); every view upwards inside is of this extraordinary timber sunshade, umbrella or hat. Rising like a giant conch shell from the old industrial quarter of central Metz, the new Pompidou was designed by an international team comprising Shigeru Ban (Tokyo), Jean de Gastines (Paris) and Philip Gumuchdjian

(London). Inside, the building is centred on a soaring lobby designed for the display of large-scale installations. Above and through this vast space, three huge concrete tubes crisscross, with windows at either end. These are the three principal galleries, reached by stairs or lift in the central 77-metre- (253-ft) tall tower standing like a ship's mast. Each space offers framed views of the city's monuments; each is entirely free of columns, and so offers seamless spaces for showcasing art. The tower, meanwhile, winds up to a rooftop café-restaurant, a viewing gallery and a studio intended for live performances, particularly of an experimental type. From up here, the building looks and feels more like the big top of a circus: a circus for the Arts.

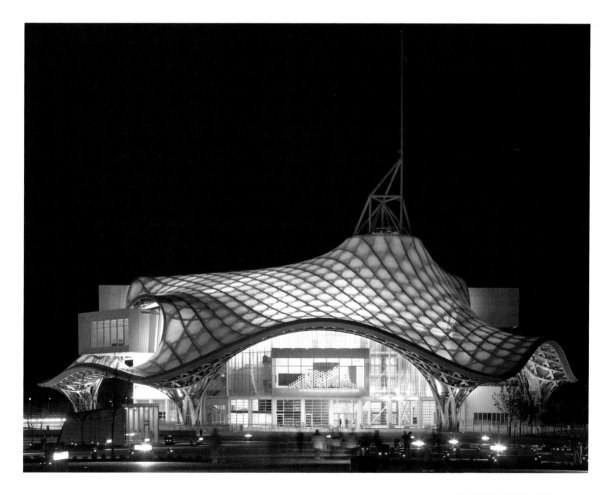

OLYMPICS VELODROME

HOPKINS ARCHITECTS 2011 GREENWICH, LONDON

A welcome relief, along with Zaha Hadid's wave-like Aquatics Centre, the Velodrome was one of just two buildings of architectural distinction designed for the London 2012 Olympics. The 6,000-seat Velodrome provided an elegant arena for cycling events; the aim, after the Games, was to add a mountain bike course and a road-cycle circuit to create a "VeloPark" for local people and sports clubs as well as a training track for Olympian cyclists of the future. The Velodrome's roof featured a distinctive double-curve that prompted Londoners to name the arena the "Pringle" after the salty snacks that do, indeed, share the same shape. The tautness and sense of constrained energy embodied in the design of the Velodrome were intended to reflect the same qualities found in

the design of racing bikes and the events they star in. In this, the architects and engineers – Expedition Engineering – succeeded. Inside, the curving timber track was a thing of sculptural as well as functional beauty, while the way in which the two tiers of seats surrounding the walls were divided by a giant window offering spectators 360 degree views of the surrounding Olympic Park and out to the London skyline was a device worthy of a Gold Medal. It just seemed a shame that this elegance and sporting purpose was overshadowed by lacklustre design elsewhere in the Olympic Park and, in particular, by what purported to be Europe's biggest shopping mall. But, Britain 2012 was far keener on shopping than sport.

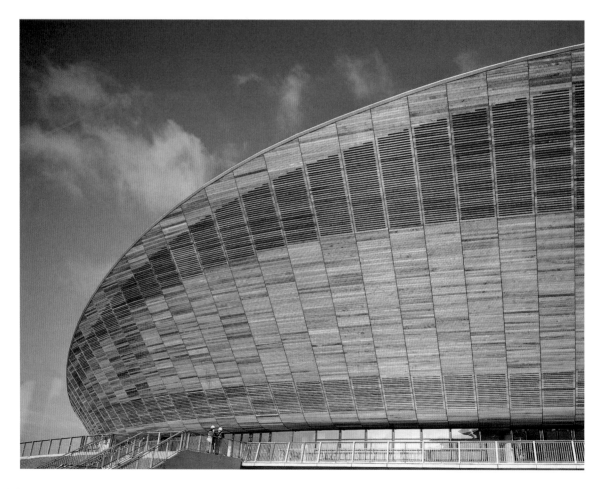

ROYAL SHAKESPEARE THEATRE

BENNETTS ASSOCIATES, 2011 STRATFORD-UPON-AVON, ENGLAND

From a distance, and peering over the rooftops of Stratford-upon-Avon, this extensive theatre complex looks like a town in itself. With its tall brick tower and variegated roofline, it might be mistaken – if you squint – for some half-remembered Italian hill town. In fact, this is very much the effect Bennetts Associates, the architects charged with redesigning and making sense of this national memorial to William Shakespeare, had been hoping to achieve. This is because the theatre grew over time, and through tragedy – it was ravaged by fire in 1926 – over several generations. One part, including the Swan Theatre, was completed in 1879 in a flamboyant Victorian Gothic style. The main part of the post-fire theatre complex was by Elisabeth

Scott; dating from 1932, it looked rather like a contemporary factory on the outside, yet inside it was all carefully considered Art Deco charm, although the theatre itself was so big that actors compared treading its boards to "speaking from Calais to the cliffs of Dover". It was also the first major public building in Britain to have been designed by a woman. By 2010, the complex had been added to, remodelled, renovated and woven into a practical yet picturesque whole. With a new auditorium, an arcade linking the buildings together, new public spaces, cafés and a tower acting, as Rab Bennetts says, as "an anchor, mooring a fleet of theatrical buildings", the RSC won many new friends without losing many, if any, of its old ones.

MODERNISM

"LESS IS MORE." MIES VAN DER ROHE

This is the core of the book and the fast-spinning hub around which so much twentieth-century architecture turned. The Modern Movement had many sources, and these have been debated, confirmed and denied many times over the last quarter of the century. At this distance what still seems to hold true is that, like the Arts and Crafts movement, Modernism was a moral force and a philosophical investigation as much as it was revolution in aesthetic sensibilities. Of course looks mattered – although you will find some real brutes here – yet one of the principal ideas driving Modern architecture was that buildings should be first and foremost functional machines for performing various programmes; and if this makes them sound like washing machines ... well, some of them are. Le Corbusier, the greatest of the Modernists, tired quickly of the word "functional". He wished to create a form of architecture that was truly of the century, a celebration of the machine age and yet poetic. And here lay a struggle or contradiction within Modernism. On the one hand there were puritanical architects who revelled in the idea of a crisp, clinical, machine-like aesthetic that brooked no decoration and suffered no poetry. On the other, there were those who saw in Modern design a new form of lyrical expression. Among these were architects like Le Corbusier or Oscar Niemeyer who may have spouted all the right words about the creation of new forms of decent architecture for the masses and yet ended up designing one-off monuments as if they were the successors of Michelangelo and Borromini rather than the social scientists architects were meant to be in the mid-twentieth century.

As the twentieth century progressed, this contradiction and division in the ranks became increasingly clear. Even as the certainties of the Modern experiment were crumbling at the end of the 1960s and the beginning of the 1970s, there were those architects who thought systems, prefabrication and no concessions to appearances was the one true path and those who plunged deeper into the unfathomable waters of formalism. If this makes Modernism sound like a religion that had begun to split into factions, then perhaps this is how it was. What began as a recognizable creed with a clear message of health, light, openness and honesty after the blood and mud of World War One became a diaspora of contradictory and even warring ideas after half a century of relentless experimentation. The difference between the concerns of Ludwig Mies van der Rohe and a local authority architect toiling on the design of a housing estate in London could hardly have been more different even though both would mouth many of the same formulas and Modernist mantras.

Yet, in whatever shape or form Modern architecture arrived, two things are clear. The first is that Modernism was not simply a style: but more of an attitude, a determination to break with the past and free the architect from the stifling rules of convention and etiquette. The second is that at the very same time architects were celebrating the Modern building's machine-like qualities, so they began to lose out to armies of engineers and contractors; for if form must play second fiddle to function, who needs an architect? The wisest Modernists – Mies perhaps above all – knew that the architect could create and shape an aesthetic of minimal form aiming for a state of perfection that no one but an artist would be likely to find. Less in Mies van der Rohe's case was indeed more, yet for many architects, the Modern building meant less is less.

APARTMENT BUILDING

AUGUSTE PERRET, 1903 PARIS, FRANCE

The Romans made extensive use of concrete in their buildings 2000 years ago; but reinforced concrete, the material that made possible so many of the most adventurous buildings of the twentieth century, was almost another 2000 years in the making. Available from the 1890s, it captured the imagination of the young French architect Auguste Perret (1874–1954) and his brothers Gustave and Claude with whom he set a construction firm, Perrets Frères Entrepreneurs, after completing his studies at the Ecole des Beaux-Arts in Paris. The apartment block, overlooking a park in rue Franklin, Paris, was Perret's first significant building and much impressed the youthful Le Corbusier when he worked with the brothers in the winter of 1908–9.

The block comprises a simple reinforced concrete frame, almost unheard of at the time, infilled with concrete panels. In the spirit of the time, Perret had these decorated with floral Art Nouveau designs; whether this was a response to fashion or a polite way of disguising the unfamiliar brutality of concrete construction is hard to say. Either way, the building marked the beginning of a trend for concrete apartment blocks boasting large windows and generous, airy interiors. The block was topped with a roof garden. The Perret brothers themselves used the ground floor as an office for several years.

CARSON, PIRIE AND SCOTT STORE

LOUIS SULLIVAN, 1904 CHICAGO, ILLINOIS, USA

Originally the Schlesinger and Mayer store, this 12-storey commercial block in downtown Chicago did much to shape the modern office block, although it was and remains a grand and glittering shop. Only the first two floors of Sullivan's building are decorated – and very lavishly so – while the upper ten storeys rise cleanly and clearly with their big, picture windows to the architect's signature "attic" at the very top. The floorplans are those of almost any mid to late twentieth-century high-rise, city centre office block. Even then, the building clearly follows Sullivan's base-central shaft-capital approach to the design of tall buildings: the clean-cut, straight up and down was still a long way in coming.

Sullivan (1856–1924) trained at the Massachusetts Institute of Technology, Chicago and the Ecole des Beaux-Arts, Paris. In many ways, he was the link between nineteenth- and twentieth-century architectural forms and sensibilities. He is best remembered, aside from his superb buildings, for the conclusion to his 1906 essay: "It is the pervading law of all things organic and inorganic, of all things physical and metaphysical, of all things human and all things superhuman, of all true manifestations of the head, of the heart, of the soul, that the life is recognizable in its expression, that form ever follows function. This is the law …"

LARKIN BUILDING

FRANK LLOYD WRIGHT, 1905 BUFFALO, NEW YORK, USA

The Larkin Building was demolished in 1950. Its brief life, however, is no measure of its immense importance: this was the first truly modern office block, a building designed inside and out to match purpose and function in a near-scientific manner. It was also the very first air-conditioned office and the first to be based around a central atrium.

The Larkin brothers more or less invented the mail order business; they needed a large supply of well-educated, diligent clerks to process a huge number of intricate orders. Lined in serried rows at the smart desks designed for them by Frank Lloyd Wright (1867–1959), these early office workers were in certain ways no more and no less than the victims of the revolution in organizational thinking led by Frederick Taylor (1856–1915), father of the school of Scientific Management that led to Henry Ford's mass-production techniques, time and motion men and lifelong tedium for the twentieth-century white-collar worker. Whatever the limitations and inhumanity of Taylor's findings, the Larkins' fast turnover business or Wright's design, the Larkin Building remainsas radical today as it was in 1905 when just 5 per cent of the US population toiled in offices compared with over 50 per cent by the end of the century.

STEINER HOUSE

ADOLF LOOS, 1911 VIENNA, AUSTRIA

The Steiner House was often used to illustrate stripped-bare Modern design in books promoting a revolutionary approach to architecture in the wake of World War One. Yet, it was only the back of the house that was ever shown: the front was compromised by the insistence of the local planning authority that it must have a pitched roof. Canny Loos gave the Steiner House a roof that curved up from the ground floor front and on to a severe back that looked like the front he had wanted to begin with. In this sense the Steiner House is a curiosity. However, in intent this reinforced concrete house was among the very first buildings hinting at what an up and coming generation of Germanic architects might do and did.

Adolf Loos (1870–1933) was the son of a stonemason; he studied at the Technische Hochschule, Dresden, before spending three years in the United States where he worked as mason, floor-layer and dish-washer, before settling in Vienna in 1896. An early commission, the Museum Café in Vienna, was known as the Café Nihilismus because of its stark lack of decoration. In 1908 he published his famous essay, "Ornament and Crime", which equated decoration with decadence and criminality; Loos had inspected criminals in Vienna's prisons and found they were often tattooed, something no civilized, law-abiding citizen could possibly condone. He admired the notion of the decorous "English gentleman" and was always impeccably dressed.

GOLDMAN AND SALATSCH BUILDING

ADOLF LOOS, 1911 VIENNA, AUSTRIA

"Modern man, the man with modern nerves", wrote Loos in "Ornament and Crime", "does not need ornamentation; it disgusts him." Unhappily for Loos, it was the very lack of ornamentation that set the press, public and planners against the Goldman and Salatsch Building when the scaffolding was first taken down. The Viennese, with their passion for opera and baroque cakes, were aghast at the nakedness of this supposedly refined tailors' store. The owners, Leopold Goldman and Emanuel Aufricht, took fright and a second competition was held to complete the building which, in the event, Loos won as he had the first. The result is a handsome and well-polished corner block in the heart of Vienna that marries a neatly tailored cleanness of line with lavish materials.

The base of the building is granite and its lower floors are lined with green Greek Cipollino marble. The pillars bestriding the mezzanine windows were cast in zinc and wrapped in bronze. The interior of the shop was fitted out with every extravagance possible behind the label "austere". Above the shop, a plain, stucco façade is punctuated with windows, some of which appear to rest on bronze window-boxes. The Goldman and Salatsch building is not just a lovely thing; it announces the junction elegantly and commandingly. It has worn its age like a well-pressed suit, cut from the finest cloth.

FAGUS-WERKE

WALTER GROPIUS AND ADOLF MEYER, 1914 ALFELD-AN-DER-LEINE, GERMANY

In the quest as he saw it to "wrest the impression of corporeality from unsubstantial materials", Walter Gropius (1883–1969) designed one of the first buildings that we associate with the look and style of Modern Movement architecture. While working in the office of Peter Behrens, Gropius, the future founder of the Bauhaus, met Adolf Meyer (1881–1929), a cabinet-maker turned architect. The two designed a brick, steel and glass factory for making shoe lasts that abandoned the apparently solid structure of architecture to date. The corners of the famous administration block were realized almost entirely in glass. In fact, here, for the first time, the core of a building was

effectively surrounded in an envelope of glass.

There had been much discussion in Germany in the previous decade – and certainly since the setting up of the Deutsche Werkbund in 1907 – about the contribution architecture could make to the public image of industrial manufacturers. Behrens had pointed the way with the AEG Turbine Hall in Berlin (p.34); Gropius, whose influence was to become international and all-pervading in the coming decade, took the next step and created a factory that was not simply elegant and refined but overtly Modern. This was Gropius's first independent commission. It could hardly have been more significant, and was to set the style of modern factories worldwide.

HOLLAND HOUSE

H. P. BERLAGE, 1914 CITY OF LONDON, ENGLAND

Berlage designed this colourful, Jacob's coat of an office block for Muller, a Dutch shipping company, in one of the City of London's typically narrow streets. It was his only work in Britain and remains as much a curiosity as it was at the time of its construction, a pointer towards the office of the future. Holland House might look as if it is made from solid masonry walls, but beneath its green glazed tilework and polished black granite plinth, it is no more and no less than a steel-frame, housing some of the earliest open-plan offices complete with moveable partitions. The granite plinth appears to frame the building, rising over its doorways and forming giant flat pilasters at either end of the Bury Street façade. The lobby is highly decorated, although the logic of the steel frame construction is openly, or "honestly" as architects liked to say, expressed.

If Holland House shows Modern tendencies, Berlage nevertheless thought of himself as a traditionalist; he attended the very first meeting of Congrès Internationaux d'Architecture Moderne (CIAM) in 1928, but declined to join this fertile seedbed of young radicals. Holland House has since been extended unsympathetically; Berlage's design, however, remains intact and a genuine surprise to anyone who thinks of British architecture of the period as "Wrenaissance" domes and columns.

MODEL FACTORY, WERKBUND EXHIBITION

WALTER GROPIUS AND ADOLF MEYER, 1914 COLOGNE, GERMANY

Just before Gropius went off to fight in Kaiser Wilhelm's army, he produced this hugely influential design for a model factory. Although the core and roofline of the administration block are clearly influenced by Frank Lloyd Wright, the twin stair towers – streamlined glass structures – were a new device that was to influence countless architects, beginning in Germany, after World War One. The factory was very much a model for future industrial buildings around the world, with its swish office block fronting a simple workshop separated by a courtyard behind. Here, the clearly expressed intention was that the factory itself would be one of the key expressions of a manufacturer's image. No longer

a "dark, satanic mill", the modern factory was to be shown off not just to visitors, but in advertising and publicity campaigns.

The Werkbund Exhibition itself was an important event, architects divided between those, like Gropius, who believed that modern buildings could be all but mass-produced like cars and domestic goods, and those who insisted that the architect's role was to give each new building a distinctive character of its own. The glazed rear elevation of the office block was to influence the self-conscious "machine aesthetic" of a wide variety of building types, from schools to railway stations, in the 1920s and 1930s.

HENNY HOUSE

ROBERT VAN'T HOFF, 1919 UTRECHT, THE NETHERLANDS

Robert van't Hoff (1887–1979) was so taken by the writings of Frank Lloyd Wright that he went to the United States to work with the master for a year (1913–14). On his return he designed what must be one of the very earliest Modern houses in Europe. Although clearly influenced by Wright – it has much of the look and overall design of, say, Wright's Gale House in Oak Park, Illinois (1909) – the Henny House is more restrained than anything Wright built. Its reinforced construction is severely expressed and the house has a determinedly elemental character, without fuss or frills. The concrete slabs are painted grey to identify the logic of the construction.

The house was begun almost immediately after the end of World War One. It sits on an immaculately groomed lawn entirely separate from the world around it; it must have seemed quite shocking when first built. For van't Hoff and his client, at least, the age of decadent, bourgeois European architecture, whether Neo-Baroque or Art Nouveau, was over. The Henny House was an early attempt to show that not just architecture but even the home could be freed from egotistical individual expression and reinterpreted in an objective and universal manner; that was the idea, anyway.

Van't Hoff joined the De Stijl group of artists and architects gathered around Theo van Doesburg in Leiden, but broke away in the early days. From 1937 he lived in England, although spent as an architectural force.

NOTRE DAME DE RAINCY

AUGUSTE PERRET, 1922 PARIS, FRANCE

Although borrowing some of the basic elements from Gothic parish churches – the soaring bell tower, long nave and aisles – Perret's Notre Dame was a demonstration of the liberating properties of reinforced concrete. Inside, all is light, reason and decidedly Modern. The barrel-vault above the nave is supported by tall (11-metre/35-ft) and slender (35.5-cm/14-inch) concrete pillars that also mark the division of the barrel-vaulted aisles into twelve bays. The effect is magnificent and comes as a complete surprise after the conventions of the bell-tower and the massive construction of the west front. So sparing is the construction of the nave that the walls are almost all glass, an effect medieval architects all but obtained with stone, a much less yielding material than Perret's concrete. The interior of this impressive church has had a profound influence on much twentieth-century architecture. It showed, aside from the new possibilities of concrete construction, how new materials and new ways of designing were not incompatible with a sense of immateriality and the spiritual dimension of life.

After World War Two, Perret was involved in the reconstruction of Le Havre; many visitors find his vision of the city too severe, even if they are usually transfixed by one of his very last designs, the Church of St Joseph, which takes up where Raincy left off.

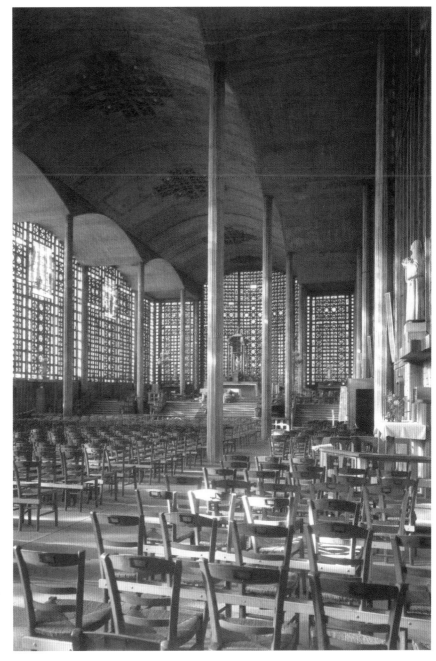

SCHINDLER HOUSE

RUDOLF SCHINDLER, 1923 LOS ANGELES, CALIFORNIA, USA

Rudolf Schindler (1887–1953) left his native Vienna for California shortly before the outbreak of World War One. He saw the West Coast as virgin territory for modern architecture, saying "I believe that climate and character, in company with a further genuine development of spatial architecture, will make Southern California the cradle of a new form of architectural expression." This it did and especially when Schindler built this remarkable single-storey, timber-framed house in West Hollywood. Hidden by a bamboo screen that sounds like the sea as it sways in the wind, the house occupies just about of all of its garden site, with the interior and exterior blurring into one another.

The house is made up of four studios, a guest wing and garage. Doors are sliding screens, light filters through canvas walls, and the whole house has an air of modern informality that is quite remarkable for its time. The minimal interiors with their concrete floors, and elemental furniture and fittings were to influence architects and designers much later in the century. The rooms interlock with the garden so that with the screens open it is difficult to tell where one ends and the other begins. Since Schindler's death, the house has been lived in by many well-known artists and writers, including the musician John Cage and the architectural historian Charles Jencks. At the end of the century it has become a museum and shrine to this revolutionary and bohemian architect.

LE ROCHE–JEANNERET HOUSE

LE CORBUSIER AND PIERRE JEANNERET, 1923 AUTEIL, PARIS, FRANCE

Le Corbusier was arguably the century's greatest architect. A profound and original thinker, a brilliant polemicist and equally inspired self-publicist, he tried harder than almost anyone to give a new shape to what he saw as a new age. Like Picasso, he moved through many stylistic phases and the great works of his sixties seem far removed from the radical, yet exquisite white villas of his thirties.

The Le Roche–Jeanneret House established Corb's early style: a first floor (or *piano nobile*) raised on pilotis (free-standing columns), double-height living spaces, internal ramps and roof gardens. Proportioned according to a strict geometry, this modern urban "semi" proved the extent to which classical geometry could give rise to a new architecture free from the corsetting restraints of traditional

Beaux-Arts thinking. Not only was the house a "machine for living", to use Le Corbusier's famous phrase, but it was also an expression of his idea of architecture being the "masterly, correct and magnificent play of masses brought together in light."

Le Corbusier was born Charles-Edouard Jeanneret at La Chaux- des-Fonds in Switzerland where he trained as a metal engraver before setting out on a tour of Europe, during which he learned to become an architect partly by sketching and partly by working in the offices of Auguste Perret in Paris and Peter Behrens in Berlin. His pseudonym is a play on an old family name Lecorbesier and the nickname Corbeau (crow) because of his physical and, as he saw it, psychological resemblance to that solitary bird.

SCHRÖDER HOUSE

GERRIT RIETVELD, 1924 UTRECHT, THE NETHERLANDS

This is a Mondrian painting transformed into a house by Gerrit Rietveld (1888–1964), a cabinet-maker and jewellery designer who joined the De Stijl group of artists and architects in 1918, a year after its foundation. Influenced as much by their puritanical Calvinist backgrounds as by radical notions of what art and architecture could be, the members of De Stijl aimed to frame the strict fruits of their imagination within the strictures of the 90-degree angle. So much so, that when you open a window in Rietveld's jewel-like house in Utrecht, it can only be held open at – you guessed – 90 degrees.

The Schröder House is built on a series of frames, based on the cube, which project in and out of the main structure like a sequence of Mondrian canvases grouped tightly together. Despite (or because of) the rigour of the plan and elevations, the house is gloriously light and enjoyable to be in. Inside, sliding partitions can be moved aside to create smaller or larger rooms. The furniture was designed to be all of a piece with the house, while the colour scheme – flat planes of red, white, yellow and blue – was taken directly from Mondrian's restricted palette. Perhaps because the client, Truus Schröder-Schräder, was involved very closely with the design, the house is remarkably practical – a painting for living in. The only low note is that the house is sited on a dreary avenue and tacked uncomfortably onto the end of a row of dull hipped-roof brick houses.

PAVILLON DE L'ESPRIT NOUVEAU

LE CORBUSIER, 1925 PARIS, FRANCE

The sensation of the 1925 Exposition Internationale des Arts Décoratifs et Industriels Modernes, this striking pavilion was intended to represent a typical flat from an apartment block of the future. Le Corbusier had prepared the idea some three years earlier, working in collaboration with the painter Andrée Ozenfant. Together they launched and edited their own magazine, *L'Esprit Nouveau* (1920–25) in which Corbu wrote the essays that made up his famous polemic *Vers une Architecture* of 1923. "We have acquired", wrote Corbu in *L'Esprit Nouveau*, "a taste for clean air and full sunlight ... the house is a machine for living in, bathrooms, sun, hot and cold water, temperatures which can be adjusted as required, food storage, hygiene, beauty in harmonious proportions."

Much of this has come to pass, despite the fact that Le Corbusier is still accused of masterminding hideous, low-rent public housing at the end of the century by those who know him only by his mysterious name.

To see the pavilion in 1925 was something quite as shocking as a glimpse of stocking had been ten years earlier. The pavilion was rooted around a mature tree which appeared to grown up through the "roof garden". It boasted a double-height living room complete with sleeping gallery, avant-garde artworks and furnishings. It still looks new 75 years on. Hidden behind a screen for the opening ceremony by the exhibition's organizers for reasons of good taste, the pavilion won the top prize.

SOVIET PAVILION

KONSTANTIN MELNIKOV, 1925 PARIS, FRANCE

Less than ten years on from the design of this pavilion, along with Le Corbusier's the most original at the "Arts Décoratifs" exhibition of 1925, Konstantin Melnikov's (1890–1974) career was effectively at an end. His Constructivist style was rejected by Stalin and his cronies as Social Realism, and an exotic Classicism came to dominate architectural design in the Soviet Union. Until then, Melnikov's own red star had been very much in the ascendant; he was chosen to represent the radical young Communist nation (Lenin had died the year before) at Paris. His design was one of the first built expressions of revolutionary Constructivism and was extremely impressive. The structure was built of timber. What was radical was the plan, a rectangle riven through as if by bolts of lightning in the guise of long, diagonal entrance stairs. These passed under what looked like steel beams crossed liked swords embellished with graphics that drew on the Constructivist revolutionary slogans of the previous eight years.

Although this style of architecture reached a dead end in the Soviet Union, it became a kind of visual folklore among designers seeking forms of radical expression throughout the twentieth century. In fact, it was to enjoy its finest hours in the capitalist west during the 1990s in the work of such architects as Zaha Hadid (p.441) and Daniel Libeskind (p.349).

CAFÉ DE UNIE

J. J. P. OUD, 1925 ROTTERDAM, THE NETHERLANDS

Jacobus Johannes Pieter Oud (1890–1963) was made City Architect of Rotterdam when he was just 28. This explains why such a lofty-sounding public servant was engaged in the design of what was the city's most fashionable hang-out, the Café De Unie. Oud's major work was in public housing, at which he excelled. The Café De Unie represented an early phase in his career when he was a part of the De Stijl group and, like Rietveld, attempting to turn what were essentially two-dimensional images into three-dimensional buildings.

The Café De Unie succeeded in part because the interior was very simple, but also because what the café needed to draw attention to itself in a long and regular avenue was a striking façade. The front was much like a giant Mondrian painting. Or, as Oud said himself, "modern architecture will increasingly develop into a process of reduction to positive proportions, comparable to a modern painting." The façade – which is really all that Oud designed himself – was also intended to be a provocation, making no attempt to fit in with the buildings on either side of it. The café was destroyed in 1940, but has since been rebuilt and is just as striking to look at today as it must have been in 1925.

BAUHAUS

WALTER GROPIUS, 1926 DESSAU, GERMANY

"The Bauhaus", said Walter Gropius the school's founder-director in its first prospectus in 1919, "strives to collect all artistic creativity into a unity, to reunite all artistic disciplines – sculpture, painting, design and handicraft – into a new architecture." The new architecture came in 1926 when this radical art school moved from Weimar, where it had fallen from political favour, to Dessau, a small provincial German capital. Here, Gropius and Adolf Meyer were able to design a building that expressed their artistic ideals. The severe yet glamorous concrete and glass complex comprised workshops (behind the famous curtain wall), the City of Dessau Technical School (on the other side of a road bridge; the road was never built), administrative offices and Gropius's studio (located in the bridge), a student housing block (complete with gym) and a canteen and hall (in a single-storey link between the students' rooms and the classrooms and workshops). The building was a powerful advert for the school which, hugely influential worldwide, was always beset by problems, either academic (what to teach and how) or political (it was always seen as leaning too far to the Left).

The school's graduates did much to spread the Modern Movement gospel. Gropius resigned in 1928; the school was closed by the Nazis in 1933. It has since reopened and the buildings have been thoroughly restored.

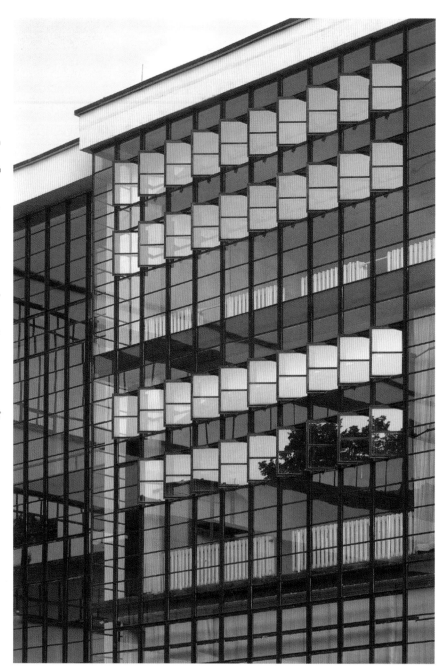

NEW WAYS

PETER BEHRENS, 1926 NORTHAMPTON, ENGLAND

Behrens was 58 years old when he designed New Ways for Bassett-Lowke, the man who designed and built model railways that were as popular in Germany as they were in their native England. Behrens was at the height of his powers, successor to Otto Wagner as head of the Vienna Academy of Arts and architect

of the magnificent IG-Farben chemical factory in Hochst. His attempt at designing a Modern house was fairly lame and by the standards of, say, Le Corbusier, rather tired. In England though, the Basset-Lowke house appeared to

be avant-garde. This was not surprising at a time when Basset-Lowke's contemporaries considered the Arts and Crafts housing of Letchworth and Hampstead Garden Suburb a little too radical for comfort. Nevertheless, New Ways proved that it was possible to import the new European architecture to England, albeit in a soft-focus guise.

Much like the Steiner House in Vienna by Adolf Loos, it is the rear, or garden elevation, of New Ways that is always shown in the progressive press; the front of the house was less radical still, as it had to make some concessions to its tweedy neighbours. As a bridge to Continental Europe, however, New Ways has a significance beyond the less than stunning impact of its design.

LOVELL BEACH HOUSE

RUDOLF SCHINDLER, 1926 NEWPORT BEACH, CALIFORNIA, USA

This famous beach house for Dr Lovell was much criticized at the time of its building by young US moderns for being too "tricksy". It was excluded from the seminal International Style exhibition curated by Philip Johnson and Henry Russell Hitchcock held at the Museum of Modern Art, New York, in 1932. In fact the house is as ingenious as it is delightful to live in. Based around a large, double-height living room overlooking the Pacific Ocean, it is raised on five exposed concrete frames. This raises the living accommodation above the beach and the street and provides a covered, open area complete with fireplace for barbecues. The second storey is cantilevered into the double-height living space, providing a balcony, bedrooms and a way of handling space that continues to delight and intrigue at the end of the century.

Schindler was a loner, and the houses he designed offered a freedom to their owners that was not always appreciated by contemporary critics. In his own house in West Hollywood he liked to sleep on the roof. This was daring in the early 1920s when beach culture was just beginning to be enjoyed by the professional classes. The combination of a complex structure and a plan that offered a way of life that had yet to come into its own made the Lovell Beach House hard to understand for East Coasters and those brought up on Victorian mores.

HOOK OF HOLLAND HOUSING ESTATE

J. J. P. OUD, 1927 ROTTERDAM, THE NETHERLANDS

Oud's career was meteoric. Having studied in Amsterdam, Delft and Munich, he became one of the founders of the De Stijl movement in 1917. The next year he became City Planner for Rotterdam and designed a series of remarkable housing estates. Severe, logical and functional, these low-cost housing schemes were also elegant and humane. They have matured well and survive today.

Perhaps the most approachable of Oud's three major schemes is the Hook of Holland housing. The two-storey buildings run in low and emphatic horizontals along the new streets; although the blocks read as single entities from a distance, close up each house is clearly identifiable with its own separate entrance and walled garden. The two main blocks are characterized by rounded ends that provide accommodation for small shops. What Oud showed in this exemplary scheme is that the new style of mass housing could be rigorous and yet realized on a notably humane scale. The houses face on to conventional streets and are easy to identify unlike those of later Modern housing estates. Oud went on to build much praised show housing in the Weissenhof district of Stuttgart (1927), but thereafter appears to have slowed down and almost disappeared from practice. He turned down the chair of architecture at Harvard University having left his official post in Rotterdam in 1933 and built little for the rest of his life with the major exception of the rather formal and heavy handed Shell Building, The Hague (1942).

RUE MALLET-STEVENS HOUSING

ROBERT MALLET-STEVENS, 1927 PASSY, PARIS, FRANCE

The grand rue Mallet-Stevens is a bravura expression of Cubism applied to architecture, although its blocky concrete houses and apartments have often been labelled Moderne, a faintly patronising tag suggesting whimsy rather than substance, rigour or Modern. This Paris street remains a surprise: it is all of a piece and a rare example of Art Deco urban planning.

Mallet-Stevens (1886–1945) studied and later taught at the Ecole Spéciale d'Architecture in Paris. With Pierre Chareau, he founded the Union des Artistes Modernes. Much influenced by Josef Hoffmann and Charles Rennie Mackintosh, his architecture was almost backwards looking by the late 1920s when Le Corbusier was coming into his own with a radical approach to the design of the home. Unlike Le Corbusier's, the plans of Mallet-Stevens nominally Modern houses and apartments were traditional. Nevertheless, Rue Mallet-Stevens stands out as a memorable and convincing composition. In the event, it was a short-lived cul-de-sac in the history of architecture. Cubism, a form of painting devised by Georges Braque and Pablo Picasso between 1905 and 1910, aimed at depicting a sense of three-dimensional space without the use of perspective. It was a difficult concept to translate into architecture; Mallet-Stevens and his Czech contemporaries adapted the style mostly in terms of surface appearance.

WEISSENHOFSIEDLUNG

LUDWIG MIES VAN DER ROHE (DIRECTOR), 1927 STUTTGART, GERMANY

The creation of the Weissenhof housing estate on the edge of Stuttgart, under the direction of Mies van der Rohe (1888–1969) was a significant achievement. Here, for the first time, Modern Movement architects were able to plan a part of a city on new lines and attempt to prove that it was possible to build beautiful, airy, functional, low-cost urban housing for those on low incomes. The cast of designers involved in the project included Le Corbusier (with Pierre Jeanneret), Walter Gropius, J. J. P. Oud, Peter Behrens and Hans Scharoun. Although each architect had a recognizable approach of his own, this arrangement of simple white houses and apartment blocks had a unity of design: the young turks of the Modern Movement could clearly work together.

The exhibition was sponsored by the Deutscher Werkbund and left a legacy of what were to have been 21 permanent houses – some since much changed, others demolished – and Mies van der Rohe's impressive apartment block, a design that was to set the tone for much European and US housing in subsequent years.

The Weissenhofsiedlung gave ordinary Germans an opportunity to see what a Modern city might be like. However, when the Nazis were voted into power six years later such light and airy Modern housing went by the board. When Modern housing made its reappearance in Germany after 1945, it was never able to be quite so delicate and idealistic. Its lessons had still to be learned in the 1990s.

SCHOCKEN DEPARTMENT STORE

ERICH MENDELSOHN, 1928 STUTTGART, GERMANY

After the design of the sensational Einstein Tower (p.83), Mendelsohn was heavily involved in the design of factories and private houses in various parts of Germany. Yet, it was the design of a department store for Schocken that pushed his style further towards a convincing fusion of Expressionism and Modernism. The Stuttgart store was rooted around a central courtyard in the city centre. The two dominant façades, one to the main street the other following the drop of a steep side street, were linked by a striking stair tower cantilevered from the main body of the building and striated with steel bands to give an impression of exaggerated height

as well as the intensity of a compressed spring. Mendelsohn also imbued this energetic building with further drama by designing vast letters spelling out the name of the store. Finally, the magnificent theatricality of the Schocken store was set brilliantly against the grand and fussy nineteenth-century buildings without undermining their stately presence.

Mendelsohn had the ability of introducing radical architecture into city centres without undermining their character or integrity, and – quite the reverse – of raising their sights and souls. All this with a department store. It was demolished in 1960.

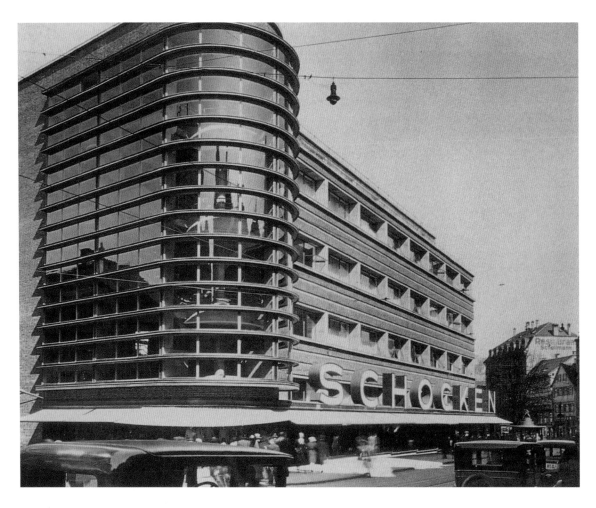

BATA SHOE SHOP

LUDVIK KYSELA, 1928 PRAGUE, CZECH REPUBLIC

In the 1920s Czechoslovakia was noted for its highly accomplished and progressive architecture. The Bata shoe shop by Ludvik Kysela (1883-1960) looked as up-to-the-minute sixty years after it was built as it was ahead of the clock in 1928. Essentially it is a simple building of the sort that became almost routine in European cities over the next three-quarters of a century; at the time it must have been a revelation. Its very clarity is what has made it special both in the 1920s and at the end of the century. This clarity is achieved by facing the seven-floor concrete structure with a wall of what is as far as possible sheer glass, offset by minimal bands of white opaque glass. As evening falls, the building lights up in contrasting layers of clear and milky tungsten and fluorescent. The building was designed for the Bata shoe company, which was to open shops in many parts of Europe selling cheap but decent footwear. The company had its own design and architecture department with whom Kysela worked closely.

The Bata shop has become an icon of Modern design, its clarity and more than bearable lightness of being a rebuke to the formal excesses of late-flowering Modernism and the excrescences of what generally passed for Postmodernism. This, then, is a good example of a simple building that acts as a benchmark for design that came after.

ZUYEV CLUB

I. A. GOLOSOV, 1928 MOSCOW, RUSSIA

The original sketches of this Moscow club were by Konstantin Melnikov who proposed a building composed of five glass cylinders. The design was handed over to I. A. Golosov (1883–1945) who retained just one glass cylinder. Even then, this has a dramatic impact on Lesnaya Street at it thrusts up from the pavement through the rectangular bulk of the building. The plan of the club is directed at all points to this distinctive corner tower.

This was one of several large factory clubs built in Moscow in the 1920s. Apart from the social function they performed, their designs encompassed the stylistic battles Soviet architects fought in that difficult decade as the early ideals of the October Revolution gave way to Stalin's Terror. Revolutionary architects fell out with one another as they struggled between the more rational designs of "Constructivists" like Vesnin and Ginzberg, and the more expressive or flamboyant work of (to make matters complicated) the so-called "Rationalists" including Melnikov and Golosov. The battles were effectively ended by Stalin's adherence to a Soviet Classicism from about 1935. Golosov's other notable designs (none built) included those for the Palace of Labour (1923) and the Palace of Soviets (1934).

SILVER END HOUSING ESTATE

THOMAS TAIT, 1928 CHELMSFORD, ESSEX, ENGLAND

This was a very English introduction to Modern architecture. Tait's houses look Modern at first glance, but are in fact rather conventional brick suburban villas treated to a hint of European Modernism with flat roofs, horizontal windows and a lick of white paint. Nevertheless they are a beginning. The estate was commissioned by the Crittall window company, which established itself in the 1920s with steel window frames that were designed to match the aspirations and needs of contemporary architects. Silver End was designed as a model estate for Crittall's employees. The inhabitants were to act as guinea-pigs to see how the new windows coped with damp and deleterious English weather over time.

The houses are laid out on Garden City lines, in picturesque rather than formal groups. Most are built of brick and painted white. Their plans are conventional. Nevertheless, Silver End proved that it was possible to drip feed new ideas from continental Europe into Britain, although the bulk of private housing built in Britain throughout the rest of the century tended to be in faux historic styles such as Georgian and Tudor. Silver End continues to be well looked after and Tait's quixotic would-be Modern houses have stood the test of time.

GERMAN PAVILION

LUDWIG MIES VAN DER ROHE, 1929 BARCELONA, SPAIN

Like Le Corbusier, another twentieth-century giant, Ludwig Mies van der Rohe, had no formal architectural training. Born the son of mason and stone-carver in Aachen, Mies was to bring Neoclassical architecture bang up to date with what appeared to be a seamless sequence of cool, masterful and – for the most part – beautifully crafted buildings in Europe and the United States. The first of these was the hugely influential German Pavilion designed for the International Exhibition at Barcelona. Mies had built and designed much before, yet the Pavilion was the first of his temple-like structures and very much a symbol of the new European architecture.

Restored to its original state, the Pavilion is disarmingly simple. It comprises a concrete slab (the roof) supported by slim, cross-shaped and chrome-plated steel columns. Underneath the slab and between the column, Mies has slid flat planes of glass and polished travertine; the panels both enclose and expose the space beneath the roof. Sunlight reflects off the Pavilion's twin pools and dapples from the glass and travertine panels of onyx and marble. Although there is nothing but space inside the Pavilion, it feels deeply luxurious. Mies provided a few of his new and soon-to-be famous Barcelona chairs inside for rest and contemplation. "Along this path", said Mies, "industry and technology will join forces with the forces of thought and culture'.' And, who, cooling off inside this Pavilion on a sunny day, would dare to disagree?

SEASIDE HOUSE E.1027

EILEEN GRAY AND JEAN BADOVICI, 1929 ROQUEBRUNE–CAP MARTIN, FRANCE

Eileen Gray (1878–1976) was born into a landed Irish family, but rather than doing the right things by her family – marrying a decent chap, breeding and ordering servants about – she went to Paris and became a successful, if unsung, designer. From the mid-1920s she produced furniture, lamps, rugs and mirrors that have become classics of twentieth-century design. Although not an architect, she also designed this summer house for herself and her lover Jean Badovici: together they were "E.1027", their initials translated into numerals. Standing on stilts and overlooking a beautifully shaped bay, the house was much admired by Le Corbusier, who stayed here frequently, and drowned in the sea nearby

in 1965. Inside the house was designed as a Modern *gesamtkunstwerk*, although Gray herself was always a free spirit and never aligned herself with an artistic or architectural movement. Her designs were made from costly materials and so her clients had to be wealthy. This is something of a shame, as in the two houses she designed, Gray displayed a warmth and grace that was all too often lacking in Modern Movement mass housing. E.1027 boasts many details that, for Gray, were no more than common sense, but which seemed new to visiting architects who were rarely as practical as their manifestoes liked to claim. Her furniture later achieved "classic" status.

LE MARBEAUF SHOWROOM

ALBERT LAPRADE AND L. E. BAZIN, 1929 PARIS, FRANCE

Contemporary photographs of this extraordinary Citroën carshowroom never fail to delight. Perhaps this is because the brand new cars with their vertical radiators, headlamps on stalks, voluptuous wings and exposed running boards seem so much older than the glass-fronted building. Laprade and Bazin stacked the cars on a sequence of cantilevered concrete galleries overlooking a six-storey void (or atrium) faced with sheet glass from floor to ceiling. A door on the other side of the great window allowed motorists buying a Citroën to drive in to the garage at the back of the showroom in their old car through one door and to drive out in a spanking new model through the other. Cars and Modern architecture had been closely connected by Le Corbusier in his hugely influential work *Vers une Architecture* (1923) and photographers like Frank Yerbury, who made the Marbeauf Showroom world famous with his striking glass-plate images, played up this relationship between the fruits of the machine age and the new architecture that served them. Sadly, the showroom has long gone, which is a shame because it would have been fashionable again at the end of the century and perfect for the display of modern cars.

MELNIKOV HOUSE

KONSTANTIN MELNIKOV, 1929 MOSCOW, RUSSIA

This was the only private house built in Moscow during the Soviet era. The authorities were so taken with Melnikov's extraordinary design that they even bailed him out when he ran out of money during construction. The house comprises two intersecting cylinders, one taller than the other. The cylinder facing the street, close to Arbatskaya Metro station, is faced with a wall of glass topped with a roof terrace; the second cylinder contains the architect's studio and bedroom, designed rather mysteriously as a "sonata for sleep". These remarkable rooms are 5 metres (16 ft) high and lit by beehive-like hexagonal windows. These are not randomly placed but a part of the complex geometry of thestructure of the house, based on 200 hexagonal

"modules", 140 of which are infilled with brick and 60 of which are windows. You could try drawing the grid for yourself, but it might tie your brain in knots.

Melnikov filled the house with ingenious gadgetry, including speaking tubes, a waste-disposal system and sliding doors that served two openings. The house was partly restored in 1990–91 and at the end of the century is still lived in by Melnikov's son. Although decidedly eccentric and not a house that every family would find easy to live in, the Melnikov house is a brave attempt to rethink domesticity and the architecture that frames it. That it has survived intact and longer than the USSR is a fact more remarkable than the design itself.

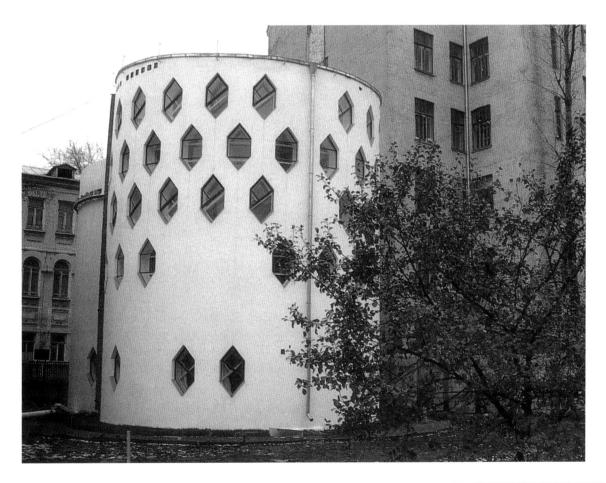

SCHOCKEN DEPARTMENT STORE

ERICH MENDELSOHN, 1929 CHEMNITZ, GERMANY

Chemnitz was to become Karl Marx Stadt when Germany was split in two in the 1950s and this Prussian city found itself under Communist rule. Of all the buildings that best expressed the values of capitalism and the consumer society, Mendelsohn's Schocken store in Chemnitz was surely the most impressive. Completed in time for the Wall Street Crash and Weimar Germany's fall into Nazidom, it was the most brilliant streamlined building in Europe, fusing Modern razzmatazz with the rigours of German Modernism.

The manner in which the clean bands of the street front sweep round in a smooth and uninterrupted curve is quite breathtaking. The top three floors were zoned back to meet local planning regulations; this gave the store the feel of a great modern ocean liner at berth in the city centre. This was appropriate, as Le Corbusier had been championing the ocean liner in his writing (notably in *Vers une Architecture*, 1923): the liner was the Parthenon of Modern times. The Shocken store also demonstrated how effective Modern architecture could be at night, with its elongated bands of glazing lit up and giving the street an energy appropriate for the speed and (perhaps spurious) glamour of the motor age. The store was badly damaged by Allied bombing during World War Two. It has long proved that the most striking Modern building has its place in city centres.

LOVELL HOUSE

RICHARD NEUTRA, 1929 LOS ANGELES, CALIFORNIA, USA

This is one of the century's most glamorous and desirable houses. What Dr Philip Lovell, the client, described as a "demonstration health house" was designed by Richard Neutra (1892–1970) and built on a steep hillside with magnificent views. From the street the house appears to be single-storey; appearances can certainly be deceptive, for once inside it drops several storeys down the hillside, its breathtaking balconies held in place by a lightweight steel frame that was erected in just 40 hours. As well as a house for Lovell, the Neutra building was also an experimental open-air school. This was the era of sun-worship and the new clean, white, open architecture. If it looks more German than 1920s Californian, this is because Neutra was an Austrian who trained with Adolf Loos in Vienna and then worked with Erich Mendelsohn in Berlin. He moved to the USA in 1923 and worked with Frank Lloyd Wright, and from 1925 with his fellow Austrian Rudolf Schindler in Los Angeles.

The Lovell House was proof that standardized factory components could be used to create radical and beautiful homes. The design makes extensive use of identically sized glass and concrete panels. Its interior is fitted out to a very high standard. Always a star, the house played a leading role in the Hollywood movie *LA Confidential* in 1997.

WITTGENSTEIN HOUSE

PAUL ENGELMAN AND LUDWIG WITTGENSTEIN, 1929 VIENNA, AUSTRIA

"Whereof we cannot speak, hereof we must be silent."
This is the famous conclusion of the *Tractacus Logico-Philosophicus* (1921) by Ludwig Wittgenstein (1889–1951), a classmate of Adolf Hitler's and one of the greatest, if most misunderstood, philosophers of all time. Having published the *Tractacus* and decided that it solved all problems of philosophy, Wittgenstein abandoned the subject, broke down, and became a teacher in an Austrian backwater. In 1929, his sister Margarethe Stonborough–Wittgenstein wooed him back to his native Vienna with a promise of work with her architect Paul Engelman (1891–1965) on the design of her new house. Engelman had been a student of Adolf Loos (p.149) and this is evident in the look of this severe, geometrical

structure. The Modern exterior belies the bourgeois interior: the Wittgensteins were a very grand and wealthy family and Margarethe enjoyed entertaining. Her brother's contribution was to refine and re-refine the proportions of the rooms – he had a new ceiling torn down because it was a millimetre or two out as far as his piercing eye saw it – and in the lovingengineering-based details that give the house its unbalanced character, at once puritanical and hedonistic.

Wittgenstein trained as an engineer before turning to mathematics and philosophy. Working on this house caused him to return to the latter. He was always fascinated with architecture, but once the house was complete, remained all but silent on the subject.

SIEMENSTADT HOUSING

WALTER GROPIUS, 1930 BERLIN, GERMANY

The two apartment blocks, one four-, the other five-storey, Walter Gropius designed for this factory estate were to be repeated in one form or the other across the world in the ensuing 60 years. This is what Modern apartment blocks tend to look like. The idea behind them was essentially humanitarian. While working and teaching at the Bauhaus, which he left in 1928, Gropius was exercised with the question of how to rehouse industrial workers in modern homes that could be built in city centres at the same density as traditional urban housing yet with a maximum of sunlight and air. When Siemens asked him to plan and supervize the design and construction of their new factory estate in Berlin, he had his opportunity to solve the problem.

Sited on parkland lawns, Gropius's pure white blocks packed a great density of housing into clean-cut blocks aligned on a north–south axis to benefit from as much daylight as possible. Each landing gave access to just two flats to rid the plan of corridors and to give residents a sense of having a private entrance of a sort. The whiteness of the blocks and their rather antiseptic quality was perhaps a statement of intent by the architect: those who toiledin industrial factories came home to escape fumes and dirt and to clean themselves mentally and physically in preparation for the next day's toil.

HILVERSUM TOWN HALL

WILLEM MARINUS DUDOK, 1930 HILVERSUM, THE NETHERLANDS

Influenced to an extent by Frank Lloyd Wright and the Amsterdam School, Dudok (1884–1974) was a military engineer turned architect who developed a complete, bricky and monumental style of his own. Whether designing a school, public baths or town hall, he approached the brief with a surety of form that he was never to stray from. Hilversum Town Hall is the grandest and most evolved of Dudok's heroic essays in powerful and unrelieved brick verticals and horizontals. It has the curious quality of appearing to be a cathedral, a factory and a crematorium all at once. There is nothing likeable here, yet the effect is deeply impressive and the rigour with which the building is carried through – both in terms of plan and in the quality of construction – exemplary.

Dudok was born in Amsterdam, trained at the Royal Military Academy, Breda and became director of municipal works at Hilversum (1915–27) and municipal architect then on. His work was to influence Charles Holden, the British architect, who softened the Dutch master's monumentality in such designs as Arnos Grove Station (p.48) on the London Underground. The style was then used for municipal works in Britain, and the influence of Hilversum can also be seen in Sir Giles Gilbert Scott's transformation of Bankside Power Station, Southwark, London into a grand, if unlovable, civic temple.

VILLA SAVOYE

LE CORBUSIER, 1931 POISSY, FRANCE

"Through the balcony-like projection of the floor over the *pilotis*, the entire façade is extended beyond the building skeleton. It thereby loses its loadbearing character ... and thus has freedom of composition." The Villa Savoye marks the climax of a sequence of perfect, white, freestanding villas Le Corbusier built on the suburban fringe of Paris from 1922. The Villa Savoye is at once the most delicate and ethereal and as magical and as satisfying as the best of Palladio's villas of the sixteenth century.

Appearing to have landed on stilts as if from outer space, the Villa Savoye offered a truly revolutionary way of living. Visitors arriving by car from Paris parked out of sight in a garage reached between *pilotis* (stilts or columns). They entered the house though a glass box beneath the main floor, washed at a prominently located basin and then climbed by ramp or stair to the main living floor. The miracle of this is that what was outdoors and what was indoors was unclear: the villa is a homage to light and air as well as to a complex geometry and plan that can be quite baffling on first encounter of even the closest kind. The roof is a terrace for sunbathing.

This special house was left for many years to run to seed. However, it has since been restored and is open to the public.

ROYAL CORINTHIAN YACHT CLUB

JOSEPH EMBERTON, 1931 BURNHAM-ON-CROUCH, ESSEX ENGLAND

The Essex town of Burnham-on-Crouch is not the sort of town in which anyone would expect to encounter modern architecture of any distinction, if at all. Yet, the Royal Corinthian Yacht Club still goes about its comfortable work in this east coast English town with great distinction.

Designed by Joseph Emberton (1889–1956), it was one of the first Modern buildings of any noteworthy scale in Britain. Emberton himself designed in a number of fashionable styles and cannot be considered a dedicated Modernist along the lines of his Dutch, French, German and Austrian contemporaries. The Yacht Club is not even as Modern as

it first appears: it is built largely of brick in the English way, although a certain degree of steel in the construction allowed for its distinctive cantilevered balconies. From an English point of view in 1931, a building might look Modern if its setting warranted it. As Emberton's design was clearly "nautical" in spirit, it was quite acceptable and even to be welcomed. Elsewhere, such a clear, open and elegant building would have been frowned upon.

It is significant that when the building won an award soon after its completion, this was given in view of its nautical character and not because of its modernity.

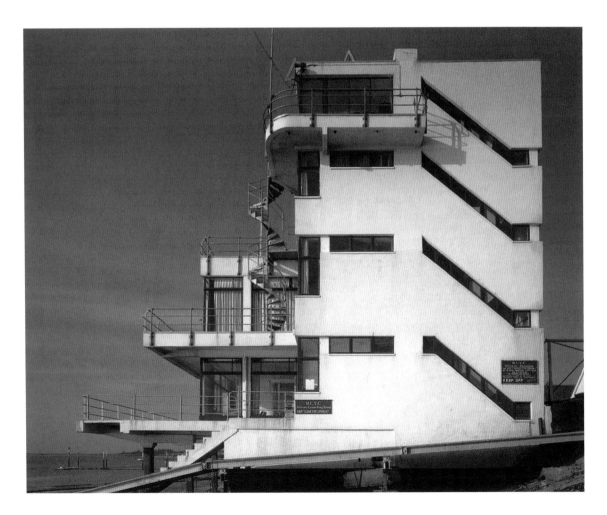

BIJENKORF DEPARTMENT STORE

WILLEM DUDOK, 1931 ROTTERDAM, THE NETHERLANDS

Sadly, this forceful building was badly damaged in a bombing raid in 1940 and demolished when Rotterdam was rebuilt after World War Two. The loss is particularly poignant as Rotterdam is, from a strictly architectural and urbanistic point of view, now one of the most Modern cities in the world. Dudok's Bijenkorf Store was the most overtly Modern of his creations. The design is based on the idea of a store being made up of a number of street markets superimposed on one another and enclosed in glass. These highly glazed markets expressed as relentless horizontal elements are brought together at the vertical, slab-sided entrance tower.

At one and the same time, each separate element of the store is clearly expressed in the transparent architecture, and they are joined by the horizontal bands held in check by the tower. Thus, the design had immense visual strength, combining a sense of freedom of plan within a powerful, if abstract, order. Even if you have little interest in shopping, this is one of those stores you would want to visit time and again just to watch the play of light on its façades and to see that wonderful abstract clock marking the hours. Soon after the store's completion, Dudok moved to The Hague where he became the Town Planner.

TRADE UNION HOUSE

MAX TAUT, 1931 FRANKFURT-AM-MAIN, GERMANY

Max Taut (1884–1967) was highly influenced by the reaction to Impressionism referred to as *Neue Sachlichkeit* (New Objectivity), a label that was coined by the art critic G. F. Hartlaub in 1924. What did a *Neue Sachlichkeit* architecture do to counteract Impressionism? Build in the clearest cut way with powerfully expressed concrete frames, that's what. This was Taut's – who saw Impressionism as soft, woolly and unfocused – new objectivity, and it is seen at its most extreme and convincing in the design of the Trade Union House in Frankfurt.

A highly controlled and rational structure, the Trade Union House is composed of identical symmetrical elements and forms a very determined picture of German logic. The building made its mark right up until the end of the twentieth century: countless office buildings were designed along the same severe lines.

Although strict, the Trade Union House is not without its poetry. As for Taut, he was effectively banned from architectural practice throughout the Hitler years. At the end of World War Two he returned to prominence as one of the most important teachers of the time; he was based at the Hochschule für Bildende Künste in West Berlin between 1945 and 1954.

DAILY EXPRESS BUILDING

ELLIS CLARKE, RONALD ATKINSON, OWEN WILLIAMS, 1932 FLEET STREET, LONDON, ENGLAND

Britain's national newspapers abandoned Fleet Street, their traditional home, at the end of the 1980s as new technology enabled them to separate journalists from printers. In 1989, the *Daily Express* deserted this glorious Art Deco headquarters, an unforgettable words-factory, with one of London's most famous, popular and dazzling interiors. The main body of this concrete-framed, glass-wrapped building was designed by the engineer Owen Williams (1890–1969). For what is essentially a factory, the building is very glamorous. Sited in one of the City of London's busiest streets and in the shadow of the dome of St Paul's Cathedral, perhaps it had to be. The distinctive black glass façade gave it its popular, if satirical, nickname – the "Black Lubianka".

The entrance hall, designed by Ronald Atkinson, is like a still from a Busby Berkeley extravaganza. The approach to the Hollywood stair is based on the entrance to Cleopatra's tomb, complete with chrome-plated snake handrails. Electric light dances from steel stalactites hanging from the cha-cha-cha ceiling. Ritzy metal relief sculptures depict jingoistic scenes of imperial enterprise. The total effect of the building is one of immense verve, reflecting the confidence of newspapers at the very height of their success in the 1930s.

MAISON DE VERRE

PIERRE CHAREAU AND BERNARD BIJVOET, 1932 PARIS, FRANCE

The Maison de Verre is no lie: aside from its filigree steel frame, it is built almost entirely from glass and is one of the most extraordinary houses of the century. Hidden from view in a courtyard, it is an outgrowth of an old house and capped by its top floor – the old lady who lived here refused to move and so the Maison de Verre was unable to grow to its full height. Even so, it is a thing of light and grace and the imagination, perhaps the most perfectly realized *machine à habiter*. It was designed by Pierre Chareau (1883–1950) and Bernard Bijvoet (1889–1979) for Dr Dalsace, an eminent Parisian gynaecologist and was meant to represent the notions and virtues of hygiene and medical efficiency. Despite this, it is also very beautiful.

The most impressive part of the house is the spacious, double-height living room, which boasts floor to ceiling windows, exposed steel columns and a gallery. This style of "loft living" took another 50 years to become popular among middle-class professionals, and, even then, few have created such a radical and liveable home from this very open arrangement of space and from the unabashed use of industrial materials. The glass bricks that Chareau made such extensive use of were brand new in 1932. Chareau emigrated to the United States in 1940 where he was to build a second special house, this time for the painter Robert Motherwell at East Hampton, Long Island.

BOOTS FACTORY

OWEN WILLIAMS, 1932 BEESTON, NOTTINGHAM, ENGLAND

Owen Williams, the structural engineer, designed this great factory at a time when few architects could have managed the brief with such confidence. Boots the Chemists was and is a hugely successful high-street chemist. At the beginning of the 1930s, the company decided to pull its manufacturing and distribution arms into one building on the edge of Nottingham. Williams came up trumps with a spectacular and airy design based on a widely spaced forest of mushroom-headed concrete columns. The building is arranged on four storeys, with galleries penetrating the floors at frequent intervals. The result is one of the sunniest factories of its time and a building of great and simple logic that, more than 60 years on from its completion, is still serving its original purpose extremely well.

Owen was educated at London University and worked in railway and aircraft design before moving on to architecture. After Beeston he designed the swimming pool at Wembley Stadium (1933), a pioneering Health Centre in Peckham (1936) and the Synagogue at Dollis Hill (1938). Until the arrival of the Danish engineer, Ove Arup, in the early 1930s, Williams was perhaps the only British-based engineer who understood intuitively the relationship between the forms of Modern architecture and the possibilities of new structural techniques.

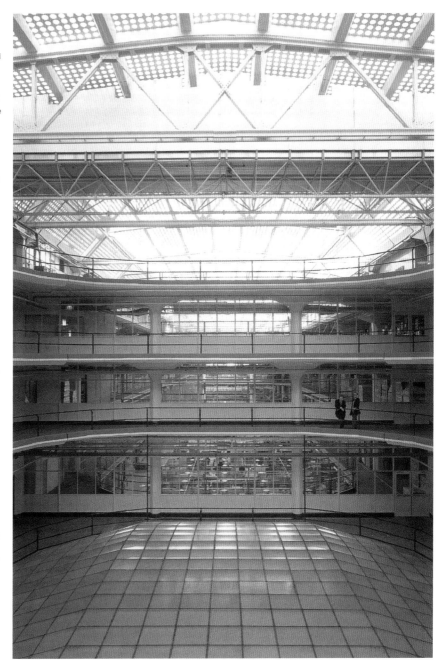

NEW FARM

AMYAS CONNELL AND BASIL WARD, 1932 HASLEMERE, SURREY, ENGLAND

The Modern house came to Britain much later than elsewhere in Continental Europe. This was due as much to Britain's island mentality and endemic nostalgia as it was for a lack of architects with new ideas. New Farm, by Amyas Connell (1901-1980) and Basil Ward (1902-1976) was a brave stab at Constructivist design in rural Surrey, a gentle English landscape better known for its houses by Lutyens and gardens by Jekyll than for cutting-edge Continental design.

New Farm is characterized by the severe planes of its thin concrete walls and by its glazed stair-tower. When completed, the house was photographed for the *Architectural Review* as part of this influential magazine's late coming to the Modern Movement. When the glass plate negatives arrived, the editors – then under the inspired direction of Hubert de Cronin Hastings (1902–84) – were disappointed by the patchy quality of the concrete walls. They had their art editor paint them white on the glass plates so that, when published, they gleamed smooth and whiter than white. This was proof that the Modern Movement was as much a tool of propaganda as it was a new way of designing, building and living. Since then, New Farm has settled happily into life in a most English country garden. Most recently it has been bought by a car designer and his family who wish to rescue it from 65 years of Surrey sleep.

PAIMIO SANATORIUM

ALVAR AALTO, 1933 PAIMIO, FINLAND

Alvar Aalto (1898–1976) is one of the greats of twentieth-century architecture. His ability to reconcile natural forms with machine-age design remained pretty much unchallenged at the end of the century. He got off to a flying start, working on the design of this pristine sanatorium in the remote forests of southwest Finland when he was just 30. The building expressed the hopes of more than 50 local Finnish communities who paid for its design and construction. What they got for their money, and confidence in a brilliant young architect, was a model hospital, the plan of which – and to an extent its style – has been copied around the world ever since its completion. The slim and elegant buildings comprise separate accommodation for patients and staff. The former occupy the famously photographed block that ends with ship-like balconies projecting out into the forest landscape. Patients' rooms are awash with daylight for as much of the year as possible and, although simple throughout, the building is beautifully detailed. It is built of concrete and painted white.

Throughout its design, Aalto worked closely with the sanatorium's doctors. The result is a very successful building both formally and functionally. It is still very much in use at the end of the century with the spectre of tuberculosis haunting Europe afresh.

ISOKON FLATS

WELLS COATES, 1934 LAWN ROAD, HAMPSTEAD, LONDON, ENGLAND

Although rather ungraceful, the Isokon Flats (named after the furniture factory of Jack Pritchard, the model Modern client who commissioned them) are important as the first of a type of residential building that never quite got going and yet could be successful again in the twenty-first century. The "existenzminium" flats grouped here on four floors and giving on to heavily defined exterior galleries, were designed for a new generation of highly mobile intellectuals and artists. People would come and go on short leases when they needed to be in London and to walk and talk on Hampstead Heath.

The idea had its roots in the Swiss Pavilion, Paris (Le Corbusier, 1930) and the Narkomfin flats, Moscow (Moisei Ginzburg, 1929). The block boasted a club room and bar designed by the Bauhaus architect Marcel Breuer. Its architect was the flamboyant Wells Coates (1895–1958), born in Tokyo, raised in Vancouver and who worked for several years as a journalist for the London *Daily Express* before turning to architecture and design. Coates was, perhaps, to become better known in the public eye as a designer of what were, for their time, very successful wireless (radio) sets rather than buildings. Nevertheless, the Isokon Flats were a notable attempt to establish a new way of life beyond the confines of the standard city flat and the English suburban semi. Neglected for many years, the Isokon Flats are being restored at the end of the century.

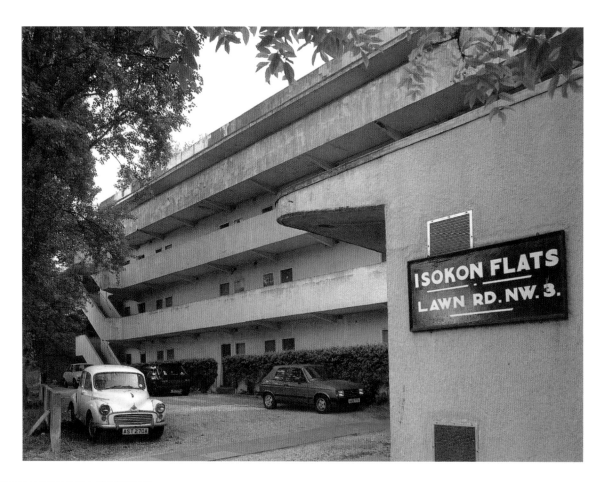

PENGUIN POOL

BERTHOLD LUBETKIN AND TECTON, 1934 REGENT'S PARK ZOO, LONDON, ENGLAND

Lubetkin (1901–90) was a Russian émigré who came to London via the October Revolution of 1917. Feisty, mercurial, charming and a great storyteller, he soon made his mark with the English intellectual elite. One of his earliest commissions was from the Director of London Zoo. A penguin pool might sound a very modest proposition, but in Lubetkin's hands it became one of the iconic architectural designs of the 1930s. Working with the brilliant Danish engineer, Ove Arup, Lubetkin shaped the pool around a balletic spiralling of concrete ramps above the blue pool. The penguins seemed happy and this romantic, rational, structure continues to serve its original purpose, delighting both visitors and penguins. It was restored by Lubetkin and Avanti Architects in 1985. Lubetkin went on to design other animal pavilions at Regent's Park and Whipsnade Zoos as well as some of the best accommodation for the human zoo in Highgate and the old London Borough of Finsbury. A lifelong Communist, he gave up architecture in the 1950s over a row over the design of Peterlee, a New Town for miners, and retired to become a pig farmer. He was chivvied from his lair by fans in the 1980s and awarded the Royal Gold Medal for Architecture duly, if late in the day.

HIGHPOINT 1

BERTHOLD LUBETKIN AND TECTON 1935 HIGHGATE, LONDON, ENGLAND

After working briefly with Jean Ginsburg in Paris (1927–30), Lubetkin came to London and established Tecton, the cooperative practice he effectively dominated. Tecton's first major venture into housing was Highpoint 1, a block of 64 flats set on eight floors of a gleaming white, double-cruciform tower on Highgate Ridge. From this suburban eyrie, residents commanded the sort of views Le Corbusier had dreamed of in his plans for ideal modern cities in which professional people would live in airy, gracious flats each with a balcony and magnificent views and set above urban parkland. Highpoint 1 comes pretty close to fulfilling Corbusier's dream. In fact, the legendary French architect came to visit when the flats were new and gave them his approval. The design was originally considerably more substantial than the block that was built. Before the concrete was poured, Lubetkin had met up with Ove Arup, the émigré Danish engineer, who showed him how Highpoint did not need a substantial concrete frame: the walls could be designed to carry their own weight.

The block became home to many famous figures in the Modern Movement, not least the landscape gardener, Geoffrey Jellicoe, who lived here until his death in 1995. Looking out from his apartment across miles of wooded landscape, Jellicoe said he didn't need a garden of his own.

HOOVER BUILDING

WALLIS, GILBERT AND PARTNERS, 1935 PERIVALE, LONDON, ENGLAND

The German émigré historian Nikolaus Pevsner described this Art Deco palace of labour as "perhaps the most offensive of the modernistic atrocities along this road [Western Avenue] of typical by-pass factories." That was nearly 40 years ago; tastes have changed. In a later history of London architecture, Edward Jones and Christopher Woodward describe the Hoover Factory as "a serious attempt to dignify the workplace". And indeed it was.

The Hoover Factory survived several threats of demolition in the 1970s and 1980s; it is now a Tesco superstore. Hoover is the world-famous maker of vacuum cleaners and other household appliances; in London, its workers were treated to a splendid cinematic entrance, a bright and breezy top floor canteen (its design adopted by the Van Nelle Factory, Rotterdam, p.363), and a Modern cornucopia of architectural details drawn from such diverse sources as Mendelsohn's Einstein Tower at Potsdam, Hoffman's Palais Stoclet in Brussels and Mackintosh's Glasgow School of Art. Whatever, the building has become a favourite London landmark over the years, celebrated in song by Elvis Costello and a happy distraction from the horrendous traffic jams that build up morning and evening on this main western exit from the city. Even the great Professor Doctor Pevsner could be wrong.

DE LA WARR PAVILION

ERICH MENDELSOHN AND SERGE CHERMAYEFF, 1935 BEXHILL-ON-SEA, EAST SUSSEX, ENGLAND

This delightful seaside pleasure palace was designed by Erich Mendelsohn, after he left Nazi Germany and before he went to Palestine, and Serge Chermayeff (born 1900), the Russian-born, Harrow-educated dancer and window dresser, who graduated to architecture in time to work for three years with his famous Prussian partner. Mendelsohn and Chermayeff won an open competition to design the pavilion, their prize £150. They were immediately attacked by members of the British architectural profession in a display of vicious chauvinism and anti-semitism that encouraged Mendelsohn to move from what he imagined to be the liberal sanctuary of Great Britain, home of fair play and decency.

The De La Warr Pavilion is both fair and decent, a design of great clarity and a building of lightness and delight. It faces the sea in a swirl of stairs, walls of glass and shining white concrete. It contains and frames a sun-lounge restaurant, library and an auditorium that was to have a major influence on the design of the Royal Festival Hall, London (1951). The pavilion is all the more surprising for being set, on its roadside, against a decidedly unquiet sea of harsh red brick and brittle terracotta Victorian apartment blocks. In fact, it is quite remarkable to find such a distinguished Modern building in this south coast gerontocracy. Yet, it is much loved by local people, and in the latter part of the 1990s was the subject of an extensive restoration by the architects Troughton McAslan.

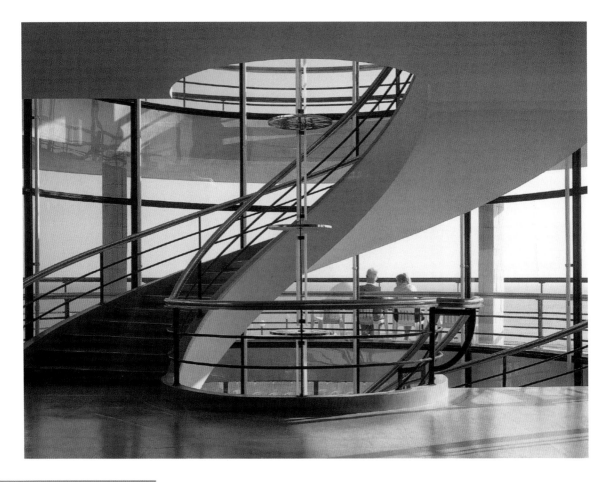

CASA DEL FASCIO

GIUSEPPE TERRAGNI, 1936 COMO, ITALY

A breathtaking building. Giuseppe Terragni (1904–41) was just 28 when he was commissioned to design this meeting hall and local headquarters for Benito Mussolini's Fascist Party in the lakeside town of Como. He had already designed a superb block of pristine white flats elsewhere in Como (Novocomum, 1928), but this still owed something to the Russian Constructivism the young Terragni abandoned as he discovered, in the design of the Casa del Fascio, a remarkably effective and compelling middle way between Classical and Cubist architecture. The result is a building that, if not timeless, has the qualities of a de Chirico townscape brought to haunting life. The building, which faces Como's cathedral across a sun-bleached piazza, is

a travertine-clad, concrete-framed box: the centre is a floor to ceiling glass courtyard entered from the cathedral side through an impressive parade of 16 glass doors. Each side of the building, however, is arranged differently, the concrete frame exposed or closed in a complex play of geometry. Here the building appears to be impermeable; there, it is possible to see into its core. This is a game the architecture enthusiast can never tire of. Yet, the building is also icily calm and dignified. It has a very special presence and is surely one of the century's top ten buildings.

Since the fall of Mussolini in 1943, it has been the Casa del Popolo, but although open to the public, it is the local headquarters of the Carabinieri.

FALLING WATER

FRANK LLOYD WRIGHT, 1936 BEAR RUN, PENNSYLVANIA, USA

This is the enigmatic, eclectic and long-lived Frank Lloyd Wright at his very best. Falling Water never fails to surprise and delight visitors who trek here through the prolific woodlands of rural Pennsylvania. It was designed as a romantic retreat for the publisher Edgar Kaufman. Having found the site – a waterfall roaring over ancient rocks, Wright anchored the house as closely as he could to the water. In effect, the house is a series of great horizontal trays pivoted around and held up by a central tower, which is also a chimney. So, although Wright claimed that the section of the house was adopted from an ancient Mayan temple, Falling Water is also like a great tent realized in concrete, timber, steel and glass rather than canvas or buffalo hides.

The house is a Wright *tour de force*: the architect's determining hand is seen everywhere, in every last detail. And yet, far from being precious, the house is liberating. How does Wright manage this? Perhaps, because from anywhere in the house, there are complex views out taking in unexpected vistas of the building as well as the primordial landscape. This is one of the most photographed and most famous houses in the world and it deserves to be. It is at its best out of season when you can have the place almost, if not quite, to yourself: the ghost of Frank Lloyd Wright is always looking over your shoulder.

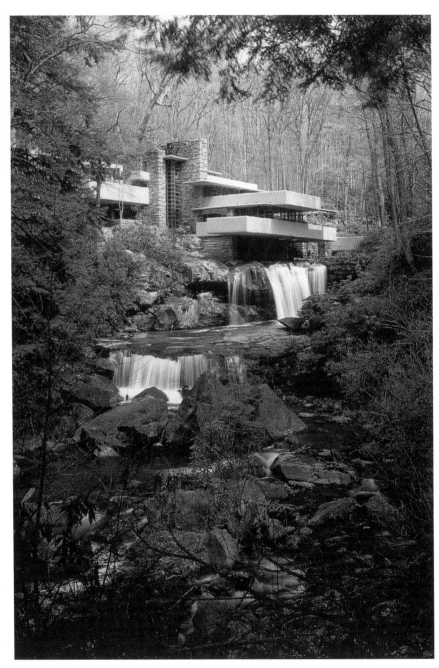

PETER JONES STORE

WILLIAM CRABTREE, 1937 CHELSEA, LONDON, ENGLAND

Clearly owing a debt to Mendelsohn's Schocken stores (pp.168, 176), Crabtree's Peter Jones is one of the few Modern buildings in London that knows how to turn a corner. For most architects, this simple and graceful act is something quite beyond them. And, yet it is this simple device that makes Peter Jones such a well-loved shop. Crabtree swept his indefatigably elegant glass screen around Sloane Square and into King's Road with panache. Unlike Mendelsohn who performed the same trick with defiant bands of horizontal glass, Crabtree's glazing emphasizes the vertical and so walks around the building rather than rushing it as Mendelsohn does. Beyond this, the building

is a simple frame containing triple-height galleries and a fine spiral stair. It is light and airy and impossible to get lost in. The top floor is set back, Mendelsohn style, like an ocean liner.

What is remarkable here is that the shop was designed for the deeply conservative top end of the British middle class who, on the whole, preferred mock Tudor beams and Neo-Georgian pediments to the new streamlined Modern architecture arriving from the Continent. Crabtree was able to convince them that Modern architecture was not some dangerous foreign perversion, and that surely was a feat worth recording.

MUSEUM OF MODERN ART

PHILIP GOODWIN AND EDWARD STONE, 1939 NEW YORK CITY, USA

Widely used in ropaganda extolling the virtues of Modern design in the United States, the Museum of Modern Art was the first major International Style building on the east coast. As crisp as Gropius's Bauhaus (p.162), the Museum of Modern Art is, in effect, a very simple container with a cool, clinical façade. The six-storey building comprises a basement lecture theatre, a lobby and gallery at street level, two floors of exhibition space, a third-floor library, fourth-floor offices and a club room with terraces under the concrete "sunshade" at the top.

It is significant that in the USA, the Modern Movement arrived with the tag "International Style", a brand dreamed up by the architect Philip Johnson and historian Henry-Russell Hitchcock. It demonstrated that for many US architects, Modern architecture was simply one more style in the great panoply that led from Classical to Gothic, from Art Nouveau to Art Deco. To an extent this was true: in Europe, the Modern Movement had risen from and was a part of a cultural and artistic revolution. It was often wrapped up in left-wing political gambits, which it why its progeny were banned by the Nazis. In the States, Modernism was freed of political and social undertones: all that really mattered was style. And that was something Philip Goodwin and Edward Stone (1902–78) gave the Museum of Modern Art.

ROCKEFELLER CENTER

REINHARD, HOFMEISTER, ET AL,1940 NEW YORK CITY, USA

Ice rink. Christmas tree. Fairy lights. Radio City. The Rockefeller Center is a magnificent and generous fusion of rampant capitalist enterprise and civic delight. It is a huge complex of ten giant buildings – some very tall – grouped with bravura and brilliance on a 12-acre site bounded by New York's Fifth and Sixth Avenues and by 48th and 51st Streets. The buildings build up from the pavement to a climactic peak, like a man-made mountain range. Each steel-framed behemoth is clad in expensive stone, granite and marble, while finishes throughout the complex are as good to look at as they are to touch. Passageways through the complex connect the various buildings, binding them to then whole.

It is rare that a complex given to generating capital and maximizing profit has been so generous and civically minded. The Center was started in 1930 and its Art Deco styling dates from then. During its decade of construction, the architects stuck to this style – to have changed it would have undermined the coherency of the ambitious whole – creating what looks like a giant Mayan temple complex seen through the distorting mirror of the mid-twentieth century. The Rockefeller Center broke no new technological barriers but it was an inspired example of grouping modern buildings to create a twentieth-century equivalent of the Roman forum.

PAMPÚLHA YACHT CLUB

OSCAR NIEMEYER AND LÚCIO COSTA, 1942 PAMPÚLHA, BRAZIL

Oscar Niemeyer is one of the century's greats, an architect who has made poetry from concrete, and who ranks with his mentor, Le Corbusier, as one of the most memorable form-givers of the Modern Movement. Born in Rio de Janiero and in love with its sensual setting and atmosphere – its mountains, beaches and beautiful people – Niemeyer's take on Modernism was quite unlike that of austere and angst-ridden intellectual Europeans. His architecture was a celebration of life and nature, an attempt to harmonize natural beauty with the possibilities of Modern design, technology and materials. On the whole he was to succeed triumphantly.

His first significant project, built at a time when Brazil was at war with Germany and Italy, was a pleasure village – Pampúlha – for the wealthy. Here, as Hitler challenged Europe and the Japanese practised unspeakable cruelties in the Far East, Niemeyer experimented with the form of bright new architecture in the guise of a glamorous yacht club and casino. The lightness and elegance of the yacht club, with its twin inverse-sloping roofs, was to influence many buildings of the 1950s in other towns and cities given over to hedonistic pleasure, notably Miami, Havana and Los Angeles. Although a frivolous project, the design of Pampúlha allowed the young Niemeyer a chance to experiment with the forms of Modernism and to adapt a European way of thinking to the sensuous nature of Brazil, which was the cradle of Modern architecture in Latin America.

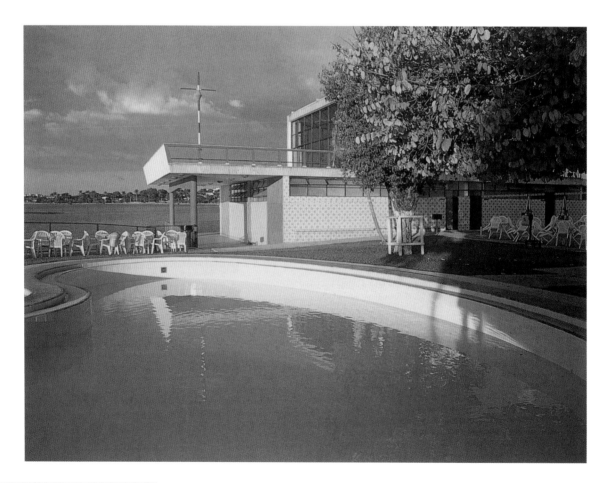

MINISTRY OF EDUCATION AND HEALTH

**LÚCIO COSTA, OSCAR
NIEMEYER AND LE
CORBUSIER, 1943**
RIO DE JANIERO, BRAZIL

Le Corbusier visited Rio in 1936
and was invited to draw up plans
for this new ministry building;
Lúcio Costa (1902–98) and Oscar
Niemeyer were invited to join
him and to see the sculptural
building through to completion.
The result was a quiet triumph,
Corbusier's concrete architecture
reworked for Rio's dazzling
climate. The most distinctive
feature of the buildings, its
permanent sun-louvres (*brises-
soleil*), hide its internal life so
that the ministry appears to be
a vast and beautifully controlled
sculpture rather than a machine
for working in. It was this building
that introduced Latin America to
Modernism. And there seems
little doubt that Le Corbusier
benefited from working on
the Rio ministry: his postwar
successes owe a debt to the
experience of working with the
sun in Rio.

Until Le Corbusier's visit,
Latin America was a Modern
Movement free zone the change
that came in little more than a
decade was remarkable. Sadly,
the standard of formal design set
by Niemeyer and Le Corbusier
was rarely matched and never
excelled. The success of the
ministry building was to lead
Niemeyer on to the design of
the centre of Brasília in the mid-
1950s, from when he dominated
the Brazilian architectural
landscape until exile following the
military coup in 1964.

KAUFMAN HOUSE

RICHARD NEUTRA, 1947 PALM SPRINGS, CALIFORNIA, USA

The alluring Kaufman "Desert" House is undoubtedly a Modern masterpiece. It was yet another perfect home for Edgar Kaufman who had, a decade earlier, commissioned Frank Lloyd Wright to design Falling Water (p.196). Although a large house, complete with servants' quarters, it sits so low in its spectacular setting that it seems no more than a super-sophisticated shack. Until you get up close: then Neutra's genius and sheer finesse show at every turn. The house opens up into the landscape like some enormous yet unshowy flower: walls slide back to let the outside world into the interior and there are magical moments when inside and outside blur together seamlessly. This is a perfect summer retreat, well able to cope with heat and sun and to make the best of them.

The Kaufman House marked, perhaps, the zenith of Neutra's career, one that had taken him a very long way indeed from turn of the century Vienna. He believed that a house like this, designed to become a part of the landscape it adorned, was a "harbour for the soul". Despite the ultra-modern appearance of the Kaufman House, Neutra condemned design that was merely fashionable: he wanted to create a "slice of eternity". In the design of the Kaufman House he got as close to achieving this goal as any twentieth-century architect ever did.

EQUITABLE SAVINGS AND LOAN ASSOCIATION HEADQUARTERS

PIETRO BELLUSCHI, 1948
PORTLAND, OREGON, USA

This crisp, elegant and supremely taut building might have been designed and built at any time in the 1980s or 1990s for a Western city centre. In fact it dates from 1948. Pietro Belluschi (1899–1994) created what was probably the first smooth-skinned office building, a type that has been repeated endlessly ever since. The skin of the building is almost flush, like the skin of a snake; or, perhaps, this is architecture created by a cheese wire. The specification of the building was very much up to date with double glazing, solar-tinted windows and air-conditioning, demonstrating clearly the technological advances made in the United States during four years of intense war production and an investment in research and development.

Belluschi was born in Ancona in Italy. He studied at Rome and then in the United States at Cornell University. In 1943 Belluschi founded his own office in Portland, which was taken over by the giant Skidmore, Owings and Merrill in 1950. From 1951 to 65 he was Dean of the School of Architecture and Planning at the Massachusetts Institute of Technology, but set up in practice again in Portland in 1965. His later concerns were a continuation of the theme established by the Equitable Savings Building: how to make an architecture that was a smooth, polished and, it seems, anonymous container of contemporary functions.

EAMES HOUSE

CHARLES AND RAY EAMES, 1949 NO 8, PACIFIC PALISADES, CALIFORNIA, USA

This brilliant house by the husband and wife team Charles (1907–78) and Ray (1916–88) Eames was one of the first to be built entirely from off-the-peg industrial components and to make this form of construction glamorous. The house was one of a number of experimental houses commissioned by John Entenza, publisher of *Arts and Architecture*. Entenza wanted to show a postwar public, hungry for ideal new homes, that modern architects could offer more for their money than conventional house-builders. His "Case Study" programme was a success: the first six houses, made of timber and completed by 1948, attracted 370,000 visitors.

The Eames House consisted of a two-storey living space and studio divided by a courtyard. The exterior was a glamorous machine, echoing the forms of a traditional Japanese house, while the double-height interiors were a revelation: light, airy, open and still looking and feeling Modern 50 years on from their completion. The Eames had a gift for creating a Modern look that was easy on the eye, comfortable and relaxed with none of the repressed earnestness of contemporary European design, nor the work ethic aesthetic of Chicago and New York. The Californian climate had brought out the best in Rudolf Schindler and Richard Neutra: it did the same for Charles and Ray Eames.

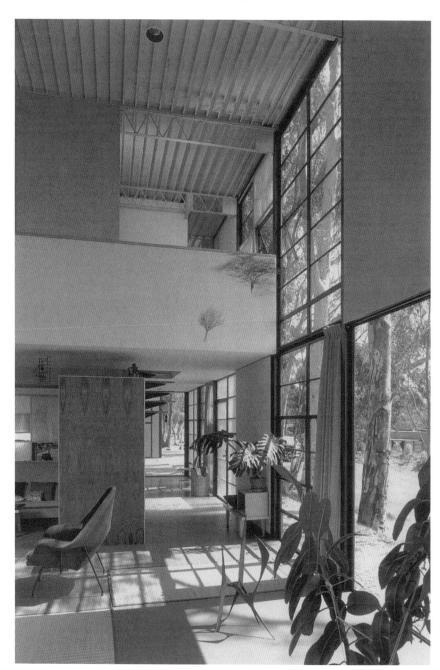

GLASS HOUSE

PHILIP JOHNSON, 1950 NEW CANAAN, CONNECTICUT, USA

Philip Cortelyou Johnson, born in 1906 into a wealthy New England family, was the most influential early protagonist of European Modern Movement ideas in the United States. Much later, he was to become champion of Postmodernism, Deconstructivism and just about every other "ism" architects were to dream up in the last quarter of the century. The uncrowned king of US architecture, Johnson was able to make and break careers. A witty, urbane character, he studied philology at Harvard before becoming the first director of the Architecture Department of the Museum of Modern Art, New York, from 1930 to 1936. The hugely influential "International Style" exhibition he curated at MOMA

with the historian Henry-Russell Hitchcock in 1932 brought the work of the European masters – principally Mies van der Rohe – to light in the United States, although Johnson seemed unaware, or was simply dismissive, of the work of Schindler in California. Having visited Mies in Germany, from 1930, and flirted with Nazism, Johnson trained as an architect under Gropius and Breuer at Harvard (1940–43).

In 1949 Johnson built his Glass House retreat, clearly inspired by Mies, in the woods at New Canaan. An exquisite steel-section and sheet glass pavilion, it remains one of the most perfect and undiluted essays in Modern Movement design and propaganda.

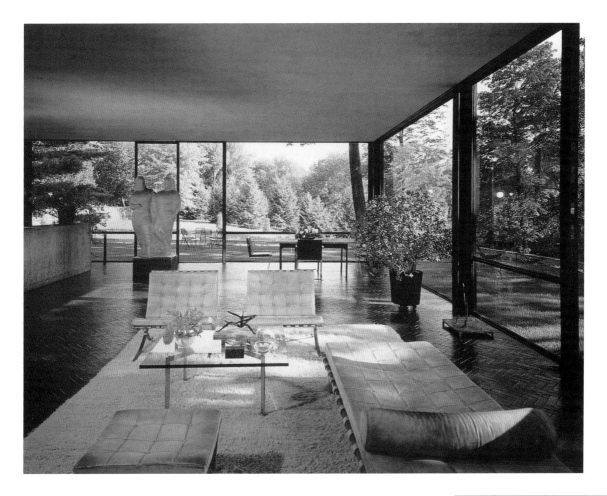

FARNSWORTH HOUSE

LUDWIG MIES VAN DER ROHE, 1951 PLANO, ILLINOIS, USA

Ludwig Mies van der Rohe arrived in the United States in 1937. He had succeeded Gropius as Director of the Bauhaus in 1930 but the school was closed by the Nazis in 1933. Finding it impossible to realize his form of Platonic Modern architecture, Mies left to teach at the Illinois Institute of Technology, for which he built a new campus from 1940.

Dr Edith Farnsworth commissioned him to design a weekend retreat in rural Illinois in 1946. The result is one of the most perfect expressions of the Modern Movement dream, a pavilion of light, transparency, tautness and weightlessness. It is one of those buildings that, first seen, sends a shiver up the spine. It is chaste: it is also sublime. The living space – a single room measuring 23 by 8.5 metres (77 ft by 28 ft) and divided only by a central

kitchen and bathroom core – is raised above the flood plain of Fox River on eight white steel I-section beams. These seem barely to touch the glass box they support, while the horizontal planes of floor and roof seem to float almost independently of the I-beams. The whole assemble is extraordinary: free-floating, yet as taut as a drawn bow; ethereal, yet as strong and substantial as so few materials can be.

In moving to the States, Mies encountered the wealth that enabled him to realize some of the most refined architecture of any century. It was not one-way traffic, however. Mies went on to design offices and apartment blocks that were hugely profitable for developers; not for nothing did American business executives say "Mies means money".

LAKE SHORE DRIVE APARTMENTS

LUDWIG MIES VAN DER ROHE, 1951 CHICAGO, ILLINOIS, USA

The twin Lake Shore Drive apartment blocks were Mies's dictum "less is more" taken to a new extreme. Their utter simplicity – or what appears to be utter simplicity when first seen – is the result of immense thought and calculation. The blocks are supported by Mies's trademark I-beam steel sections that rise the height of the buildings. These give the 26-storey blocks a powerful vertical emphasis and an equally powerful abstract quality. This abstractedness is heightened by the way in which the two blocks are related: situated at right angles to one another, the broad front of one meeting the narrow side of the other. Walking around them, they appear to waltz slowly around one another in a configuration that seems to change with each step. Neither of these purist, Platonic blocks can be said to have a front or a back. They are designed as perfect shapes: nothing is allowed to upset this purity. This includes the blinds protecting the floor-to-ceiling windows of individual apartments from the glare of the sun. Originally, these were uniform, so that no one detail – a colourful blind, a florid curtain – was able to challenge the purity of the whole. The messiness of everyday living – laundry, storage, car parking – was swept beneath the twin blocks. The influence of the Lake Shore towers on twentieth-century architecture has been incalculable.

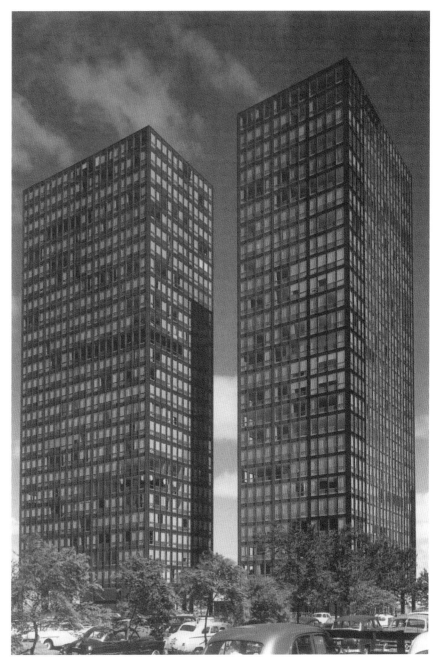

ROYAL FESTIVAL HALL

LCC ARCHITECTS DEPARTMENT, 1951 LONDON, ENGLAND

The one lasting legacy of the 1951 Festival of Britain held on London's South Bank, the Royal Festival Hall was one of the first major Modern public buildings in Britain. Commissioned in 1948, it was designed by a team led by Leslie Martin (born 1908) and Peter Moro (born 1911) for the London County Council. The building took its aesthetic cue from Modern architecture in Scandinavia, but its form was determined by the need to find a way of constructing a sound-proof auditorium. Not only did the Bakerloo Line of the London Underground run beneath the building, but planes flew overhead, Waterloo mainline station was in whistling distance (in the days of steam locomotives) and trains from Charing Cross station rumbled across Hungerford Bridge alongside the new building. Martin's solution was what he described as an "egg in a box": the 2,740 seat auditorium would be lifted into the very centre of the structure. It was an ingenious solution and one that never fails to delight and baffle visitors to this building; the auditorium floats serenely and magically above lobbies, bars, cafés, shops and exhibition space.

The Royal Festival Hall was built in concrete at great speed, although to a high standard. The original river front was temporary. Martin left the LCC in 1956, but the front was redesigned very much the way he had intended in 1964.

BRYNMAWR RUBBER FACTORY

ARCHITECTS CO-PARTNERSHIP, 1952 EBBW VALE, SOUTH WALES

Unemployment in Ebbw Vale, a coal mining district of South Wales, reached 82 per cent shortly before the outbreak of World War Two. When a socialist government was voted overwhelmingly into power in Britain in 1945, it promised to revitalize and help this downtrodden area. The government paid for this imposing new factory, designed for the manufacturer of rubber goods by the socialist practice Architects Co-Partnership with the idealistic and inventive engineer Ove Arup. It was an expensive gesture and ultimately proved to be an economic folly. The factory has long been closed – and the object of several failed attempts to save it from demolition – and Ebbw Vale remains a poor area.

At the time of its design and construction – stretched out over seven long years – the Brynmawr Rubber Factory was one of the finest buildings of its kind, as well as one of the most altruistic. Not only did workers and management use the same entrance and canteen (enlivened by contemporary artworks), but working conditions – because of the architecture – were among the best to be found anywhere in Britain, although that isn't saying much for a country that, even at the end of the twentieth century, relies heavily on some of the cheapest and most easily dispensable labour to be found in Europe.

The design of the factory was based around a grid of nine spectacular concrete domed vaults, each measuring 26 by 19 metres (85 ft by 62 ft); it was light, airy, handsome and doomed from the start.

UNITÉ D'HABITATION

LE CORBUSIER, 1952 MARSEILLES, FRANCE

This titanic building was designed to house 1,600 working-class Marseillaise. Well before the end of the century it had become one of the most fashionable addresses in the great Mediterranean seaport, populated almost entirely by middle-class professionals. Who could blame them for wanting to live here? This was no cheapskate local authority housing block, but the representation, in thousands of tons of weather-boarded and bush-hammered concrete, of social and architectural ideals Le Corbusier had been struggling with for 30 years. In effect, the 337 flats on 17 storeys above the streets of Marseilles, are interlocked around central streets within the building and raised on massive concrete supports above a beautifully maintained park. The flats boast double-height living rooms and each, because of the concrete construction, is quiet and well insulated. On the fourth floor there is a hotel (Hôtel Le Corbusier) and a variety of shops including a poodle parlour. The roof with its surrealistic landscape of vents and towers, swimming pool and spaces to play has become an icon of Modern design at its most sculptural and challenging.

   Le Corbusier designed five more Unités (Nantes-Reze, 1957; Berlin, 1958; Meaux, 1959; Briey-en-Fôret, 1960 and Firminy-Vert, 1968), but these were compromised and the original remains unchallenged.

SÄYNÄTSALO TOWN HALL

ALVAR AALTO, 1952 SÄYNÄTSALO, FINLAND

Aalto did more than almost any other Modern architect to connect his buildings to Nature. And, this is why his centenary in 1998 was so widely and enthusiastically celebrated. Perhaps his concern for Nature was natural enough for a Finn brought up in a largely unspoilt land of lakes, woods and wildlife; perhaps it was his time as a front-line soldier during World War Two that encouraged this great architect to see Nature as the balm for the machine-like quality of modern architecture and urbanism.

Shortly after the war he designed this romantic and much-loved town hall, or civic centre, in rural Finland. A huddle of elegant brick, timber and copper pavilions mounted on a capitol-like plinth and connected by stairs planted with grass and meadow flowers, the complex offers both intimacy, adventure and great spatial play. In short, it is a delight and a perfect answer to anyone foolish enough at the end of the twentieth century to say that Modern architecture is inhuman. Somewhere else, yes, but not here. The centre includes a council chamber as well as a public library, post office, bank and shops.

Sadly, the hand-crafted bricky style of Säynätsalo was to be much copied, without much inspiration, in Britain and elsewhere in Europe in the 1970s as an antidote to the unpopularity of concrete estates and "high rise horrors". The original is peerless.

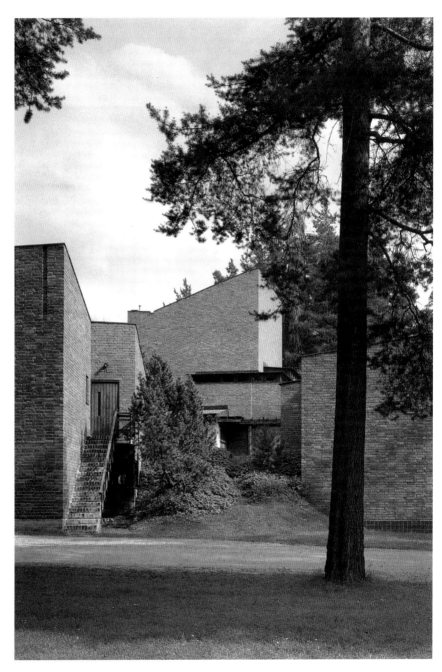

LEVER BUILDING

SKIDMORE, OWINGS AND MERRILL, 1952 NEW YORK CITY, USA

The Lever Building is one of the most influential of all twentieth-century buildings. From the perspective of the end of the century it might look like any other office block, but that's the point: countless thousand office blocks look like the Lever Building.

Consisting of a two-storey slab around a central courtyard and a 21-storey curtain-wall tower, the design owes much to Mies van der Rohe and the International Style aesthetic that permeated the United States from 1932. The fact that the building was much copied is largely, perhaps, because Skidmore, Owings and Merrill (SOM) were not just clever designers, but they had managed to get under the skin of the newly emerging postwar corporate America and, in the process, created a house style for it. The firm was founded in 1936 by Louis Skidmore (1897–1962) and Nathaniel Owings (1903–84), who were joined three years later by John Merrill (1896–1975). The partners established a form of architectural teamwork: anonymity ruled the roost and there were to be no prima donnas. Offices were soon established in Chicago and San Francisco as well as New York. If SOM did have a star at the time, however, it was Gordon Bunshaft (1909–90) who was the creative talent behind the design of the green-skinned Lever Building. His later masterpiece was the Ford Foundation, New York (p.244).

HUNSTANTON SCHOOL

ALISON AND PETER SMITHSON, 1954 NORFOLK, ENGLAND

The Smithsons, Alison (born 1928) and Peter (born 1923), were a fashionable and formidable duo who will be forever associated with the tag New Brutalism and remembered for the aggressive housing they built for the London poor (Robin Hood Gardens, 1972) and for the Mies-inspired school they built at Hunstanton on the north Norfolk coast. Normally portrayed in bright sunlight, photographs have never prepared visitors to this symbol of the New Brutalism for the bitingly cold winds that scythe across the North Sea here from Siberia and the Arctic; the school can be very cold, a condition not helped by the extensive glazing, which has tended to fall out as this exposed building expands and contracts. The school was proof, despite the propaganda, that Modern architects were not necessarily functionalists: "functionalism", like New Brutalism, was often just a fashionable, and for most architects, irritating tag.

Hunstanton School certainly looked the part and was widely published at the time of its completion. Formally, it is satisfying, a neat, logical plan realized in exposed industrial materials and free from any form of gratuitous expression, much less decoration. The Smithsons redeemed themselves a decade later with the Economist Building, London (p.235).

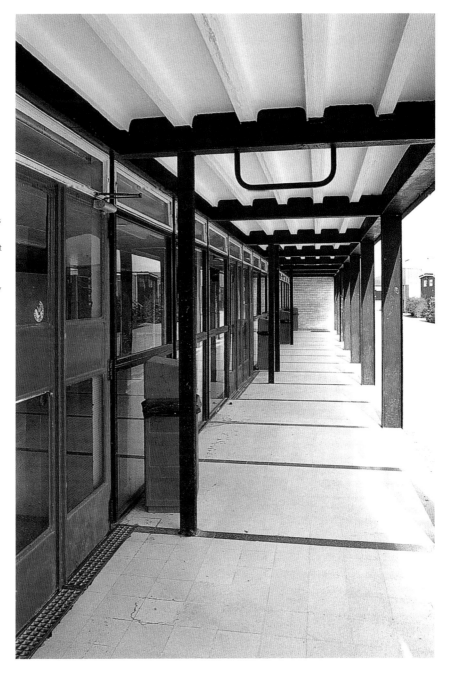

GENERAL MOTORS TECHNICAL CENTER

EERO AND ELIEL SAARINEN, 1955 WARREN, MICHIGAN, USA

The Saarinens, father (Eliel, 1873–1950) and son (Eero, 1910–61), arrived in the United States in 1923. Eero studied sculpture in Paris – which is evident in his work – and architecture at Yale before joining his father in practice in Ann Arbor, Michigan in 1937. He set up shop in his own right in Birmingham, Michigan in 1950. Before Eero soared into the realm of sculptural fantasy, he was commissioned to design and masterplan General Motors' ambitious 330-acre Technical Center, which was to include 25 buildings gathered around a lake on a revolutionary style of business "campus". Working with his father, Saarinen created a regimented parade of handsome, Mies-inspired, low-rise blocks in steel and glass. Their cool geometric perfection was set off by

two baroque elements: the domed lecture theatre, covered with a reflective skin of aluminium, and the water tower, a beautiful aluminium ellipse mounted high above the lake on three long legs.

The Technical Center was a way of showing that corporate America had come of age: grim, makeshift factories and faceless counting houses had given way to a form of business that invaded the territory of universities and monasteries before them. Perhaps it was all a bit of sham – General Motors – informal motto: "what's good for General Motors is good for the world" – was hardly the most altruistic corporation, yet Saarinen imbued it with a Platonic perfection and a state of what looked like grace, even if was nothing of the sort.

ARVESU HOUSE

ALEJANDRO DE LA SOTA, 1955 MADRID, SPAIN

This special house was demolished in 1987. What a waste. It was one of the quiet masterpieces of Alejandro de la Sota (born 1913) and was designed as a retreat from the sheer busyness of the world. The idea was for a very private house screened by an enigmatic brick wall that, in the architect's original design, had no windows. All daylight would come from the south-facing garden front and from skylights. In the event de la Sota's client demanded windows and a few apologetic specimens did indeed peek through a wall that looked as if it had been woven.

This curious use of brickwork would have made sense if you could have seen the house in daylight: the sun played on its weave creating an entrancing dance of shadows. This imbued the house with not only warmth and life but a sense of age that few Modern architects were able to evoke – assuming they wanted to. On its garden side, the house featured extensive glazing, a balcony running from one end to the other and a garden that sloped down to a circular pool. The interior, a place of curves too, flowed easily and elegantly and featured one of the most satisfying of all Modern stairs, a graceful realization of a single curve sketched with a pencil. A perfect example of how less can indeed be more.

CAPUCHINAS CHAPEL

LUIS BARRAGÁN, 1955 COLONIA TLALPLAN, MEXICO CITY, MEXICO

A lyrical work by a great poet and colourist, the Capuchinas Chapel was also an expression of Luis Barragán's outgoing spirit. When asked to redesign the chapel on a small scale and on a very modest budget, Barragán offered to build something a little more ambitious and paid for the extra works himself. Perhaps this could be seen as "vanity architecture". Even if it were, the result was very moving and in the right light – most of the year – achingly beautiful. The chapel is designed with daylight filtering from a lattice and a tall, thin stained glass window at its west end. This finds its way to the altar which is crowned with a simple gold *reredos* (wall-hanging) by Mathias Goeritz that captures and diffuses the last of its abstracted beams.

The materials used throughout are simple – roughcast plasterwork, concrete, timber planks – but the colours and the fall of light here are truly sublime.

Barragán did not train as an architect: his introduction to the Modern Movement was gradual, and while he moved towards a romantic Modern aesthetic very much of his own, his passion for such buildings – and gardens, always gardens, such as those of the Alahambra in Grenada which he loved – shone through in all his light-filled, life-enhancing designs.

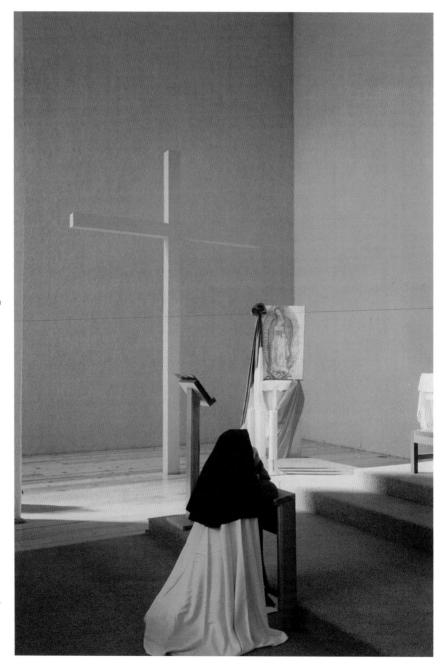

CROWN HALL

LUDWIG MIES VAN DER ROHE, 1956 CHICAGO, ILLINOIS, USA

Having finally broken with Nazi Germany in 1937, Mies took up a teaching post at the Armour (later the Illinois) Institute of Technology, Chicago a year later. In 1940 he was asked to mastermind a new campus, which he designed as a kind of minimalist Greek Acropolis except that, unlike the Greek model, Mies' ideal "city" was all on the level and decoration non-existent. Here, if anywhere, his ascetic philosophy of "less is more" is most clearly expressed.

The heart of the campus is the Crown Hall, a large single space building measuring 67 metres (220 ft) by 36.5 metres (120 ft) by 6 metres (20 ft) high. Like other of Mies's finest buildings, it appears to be floating off the ground and seems to be little more than a volume of air contained within two long slabs of steel. This illusion is helped by the approach to the Hall, which is reached up two flights of stairs that also look as if they float in thin air. Except for the fact that the hall stands on a solid, yet all but invisible, basement it really does have an ethereal and otherworldly character, saved by the life students bring to it. Thrilled by the industrial possibilities of US architecture, Mies built the superstructure of the Hall from four giant prefabricated steel girders that were driven to the site. In fact, like all Mies's US buildings, stringent fire regulations meant that what appear to be exposed structural steel beams are, in fact, a bit of a fraud: they are effectively a form of severe decorative cladding over an internal structure of steel and concrete designed so that in a blaze the steel girders would not buckle.

MAISONS JAOUL

LE CORBUSIER, 1956 NEUILLY-SUR-SEINE, FRANCE

In the 1950s, Le Corbusier turned away from the machine-like aesthetic of his early years and developed a moody architecture that was highly individualistic and responsive to site and locale rather than to purely abstract ideas of what was rational, revolutionary and deterministically futuristic. His new trademarks were raw, board-shuttered concrete, vaulted roofs and tough and rugged forms. Despite their overt toughness – a muscularity that helped give rise to the very rough and tough Brutalist school of design in Britain – the Maisons Jaoul are delightful, womb-like houses to live in.

Built of brick and concrete, the pair are set at right angles to one another and dig deep into their shaded site. Gardens are at basement level, roofs are planted with grass. The house interiors are a revelation, with their vaulted ceilings; they are quite unlike the clever, white, urbane villas and apartments we associate with Corbusier in his first forays into Modernism. Instead they have a gently brooding quality: you feel like curling up like a cat or dog inside and dreaming long dreams.

Although romantic and superficially fortress-like, the Maisons Jaoul are rationally planned, their proportions rooted in Corbusier's "Modulor", a personal and possibly idiosyncratic reworking of the rules of Classical proportion. This pair of houses on the fringes of Paris were hugely influential, their design echoing as far afield as downtown Tokyo and the Sussex coast.

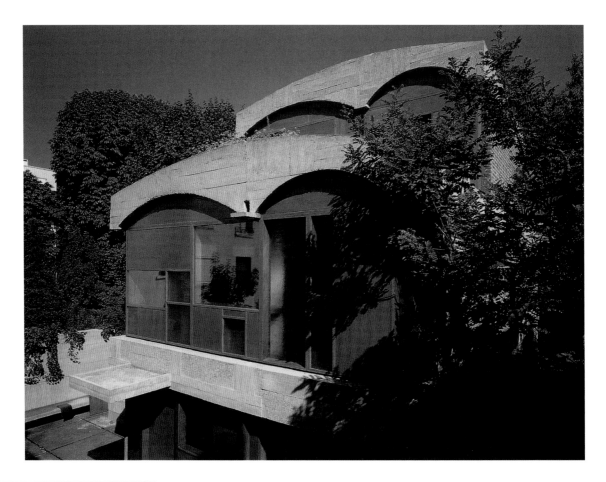

PEACE PAVILION

KENZO TANGE, 1956 HIROSHIMA, JAPAN

The atomic bombs dropped by US B-29 bombers on Hiroshima and Nagasaki in April 1945 prompted the Japanese surrender and the end of World War Two. The bombs, said Emperor Hirohito in an infamous broadcast, meant that the "war was not necessarily proceeding to Japan's advantage". Where the centre of Hiroshima once stood, Kenzo Tange (born 1913) was commissioned to design a Peace Pavilion that was also to form the core of the reconstructed city. The result is a strong and simple cultural hall aimed at reconciling the forms of traditional Japanese temples with Modern concrete architecture.

Tange, who was born in Osaka and studied in Tokyo, had spent the war years thinking about ways in which Japanese architecture might face the future. The goal he set himself was to bring together the two extremes of ancient Japanese art, *Yayoi* (equivalent to the Greek Apollonian, rational, world view) and *Jomon* (equivalent to the Greek Dionysian, or irrational force). Tange was to work through this conundrum with increasing rigour in the 1960s; the Peace Pavilion was only a beginning. The young Tange had worked in the office of Kunio Mayekawa in Tokyo. Mayekawa had trained with Le Corbusier; like Tange, it was the poetic quality of Corbusier's architecture that caught his imagination and which was to have a profound effect on Japanese design after the war.

SHODHAN HOUSE

LE CORBUSIER, 1956 AHMEDABAD, INDIA

This superb Indian house has the appearance of some sort of three-dimensional mathematical puzzle. In fact its complex concrete façade – more of a screen, perhaps, than a façade – is a floor-to-roof sunshade, and a very effective one too. The villa itself is hidden on no fewer than seven floors behind the deep concrete *brise-soleil*, the floors connected, as in Corbusier's Villa Savoye (p.181) of nearly 30 years before by ramp. The principal rooms are on the first floor; above this large villa are three self-contained but interconnecting apartments. Under what looks to be free-floating concrete parasol at the top of the building, there is a hanging garden. There are also plenty of spaces to sit outside, protected from the 40°C (104°F) midday sun, and to look over the gardens and swimming pool.

Here, in Ahmedabad, Corbusier pointed the way to a new type of house for blazingly hot climates without the need for wasteful air-conditioning and complex building services. However, the fact that the Shodhan House remains a one-off lies partly in the fact that it is so "primitive": in 1950s' India, the wealthy often wanted to show that they could afford luxuries like air-conditioning and to prove that anything the Americans could do, they could do too. At the end of the century, any sane person – or aesthete – having the choice between a hermetically sealed air-conditioned box and this intriguing, multi-layered house, so very aware of the changing elements, would know which one to move into.

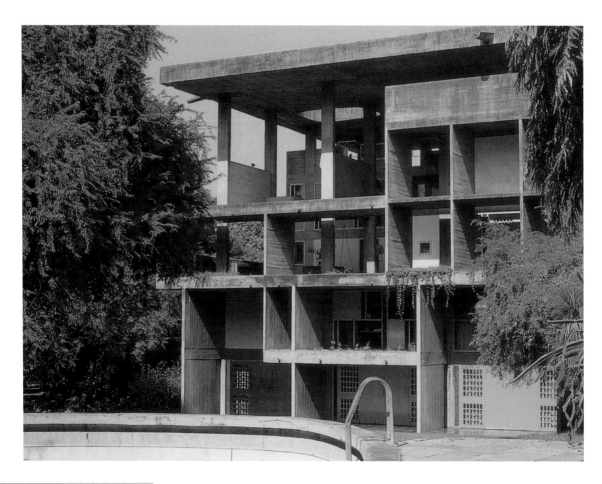

COURTS OF JUSTICE

LE CORBUSIER, 1956 CHANDIGARH, INDIA

Punjab was one of the new states formed in the newly independent Republic of India in 1947. It needed a capital. And remarkably it got one that in its curious and iconoclastic way is one of the wonders of the urban world. The new city, Chandigarh, was masterminded by a team of Indian architects and planners working under the direction of Le Corbusier who had been persuaded to work in India by the British architects Jane Drew and Maxwell Fry. Le Corbusier designed the core of the city and its principal official buildings – the Courts of Justice, the Palace of Assembly, the Governor's Residence and the (later) Court of the Open Hand. What Le Corbusier created here was magnificent sculpture – a sculpture that works as architecture – brought together under the dazzling Punjabi sky. The prime consideration was

water and shelter from a sun that is merciless in summer. So, the Courts of Justice stands on the edge of a man-made lake. By night the lake brims with starlight. The façade of the Courts form a complex or sunscreen, which really does keep the sequence of courtrooms and waiting rooms inside cool. The dense mass of the concrete walls helps a bit too.

As with his other buildings here, the Courts of Justice is a flamboyant sculptural gesture, alien to the historic artistic landscape of India and yet a part of it. Perhaps the happy thing here is that Le Corbusier and his European colleagues were able to build only so far and no more: the result is a city which brings the most sophisticated and romantic architectural sculpture together with the miasmic world of the modern Indian city.

CASE STUDY HOUSE NO 21

PIERRE KOENIG, 1958 LOS ANGELES, CALIFORNIA, USA

The Case Study houses always seem so perfect. This is partly because they nearly all share a purity of line and because they have been so memorably photographed by Julius Shulman, a craftsman behind the lens, who has handed down to us images of what a perfect mid-twentieth-century West Coast way of life was meant to have been. When faced with the clutter of our own homes and the density of the fabric of most world cities, houses like Case Study No 21 designed by Pierre Koening (born 1925) are hugely enticing. They were meant to be dreams made real, or as the architect Richard Neutra put it, a "harbour for the soul" and a "slice of eternity".

Koenig's house was a showcase of contemporary building technology, domestic design, furniture and fittings. It was meant to show just how relaxed and easy Modern living was; the entire house is premised on the idea of easiness and accessibility. Roll your jeep up under the steel-framed *porte-cochère* (not that you would have called it that in Fifties' California), ease out and in to the fully glazed kitchen, fix yourself a drink and out onto the sun lounge for a laid-back evening watching the sun set over LA. Bring together the latest in refrigerator design with a Zen-inspired pool and rock garden, the chasteness of Mies van der Rohe with the voluptuousness of the latest plastic and steel-framed furniture and you have a home that's as stylish, as sophisticated and as relaxed as the conceit of California itself.

SEAGRAM BUILDING

LUDWIG MIES VAN DER ROHE, 1958 NEW YORK CITY, USA

"Mies means Money", said US property developers, watching in awe as this inspired Modern Movement giant raised towers of steel and glass in Chicago and paved the way for the global office block that in lesser hands was to prove a large part of the undoing of the Modern Movement in the public eye. When Mies came to New York the meaning of the developers' phrase was turned on its head with the Seagram Building. Here, Mies certainly meant money: this sheer, 38-storey headquarters for the Canadian distillers, was clad in bronze and cost a mint. It was, and remains, one of the greatest achievements of the Modern Movement, a purist building standing in its own exclusive plaza and not only owing nothing to the world around, but looking with a kind of silent disdain on the busy streets and even busier architecture it surveys.

The Seagram headquarters was to have been a much lesser building; it was the president of Seagram's daughter, Phyllis, who brought Mies into the picture. The result is breathtaking. Designed with help from Philip Johnson, the building soars effortlessly from its plaza set back from Park Avenue into the Manhattan skyline. The vertical emphasis of the building is as emphatic as it is relentless. This is the building that launched far more than a thousand corporate headquarters. It is by far the best of them.

PIRELLI TOWER

GIO PONTI, 1959 MILAN, ITALY

The Pirelli Tower is the first monument in a profoundly monumental city to greet the traveller who comes to Milan by train. The 34-storey tower is very unlike the steel and glass towers pioneered by Mies and Skidmore, Owings and Merrill in New York and Chicago. In this case a team of architects and engineers, including Pier Luigi Nervi and led by Gio Ponti (1891–1979), developed a sophisticated concrete skeleton that allowed the building to rise high while maintaining a delicate, streamlined profile. The result is a distinctive building that represents an alternative to the steel and glass shoeboxes that have littered the skyscapes of so many cities across the world. It also marked a high point in the long career of Ponti, an eclectic designer who had founded the art, architecture and design journal *Domus* in 1928, and edited it until his death.

Ponti, who was born, educated, lived and died in Milan, spent his first years as an architect working in a stripped Neoclassical style – one of the hallmarks of Italian Fascist design – yet lacing his buildings with gorgeous and even Surrealist interiors. His change of heart appeared to come with the design of a Modern pavilion for the Catholic Press Exhibition held in the Vatican City in 1936. His two Modern masterpieces were chasteand simple, although impressive: the Superleggera chair of 1957 and the Pirelli Tower.

ALTON WEST ESTATE

LCC ARCHITECTS DEPARTMENT, 1959 ROEHAMPTON, SURREY, ENGLAND

Architecturally, if not socially, this was one of the more successful attempts made at exporting Le Corbusier's L'Unité d'Habitation from warm and sunny Marseilles. This vast aggregation of local authority flats sits together in carefully considered concrete blocks that stand on *piloti* and overlook the dreamy landscape of Richmond Park, a vast acreage of plantations, herds of deer, exquisite eighteenth-century buildings and a famous escape for Londoners in need of fresh air and a Sunday afternoon walk with the dogs.

Sadly, few of the middle-class dog walkers who stroll across Richmond Park have much good to say about Alton West Estate, which steals a significant part of a once famous view from here of central London and St Paul's Cathedral. Rusting cars, litter and louts do not help

make an English L'Unité out of Alton West, nor Marseilles from Roehampton. Nevertheless, the six- and twelve-storey blocks of flats are nicely arranged and thoughtfully designed. They occupy a kind of annexe to Richmond Park and the tall blocks are interwoven by staggered rows of single-storey houses for the elderly.

It is significant, however, that although the standard of design here and the setting is considerably higher than those of council estates almost anywhere else in British cities, Alton West is not much fun. Perhaps the British do find it genuinely hard to live in blocks of flats or perhaps they are simply too poor to enjoy the life lived by the professional classes who occupy L'Unité d'Habitation so successfully. Still, at Alton West, they did have the park.

MONASTERY OF SAINTE-MARIE DE-LA-TOURETTE

LE CORBUSIER, 1960
EVEUX-SUR L'ARBRESLE,
FRANCE

This is a building that you need to experience at length for it to make sense. To many this superb monastery seems ugly, but it grows on you so that you come to understand why so many believe this to be one of the greatest buildings of any era. It is the home of an Order who live to work and pray. Although the roughcast architecture is stripped to material basics, it is profoundly rich in terms of the way Le Corbusier handled space and brought light to play on walls and interior surfaces. The monastery is gathered around a cloistered garden with the highly expressive church on the north side. The public rooms are at ground level with two floors of narrow cells above them. The monastery is full of sculptural invention: each mysterious pyramid or tower serves a distinct purpose, bringing light, in angelic play, into the recesses of a mind-game of a building that serves to inspire as much as it does to strip away the Modern world it owes its architecture to.

PLAZA OF THE THREE POWERS

OSCAR NIEMEYER AND LÚCIO COSTA, 1960 BRASÍLIA, BRAZIL

The plaza at the core of the new Brazilian capital is reached by a 9.6-kilometre (6-mile) long avenue planned by Lúcio Costa. Do not try walking it on a steamy day. Brasília was, and remains, a heroic political and urbanistic statement. This is a great new city and boy can you feel the weight of that intent. The problem here is a simple one. The climate threatens the monuments designed by the brilliantly facile Niemeyer, while the heart of the city stands remote, physically and symbolically, from the shanty towns that surround it. The idea of Brasília though impresses in much the same way as the building of the Opera House on the Amazon at Manaus does. It was always a brave and vainglorious

concept. At the end of Costa's avenue stand the thrilling shapes of Niemeyer's Congress building and its attendant administration block. This sculptural group rises effortlessly from the Plaza of the Three Powers. Since it was first built, it has retained the power of surprise and dramatic composition. The difficulty in coming to terms with these buildings is that they really do seem pretty inhumane: designs that belong to the drawing board and the grand architectural model.

Niemeyer continued to work on and off on the design of Brasília until 1979. By then, nature had already got to work on his monuments: Brasília will only ever be perfect in the architect's imagination.

CHILDREN'S HOME

ALDO VAN EYCK, 1960 AMSTERDAM, THE NETHERLANDS

A home at the end of the century to the Berlage Institute (an architecture centre), this former orphanage was an ambitious and highly influential attempt by Aldo van Eyck (born 1918) to reinvent officious civic buildings. It was conceived as a small city made of single-storey pavilions that were linked by a pattern of courtyards. As such it would be an enjoyable experience to wander through, and full of daylight. In practice it was never so attractive; the concrete panel and glass brick construction soon tired and the building lost its lustre. The ideas behind it, however, remain valid as they show an alternative to the banal, hermetically sealed, box-like buildings that dominate city centres worldwide and which make no one particularly happy save

the boss with the wood-panelled office and cocktail cabinet in the corners with the best views.

Perhaps the difficulty with van Eyck's architecture is that it posits a humane world, yet realizes it in materials that are often too tough for comfort. As a result, they appear to be unyielding.

Van Eyck was born in Driebergen, The Netherlands and educated in Zürich, Switzerland. An influential and garrulous teacher, he was also the editor of he architecture magazine *Forum*. Van Eyck has had a major influence on the work of many European architects in search of a form and organization of Modern architecture that creates spaces for people to interact rather than impressive, yet isolated monuments.

KURASHIKI CITY HALL

KENZO TANGE, 1960 KURASHIKI, JAPAN

Tange was perhaps the architect most influenced by the forms of Le Corbusier: he took them home to Japan and made something new and convincing with them. This was far from easy. Corbusier's forms were extremely powerful and highly personal, and it was only too simple to ape the master's designs rather than to reinterpret them or else to adapt them to new locations and climates.

In the design of the City Hall at Kurashiki, Tange can be seen to be moving towards a personal view of Le Corbusier, working hard with the idea that traditional Japanese architecture could be translated through Brutalist concrete structures into something new, yet with a soul rooted in the distant past. In

the immediate postwar period and as the Japanese economy made its spectacular recovery, Tange's approach appeared to make good sense. Japan might have been ready and willing to move forward rapidly into a new machine age, yet its culture and sense of pride had been badly damaged by the experience of misguided imperial conquest and a notably savage war. What Tange offered in buildings such as the City Hall at Kurashiki was Modernism and certainty at one and the same time. With its narrow, slitted window openings and beetling concrete cornice, the building has a fortified manner that was to be echoed in Tange's later projects culminating in the Yamanashi Press and Broadcasting Centre (p.380).

KEELING HOUSE

DENYS LASDUN, 1960 BETHNAL GREEN, LONDON, ENGLAND

Born in London in 1914, Denys Lasdun trained at the Architectural Association, London, and designed most of his buildings there. He first worked for Wells Coates, before joining Berthold Lubetkin at Tecton. During World War Two Lasdun served as a Major in the Royal Engineers, building airfields for Allied fighter squadrons at the beginning of the invasion of Nazi-occupied Europe in summer 1944. After the war, his attention was turned to rehousing Londoners bombed by the Luftwaffe and V1 and V2 rockets. There were various plans at the time to rebuild damaged housing in London's East End. Lasdun built two unusual "cluster" blocks in Bethnal Green, one of eight, the other of fifteen storeys. The idea was to offer families spacious flats leading off from a central service core. Each flat would be surrounded by daylight and enjoy a variety of views. In practice, the flats needed a degree of maintenance local authorities were either hard-pressed or unwilling to fund, which led to the slow and sad decline of Keeling House despite its popularity with residents. Rightly, they felt that if moved elsewhere they would never find such generous amounts of space and light again. The fate of Keeling House became a *cause-célèbre* in conservation circles in the 1990s as the Modern Movement itself seemed more and more like a distant historical episode.

PAN-AM BUILDING

WALTER GROPIUS AND PIETRO BELLUSCHI, 1963 NEW YORK CITY, USA

How the mighty fell. It is hard to connect Gropius, founder of the Bauhaus and one of the most important pioneers of the Modern Movement, with this bulky skyscraper looming over Grand Central Station. It's enough to make one sit down and weep. Gio Ponti and Pier Luigi Nervi had only recently shown how well a building of this scale could be made to work (p.224). Gropius's design was bombastic, although there are signs that he was hoping to mitigate its bulk. The building's ten-storey base respects the cornice line of Grand Central Station, before the 49-storey tower shoots up above it. The tower itself is designed to appear to be cast in sections, but even then it has a weighty look that Mies van der Rohe avoided with flair in the design of the Seagram Building (p.223).

For several years this lozenge-shaped tower was used as a helicopter landing pad. No one who has arrived in Manhattan by Pan-Am helicopter will ever forget the experience. Tragically, a helicopter slipped off the top of the building in bad weather and this *Bladerunner* experience has since been denied future generations. Gropius designed some more subtle buildings in Berlin in the years left to him, although he continued to live in the USA. The Pan-Am Building is perhaps the physical zenith and cultural nadir of his career at one and the same time.

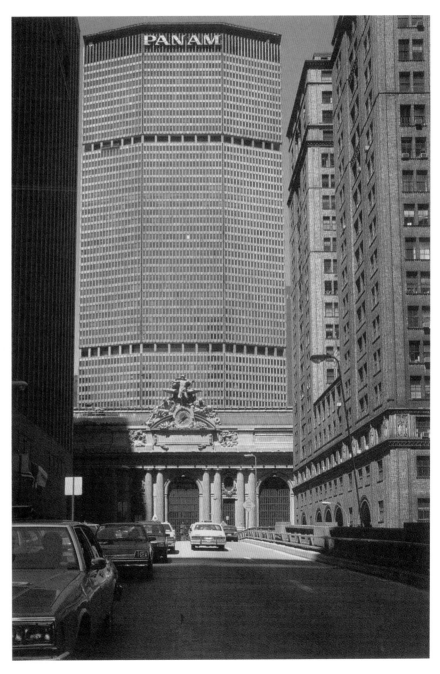

APARTMENT BLOCK

ALEJANDRO DE LA SOTA, 1963 SALAMANCA, SPAIN

It would be easy to walk past this apartment block. It stands six storeys high in a narrow street in the centre of Salamanca. The ground floor is home to a variety of dusty and shabby shops. At least one or two are normally boarded up or for let. But if you bother to look up, you will soon see why it deserves recognition. Instead of scruffy concrete or cheap render, the walls are faced in handsome and well-dressed local Salamanca stone. This simple fact imbues the block with a certain grandeur. This might be the home of ordinary people, but the materials employed are aristocratic. And then there is the key detail that makes a simple block of flats humane and likeable: the projecting windows or *miradores* designed so that those inside can peep up and down the street as people always have done in the traditional houses of this part of the world. Because the street is narrow, the *miradores* cannot project very far, yet the fact that de la Sota insisted on them is an encouraging sign: a Modern architect knew when to pay heed to local tradition and to incorporate it convincingly into an otherwise rational, shoe-box construction.

The detailing of the *miradores* is particularly satisfying – the glass is supported by clearly expressed steel brackets that seem to cling to the warm stone walls with a limpet-like certainty.

CASTELVECCHIO MUSEUM

CARLO SCARPA, 1964 VERONA, ITALY

This was an important project in the history not so much of conservation, but of the reuse of historic buildings. This issue became increasingly important in the years following World War Two. Not only had the war itself witnessed the destruction of very many historic buildings, but rapid new development in the 1950s – notably in Germany and Italy – meant the destruction or usurping of even more. Increasingly, too, old buildings, notably churches, lost their purpose. If they were not to be demolished or a burden on those charged with their upkeep, what useful role could they serve? And if they were to be converted, how could this be done without undermining their structural and aesthetic integrity? At Castelvecchio in Verona, Carlo Scarpa (1906–78)

showed the way forward. The Venetian architect transformed the medieval castle into a museum and art gallery with the lightest of touches.

The project began in 1956 and was carried out over the period of a decade. Scarpa's genius was to make the lightest, smallest and most delicate interventions into the fabric of the old building and yet each of these spoke of an intelligent and highly tuned modern sensibility. Here was proof that the work of ancient and modern architects could sit happily together, one enhancing the aesthetic and logic of the other. Scarpa's ability to surprise and delight with the simplest architectural gesture has helped make this museum a model of its kind.

FACULTY OF MECHANICAL ENGINEERING

ALFRED NEUMANN AND ZVI HECKER, 1964 HAIFA, ISRAEL

It took some while before Israeli architects began to find a recognizable voice. When it came, it was hard and clear and one that had been learned in the heat of the desert and, perhaps, in the mentality of defence. Many of the most impressive Israeli buildings have the look of modern fortresses. This makes sense in a country continually threatened with invasion. Yet, such buildings are also defences against a climate that can be a hard enemy too.

Neumann (born 1924) and Hecker (born 1931) designed the Faculty of Mechanical Engineering at Haifa – only one of several planned pavilions was built – as a shelter from the sun that did away with the complications of the *brise-soleil* that had been devised by Le Corbusier and developed by many architects,

not least Corbu himself, ever since. The solution at Haifa was to design the whole structure of the building as a concrete sunshade – thus its dramatic façades in which the windows, invisible from almost any oblique angle, slope steeply down and backwards into the depth of the reveals to keep the sun at bay. This represented an important, energy-saving move away from flat-fronted buildings that required too much in the way of ingenuity, inconvenience and electricity to keep them cool and their interiors free from glare.

To an extent, the Faculty of Engineering was also a way of connecting contemporary Israeli architecture with ancient precursors such as temples in the guise of ziggurats.

ECONOMIST BUILDINGS

ALISON AND PETER SMITHSON, 1964 ST JAMES'S, LONDON, ENGLAND

The Smithsons redeemed themselves after the strictures of Hunstanton, (p.213) with the Economist Buildings, a handsome trio of small towers – publishing offices, bank and club – grouped informally on a tiny, stepped and ramped piazza off one of central London's finest eighteenth-century streets. That the new buildings and their Georgian predecessors sit so well together is as surprising as it is pleasing. Packing a group of smallish blocks together in a new city piazza made much sense in this sensitive area. At the time of their construction, the centre of London was being ruined by a rash of vile and foolish office blocks that were designed to make as much money for developers as quickly as possible before someone noticed that something was going horribly wrong and put a stop to it. London's powerful conservation lobby gained its teeth at this time; it is significant that it has never had a problem with the Economist Buildings. As well as being thoughtful and well constructed they are well mannered and do no try to "fit in" stylistically with their Georgian neighbours. There is no need, as the Smithsons proved, for them to do so.

When Peter Smithson, in later years, went on to berate errors made in British urban architecture in the 1960s, it was easy enough to listen to him. Whatever else, he had the Economist Buildings behind him.

FONDATION MAEGHT

JOSEP LLUÍS SERT, 1964 ST-PAUL-DE-VENCE, FRANCE

One of the most magical of all art spaces, the Fondation Maeght, shows some of the twentieth century's greatest art in galleries and courtyards designed by the Catalan architect Josep Lluís Sert (1902–83). In the blissful climate of St-Paul-de-Vence, Sert shaped an architecture from brick and concrete that was remarkably open and free. This is the antithesis of the work of Mies van der Rohe: at once sculptural, playful and as open as possible to the elements. Even on a rainy day, doors can be kept open. There is a refreshing lack of preciousness in evidence here which adds to the pleasure of Sert's sensual design. If the building picks up a sculptural trick or three from Miró and

Braque, this is clearly intentional; there is no Postmodern irony involved, just a knowing and rather gentle whimsy that suits the location well. Appropriately, Sert went on to develop the ideas guiding the Fondation Maeght further with the Fundación Joan Miró (1975) in Barcelona. The architect was born and educated in Barcelona. He worked for Le Corbusier and Pierre Jeanneret in Paris between 1929 and 1931 before setting up on his own back in Barcelona in 1931. When Franco took the city, he left for the USA where, in 1953, he became Dean of the Graduate School of Design at Harvard. He returned to his native city, and it is nice to be able to say that his last buildings were his best.

PARK HILL AND HYDE PARK ESTATES

J. L. WOMERSLEY, ET AL, 1965 SHEFFIELD, ENGLAND

These vast local authority estates were in no way cynical attempts to rehouse Sheffield's working classes in modern slums, although today they might seem that way, and much here has either been demolished or rebuilt. The idea, based in part on Le Corbusier's hugely influential L'Unité d'Habitation in Marseilles was to build a modern version of traditional streets of terraced houses but in the sky rather than on the ground. The "houses", or duplex apartments, were entered by individual front doors leading off "access decks" (or streets in the air) and gathered together in Brutalist concrete blocks connected by concrete bridges. The "access decks" and bridges proved to be a perfect way for muggers and burglars to race through

the estates, and have since been demolished. Clearly these monumental and relentless housing blocks were designed, despite their formidable appearance, for a more innocent age.

The designers from Sheffield City Architects Department who were involved in the project were much influenced by Le Corbusier and the Smithsons (p.235). The forms they created – tough, stark, gridded – were meant, in part, to reflect the tough, stark and gritty world of poor, working-class life in the northern England of the 1950s; but what hope they were meant to give people is unclear. Sheffield was not Marseilles, lacking the sun, warmth and vibrant street and café culture that might have redeemed these craggy and daunting housing estates.

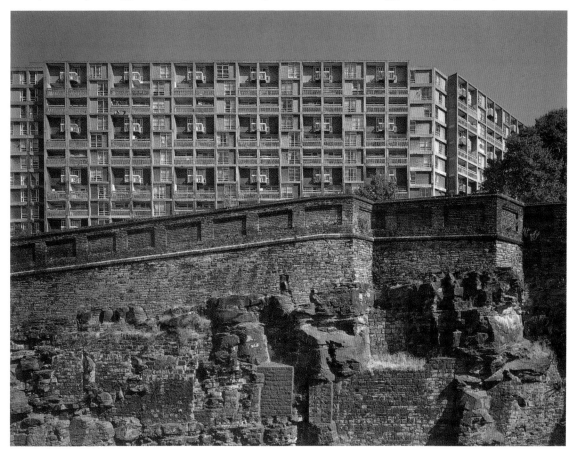

CENTRE POINT

RICHARD SEIFERT, 1966 LONDON, ENGLAND

The beehive concrete sections, slim profile and catwalk stance of this 34-storey Pop-era office block have all helped endear what was once the most unpopular building in London, built by the highly litigious developer, Harry Hyams, into a much-liked and even respected monument to Mammon. Although completed in 1966, the tower stood empty for many years. Quite why remains a mystery, but be careful how you tell the story if you do: Mr Hyams' lawyers will be waiting like vultures for you to slip up. The tower dominates many views of central London and it is unfortunate, given its latter-day popularity, that its top floor cannot be opened as a bar, restaurant and public viewing gallery.

The tower is part of a bigger development that includes flats and shops and connects directly to Tottenham Court Road tube station. The architect was Colonel Richard Seifert (born 1910) who became a household name in the 1960s and '70s: his buildings were said at the time to have had as much, if not more, impact on central London than any architect since Christopher Wren. True or not, Seifert's highly distinctive towers – beehives, drums, strutting boxes – have ridden out the ridicule. The pipe-smoking Colonel (he served with the Royal Engineers during World War Two) designed, it now seems agreed, some of the sassiest commercial buildings of the 1960s.

ST PETER'S COLLEGE

GILLESPIE, KIDD AND COIA, 1966 CARDROSS, SCOTLAND

The architecture of Le Corbusier translated well into Scotland in the 1960s. Although the climate of the south of France and the west of Scotland could hardly be more different, Corbu's roughcast concrete style could, in the right hands, be seen as a natural successor or complement to traditional Scottish tower houses with their rugged forms and tough materials. Those hands belonged to the Glasgow firm Gillespie, Kidd and Coia.

St Peter's College is a Roman Catholic seminary inhabiting a severe Victorian building that was very successfully added to by Jack Coia 1898–1981) and his team. The low-set and

rhythmic four-storey addition was in part derived from the forms of Corbusier's Maisons Jaoul (p.218) and in part by the plan of the monastery at La Tourette (p.226): the refectory and public rooms are at ground level, the seminarists' rooms stacked in tiers on the three storeys above. The ground floor led into an imposing and brooding chapel that adopted the organic plan of Ronchamp (p.101). Although the debt to Corbusier is strong, and obvious, St Peter's has a character and spirit very much of its own, a muscular architecture for those studying for the demanding life of the Catholic priesthood. It has since been abandoned and left to rot.

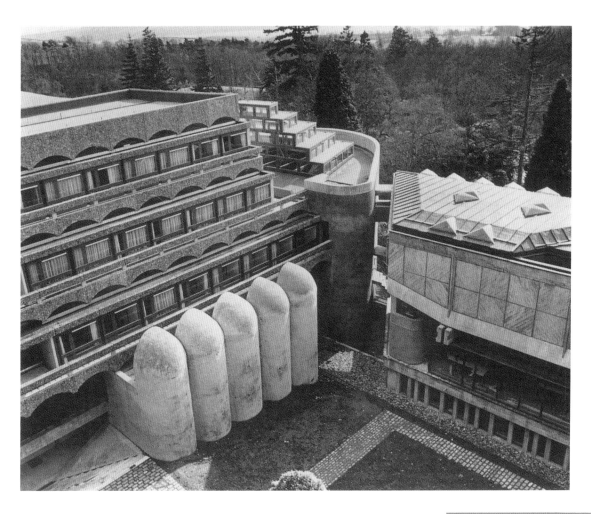

HABITAT HOUSING

MOSHE SAFDIE, 1967 MONTREAL, CANADA

One of the big surprises of the Expo '67 Montreal World Fair were the 158 beehive apartments designed by the Israeli-born architect Moshe Safdie (born 1938). Known as Habitat, this experiment in Pop-age living was to become one of the most fashionable addresses in Montreal. Habitat was Safdie's first major work. He was 29. After graduation from Montreal's McGill University, he worked with Louis Kahn in Philadelphia before going on to run his own studio.

Habitat might have seemed a surprise success with professional families, yet they were clearly able to see well beyond its prefabricated concrete panel construction to its intriguing and even poetic disposition. There were no fewer than 15 different layouts among the apartments, each with its own roof terrace and particular view. At one point it was suggested that Habitat be expanded to a total of 900 apartments, but this fell through and the houses remain an intriguing one-off in North America, although Safdie developed the idea in Israel.

After Habitat, Safdie went on to teach at the Ben Gurion University at Beersheva, Israel, before taking a post at Harvard. Subsequently, he returned to Israel where he developed a new monumental architecture based on the severe grids and geometry adopted from his experience both with Kahn and Expo '67.

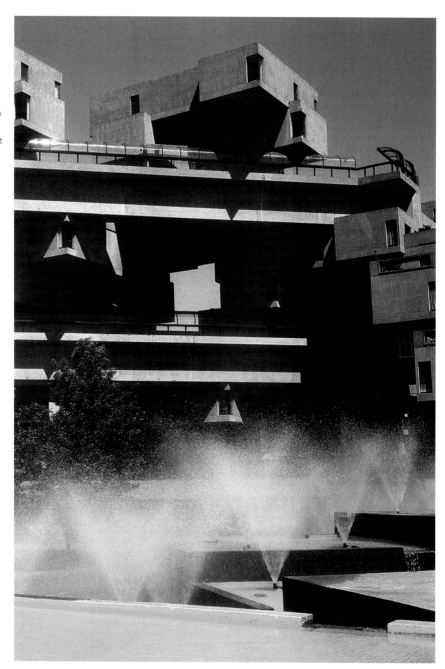

CATHEDRAL OF CHRIST THE KING

FREDERICK GIBBERD, 1967 LIVERPOOL, ENGLAND

Known both affectionately and condescendingly as "Paddy's Wigwam" – Liverpool is a city of Irish immigrants: the cathedral looks like a Red Indian tent to Liverpudlians – the Roman Catholic Cathedral is more likely to have been based on the design of Oscar Niemeyer's "Crown of Thorns" cathedral at Brasília, and even perhaps on the Gemini space capsules of the early NASA orbital launches. The cathedral, by Frederick Gibberd (1908–84), stands on a prominent site at one end of Liverpool's Hope Street: at the other end broods the almighty Gothic Anglican cathedral by Giles Gilbert Scott (p.114). Gibberd's church, although a striking design, occupies just a fraction of the terrace that was to have been one of the most imposing and brilliant ecclesiastical buildings of all times – Edwin Lutyen's vast domed Catholic cathedral. In the event, only the crypt was built. Gibberd's slighter design, built at great speed and rather cheaply, in just a few years, consists of a skeletal cone made up of slim concrete buttresses and topped with a lofty lantern filled with stained glass by John Piper and Patrick Reyntiens. Between the buttresses at ground level is a circle of chapels, each different. The congregation sits in the round bathed in coloured lights: the altar is central following the precepts of Vatican II. Restoration began on the cathedral in the 1990s.

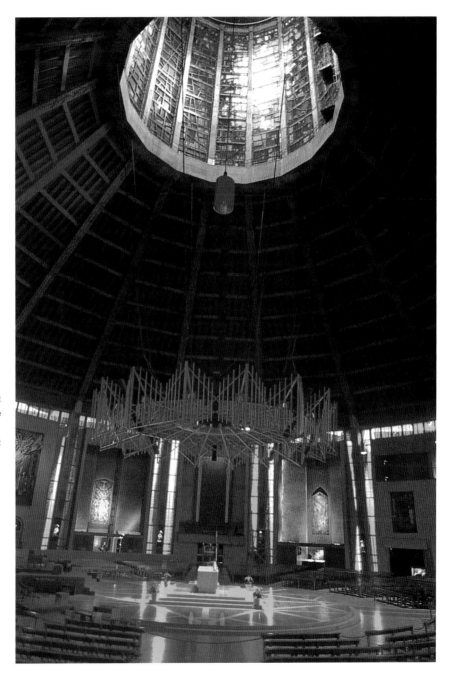

HAYWARD GALLERY

LCC ARCHITECTS DEPARTMENT, 1967 LONDON, ENGLAND

Threatened with demolition at various times in the 1980s and 1990s, the Hayward Gallery – a Brutalist concrete culture bunker on London's South Bank – has survived to become admired by younger generations for whom its bizarre, defensive architecture is an adventure rather than a threat. The gallery had a long gestation and was finally built, after long delays, between during the 1960s. It was designed a team of young "Turks" led by Norman Engleback (born 1930) under the direction of Hubert Bennett (born 1909). The heavy-duty concrete construction, although heavily influenced by Le Corbusier and the Brutalists, was considered necessary because at the time of its design there were plans to build a helicopter terminal near the gallery. Despite its menacing,

military style, the Hayward is a well finished building and was expensive to construct. Originally, and again to prevent noise from overflying helicopters, the galleries were to have been enclosed and artificially lit. In the event, the committees involved in its progress demanded daylight ("God's own daylight", said the sculptor Henry Moore) and insisted on top-lighting in the upper galleries, giving the building its distinctive roof profile.

A number of exhibitions in the 1990s – most of all Richard Long's "Walking in Circles" – gave the building the profile it needed to make it popular with a newly receptive audience. It remains a difficult building, yet as endearing as a boxer with a "cauliflower" ear.

MARINA CITY

BERTRAND GOLDBERG, 1967 CHICAGO, ILLINOIS, USA

By night, car headlamps swoop around the spiralling ramps of the car parks that occupy the lower heights of these characterful circular downtown apartment blocks: the effect is dizzying, dazzling and utterly compelling. Like two giant corn cobs, the twin towers of Marina City rise high into the Chicago skyline. Each supports 40 floors of balconied apartments over spiralling elevated car parks. If it seems odd to live so high off the ground, it seems stranger to see automobiles parked so very high off the streets they are designed to roar along. Marina City was the finest work of Bertrand Goldberg (1913–97) and one of the most imaginative and convincing examples of how to live high in the city sky. Goldberg's genius was to take advantage of a river setting and to adopt an architectural form that allowed for so very many balconies – and thus life outside – without undermining the formal strength of his highly sculpted towers. These were the antithesis of, for example, Mies van der Rohe's sleek-skinned Lake Shore Drive apartments nearby (p.207) and were considered by many critics to be kitsch. This is unfair. Once seen in real life, Marina City has much of the verve promised in the paper architecture of the Futurists and seems an ideal answer in some ways to the question of what to with the cars we say we despise yet can't seem to do without even if we live in city centres.

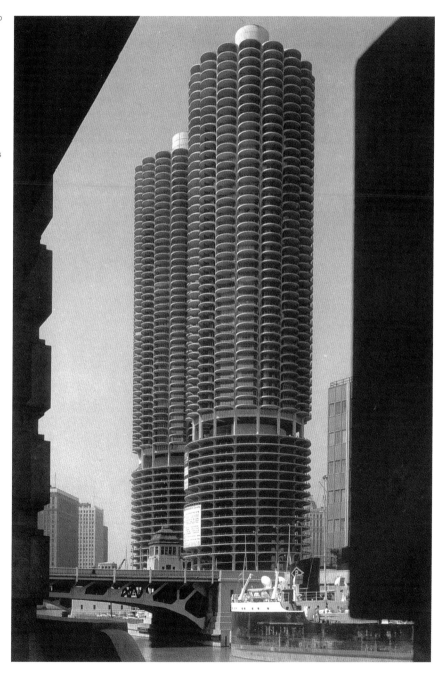

FORD FOUNDATION

ROCHE–DINKELOO, 1967 NEW YORK CITY, USA

Not for those who suffer from vertigo or agoraphobia, the Ford Foundation is, for the brave hearted, an almost unparalleled and hugely impressive achievement. The offices of the Foundation are planted on two sides of a 12-storey greenhouse or atrium. Windows open into this world of lush planting, vertiginous columns and vast sheets of plate glass; so office workers look out to the city beyond through a layer of greenery and glazing. The views can be quite surreal. Even more so, the executive suites and dining rooms occupy what seems like a perilous two-storey gallery, running along the street front on top of the gallery with nothing below but the depths of the giant atrium. Doubtless,

it was the Ford Foundation that made the atrium popular, and something of a cliché, in office buildings 20 years later. Here, though, the concept is as impressive at it was original. Also impressive, from an urban point of view, was the fact that this radical building sat flush and neatly with the line of the street.

The building was designed by Kevin Roche (born 1922), an Irish architect who worked for Michael Scott in Dublin, Maxwell Fry and Jane Drew in London before emigrating to the USA in 1948 where he became head of design with Eero Saarinen's office in 1954. Here he met John Dinkeloo (1918–81), an architect and inventor of great distinction.

CENTRE LE CORBUSIER

LE CORBUSIER, 1967 ZÜRICH, SWITZERLAND

Originally designed as a private house, the Centre Le Corbusier, completed two years after the death, shows a further turn in direction at the end of a long journey of a great artist who chose building as his most convincing medium. Here, the house is conceived as what is potentially an infinite sequence of prefabricated geometric panels that can be arranged in chess-board moves or simply a straight line. In fact, their arrangement and number is governed and determined by the umbrella roof suspended above them by a variety of steel poles and columns. The effect is rather like seeing a Greek temple with a modern building inserted beneath its pediments and between its columns. On another level, it is like looking at a sequence of abstract canvases displayed beneath a giant frame. What we can be sure of is that at the end of a long and remarkably fruitful life, Le Corbusier's capacity for invention and reinvention was far from exhausted. The man himself, however, felt he had accomplished enough, and when he swam to his death in 1965, a number of friends and observers believed that he had intended to die swimming into the sun he worshipped rather than to wait while his enormous and unprecedented talent expired.

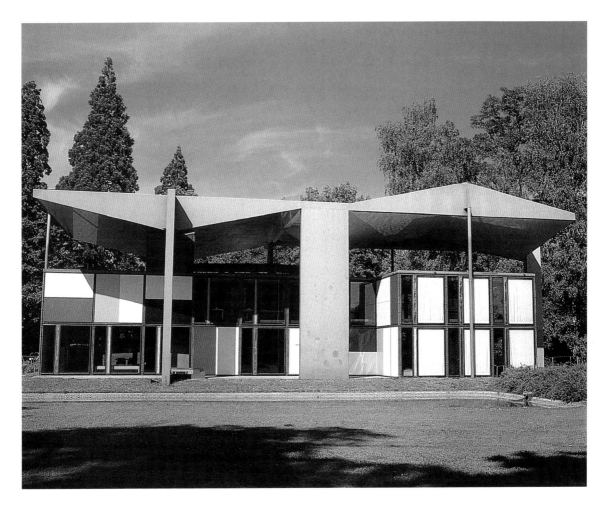

NEUE NATIONALGALERIE

LUDWIG MIES VAN DER ROHE, 1968 BERLIN, GERMANY

It might be unwise to call the Neue Nationalgalerie a
reductio ad absurdum, yet there is an unsettling feeling
in this vast and empty building that Mies had gone too far
and even lost his own exquisitely refined plot. Most of the
artworks on show here line the relentless walls of basement
galleries lit from one side by a wall of glass, or else occupy
rather breathless sub-surface rooms. The upper gallery,
housed under the great coffered canopy, supported by just
eight deeply recessed cruciform steel columns and encased
in walls of floor to ceiling glass, seems formless. On days of
low sun – of which there are plenty in Berlin – fusty curtains
are drawn across the giant windows, making the space

sombre and rather like a giant funeral parlour.

As a monument, the gallery is memorable; as an art
gallery it seems deeply unsatisfying and even wrong-headed.
It would almost be better left empty, a mid-twentieth-century
reinterpretation of a Greek temple, as cold and passionate as
a winter dawn rising over the lakes of the nearby Tiergarten.
This was the last of Mies's major buildings and the last in a
long line of purist pavilions or secular temples he had been
occupied with since at least the Barcelona Pavilion of 1929
(p.172). It is comforting to know that the hard-drinking, fine-
living architect's own Chicago apartment was comfortable,
bourgeois and even a little old fashioned.

STUDENT HOUSING

DENYS LASDUN, 1968 UNIVERSITY OF EAST ANGLIA, NORWICH, NORFOLK, ENGLAND

Looking much like twentieth-century Aztec or Mayan stepped temples, this university housing was opened the year that students across Europe and the United States took to the streets and hoped for the Revolution to come before their grants ran out and they had to get jobs, get married and settle down. The Revolution might have been a serious proposition in France or Germany, and even to an extent in the USA where the student uprisings were part of a general reaction against Washington's futile war in Vietnam. In Britain, life was cosier: there wasn't that much to rebel against. There were grants aplenty, jobs galore, great music, more freedom than many knew what to do with, and lavish university expansion schemes that meant

cheap accommodation in buildings designed by some of the country's finest architects.

At UEA, a new university set outside Norwich, Lasdun designed this cluster of distinctive pyramid blocks offering generous rooms and plenty of spaces to sit outside. Within a few years, the interiors were squalid – nothing to do with the architect – and the ziggurats, it was said, were gradually slipping down towards the lake below them. They still stand, however, a loose-fit monument to the heroic age of tertiary education in Britain when a university degree – even in the arts in which UEA specialized – was a passport to a groovy and well-paid job. As a formal composition, Lasdun's concrete pyramids stand up well.

LAKE POINT TOWER

SCHIPPOREIT–HEINRICH ASSOCIATES, 1968 CHICAGO, ILLINOIS, USA

This shimmering 196-metre (645-ft) apartment block standing in solitary splendour over Lake Michigan was designed by former students of Mies van der Rohe. It is, in effect, the realization – with Chicago money, muscle and can-do know-how – of Mies's 1921 project for a curved glass office tower, which was never built due to lack of funds and the necessary structural and glass technology. So, while it is a home for those lucky enough to be able to afford one of its 900 apartments, it is also a homage to one of the century's greatest architects built at the end of his life. And, of course, a show-off exercise in US building skills.

The tower is clover-shaped in plan and clad in a pretty much skin-tight glass cat-suit. Even Spider Man would find it hard to climb. The plan and flush glazing conspire to catch the sunlight at all times of day, although it is at sunset, as Lake Michigan appears to catch fire, that Lake Point Tower comes into its own. The sense of detachment that comes from living here – high up and away from the city centre – is a Modern Movement dream come true. From any one of the tower's apartments, residents have the feeling of looking down on the restless city beyond and below as if it were little more than a movie shown in Cinemascope. They enjoy the view of the world shared by Mies van der Rohe and Le Corbusier in the 1920s as they sought to create cities in which professional people would live in serviced flats above parkland and lakes.

SAN CRISTOBAL STUD FARM

LUIS BARRAGÁN, 1968 MEXICO CITY, MEXICO

The flamboyant Luis Barragán (1902–87) had a magnificent eye for colour, and for many people who find the strictures of, say, Mies van der Rohe too clinical and monochrome to bear, this Mexican architect offered a palette of exquisite natural pigments that made Modernism sensual, warm and, quite simply, delightful. This stud farm – house, stables, lake, gardens – outside Mexico City is perhaps the closest Barragán got to shaping an architecture, and a landscape, in which the formalism of Modern architecture was reconciled with nature, colour, animals and the good life under the sun. Here, he employed an abstract constructional geometry brought to rippling, ever-shifting life by the play of bright sunlight and shadows on water and lush,

perfumed plants and trees. The smell of horses and saddle leather is an added bonus.

Significantly, and like many of the century's most sensual and least fettered architects, Barragán was self taught. He had trained as an engineer, but as an architect he invented himself. His earliest designs were much influenced by Moroccan and Islamic architecture in general; it was only when he moved from Guadalajara to Mexico City in 1936 that he became aware of the Modern Movement. From then on he developed his highly individualand very beautiful approach to architecture: if anyone thinks Modern architecture is cold, they have never experienced anything like this superb built landscape in Mexico.

EXPO '70

KENZO TANGE, ET AL, 1970 OSAKA, JAPAN

This was the first of the world fairs to be held in Asia and it was easily one of the best, at least from an architectural perspective. The site was laid out by Kenzo Tange but architects from all around the world contributed a zoo of gloriously inventive, daring, perverse and even funny structures. Expo '70 marked, in fact, the zenith of architects' first-time around fascination with inflatable structures, fabric construction and new ways of defying the downwards pull of gravity, a force that architects have wrestled to overcome since Daedalus, the "first" (and mythologized) architect built wings to fly with his ill-fated son, Icarus, from Crete to Greece.

The zany structures that animated Expo '70 were not wasted. Many of the ideas and the aesthetics that inspired them, were to emerge in mature expressions of tented and soft, fabric-based, architecture in the last two decades of the century. They also set the tone for transportable and inflatable sets for rock concerts, for the bouncy castles of childrens' fairgrounds and the settings for art events and political galas. The idea that the Modern world could invent, use and enjoy a soft, transient architecture, as nomads around the world had done for millennia, was as surprising as it was enjoyable.

WEINSTEIN HOUSE

RICHARD MEIER, 1971 OLD WESTBURY, NEW YORK STATE, USA

Whiter than white, the single-minded architecture of Richard Meier (born 1934) is as unmistakable as it is satisfying or numbing, depending upon your point of view. Meier, the white knight of Modern architecture, saddled up his white charger in the mid-1960s, having graduated from Cornell University and worked for Skidmore, Owings and Merrill and Marcel Breuer. Over the next decade, he received several commissions to design the white houses that he has been associated with ever since. Each is a play or variation on its siblings and these houses do indeed form a close-knit architectural family. Nevertheless, they are also highly responsive to their individual sites and are thus different

from the starship villas of the early Modern Movement that appeared to have landed in green fields with no thought of what the local terrain might look or feel like.

Meier worked in loose collaboration with other "whites" who became known as the New York Five. Their theorist was the erudite Peter Eisenman (born 1932), but Meier was the one who built quietly and prolifically. The Weinstein House in New York State is a deeply satisfying Meier design, showing how many ways a cube can be cut through, rearranged, its geometric possibilities exposed. The various elements of the house appear to lock together even as they are pulling apart – a sense of being together wisely divided by an equal and opposite sense of privacy. Truly brilliant.

FLOREY BUILDING

JAMES STIRLING AND JAMES GOWAN, 1972 OXFORD, ENGLAND

Mistaken endlessly for a multi-storey car park – there is a public car park alongside it – the ugly backside of the Florey Building belies its river frontage. This is hidden because the bright orange back of this students' hostel wraps around it, keeping prying eyes at bay and holding the hoi-polloi back from the precious world of the Oxford undergraduate. The several tiers of student rooms here are held up on concrete stilts and gathered around an internal courtyard, opening on one side to the lugubrious River Cherwell below. The difficulty here is that residents are completely exposed to view and the shy or modest feel the need to keep the blinds of their floor-to-ceiling windows drawn for much of the day.

If this is perverse, then the arrangement of the rooms is even more so, particularly if you happen to be one of the unfortunates through whose room the concrete buttresses that support the building passes through at an oblique angle. And then there is the small question of how, after a few drinks in the bar, to negotiate a bed that is mounted at the top of ladder-like stairs.

Was big, braw Jim Stirling having a joke at the expense of fey intellectual students? It certainly seems that way, although as a work of sculpture, the Florey Building is nothing if not impressive.

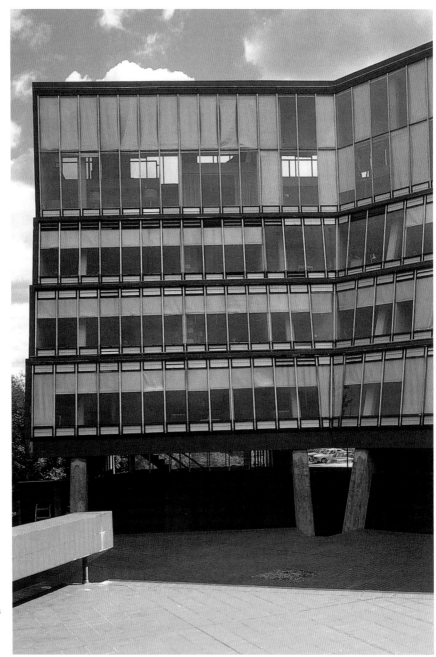

LETHBRIDGE UNIVERSITY

ARTHUR ERICKSON, 1972 ALBERTA, CANADA

An ocean liner or spaceship of a building berthed or come to land in the rural vastness of Alberta. This is Lethbridge University by Arthur Erickson (born 1924), perhaps the most important Canadian architect of the century. Here, every function and activity has been housed under one enormous roof, even student accommodation. No messy extrusions. No outbuildings of any sort. This is a powerful, and even overbearing concrete megastructure, and yet it makes å some sense in a vast landscape in which a gentler touch would make little impact. Assuming the University did want to make its mark on a boundless landscape, it certainly chose the right architect.

Erickson studied in Vancouver and Montreal. A dynamic architect, by the 1980s he had offices across the world. His buildings have, for the most part, been as ambitious in scale as his world view. They are often in spectacular locations and do their muscular best to make their presence felt in no uncertain terms. The most impressive of the earlier buildings are the Simon Fraser University, Burnaby, Vancouver (from 1963) and the Justice Building (1980), which occupies a whole city block in Vancouver. The scale and bombast of Erickson's architecture, although he has built some small wooden houses influenced by Mies van der Rohe, may be a natural reaction to the scale and power of the Canadian landscape and climate. It is hard to imagine Lethbridge University sitting well in the exquisite confines of Europe.

CENTRAAL BEHEER

HERMAN HERTZBERGER, 1972 APELDOORN, NETHERLANDS

A big yet modest building, Centraal Beheer was designed as an office for over a thousand insurance clerks whose work can hardly have been called scintillating. To make their day more of a grind than it needs be, such white-collar workers have all too often been filed into bland, sub-Miesian office blocks and bored into submission. Hertzberger (born 1932) came up with an idea that been discussed during the 1960s, yet rarely realized: the office as interior landscape. Inside what is a fairly dreary, low-lying grey concrete structure composed of a large number of interlocking pavilions is a complex office divided and subdivided into spaces that give each clerk or group of clerks a home of their own. The apparently informal layout and the relaxed attitude of management here meant that workers were allowed and even encouraged to customize their workspaces to the point where the office began to take on the look of a bureaucratic Hanging Gardens of Babylon. This was very much in keeping with Hertzberger's belief that the architect's role was not to try and determine the way people occupied a building, but to design buildings that allowed people to use them as they wanted to. Like many Dutch architects of his generation Hertzberger appeared to see no contradiction between a deep-rooted humanity and an architecture that relied almost unduly on dull concrete and drab breeze-blocks.

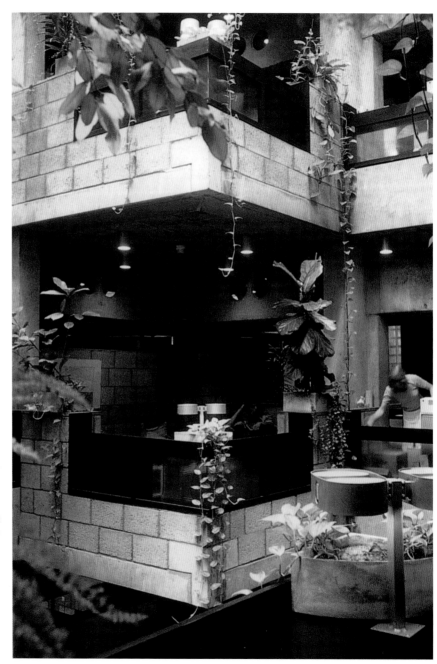

BIANCHI HOUSE

MARIO BOTTA, 1972 TICINO, SWITZERLAND

A house for a Swiss schoolteacher, this simple, geometric tower rises three storeys from a field overlooking Lake Lugano. It is made from lightweight concrete blocks and would be unremarkable save for three things: its marvellous setting against the lake and snow-capped mountains beyond, the rigour of its geometry and the enclosed, steel-mesh bridge that connects its top floor to the otherwise unreachable road alongside. The result is as simple as it is satisfying.

Mario Botta (born 1943) trained as an architectural draughtsman from the age of 15. Later, in Venice, he got to work on Le Corbusier's very last, unrealized project, a hospital for the city on water. He also worked briefly with Louis Kahn. Botta had built his first house at the age of

18 but his precociousness did not lead to preciousness. Far from it. his concerns were always with the elemental building blocks of architecture – the cube, sphere and cylinder – and in setting these in subtle juxtaposition with the Swiss landscape. In a sense, he was going back to the very beginnings of Western architecture, to the archetypal forms described by Plato. His interest in these forms, however, was far from being wholly intellectual: Botta was and is concerned very much with the craft of building and, in this sense, he is a rare talent, for many of those those who think boldly in the abstract are often at odds or removed from the process of construction. It is the two things combined that make great and desirable architecture.

TRELLICK TOWER

ERNO GOLDFINGER, 1972 LONDON, ENGLAND

A west London landmark, Trellick Tower is the most visible component of a large local authority estate designed in a heroic and Brutalist manner by Erno Goldfinger (1902–87). And, yes – Goldfinger was a friend of Ian Fleming, author of the James Bond thrillers. Although bombastic, Trellick Tower was to become a highly coveted address by fashionable young things living around the glamorous Portobello Road market in the 1990s. For several years until then it had been used as a prison in the sky for some of the area's poorest families. What the tower offered, aside from memorable architecture and stunning views all around London, were duplex flats, modelled on those of Le Corbusier's L'Unité d'Habitation (p.210), which were spacious, light and airy and with windows on both sides of the tower.

Goldfinger's monumental works have been described as the product of "structural rationalism", which makes a certain amount of sense, and yet the force and brute nature of Trellick Tower seem fairly irrational. If Trellick hadn't become so fashionable in the last decade of the century, one might be tempted to say that this is the sort of architecture one wouldn't want to bump into on a dark night. A sibling estate, without the full-on drama of Trellick was built in London's East End and, famously, Goldfinger lived in the tower (although for not that long).

THAU SCHOOL

MARTORELL–BOHIGAS–MACKAY, 1972 BARCELONA, SPAIN

This modern school divided into infant, junior and senior blocks does that clever thing: without recourse to pastiche and as if with a nod over the architects' shoulders, it recreates the urban landscape of the ancient Greek *agora* or market place. The school is a city centre in miniature with squares, terraces and stairs connecting the various parts. The symbolism is simple and satisfying: as the children progress up through the years, so they climb higher up the stairs, modelled on the tiers of a Greek theatre, with the peak of the hills that form the backdrop to the school signifying the heights yet to be attained.

The buildings themselves form a strict geometrical composition, but the severity of the plan and its cool, rational architecture is continually mollified by views out to other parts of the school, to the *agora*, its steps and the rising landscape beyond. Not surprisingly, Oriol Bohigas (born 1925) is a highly gifted urban planner who was responsible for a significant part of Barcelona's physical and cultural revival after the death of the dictator, General Franco, in 1974. His colleagues in on the Thau School project were Josep Martorell (born 1925) and the Scottish-born David Mackay (born 1933). Bohigas has been an advisor to the city of Barcelona since 1981.

KIMBELL ART GALLERY

LOUIS KAHN, 1972 FORT WORTH, TEXAS, USA

"The first thing you want in most museums is a cup of coffee. You feel so tired immediately". Louis Kahn (1901–74) felt the way most of us do when faced by a big museum full of very important art. The aching shoulders, the exhaustion, the feeling of guilt as you fail to take in the subtleties of all that Art that is meant to be good for you. And all you want is to sit down and drink a coffee. The café in this superb museum is one of the best in the world. Kahn has given it equal ranking with the galleries, and that is the work of a very civilized and intelligent man, which this Estonian architect, whose poor Jewish parents settled in the USA in 1904, most certainly was. Kahn came from nothing and gave everything back: he was a genius, up there with Mies and Le Corbusier, but his buildings were somehow warmer and, even when designed on a heroic scale, engaging.

The Kimbell is designed on a small scale. A group of barrel-vaulted pavilions are linked, interspersed with courtyards and gardens and bathed inside with the most subtle and delicate wash of daylight. The materials used throughout are the very best. This, of course, is often possible in the USA where wealthy patrons (in this case Kay and Velma Kimbell) can indulge their architects to degrees their European counterparts can only dream of. This was Kahn's favourite of his own buildings. He was right to be proud of it.

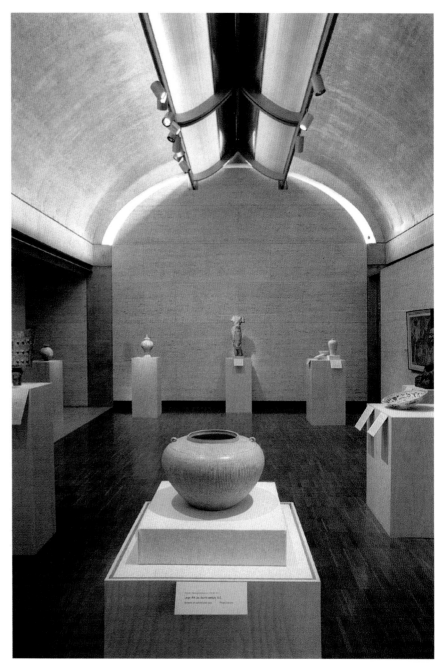

WILLIS FABER AND DUMAS

FOSTER ASSOCIATES, 1975 IPSWICH, SUFFOLK, ENGLAND

This sleek office block still comes as a surprise, for it sits in the heart of Ipswich, a country town that is about as sleepy as they come in southern England. By day, the jet black glass gives away nothing of the interior and the building is Sphinx-like in its silence. As the sun sets, the interior begins to emerge and the reflections of the town in the all but seamless glass walls vanish. This daily spectacle makes the Willis Faber building (the Dumas got dropped along the way at some point in the insurance company's more recent history) as exciting a part of the townscape as it was when it opened 25 years ago. Since then, the building has been listed as being of historical and architectural importance even though it less than the statutory minimum of 30 years old. Such is Norman Foster's reputation.

The building's skin, like an Alaïa frock, is the most fascinating part of a building that, once through its triple-height lobby and up its smooth-running escalators (in place of lifts), is really a rather conventional open-plan office for insurance clerks. Many of these work facing inwards, unable to enjoy the views out of Foster's impeccable glass screen, which reaches right down to kiss the pavement. Staff did, however, in the early days at least, benefit from a swimming pool in the basement and an immaculately maintained lawn on the roof.

NATIONAL THEATRE

DENYS LASDUN, 1975 LONDON, ENGLAND

Lasdun has always described this building as a series of terraces or architectural strata, and one sees what he means. From the outside this mountainous concrete building feels more like some strangely refined archeological outcrop than a place of public entertainment. And, from its tiered terraces, to be climbed over as if mountaineering in the city centre, there are superb views of other urban peaks, notably that of St Paul's Cathedral and Lloyds of London (p.393). Perhaps this curious way of looking at the National Theatre has helped endear itself to the public since its completion, after a long gestation, in 1975. The interior has always been popular. The three theatres are superb and the lobbies enjoyable save for the horrid

carpets – quite why the British are so obsessed with carpet in public buildings remains a mystery.

The theatre sits alongside Waterloo Bridge and dominates a particularly fine bend on the River Thames. For the most part it is finished in weather-boarded concrete and is saved from seeming brutal by the quality of the materials used and by the intriguing play of horizontal and vertical planes on which the sun plays very effectively, as does electric light at night. The back side of the building is uninspired and merely functional as if Lasdun suddenly forgot what to do without the drama of the river to prompt him.

MINISTRY OF HIGHWAYS

GEORGE CHAKHAVA 1974 TBILISI, GEORGIA

One of the masterpieces of late-flowering Soviet architecture, this urgent building is a magnificent response to its purpose. At every criss, cross, jut, angle and junction, it suggests the structure, layout and flow of fast roads. George Chakhava, its lead designer, was both an architect and the minister of roads for the Georgian Soviet Socialist Republic. Based on ideas drawn from Revolutionary Russian architecture of the early 1920s – Suprematism and Constructivism – the Highways Ministry pushed these further into what its architects called the "Space City" method. This displayed an eco-awareness well ahead of its time, with the building taking up precious little ground area, allowing nature to swarm under and through it. The walls are also adorned with climbing plants that soften the impact of this dramatic concrete megastructure. Here is a fine example of how ultra-modern design can work harmoniously with natural surroundings. It is also a building that seems ahead of its time in aesthetic as well as environmental terms, prefiguring the work of architects like Zaha Hadid who was also influenced by early Soviet design. The highways ministry demonstrates that Soviet architecture was far from being a monolithic entity in the years in which it is most remembered for row after row of characterless and grim, high-rise, concrete housing blocks blighting what appeared to be every town or city in the USSR of any size or economic worth. The ministry, although no longer a government building, is a national monument today.

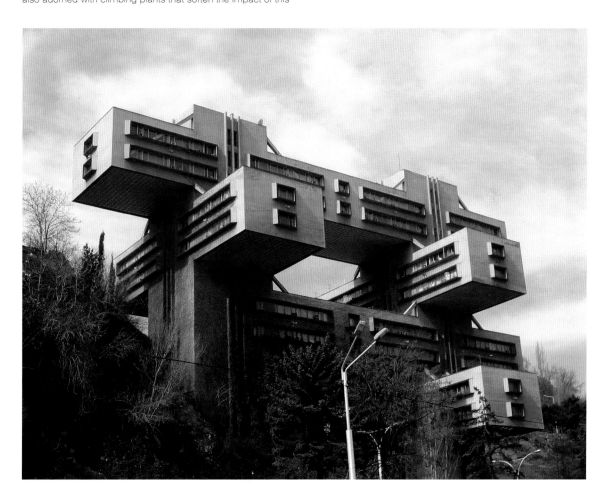

STUDENT HOUSING

LUCIEN KROLL, 1975 CATHOLIC UNIVERSITY OF LOUVAIN, BELGIUM

This was the year that Punk hit the headlines. It seems very unlikely that Lucien Kroll (born 1927) was ever a fan of the Sex Pistols, yet the university campus at Louvain he completed that year was about as punky as mainstream architecture gets.

Kroll, born and trained in Brussels, was a devout believer in the much talked about, yet little practised, notion of public participation in architecture. He genuinely believed that the users of a building should shape it with the architect acting as sounding board and guiding hand. The medical faculty and student residences attached to it have been a remarkable and perhaps unexpected success.

The buildings have grown in a rather shaggy, punk manner, but are entirely free of the bogus "community" architecture look that emerged in Britain at the same time, whereby the architect patronized users by interpreting their wishes in Toy Town, comic book forms and details.

What Kroll allowed was for students and teachers to say what they needed and wanted and then to knit together the various strands into a loose-fit architecture. So, there were odd bits of gardens here, stairs there, jutting roofs and roof terraces galore: all these things are expression of what people say they want and they are not always quite where architects, with their tidy minds, want them to be.

KALMAN HOUSE

LUIGI SNOZZI, 1976 TICINO, SWITZERLAND

Luigi Snozzi (born 1932) is one of a loosely related group of architects from Ticino who has worked on developing a rational yet romantic architecture that owes as much to Cubism and Le Corbusier as it does to landscape and site. Perhaps this is because the locale – a beautiful setting of lakes and mountains – encourages the building of houses on sites that in lesser hands would be problematic, but for the Ticino architects are a natural challenge.

The Kalman House – on one level a simple concrete box sliced and sectioned – climbs dramatically up from its hillside setting. It may be an essay in strict geometry and in the use of a minimal palette of materials and colours, yet this is the

point: the theatre of the enfolding landscape provides all the colour and decoration the house and its owners ever really need. This special relationship between house and landscape is emphasized by the bridge that juts out from the house and leads out to a pavilion from which the Kalmans can sit and look out across the mountains and watch the sun set across lake and valley.

In another less dramatic location the house would seem quite cold, if logical, intelligent and thoughtfully planned; here, the architect has played a knowing and gentle game, contrasting the mathematical construct of the building against nature's own rococo.

BYKER WALL

RALPH ERSKINE, 1979 NEWCASTLE-UPON-TYNE, ENGLAND

The Byker Wall was premised on a lie, which was not the fault of Ralph Erskine (born 1914), its popular Anglo–Swedish architect. Originally, an urban motorway was to have sliced through Byker, a working-class district of Newcastle, and the new housing, proposed to raise the spirit of this depressed area, was to be built in a way that denied the roar of speeding traffic. In the end, Newcastle's famously corrupt local councillors were either chucked out or imprisoned and Erskine need not have designed the "Wall" the way he did. Nevertheless, this local authority housing was instantly popular and has rightly become famous.

The outlying wall of informal flats and houses puts a big and friendly, if rather shaggy, arm around smaller blocks and individual houses. It is one kilometre (^{2}⁄3 mile) long and rises up to a maximum of eight storeys. The result is a cosy and well-protected urban village. Residents had a lot of say in its design and layout. Erskine is a good listener and able to produce populist architecture that never resorts to pastiche or whimsy. He was born and brought up as a Quaker in Saffron Walden and moved to Sweden in 1939. In 1998 he was appointed architect of the Millennium Village, an ecologically correct new town on the Greenwich peninsula in London.

ATHENEUM VISITOR CENTER

RICHARD MEIER, 1979 HARMONY, INDIANA, USA

Having designed a number of chaste and beautiful white villas for well-heeled New Englanders throughout the 1970s, Meier was set to take off on a global trip in the next decade during which time he was to produce one memorable museum after the other. His crisp, white, impeccable style proved to be truly international. The missing link between the villas and the museums is this shining visitor centre for the community of Harmony, Indiana.

This was Meier's first public building and is without doubt harmonious. It stands on a pristine lawn and hints at a perfect social order. Meier's buildings have the disconcerting quality of looking exactly as they do in photographs: the grass is always green, the buildings fresh back from the dry-cleaners. It consists of three storeys of rooms gathered around a lecture theatre, linked by a highly articulated web of ramps, external stairs and bridges. What Meier has done is to take a classically white box and break it apart, reassembling some of what might have gone inside – such as the stairs – outside. This accessibility is reinforced by the feeling that some of the walls have been slid away from the box and projected as screens onto the lawn. With a push here and there, you feel that you would be able to straighten the whole thing up again. It is a nice conceit: a building that expresses democracy and order at one and the same time.

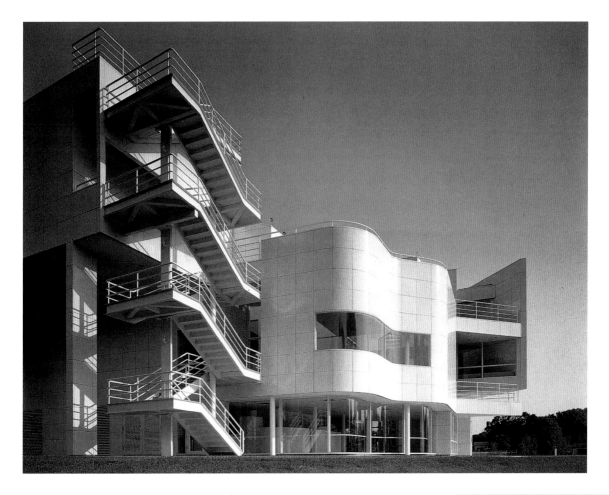

BARBICAN CENTRE

CHAMBERLIN, POWELL AND BON, 1979 CITY OF LONDON, ENGLAND

This heroic housing development was in the making for something like a quarter of a century. Despite its formidable appearance – a huge castle of solid concrete topped with high and highly sculpted towers – the Barbican is not a low-rent council estate but an aggressive aggregation of flats for City of London professionals. In fact, nearly the entire resident population of the City of London lives here.

The Barbican was built to an extremely high standard and those who live here will have nothing, or not very much, to say against it. Don't even think of entering without a guide and compass. Once inside its walls, the uninitiated are faced by dark, labyrinthine walkways that appear to lead nowhere, but in fact link together a complex arrangement of internal squares, courtyards and gardens. These are surprisingly lush and attractive when you find them, and the complex turns out to be a bit of a softie at heart, with water gardens and a waterfall, a medieval parish church, sections of the Roman wall that once bounded what was Londinium, a smart girls' school and an arts centre within its formidable boundaries.

Shortly before they were commissioned to design it, the same architects had built the comparatively bright and breezy Golden Lane estate that is situated alongside the Barbican. The contrast between the two is marked: where Golden Lane seems open and willing to engage in conversation, the Barbican is aloof and silent.

ALEXANDRA ROAD HOUSING

CAMDEN ARCHITECTS DEPARTMENT, 1979 LONDON, ENGLAND

A defiant last fling, Alexandra Road marked the end of the giant concrete local authority housing projects in London that had been such a controversial part of the British architectural scene since the 1950s. It comprises two new carless streets, one a kilometre (⅔ mile) long, running parallel to the busy electrified train line from London to Scotland. The result is an extraordinarily powerful, if utterly terrifying, experience. The ideas behind the project seem rational, yet it all seems so inhumane. If you happen to live half way down that one-kilometre street, you may well experience a sense of being quite lost to the world beyond the regimented, concrete confines of the estate. The density of occupation here (200 people to the acre) is great by British or US standards, although typical of many continental European cities. While this is fine in principle, in practice it isn't because of the way in which Alexandra Road turns in on itself, partly as a defence against the noise of trains speeding past. Car parking is provided in a grim labyrinth below the streets.

The Camden Architects department was one of the last bastions of such designs, and though architects tend to defend its last ditch attempt at grand Modernism, people breathed a sigh of relief when this bombast came to an end.

HUMBERTUS HOUSE

ALDO VAN EYCK, 1980 AMSTERDAM, THE NETHERLANDS

This multicoloured city building is a home for single parents and their children. If this sounds like a little institutional, then it is, for the building represents the powerfully cossetting operations of the Dutch welfare state in the latter part of the century. When it was built, European societies were only just beginning to come to terms with the fact that the "nuclear" family (Mum, Dad, 2.4 kids) was breaking down and that, many children would be brought up by one parent. As this realization dawned, so there appeared to be a need for local authorities and city governments to cope with what was perceived as a problem, rather than as a natural change in the Western social set up that had been brewing for many years.

The six-storey Humbertus House is a brightly painted creature composed of many different materials, of a complex arrangement of interlocking, intersecting blocks, of courtyards and roof gardens, big airy windows drawing quietly form historic precedent, of pergolas and walkways. Its informality was drawn together by a rigorous plan, as one expects from an architect who was very much a Modernist. Its complexity is rooted in van Eyck's fascination with the idea of such civic buildings being towns in themselves, with their own internal streets and squares. This is an idea that dates back to the origins of Occidental architecture, whereby the plan of each house reflected that of the city as a whole.

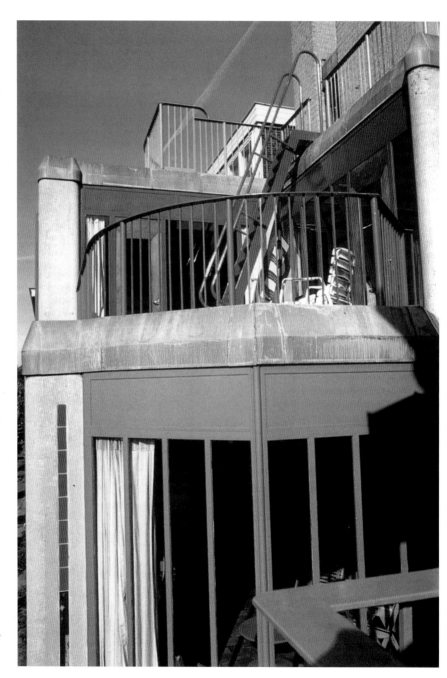

XEROX CENTER

HELMUT JAHN, 1980 CHICAGO, ILLINOIS, USA

Super sleek, the Xerox Center was very close in spirit to Mies van der Rohe's glass tower project of 1921. It rises in 45 seamless storeys above Chicago and is as poised and polished as it is silent and apparently impenetrable. Its aluminium and glass skin, as tight as tight can be, creams round the junction of South Dearborn and West Monroe Streets. This was about as far as this kind of building – 60 years in the conceptual making – could go before running out of ideas or slipping into the realm of sheer banality. The Xerox Center comes close, but Jahn (born 1940) is good enough to have something left to say.

Like Mies van der Rohe, Jahn was born and educated in Germany before moving to Chicago to study at the Illinois Institute of Technology between 1965 and 1966 where, of course, Mies had designed the campus and taught. In 1967 he joined the Chicago firm of C. F. Murphy, which he took over as principal architect in 1983.

Jahn teaches at Harvard. His buildings are characterized by the use of simple geometric shapes drawn out on a massive scale, as in the State of Illinois Center, Chicago, for example, in which the great rectangular box of the structure is cut through with a sloping glass cylinder. It is all very impressive in a controlled and slick way, but you cannot help thinking that this approach to architecture has to lead to a dead end soon.

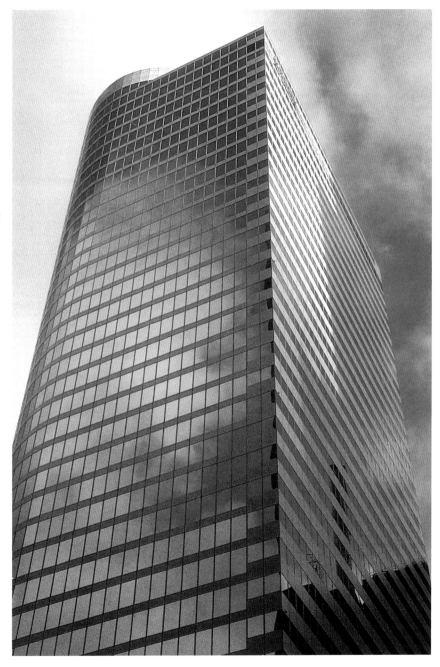

KOSHINO HOUSE

TADAO ANDO, 1981 ASHIYA, HYOGO, JAPAN

To Western eyes, the Koshino House is rather like a monastery. It consists of two wings separated by a courtyard and connected by an underground corridor. One wing contains no fewer than six children's bedrooms lined up in a row like monks' cells. The other comprises the parents' bedroom, living room and kitchen. Both are austere concrete structures, but superbly finished and lit in ways that are as haunting as they are magical.

Tadao Ando is one of the finest architects of the late twentieth century. His houses are extraordinarily beautiful, yet utterly simple and built, for the most part, from concrete blocks and slabs. There is, however, concrete and concrete,

and in Ando's hands it is a beautiful material. Most of all, Ando understands, like Le Corbusier before him, how best to let daylight play on the depths of this often misunderstood material. The light effects that play across the walls of the Koshino House belie the need for decoration of any sort – no pictures and certainly no wallpaper.

Ando's particular sense of beauty must be innate. Born into a working class family of "untouchables", he trained first as a boxer before learning to build. He had no formal training as an architect and the Japanese profession was long dismissive of his talent. However, he has become one of his country's most precious talents.

MEDICI HOUSE

MARIO BOTTA, 1982 TICINO, SWITZERLAND

Approach Botta's *casa rotonda* one way and it can seem like a giant medieval knight's helmet; approach it from another direction and it resembles a pill box. It has a mysterious quality, as perhaps do all circular buildings, but is a fine family house as well as a rigorous expression of very elemental architecture. Here Botta has chosen the cylinder and, in his characteristic way, has cut it through with slits and other openings, not enough to reveal the interior but more than enough to create a play of deep shadows that animate a simple shape and one of the primary building blocks of architecture. You can walk right through the cylinder at

ground level without entering the house. An arcade sliced through the building brings daylight into its core.

Up to this point in his career, Botta had built exclusively in the countryside and on the fringe of villages and small towns. His first urban building, an extension of the Staatsbank in Fribourg, Switzerland, was completed the same year as the Medici House. It seemed somehow overwrought as did many of Botta's later city projects. Undoubtedly, his finest work up until the end of the century remained the sequence of elemental brick houses built in his native Ticino.

ARTIST'S HOUSE AND STUDIO

GLEN MURCUTT, 1983 SYDNEY, AUSTRALIA

Glen Murcutt (born 1936) brought the Outback back to Sydney with this delightful super-sophisticated corrugated steel house. On any level it makes good sense. Raised off the ground on steel beams it has some of the feel of the Farnsworth House by Mies van der Rohe (p.206). However, it is equipped for a life dogged by worrying insects, life-threatening spiders, unexpected snakes and bush fires. Raised above ground, it also stays as cool as an intelligently thought-through house without air-conditioning can. The reflective property of the corrugated steel and extensive use of wooden blinds keeps the worst of the heat at bay.

The plan is simple: one end forms a well-sheltered balcony and the rooms follow a simple logic. When Murcutt built this house, the area on the edge of Sydney really did feel as if it were in the Outback, or close enough; in later years, as more and more Australians were able to build second homes away from the city, it became less isolated. The idea, though, remains an interesting one, combining a nostalgia for Australia's settler past, its tin-shack architecture and Modernism. Quite an achievement. Not surprisingly. Murcutt became a popular architect and was to develop the theme of this house many times.

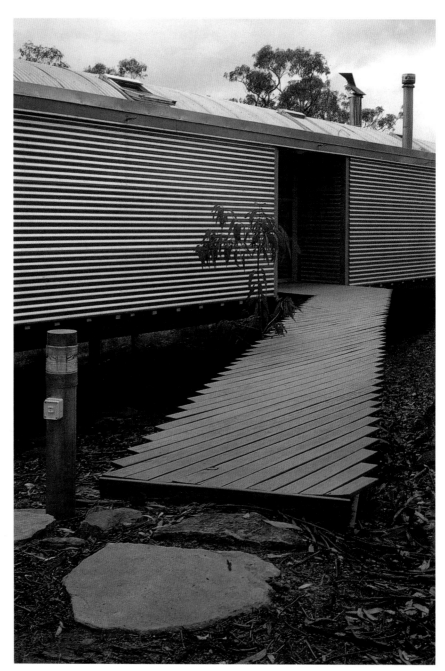

HIGH MUSEUM

RICHARD MEIER, 1983 ATLANTA, GEORGIA, USA

In the 1980s, cities across the world began to invest heavily in museums. There was a widespread belief that investment went where the quality of life was high and one of the measures of quality was the level of cultural life. Museums were popular in this sense not least because business corporations could make a soft impact on host cities by sponsoring the construction of museums and the exhibitions they mounted. In other words, there was an unspoken and reciprocal relationship between art and commerce, between businesses thrusting into the future and museums nurturing the past.

Richard Meier became the shining star of the new museum movement and has built several across the world. Perhaps none, though, has the sheer, brilliant impact of the High Museum. In a flippant mood, one could say that it is rather like a giant washing machine designed to make the past – the artefacts on show – cleaner, brighter and thus more appealing than they ever really were in daily use. Certainly, US museums have a habit of making exhibits of whatever age look brand new. Based on three cubes and a cylinder, this purist building boasts light, generous and ennobling circulation spaces and a cool dignity that is certainly very impressive.

MINISTRY OF FOREIGN AFFAIRS

HENNING LARSEN, 1984 RIYADH, SAUDI ARABIA

Richard Bryant, the renowned architectural photographer was seized by guards in this vast and gleaming building. His crime was that his assistant had scratched a tiny patch of marble flooring with his camera tripod. It was a small diplomaticincident, and the editors of the *Architectural Review* in London were able to diffuse the situation. Still, it showed the esteem in which those employed to care for this impressive building held it. The building was a significant step forwards in terms of Western architects making an effort to find a form of design that was modern yet reflected Islamic and Arabic values. So many of the buildings designed for Saudi Arabia and the Middle East were as cynical as they were trashy. Henning Larsen (born 1925) took a polar opposite approach.

Designed in the guise of a fort, the building opens up, delightfully, into an internal street based on a traditional bazaar that runs right around its core. At the heart is a soaring triangular atrium off which lie the ministry offices which are grouped around nine courtyards. So, behind its foreboding walls, the ministry unfolds like a flower; this comes as a complete surprise and was proof, at long last, that Western architects had more in mind in the Middle East than flogging off designs that had been rejected in their home countries.

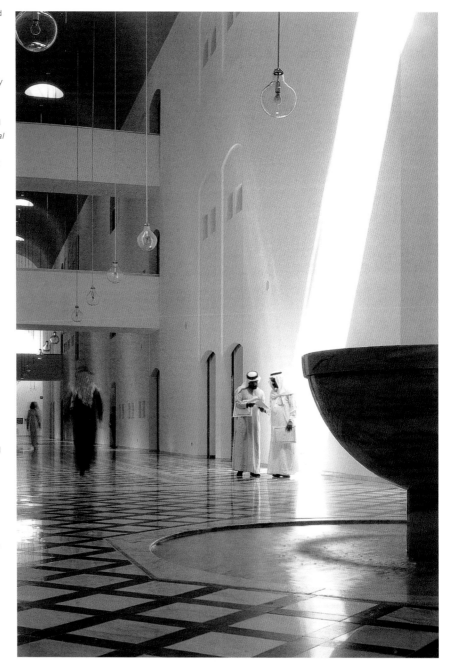

SAATCHI COLLECTION

MAX GORDON, 1985 ST JOHN'S WOOD, LONDON, ENGLAND

Charles Saatchi is an ad man who has enjoyed playing cards, racing go-karts and collecting contemporary art inspired by the world of advertising, or art that might be turned into advertising one day in the future. The art he liked, bought and championed came in a rush from 1988 when a new wave of young artists, spearheaded by the canny, media-friendly Damien Hirst, exploded out of Goldsmith's College in south London. Hirst showed what could be done in the name of art with pickling fluids, blood, semen and anything other dangerous or provocative substance.

Saatchi's genius has been to show his conquests (he would buy up a fresh young artist's entire show in one unrefusable

transaction) in a gallery that is as clean, as pure, as white and as light as the art was brutal and, to some, disgusting. He bought a former garage in a genteel stuccoed street in one of London's wealthiest suburbs and commissioned Max Gordon (1931–90), a Scottish-born architect settled in New York, to convert it. Gordon's genius was to make it look as if he had done nothing at all except to paint the walls white. In this sense, he was partly in league with a loosely connected group of architects, including John Pawson and Claudio Silvestrin (p.285) who made their names in London from the mid-1980s with an ascetic, minimalist architecture that all began with the design of chic art galleries.

HONG KONG AND SHANGHAI BANK

FOSTER ASSOCIATES, 1986 CENTRAL DISTRICT, HONG KONG

The high point of British Hi-Tech, Norman Foster's hugely impressive banking headquarters in the former British crown colony is best remembered for its enormous cost. As far as anyone can remember or tell it was the most expensive building of all time. Since then this questionable mantle has passed on later buildings and Foster's mid-period masterpiece can be looked at without a thick veil of Hong Kong dollars blocking the view.

The bank was an important symbol of confidence and permanence in a city that had a possibly healthy habit of demolishing even its grandest buildings every so many years to make way for more lucrative successors and which was to be handed back to Communist China within just 11 years of the bank's completion. This steely machine for making money in is supported by eight ladder-like masts, cross-braced with struts that, in turn, hold up the floors. Floor space is as clear as possible. Lifts, stairs, lavatories and other services are pushed right to the edge of the tower. An imposing lobby, cleverly lit by daylight scooped from the sky, rushes up into the core of the building, adding a dimension of drama and life that the building's enigmatic, machine-like exterior belies. Nearly everything here has been custom-designed and made: very cool and very impressive.

DE MENIL COLLECTION

RENZO PIANO, BUILDING WORKSHOP, 1986 HOUSTON, TEXAS, USA

One of the best of new museums and galleries that appeared in the 1980s, the De Menil Collection was also one of the least pretentious. Its form and structure derive entirely from one detail, the finely profiled concrete "leaves" that span the entire building and act as light baffles. In the frazzling heat of Houston these allow the museum to be top-lit and naturally lit all day long. The "leaves", suspended by a simple steel frame, are angled so as to make the most of available daylight without allowing direct sunlight to sear into the galleries. Dominique de Menil, Piano's patron, was insistent that her choice collection of tribal art should be benefit from being viewed in daylight. Where extra light is needed, this shines from spotlights which have been incorporated into the leaves.

The rest of the structure was easy. Walls of weatherboard are set back within the structural frame which thus acts as a sunshade around the museum. Inside, lushly planted courtyards are the only interruption in the flow of a simple and elegant plan. The galleries are not air-conditioned: this luxury is confined solely to the "treasury" (the store for the collection) located above the roof. In a city in which architectural bombast is the rule, the De Menil Collection is delightful. It is one of the softest of Piano's inspired "soft machines".

MUSÉE D'ORSAY

GAE AULENTI, 1987 PARIS, FRANCE

The Gare D'Orsay, gracing the banks of the Seine, was always a pretty railway station but little used. Designed by Victor Laloux, it dates from 1900. Just 75 years later, President Georges Pompidou decided that it should be converted into a museum, and so it was. ACT, the team who won the competition for its redevelopment, were left largely to sort out the essentials, while the second prize winner, the Milanese architect Gae Aulenti (born 1927) was commissioned to design what was to become the eye-catching interior.

The exterior remains, thankfully, pretty much as Laloux shaped and decorated it. Aulenti's interior is simple, axial and very impressive. As if wanting visitors to make sure they knew that she planned to touch this grand old countess of a building as lightly as possible, Aulenti designed an interior that looks like a substantial and elegant exhibition installation and no more. It works extremely well. At no point is the station's superb interior denied or spoilt. Visitors stroll along what was once the trackbed and are diverted into simple, temple-like pavilions to gawp at the paintings or *objets d'art* of various periods. The interior works at its best, though, when you come across vast, pretentious canvases depicting stirring events in France's faultless history, mounted on modern walls and set against the further backdrop of Laloux's wonderful vault.

HYSOLAR RESEARCH INSTITUTE

BEHNISCH AND PARTNERS, 1987 STUTTGART, GERMANY

Günther Behnisch (born 1922) designed the breathtaking tents for the Olympic Games with the engineer Frei Otto at Munich in 1972. Fifteen years later, he produced this equally daring, if smaller and much less well known, structure. A part of the University of Stuttgart, the Hysolar Research Institute was set up to investigate the possibilities of generating hydrogen through solar energy. The complex and inscrutable processes by which this might be achieved is reflected in Behnisch's good-humoured building. Here is architecture as experiment. It works well and hard for its living, yet the playful aspect is carried throughout the structure, which includes funny angles, crazy glazing and

bits of building shooting out at odd angles. Undoubtedly, it evokes a world of nutty professors beavering away in white coats and steel-framed glasses on top-secret experiments, and this is a large part of its appeal.

The building was completed the year before Philip Johnson organized the "Deconstructivist Architecture" show at the Museum of Modern Art, and was, whether Behnisch would have agreed or not, part of a move that had been gathering steam (or hydrogen) as many architects tired of the cheesy feyness of Postmodernism and, bored by the skin-tight school of super-smooth façades, appeared to want to take the whole subject to pieces and to start again.

MOUND STAND

MICHAEL HOPKINS, 1987 LORD'S CRICKET GROUND, LONDON, ENGLAND

The MCC (Marylebone Cricket Club) has for aeons been one of the last bastions of a very peculiar English male chauvinism. Florid-faced duffers, half-cut on Pimms and champagne, were still snoring away summer afternoons in the famous Lord's Pavilion as willow struck leather and Michael Hopkins set to work on this impressive and festive stand for spectators and sleepers. The fact that the MCC commissioned one of the best and most popular new buildings of its time was simply extraordinary. In fact, the age-old club, far from being repentant, commissioned Hopkins a second time and then went a step further down

the Modern line and roped in Nicholas Grimshaw (p.400) and Future Systems. Ever since, half-cut, florid duffers have been able to snooze through Test matches shaded by the white fabric tents of Hopkins' Mound Stand.

The building rests on an existing brick arcade and is held up by just six masts on the side of the pitch. These are entirely absent, or hidden from view, as far as spectators are concerned, and they enjoy a completely clear view of the action (or lack of it). The stand is ringed around with swish, fully glazed "hospitality suites" in which men in suits, as opposed to Panamas and blazers, drink large quantities of beer and ignore the cricket.

L'INSTITUT DU MONDE ARABE

JEAN NOUVEL, 1987 PARIS, FRANCE

It was this building that won many sceptics over to the pleasures of Modern architecture and excited a generation who had been brought up with Modern design and had no real problem with it. This is a bold claim, yet many observers of the architectural world were aware of something of a sea-change in public sensibilities in the late 1980s. Modern architecture was no longer a demon to wrestle with or something terribly difficult that no one without a doctorate could make head or tail of but something to enjoy, to talk and read about.

Jean Nouvel (born 1941) is a master of the popular, yet ground-breaking building. The Institut du Monde Arabe was one of the famous *grands projets* initiated in Paris by President Mitterand. On a site on the banks of the Seine, it comprises two intersecting blocks, one curved and facing the river, the other rectangular and facing south. Between the two there is a courtyard. Inside, a wide range of cultural activities and a restaurant are offered. Yet what most people long to see is the wonderful south-facing glass wall. Between sheets of glass, exquisite metal diaphragms in the guise of Islamic patterns frame lenses that open and close like the human eye to control the intensity of daylight entering the Institute. This is a brilliant example of how art, architecture and new building technology can work together to enhance one another. A *tour de force*.

CHURCH ON THE WATER

TADAO ANDO, 1988 TOMAMU, HOKKAIDO, JAPAN

Ando can do so very much with so little. The Church on the Water relies for its effect and mood on the changing seasons, beyond the great glass screen that fills its east end. The seasons here remain marked. In winter the snow lies deep and crisp and even, and the lake that frames the view through the window freezes over entirely. In summer, the skies are clear and the air warm: then, the screen is lowered out of sight and services are held with Nature as a live and spirited backdrop. Christ's cross stands here in all seasons to remind the faithful that he is with them at all times.

To focus the congregation's attention in this way makes perfect sense, and indeed the rest of this simple concrete container is without incident. Ando's architecture never offers more than it needs to in a structural or decorative sense. It relies for its effect and power on the play of light and shade, on texture, on all the senses playing together to feel an architecture rather than to feast on it with eyes greedy for incident and sensation.

Very few architects in any period have been able to get away with this. No trickery is ever involved. What is required, as Ando must have known innately, is a natural sense of place, of repose, of human sensitivity to the slightest change in temperature, mood and setting. This is architecture of rare genius, and is about as timeless as it gets.

LA GRANDE ARCHE

JOHANN OTTO VON SPRECKELSEN, 1990 LA DÉFENSE, PARIS, FRANCE

A modern counterpart to the famous Arc de Triomphe, von Spreckelsen's huge, abstract and anonymous gateway terminates the heroic axis that runs from Place de la Concorde, along the Champs Elysée, through Etoile and right up to La Défense, the terrifying mountain of offices and corporate headquarters to the west of Paris. From the steps of this visually silent monument, the eye is drawn straight through the Arc de Triomphe. From the top of the Arche, reached by a lift that climbs vertiginously up through the giant aperture, the views of Paris are stunning.

Although it serves as a monument – to the bicentenary of the storming of the Bastille and the French Revolution – the Arche has a more prosaic purpose; within its mighty white Carrara marble-clad walls are 35 floors of government offices. Given the design of the Arche, these look out into its enormous hollow centre and to north and south (depending upon which side you work on), but not to the east, as if enticing views of Paris would put bureaucrats off their stride.

The Arche is basically a hollowed out 100-metre (330-ft) cube. The design was chosen in a competition held in 1982 for which there were 400 entries. Von Spreckelsen, a Dane, was very much an unknown and it is to the credit of the Mitterand regime that, in the construction of its *grands projets*, it was so willing to employ architects from elsewhere in Europe and the USA.

IMAGINATION BUILDING

RON HERRON, 1990 LONDON, ENGLAND

A little bit of Archigram (p.439–40) came happily and eventfully to life in what was the former lightwell of a five-storey red-brick Edwardian office block in central London. Herron converted the whole building for the design group Imagination but brought it to life with this spectacular and unexpected atrium at its heart. New windows and doors were made in the white-painted internal walls on either side of the atrium and these either look on or lead over a criss-cross weave of high-level, perforated steel bridges. Above these, a voluminous fabric roof billows in the wind. This gives the building the sort of festive air that Archigram had always promised in its drawings. The roof is an entertaining addition to the local skyline. It was engineered to withstand winds of 260 km/ph (160mph). Down below, the atrium boasts overscaled pots of plants, trees, a modern baroque staff restaurant and the sort of genuinely informal atmosphere that architects have long talked of trying to create – for example at Centraal Beheer (p.254) and Hillingdon Civic Centre (p.317) – without succeeding.

In the case of Imagination, it was the client who set the tone; here work was meant to be a pleasure, not a penance. Architect and client got on so well that Herron, working with his two sons, set up shop here.

NEUENDORF HOUSE

JOHN PAWSON AND CLAUDIO SILVESTRIN, 1990 MAJORCA, SPAIN

A holiday house as artwork for a German art dealer, the Neuendorf House is a masterly composition of walls. No roof is visible from the outside, just a high concrete perimeter wall finished in a sun-burned stucco. The house is reached across fields along a stepped-stone path. This leads to a narrow, 9-metre (30-ft) high slit in the wall which, in turn, reveals an amphitheatre-like courtyard, empty save for simple stone benches flanking two sides.

The courtyard leads into an austere dining room, the heart of the house. There is nothing here save for a stone table designed as part of the architecture and sculpted wooden chairs by the great Danish furniture maker Hans Wegner. The fireplace runs the length of one wall. Other rooms are equally austere, employing the same palette of materials – stone floors, wooden benches, wooden bath tub, stone basins, smooth white concrete walls. Daylight plays through the rooms from slits and chutes and is always restrained.

The overall feeling is that of living either in a modern sculpture or in a latter-day monastery. This is not all that surprising: John Pawson (born 1949) made his name designing Minimalist art galleries and Claudio Silvestrin (born 1954) was to have become a priest or monk before turning to architecture.

TEMPLE ON THE WATER

TADAO ANDO, 1992 AWAJI ISLAND, HYOGO, JAPAN

Ando in another magical mood. This Shingon Buddhist temple dug into a hillside overlooking the Bay of Osaka is entered by a long concrete stair that passes down through the centre of a circular lake awash with gorgeous floating lotus plants. From even the slightest distance, the monks look as if they are walking down among the lilies and into the water itself. This is a lovely conceit and one that visitors never tire of watching. The watchword is simplicity: of both materials and design. On the surface, Ando has done little more, it seems, than to create an entrance. Down below, the temple opens up into a womb-like world of warm red passageways and then into a blaze of colour as the prayer hall itself is reached. This comes as a surprise, particularly for those who know how sparing Ando's palette of colours

is. Yet, these are colours – the reds and oranges – that are sacred to Buddhist monks and their rituals; they are not at all gratuitous.

Ando's temple is a good example of how an architecture of great simplicity and still rooted in the fertile ground of Modernism can be at one with Nature. It is one thing to design a build that mimics and otherwise represents the forms of Nature as in, for example, the works of Bruce Goff (p.96), Herb Greene (p.105) or Imre Makovecz (p.112). It is quite another to set a modern building quietly and respectfully into a natural setting so that the one, Nature, enhances the other, Architecture. The latter is an old and valuable lesson: the Greeks did it at Athens and Ando does it 2,500 years later here near Osaka.

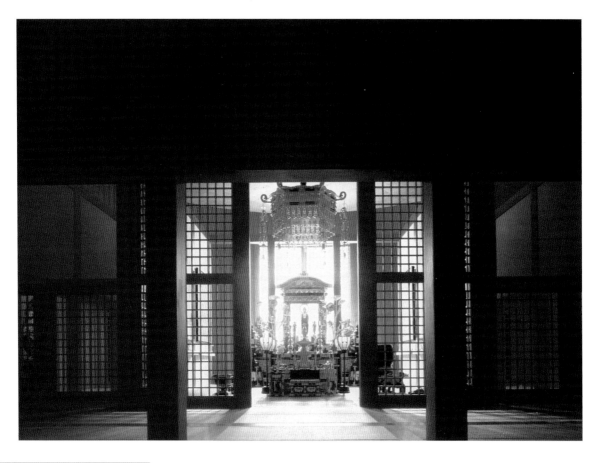

CARUSO–ST JOHN HOUSE

CARUSO–ST JOHN, 1994 HIGHBURY CORNER, LONDON, ENGLAND

Art from thrift, the Caruso House won many friends when it was first seen, often through Hélène Bînet's superb black and white photographs. A former slaughterhouse, this mews building was converted into a house and studio for very little money. The architects, Adam Caruso (born 1962) and Peter St John (born 1959) stripped the interior and inserted new elements into the tall narrow space. They left the walls in the stripped state and found that these had a rough beauty of their own, particularly when daylight was manipulated to accentuate the mood. Throughout the house, cheap but curiously pleasing materials have been used and left unadorned.

If the house has a raw character it never feels trashy or tacky. This was the era when late-flowering Postmodern architects and designers were still trying to turn MDF (medium density fibreboard) into marble using unhappy paint effects. Caruso–St John made a determined effort to get away from this rag-rolled decorators' approach to architecture. What they proved here was that a serious Modern architecture was in the grasp of the young and the hard up as long as they thought in terms of light and space and not in those of brass-effect lightswitches and deep-pile fitted carpets. A brilliant street urchin of a building.

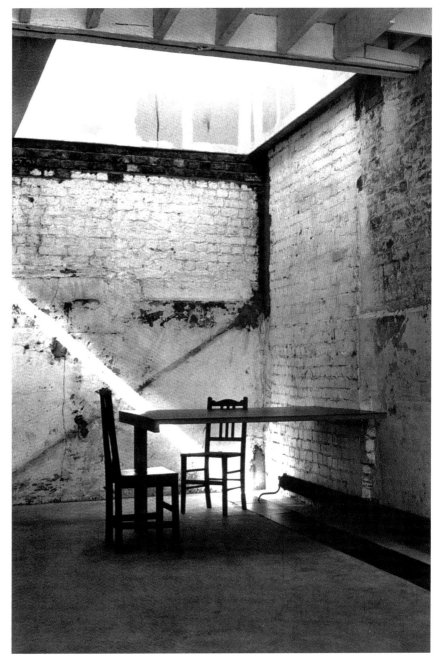

FONDATION CARTIER

JEAN NOUVEL, 1994 PARIS, FRANCE

As discreet as a fine French scent, the Fondation Cartier is an ethereal museum that, in some lights and from some angles barely seems to exist. The building is almost transparent, its interior protected by layers of screens that, stepping back from the street, have the effect of enjoyably confusing our notion of where the building begins and ends, of what is substantial and what is simply a trick of light and incorporeal architecture. This dream-like quality is played on further by the fact that the building cannot be separated from its garden that appears to pervade its interior. Meanwhile, trees on the site, were left to flourish and these spring into leaf between the layers of Nouvel's screens. The result is a delicate and exquisite building that

is as popular as it is refined, proving that accessible culture for the masses does not need to be dumbed down in the age of satellite television and computer games. Nouvel was much concerned with the idea of how to make big modern buildings appear to touch the ground and meet the city as lightly and as quietly as possible. A project for an office tower for the centre of Paris that appeared to disappear asit rose into the city's grey skies – the *Tour sans Fins*, 1989 – was much talked about at the time, but unrealized.

Architecture can be so heavy and plodding. Cities are full of the stuff. How can a sensitive architect contribute something as graceful as a ballerina at the end of the century? The Fondation Cartier was one answer.

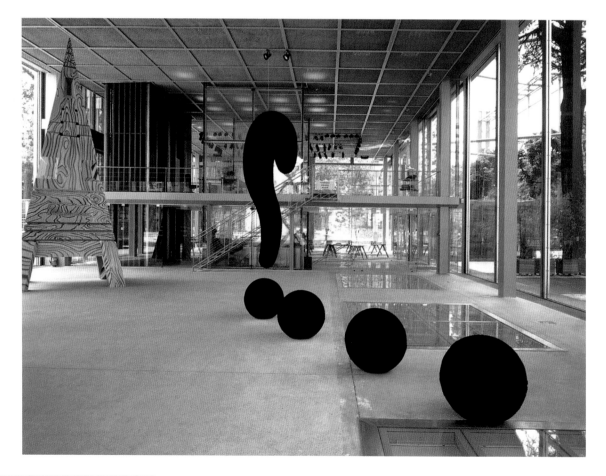

STEIN HOUSE

SETH STEIN, 1995 KNIGHTSBRIDGE, LONDON, ENGLAND

A strong reaction to the excesses and gimcrack quality – intellectually and aesthetically – to US style Postmodern design changed the face of youthful British architecture during the last decade of the twentieth century. A young generation of architects wanted a Modern world, but one that was less puritanical than that of Walter Gropius and the Bauhaus and reflected both a world that was once more affluent, more colourful and, somehow, less naive. In this house, tucked away on a formerly semi-industrial site in one of London's smartest districts, Seth Stein (born 1959) shaped a courtyard house that was Modern, had it own

distinct identity and yet borrowed cleverly and carefully from a wide range of twentieth-century sources. So, there's a touch of Le Corbusier here, Tadao Ando there; there's more than a hint of the work of Luis Barragán and, then again, references, by way of the courtyard plan, to a way of house building that dates back to Ancient Rome and even earlier

Confident use of pigmented colour and contrasting materials makes for an experience that is far from puritanical and yet the house has a sense of strength and quietude that the masters of the Modern Movement sought in their most inspired designs.

RICHARD ATTENBOROUGH CENTRE

IAN TAYLOR, 1997
LEICESTER, ENGLAND

Opened by the late Diana, Princess of Wales, the Richard Attenborough Centre for Disability and the Arts captures a particular moment in the story of British patronage: the late princess made charities, notably those concerned with the sick or disabled, a fashionable cause. This was good news for this low-key, thoughtful and elegant building that needed the kind of support that Diana was able to give it. The Centre's purpose was to train people with severe physical disabilities to become fully fledged artists. For the blind to be taught to sculpt or those with no arms to paint requires a special building. Ian Taylor provided a design that not once acts in the condescending way so many buildings for the disabled do, if not intentionally. It employs subtle changes of surfaces, acoustics and smell (the corridor lined with Cedar of Lebanon panels is a perfumed delight) to help students move about. There are no patronizing colours anywhere (why people who are disabled should have to look at lurid colours all day is a mystery), while subtle shifts of daylight and shadow are brought into the building through a top-lit atrium. The various spaces are flexible and the building has an enviable sense of determination. It is finished in simple materials and is one of those modest Modern buildings that is far more than the sum of its parts. Cleverness gives way to subtlety here.

MUSEUM OF ROWING

DAVID CHIPPERFIELD, 1997 HENLEY-ON-THAMES, ENGLAND

David Chipperfield (born 1954) pursued a determined "homage" to the early Modern Movement having left the office of Norman Foster to set up on his own in the 1980s. Influenced by traditional Japanese architecture, as were many pioneers of Modernism, Chipperfield developed an uncompromising aesthetic that could easily be perceived of as severe and unyielding. This made much sense in the fashionable shops and cafés he designed in Tokyo and London, but outside the new cosmopolis could seem altogether too cold and even aloof.

The Museum of Rowing was one of those happy accidents whereby the sensibility of the architect was seemingly threatened by local planning restraints and yet the result was happy. In this case, Chipperfield was forced to adopt a pitched roof – something he had eschewed to date – however, the roof of this handsome museum is what makes it likeable. The balance between the chaste walls and interiors and their timber roofs is exactly right and the building is all the better for it because it seems to express something about the nature of the construction of boats and of boatsheds. Planning restrictions have become increasingly tight in many parts of the world. Architects can no longer expect to pose, to set a compass on the face of the world, but are forced to stop, look, listen and to be deft and inventive.

BRITISH LIBRARY

COLIN ST JOHN WILSON, 1997 LONDON, ENGLAND

Colin St John Wilson (born 1922) liked to compare this vast pile of red bricks alongside George Gilbert Scott's exuberant Neo-Gothic Midland Grand Hotel to the work of Alvar Aalto. In particular he cited Aalto's wonderful town hall at Säynätsalo (p.211). The comparison cannot hold. Where Aalto's subtle work was gentle and natural and feels at one with its island landscape, Wilson's exterior is big, cold and obtrusive and the hard brick looks as if it has been cut with a cheese wire. The great redeeming quality of this gigantic tweed jacket is its imposing interior, which has some of the qualities of Aalto but probably more of the beautifully crafted town halls, libraries and railway stations of Sweden and Finland in the 1910s and 1920s.

The Library took many years to build, but was clearly designed to last for hundreds of years. So, oak desks and chairs (by Ron Carter) are as solid as the trees their wood came from, walls are lined in marble, heavy brass door handles and handrails wrapped in leather. The top-lit reading rooms – science on one side, arts on the other – are dignified places to study, while throughout the costly building Wilson provided ledges, nooks and corners for readers to meet.

In scale and ambition, and even in purpose, this curi-ous building – clumsy on the outside, all glorious within – resembles a grand medieval abbey revisited on London's teeming Euston Road.

GARAGE HOUSE

SETH STEIN, 1997 KNIGHTSBRIDGE, LONDON, ENGLAND

One of the best of a young generation of born-again white Modern architects in the 1990s, Seth Stein's imaginative houses take into account the new concerns of city-dwellers, like where to park the car. Car parking space had become prohibitively expensive in central London when Stein squeezed this light and airy house into a tiny plot in London's Knightsbridge, not far from the famous Harrods department store. Not only did the client want a parking place, he also wanted to look at his cars as works of art. Whether you agree or not, Dante Giacosa's design of the 1957 Fiat 500 is a lovely sculptural work. In this house it takes pride of place and can be raised in a very swish lift into what is, when the car is out for a spin, a living room.

The living room as garage is an idea that has been explored by several architects in the past – notably by Geoffrey Bawa (p.325) in Sri Lanka who designed the living room of his house in Colombo around his vintage Rolls-Royce – but never in such an ingenious way. The rest of the house is as neatly packed and organized as a small modern car.

The New Modernism of the 1990s is a style, no more and no less, and carries none of the moral baggage nor the obsession with functionalism that characterized the early Modern Movement. Stein's tiny house may be a new form of *existenzminimum*, but it has nothing to do with the quest for ideal housing for the working classes.

MEETING ROOM

CLAUDIO SILVESTRIN, 1997 HOMBRICH ART FOUNDATION, FRANKFURT, GERMANY

Built on the site of a former NATO missile base in what had been West Germany until the fall of the Berlin Wall in 1990, the Hombrich Art Foundation was the brainchild of a retired Frankfurt property developer who was also, as property developers so often were in the 1980s and 1990s a keen patron and collector of contemporary art. The Hombrich Foundation, however, was rather special. It comprised not just galleries devoted to the work of modern artists, but also studios and workshops, a cloister and cabins to stay in, a bakery, brewery and an organic farm. It was meant as a way of redressing a world that had been given over to war, a city to fast-buck architecture and farmland to agro-chemicals.

At the centre of the Foundation is this meeting room or place of contemplation by Claudio Silvestrin. A simple space, it consists of little but light falling beautifully onto warm white walls, a stone floor and benches. It is the opposite of all the architecture that has been built in "Bankfurt", as Frankfurt became known in the prosperous 1980s. And in Silvestrin's hands it works: it is one of those spaces that stops people chattering and quietens the human spirit.

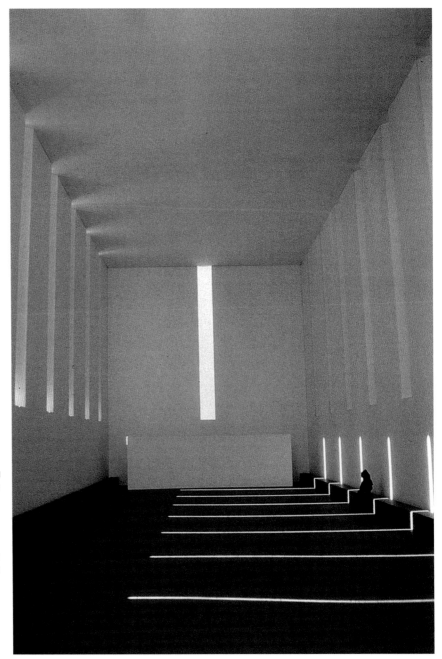

STEIN HOUSE

RICK MATHER, 1997 HIGHGATE, LONDON, ENGLAND

Rick Mather (born 1937) is an American architect who came from Portland, Oregon to London and has worked quietly on the design of refined white Modern houses, restaurants, museums and galleries. His is an approach that has developed project by project without fuss, drama or error. A well-known chain of sophisticated Chinese restaurants in London and Hong Kong – "Zen" – made Mather something of a household name among people who dined out in fashionable style in the 1980s. His proposals for delicate and difficult projects, such as the extension of the historic Dulwich Picture Gallery by John Soane or the Wallace Collection in central London, are models of architectural good manners. So, too, is this white and glass family house in north London.

Its precision, clarity and delicacy of manner are all hallmarks of Mather's unerring style of elegant restraint. Here, though, Mather went that bit further and created a house that is almost ethereal. It could hardly be described as a machine for living for it is as unlike a machine as a house can be. In this sense, Mather proved that the language of early Modernism, refined through usage and practice over many decades, had mutated into a manner of speech very different from the original strident posturing of Le Corbusier and the Bauhaus. Most of all, it was very hushed.

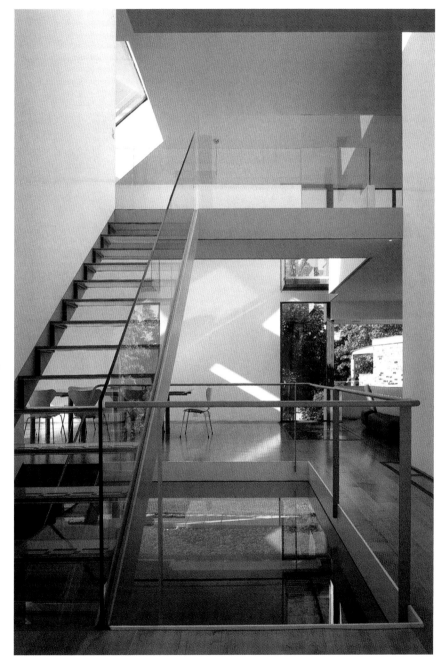

RUSKIN LIBRARY

MACCORMAC–JAMIESON PRITCHARD, 1998 LANCASTER, LANCASHIRE, ENGLAND

John Ruskin (1819–1900) was a fiery Victorian critic and seer, famous as the champion of the great English painter J. M. W. Turner and for his books *Modern Painters* and *The Seven Lamps of Architecture*. He wrote like an archangel might, looked like an Old Testament prophet and railed against bad art, poor architecture and a social fabric too thin to provide the working people of Britain with anything like a decent living or education. This handsome white library was built as a kind of entrance gate to the University of Lancaster overlooking the sands of Morecambe Bay and not far from Ruskin's romantic home, Brantwood, in the Lake District.

Its plan is in the shape of an eye (Ruskin was always asking people to look closely, to argue with the eye) and it is designed to be a modern version of the baptistery at Parma or Siena Cathedral in Tuscany. At each end of the elliptical building, tall windows – one an entrance – rise its full height. They reveal the richly coloured "treasury" or holy of holies in which Ruskin papers from previously separate collections have been garnered. The treasury and indeed the whole of the interior are finished in warm and richly coloured materials that contrast powerfully with the white, crystalline walls. It is a happy place to work in on a dark and stormy night.

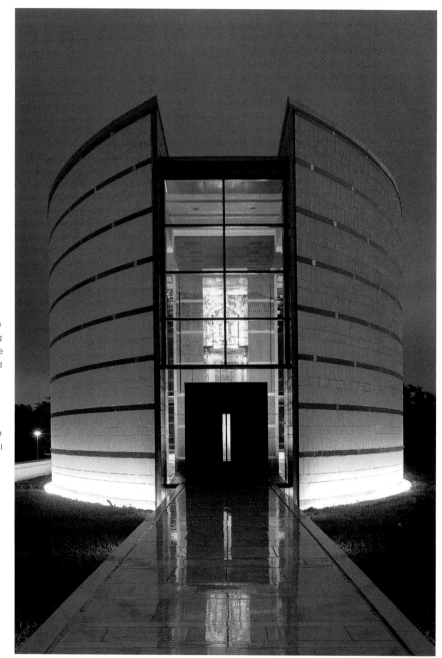

WALSALL ART GALLERY

CARUSO–ST JOHN, 1999 WALSALL, ENGLAND

Many new museums opened in provincial English towns in the 1980s and 1990s are located either in cultural ghettoes or else in converted red-brick Victorian warehouses. Caruso–St John's Walsall Art Gallery is a shining exception. And shine it does, its tall walls clad in various shades of grey terracotta that sparkle on wet, sunny days. It shines too in the sense that it is a brand new design by a firm of young architects with ideas very much of their own. It is sited in the heart of a new shopping development, and far from being the arty-smarty shops one would expect around and about a gallery, the shops here are branches of the chain stores Woolworth and British Home Stores. In Walsall, art has been brought down from Parnassus to the market place and people doing a bit of Saturday morning shopping in "Woolies" can go for coffee in the gallery's rooftop terrace restaurant.

There is nothing precious about the design of this rigorously planned building, which owes its internal logic, and thus the irregular window spacing, to the nature and scale of the collections arranged within it. It has a toughness that belies the delicacy of much of the work on show and has clearly been built to last. The one enjoyable affectation of the project is the digging of a canal basin up to the gallery at one end, a detail that has more than a touch of the great gardens of Versailles about it.

TATE GALLERY OF MODERN ART

HERZOG–DE MEURON, 2000 BANKSIDE, LONDON, ENGLAND

To build a new gallery or convert an existing building. That was the choice the Tate Gallery faced when it set about looking for a home for its ever-expanding art collection.

The problem with building from scratch was the lack of a suitable site in central London and the fact that the gallery's shrewd director, Nicholas Serota, knew that it would take a long time to steer a worthwhile new building through tortuous planning procedures. The redundant Bankside Power Station was an inspired choice. A majestic temple of power, it stands on the banks of the Thames opposite St Paul's Cathedral. It is connected to Wren's great civic temple by a lithe new footbridge designed by Norman Foster, the sculptor Anthony Caro and Chris Wise, an engineer from Ove Arup and Partners. A new Underground station links the new Tate to the West End and a new river bus service stops at Bankside.

The conversion of the mighty power station was favoured by conservationists as well as those looking forward to the pristine galleries designed by the Swiss practice Herzog de Meuron. Jacques Herzog (born 1951) and Pierre de Meuron (born 1951) run their office from Zürich and are well known for a strict yet romantic new Modern architecture which relies for much of its impact on tactile materials that belie the need for conventional decoration.

REICHSTAG

NORMAN FOSTER, 1999 BERLIN, GERMANY

Built to house the parliamentary assembly of the Second Reich, the Reichstag (1894) was a heavy-handed exercise in Neo-Renaissance style by Paul Bellot. In February 1933, less than a month after Hitler was voted into power it burned down in mysterious circumstances. Hitler blamed the Communists and used the occasion to ban all parties opposing his NSDAP (Nazi Party). It would have been demolished if Albert Speer had been able to build his giant domed assembly hall (p.54) here, but it survived both the Nazis and World War Two, during which it was further damaged by bombing. It was patched up between 1958 and 1972 and used as a museum, then dressed up in silver sheeting by the artist Christo in 1996.

In the last year of the twentieth-century, the Reichstag reopens as the new seat of a united German government – Germany having been split into capitalist West and communist East from 1945 to 1990 – with Berlin firmly back in its role as the German capital. The building has been remodelled at great cost by Norman Foster.

Its distinguishing feature is a glass dome over the assembly chamber up which visitors can climb to view the city and to watch that remarkable thing: a democratic German government in action.

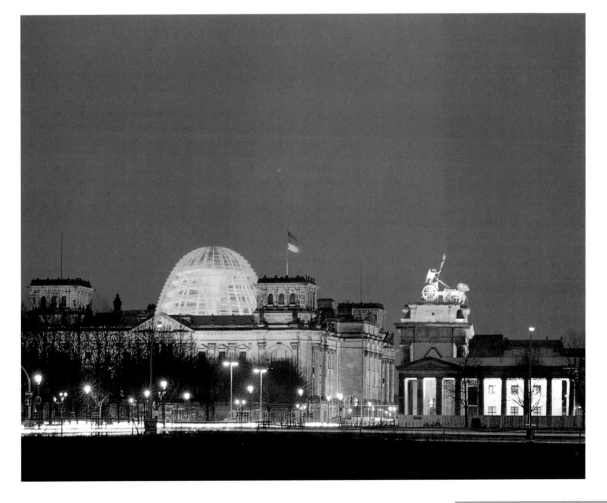

THE ARK

FUTURE SYSTEMS, 2001 DONCASTER, YORKSHIRE, ENGLAND

This exquisite butterfly of a building was designed as the heart of the Earth Centre, an ecology park built on the site of former slag heaps in South Yorkshire. Doncaster had, for many decades, been famous for its coal mines and its locomotive works. By the mid-1980s, as Britain gave up manufacturing almost anything worthwhile in favour of financial services and retailing, Doncaster had all but lost its purpose.

The Earth Centre was a thoughtful way of reclaiming land once given over to coal mining and helping to give the town a new focus. The centre's principal activities – research and the dissemination of information about ecological matters to the widest possible public – were housed in a network of pavilions. The most spectacular of these was to be an exhibition hall designed by Jan Kaplicky and Amanda Levete of Future Systems. This giant, yet gentle and low-lying, building was to have been dug into a hillside and to have resembled a huge butterfly. The triple-height interior was to have been every bit as organic as the sensuous exterior. The atmosphere inside would have been light, airy and delightful.

The Ark at Doncaster was a sensitive riposte to London's Millennium Dome (p.407), and was, at the time, one of the most eagerly awaited new buildings of the new century. Sadly, the Earth Centre went bankrupt and closed in 2004. Jan Kaplicky, an original and much missed talent, died in 2009.

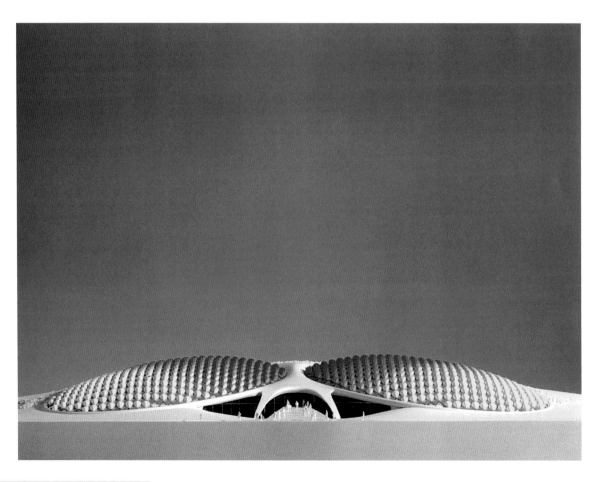

FAITH HOUSE

TONY FRETTON, 2002 HOLTON LEE, DORSET, ENGLAND

Here is one of those modest, yet magical, buildings with the power to transform the way you feel for the better, not through fashionable and expensive bombast, but with intelligence and, ultimately, the kind of subtlety you would be hard-pressed to put a price on. The Faith House is a meeting hall and place of meditation for a low-key, non-denominational Christian charitable institution. Fretton describes Faith House as being built in the spirit of a "poor village church", yet, although very cheap to build, its prefabricated and immaculately detailed timber frame touches the garden beside the old farmhouse of Holton Lee in much the same cool, abstract way as Doric temples adorned the rustic landscapes of ancient Greece.

The entrance front of this cedar-clad building is essentially a stripped classical portico seen through the price-conscious lens of the early twenty-first century. Unlike a classical temple, however, it lets you see right through two of the three bays to the fields beyond that tumble down to the sea at Poole Harbour. One bay – the entrance porch – leads, in one direction, into the central bay, a lobby fronted with a sheer glass screen. In the other it leads into the meditation room. This is a 3.5-metre (11-ft) cube, its walls painted silver and planted around with a ring of aromatic, floor-to-ceiling silver birch trunks. This room has no function other than to slow you down, to help you locate that still point in the turning world.

CISTERCIAN MONASTERY

JOHN PAWSON, 2004 NOVÝ DVÙR, CZECH REPUBLIC

In the 1990s, the chicest new fashion shops came, bizarrely, to borrow the rigorous aesthetic of the monastery, with none coming closer than the Calvin Klein store in New York, designed by John Pawson in 1995. Five years later, Pawson received a hand-written letter from a Czech engineer asking if he would like to design a monastery for a Cistercian Trappist community in Bohemia. The letter was genuine. The engineer was acting as a go-between for the monks, who rarely travel, and were shy. Somehow, the abbot had seen a picture of Pawson's Calvin Klein store. Its tables are like altars, the jacket-lined recesses like chapels, and the architecture of the space could be mistaken for the nave of a well-lit modern church. And so

it came to pass that the monks of Nový Dvùr came to London to see Pawson. If ever there were a marriage made in heaven, this was it. What the monks learned, to their delight, is that this was the commission Pawson had dreamed of for decades. A passion for Cistercian architecture had haunted his work from the outset. The resulting church at the heart of this thoughtfully modernized monastery is as haunting as it is beautiful. A drop in the floor level behind the altar, in conjunction with light entering at a low level, creates the illusion that the apse is floating in a haze of luminescence. Daylight filtering into the lime-rendered interior gives the church a radiant, muted quality. It might just make religion the new shopping.

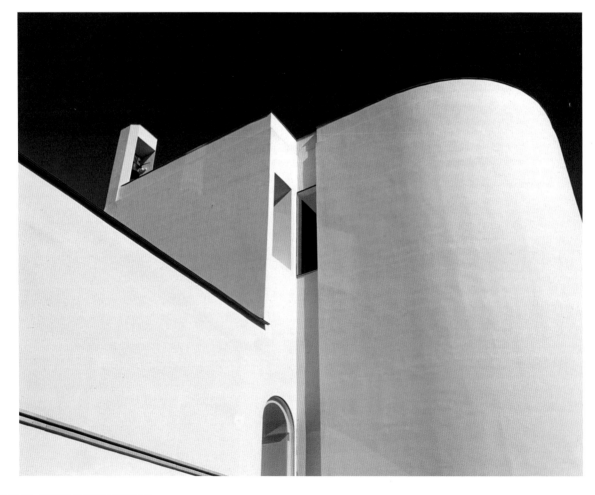

MUSEUM OF MODERN ART

YOSHIO TANIGUCHI, 2005 NEW YORK, USA

Rebuilt at vast cost, the new look MoMA is as discreet as a major downtown museum can possibly be. In fact, Taniguchi's design was criticized locally for being too low-key. There was popular support for a far more crowd-pleasing, sexed-up look by the Swiss architects Herzog and de Meuron, yet MoMA settled, perhaps wisely, on an almost Zen-like design, as far as anything remotely Zen-like is possible in the noisy sprawl and pushy rush of central Manhattan. In any case, the original MoMA (1939), designed by Edward Durrell Stone and Philip Goodwin and one of the first International Style buildings on the east coast, was never anything other than a model of preppy discretion and quiet urban manners. The next addition, by Philip Johnson, MoMA's first curator of architecture, dating from

1953, was, if anything, even more restrained.

Taniguchi's design creates a new entrance for the museum, restores the 1939 wing, adds a light-filled five-storey atrium connecting the various galleries, and brings two hooded, glazed galleries facing one another across a restored sculpture garden, one of the best-loved meeting spaces in central Manhattan. The result is all very subtle. In fact, all Taniguchi's buildings are characterized by the most subtle plays of daylight brought gently, yet persistently, into their smooth-surfaced concrete, stone and timber interiors. "At MoMA," says Glenn Lowry, MoMA's director "we aimed to have daylight wherever possible, to get away from the labyrinth-like environment we had before." They succeeded.

SANTA MARIA CHURCH

ALVARO SIZA, 2005 MARCO DE CANAVES, PORTUGAL

This fine, white geometric church by Portugal's most celebrated contemporary architect freshly adorns a small town in the Douro Valley. A simple double cube of white concrete with few windows, this is religious architecture at its most elemental. Its severe design gives little away, even though the ends of the church prove, when you meet them face to facade, to be moulded in ways that recall the work of great Baroque architects, both Portuguese and Roman. Even then, these elements are not so much stripped away as somehow melted down, suggesting that although this quietly beautiful building owes something to history, it is somehow all but outside history, too.

The ceremonial entrance is through a pair of heroic doors, measuring 10 metres (33 ft) high by 3 metres (9 ft) wide. At first they seem almost too large for this parish church; but they are a brilliant device, welcoming, when thrown open, the whole town inside on feast days and other celebrations. Inside, an equally dramatic window running the length of one side of the church offers views out to a seemingly infinite rural landscape. Another wall is curved, following the contours of the landscape and evoking the feeling, as with the great window, that the church is not just a place of the spirit but belongs to the spirit of the place. Here in the Douro Valley, Siza, an old fashioned Modern architect, proves that there is life yet – both spiritual and physical – in the design of new parish churches.

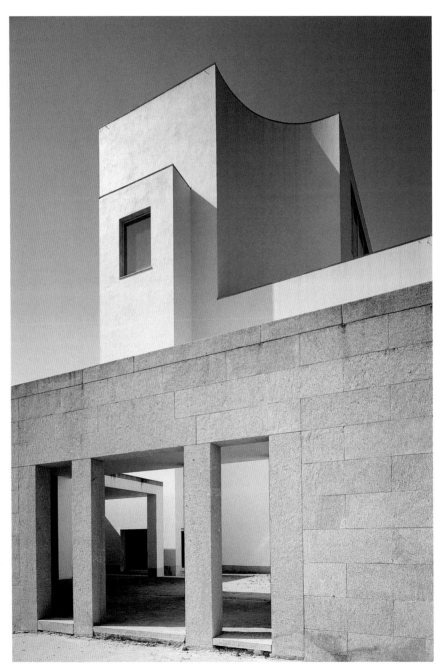

TURNER CONTEMPORARY GALLERY

DAVID CHIPPERFIELD 2011 MARGATE, KENT, ENGLAND

This is where the great English artist JMW Turner came to stare at the boisterous English Channel and to paint some of his greatest seascapes. The idea of a gallery in his name here at Margate was not so much to celebrate the nineteenth-century artist, but to encourage those who might follow in his wake and to help bring fresh economic and cultural life to what, by the end of the twentieth century had become a rather run-down seaside resort. The original design, by the Norwegian architects Snohetta (p.134) was in the guise of a concrete fin or wave braving the sea itself. Although memorable and romantic, the idea was considered far too costly and a hostage to the sea; the English Channel cuts up rough and cold on this highly exposed corner of the country. David Chipperfield's replacement design is less dramatic than Snohetta's, but it faces the sea with confidence and has the look of a large artist's studio that seems apt. Inside, the gallery has a raw, if crafted, feeling ideal for allowing works of art to take pride of place. What matters most for the architect here is the quality and play of daylight inside the individual galleries. Turner thought the light here at Margate "the loveliest in Europe", and he, if anyone, knew. This is very much the architecture of modesty: robust and intelligent and set against the desire of many contemporary architects and their clients to let rip and show off.

POSTMODERNISM

"LESS IS A BORE." ROBERT VENTURI

Here are some of the most colourful pages in this book. "Less is a bore", wrote Robert Venturi (p.309) in his widely read and all too well digested book *Complexity and Contradiction in Architecture* (1966). Venturi might have thought 50 years of Modern Movement architecture a bore, yet the complex and contradictory architecture he proposed as a riposte and way out of the tenacious grip of the Modernist trap proved to be a bigger bore altogether. Architects with a light touch could get away with making outlandish and funny buildings, but there were precious few of them. Freed from the binding corsets of Modernism, most of those who tried on Postmodern dress soon discovered that letting it all hang out was neither seemly nor decorous. On the whole it was plain dumb.

Postmodernism in some form or other was probably inevitable. The Modern experiment had become tired and corrupted in any case; it badly needed a rest. Architects meanwhile were, like anyone else who lived through the 1960s, bombarded with new forms of imagery from Pop culture, advertising, television and new movements in art in which the collage and irony played king and queen. It was not long before buildings emerged that were collages of earlier styles, making knowing references to famous designs. Before too long Philip Johnson had dressed a Manhattan office block in the guise of a skyscraping Chippendale cabinet (p.323). How we were meant to laugh. Ooh, Philip, you are a wag. And anyone who didn't want to know was simply a bore.

There was, though, another side to Postmodernism that was ultimately more interesting and worthwhile. This stemmed from investigations into history and context by architects in various parts of the world who were struggling to reconcile history and local precedent with Modern designs. The Torre Velasca in Milan by BBPR (p.308) springs to mind as does, much later, such striking monuments to the memory of a specific place as Daniel Libeskind's Jewish Museum in Berlin (p.349).

Such buildings have little to do with the gimcrack excesses of US "Po-Mo", although they are certainly Postmodern. Perhaps a parallel can be drawn here between the Modern Movement as it emerged in Europe – zealous, puritanical, intense – and in the US, as the International Style – chic, amoral and relaxed. Nevertheless there were architects who seemed to be well equipped to play a complex, if outlandish, game, and to score lots of points with buildings of great verve and character that were neither puerile nor kitsch: James Stirling and Michael Wilford's Staatsgalerie in Stuttgart was one example (p.331), Frank Gehry's Guggenheim Museum in Bilbao another (p.347).

At the beginning of the twenty-first century, buildings that transcend the early posturings of an architecture struggling to free itself from Modernism, such as those by Gehry and Libeskind, have begun to emerge. Such architects have moved away from the concerns of self-conscious Postmodernists and, if anything, their work is moving in a modern Organic direction. Perhaps, though, labels again prove to be their own undoing; it is just as likely that these designers are simply free spirits whose work is hard to pin down. Whatever, both Gehry and Libeskind have proved that modern architecture can be highly expressive and play emotional mind-games without needing to be funny or crudely subversive. After all, how subversive can a corporate headquarters be even if clothed in fancy dress?

The fashion for outrageous clothes, however, was ultimately short-lived. It also produced its own reaction. By the early 1990s, young architects the world over were returning to a clean-cut Neomodernism; if this lacked the energy and crusading spirit of the white architecture of the 1920s, it was some sort of attempt to sweep the boards clean and to start again after two decades of mostly silly, cardboard cut-out design.

TORRE VELASCA

BBPR, 1958 MILAN, ITALY

Here is a very literal expression
of the idea of the "High Game
of Architecture", or else the
beginnings of Postmodernism.
The Torre Velasca, a 26-storey
office tower in the heart of
Milan, can be looked on either
as an example of architectural
wit, a game played high
into the Lombardy sky, or a
brave attempt to reconcile the
demands of mid-twentieth-
century property development
with those of traditional
design. For, quite clearly, this
idiosyncratic building, is a
modern representation of a
medieval Italian tower. With its
top eight storeys cantilevered
out from the main body of the
building and a framework of
what look like buttresses, the
Torre Velasca distantly echoes
the forms of the medieval
Castello Sforzesco, one of
Milan's principal attractions. Just
two years before its completion,
BBPR, the team that designed
Torre Velasca, had designed
a museum installation inside
the walls of Castello Sforzesco.
The team comprised Gianluigi
Banfi (1910-45), Ludovico
Belgiojoso (born 1909),
Enrico Peressutti (1908–73)
and Ernesto Nathan Rogers
(1909–69), uncle of Richard
Rogers, who formed BBPR
in 1932. From early on their
concern was to challenge the
dogmatic nature of Modernism.
For them, architecture needed
to be rooted in specific places
and to respond to local building
traditions: Torre Velasca is the
high point of beliefs that were to
be taken up widely in the next
three decades.

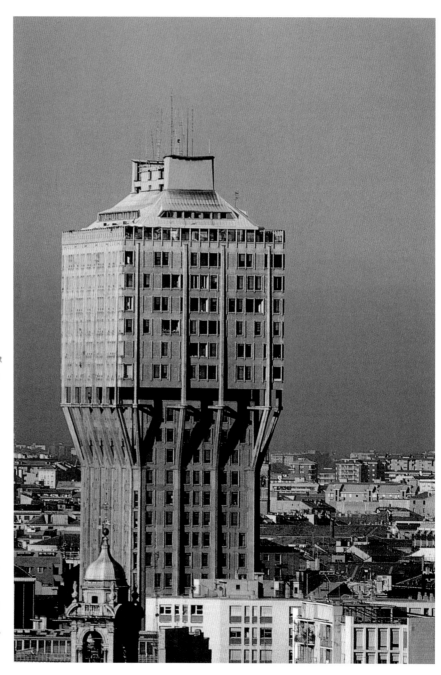

MOTHER'S HOUSE

ROBERT VENTURI 1964 CHESTNUT HILL, PHILADELPHIA, USA

One small house for an architect, but a giant leap for architecture. The Mother's House by Robert Venturi (born 1925) is generally taken as the first knowing step into the choppy seas of Postmodernism. Why? Venturi was the first architect to publish a Postmodern theory of architecture. His book, *Complexity and Contradiction in Architecture* (1966), was written at much the same time as the Mother's House was built – it really was for his mother; many good young architects with wealthy and adoring mums start this way. Venturi's basic premise was that "less is a bore", a witty riposte to Mies van der Rohe's famous maxim "less is more". Instead he offered an architecture that took into account all the richness, oddities, quirks and even embarrassments of the world it occupied and tried to represent. So, anything could go, more or less. An architect could drop "quotes" into his buildings whenever and wherever he wanted to and these could be interpreted as knowing and amusing. Why shouldn't a Modern architect stick Classical mouldings onto a new building? Why not raid the picture book of history? As a reaction against the puritanical strictures of Mies and the increasing banality of international architecture, Venturi's musings seemed to make sense. *Complexity and Contradiction in Architecture* was destined to have widespread influence, yet the architecture that it gave rise to was never really much fun and rarely inspired.

The Mother's House speaks for itself. Compare it to Le Corbusier's Villa Savoye at Poissy (p.181).

LINCOLN CENTER

PHILIP JOHNSON, ET AL, 1966 NEW YORK CITY, USA

A mighty Renaissance piazza, translated to Manhattan by way of what looks suspiciously like Fascist Italy – it would have fitted well into Mussolini's EUR (p.59) – the Lincoln Center is representative of the "historicist", or early Postmodern approach to urban design and architecture. This rather odd cultural plaza was laid out by the grand Beaux-Arts architect and planner Wallace Harrison (1895–1981) who had previously worked on the Rockefeller Center (p.199) and the United Nations complex on Manhattan's eastern seaboard (1947–50). Harrison designed the rather spookily arcaded Metropolitan Opera House (1966) while Philip Johnson designed the New York State Theatre (1964)

and Harrison's partner Max Abramovitz (1908–76) designed the Philharmonic Hall (1962).

The Lincoln Center marked the start of a new formalism in US architecture and the beginnings of a new-found obsession with history and European urbanism. It remains a somewhat cool and aloof space and has never seemed quite at home in Manhattan's busy grid of commercial skyscrapers. It looked at its best in Mel Brooks' movie, *The Producers*, when the stars, Max Bialystock (Zero Mostel) and Leo Bloom (Gene Wilder), hit on the idea of making millions by producing the worst play on Broadway, "Springtime for Hitler"; Brooks could not have chosen a more apt setting.

PORT GRIMAUD

FRANÇOIS SPOERRY, 1969 FRANCE

Port Grimaud is a fantasy seaside fishing port, a playground for wealthy things with yachts and time on their hands. It was the creation of François Spoerry (born 1912) and its make-believe architecture is realized mostly in concrete, although few visitors to this holiday village would guess it. Ersatz creation it might be, yet Port Grimaud works. Spoerry caught the feeling and character of a Mediterranean fishing port with quiet aplomb and reinterpreted it with a sure and gentle touch for those who wanted an escape from the Modern world with all mod cons secretly on tap. Port Grimaud, however, is not alone. Throughout history, architects and their patrons have tried, with varying degrees of success, to design oases of the historical and romantic imagination. Poor, "mad" Ludwig II of Bavaria and his fantasmagoric palaces, Neuschwanstein chief among them, springs to mind. So, of course, does Walt Disney, who adapted Neuschwanstein for his Sleeping Beauty's castle.

The model, if there was a specific one, for Port Grimaud and its British counterpart – Portmeirion by Clough Williams-Ellis in north Wales – was the picturesque Italian seaside village, Portofino. Portofino became a symbol of the perfect holiday escape for those in love with architecture and an azure sea. Port Grimaud remains hugely popular and has been much copied in spirit, if not in such loving detail, since.

HYATT REGENCY HOTEL

JOHN PORTMAN, 1974 SAN FRANCISCO, CALIFORNIA, USA

An innate commercial flair has ensured that John Portman (born 1924) has developed and designed some of the world's most significant hotels. Portman wanted to be able to shape both the look and the programme of his buildings, and he has succeeded in spectacular style. His trademark has been the giant hotel lobby, a vast and glittering space shooting up in the far heights of the buildings, animated by glazed "wall-climber" lifts, lit as if part of a funfair, as well as by glittering shops and cafés. In this way, Portman brought the grand drama of the great US railroad stations together with the razzmatazz of Hollywood. These were very exciting places

to be when they first raced up in the 1970s, but much belittled by Portman's fellow architects who thought them outrageous. Whether in the design of hotels or shopping malls, they would soon be following in Portman's giant and pioneering footsteps.

Portman was born in Walhalla, South Carolina. He trained at the Georgia Institute of Technology setting up his own architectural practice there in 1953. Success came with his breakaway hotels, and through the 1970s he built very many of them. The Hyatt Regency in San Francisco, is, perhaps, the most dramatic of Portman's hotels.

PIAZZA D'ITALIA

CHARLES MOORE, 1978 NEW ORLEANS, LOUISIANA, USA

A Postmodern confection for the Italian, and more specifically the Sicilian, community of New Orleans, Piazza d'Italia is a genuinely entertaining urban set design that pokes fun at the pomposity of Classical architecture while revelling in its theatrical quality. The centrepiece of the circular piazza is a fountain based on the map of the heel of Italy. From the spandrels of the "ironic" screen above, twin heads – portraits of the architect – spout water. Originally, the scheme was to have been more ambitious than it is, with a flamboyant Italian restaurant leading off the large ochre triumphal arch and its "Deli" order pilasters.

Moore (1925–93) had long worked on subverting the canons of architecture. Born in Michigan and educated there and at Princeton, he set up his own practice in Connecticut in 1970, working as part of a wider team with other offices. Moore had a great interest in breaking down the conventional barriers of internal and external spaces, beginning with the design of his own house in Orinda, California (1962). It was a theme he pursued throughout his career. Whether you find his later work engaging or nor depends upon the nature of your sense of humour, a quality many architects deny themselves once they graduate. Piazza d'Italia is funny, but the same thing may not be true of a Berlin housing scheme (1980) in which a Disney-like steamboat motif is mixed with clipped, military Prussian Classicism.

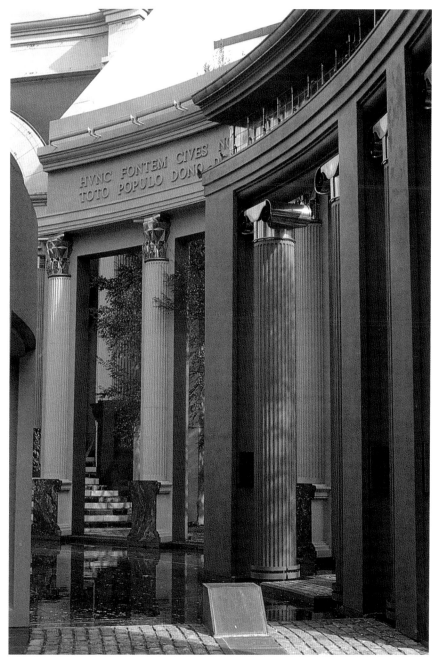

WALDEN 7

TALLER DE ARQUITECTURA, 1975 ST JUST DESVERN, BARCELONA, SPAIN

A huge block of flats resembling a fairy-tale castle from a distance, Walden 7 is less attractive close up. For many years, the block was surrounded by netting as tiles once attached to the walls hurtled to the ground. This was exciting but rather disconcerting. Walden 7 is interesting for being one of the major stepping stones leading to the extraordinary sequence of prefabricated Neoclassical housing projects designed in France by Ricardo Bofill (born 1939) and his Taller de Arquitectura (p.62–3).

The son of a wealthy Catalan builder, Bofill studied in Barcelona and Geneva before buying an old cement factory near Walden 7 and filling the former silos with fellow architects and with artists, poets, musicians, pets and parrots. It all seemed like a set from a Fellini film, and as surreal in practice as a scene from one of Buñuel's. Remarkably, this iconoclastic practice thrived and especially so when Bofill turned it away from early experiments in Brutalism to a reworking of local traditions – as, supposedly, in the design of Walden 7 – and then to an industrial Neoclassicism. Taller de Arquitectura was certainly fascinating, and not a little infuriating, but what puzzled most was why so many French cities were willing to adopt such crazy stuff.

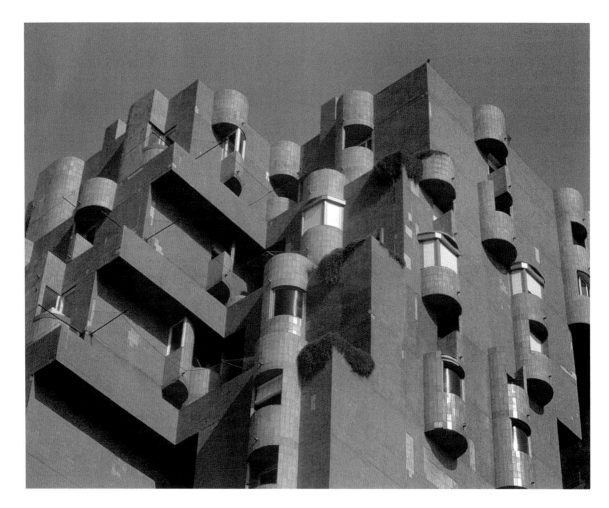

BEST SUPERMARKET

SITE, 1975 HOUSTON, TEXAS

James Wines (born 1932) pioneered a programme of what he called "De-architecture" in the 1970s aided by various members of his design team SITE (Sculpture in the Environment). The idea was quite funny in a *Beavis and Butthead* kind of way. But, once you have sniggered at the artfully tilted and broken façades of no more than three of the Best supermarkets SITE designed, the joke has worn pretty thin. Architecture just isn't very funny (except unintentionally) and Wines was trying a little too hard. What the hell; supermarkets are extremely boring buildings at the best of times and at least the Best buildings raise a smile the first time you see them. Perhaps regular customers laughed too for the first few months, but they probably got to worrying about the price of frozen corn cobs and treated the buildings like any other store. So, while the Best supermarkets appear to be subverting the sacred world of US retailing, they are doing no such thing. In fact they are superb adverts and have done much to promote the chain even to those who, smiling at the pictures, will never get to the Almeda-Genoa Shopping Center, Houston, Texas.

EATON CENTRE

ZEIDLER ROBERTS, 1977 TORONTO, CANADA

The mother of all modern shopping malls, the Eaton Centre is also one of the finest and, if you like this sort of thing, among the most convincing. This, perhaps, is because its architecture is more than skin deep. It has integrity, which cannot be said for the plague of shopping malls that has ravaged the face of so many countries worldwide in the last two decades of the twentieth century. Mall culture encouraged people off the streets and into a hermetic, safe and, above all, controlled world in which everything is a given and human beings are transformed into zombies, passive machines for shopping. This is not everyone's view, and certainly not if you happen to live in Toronto where the winters are bitterly cold and the only way to survive is to stay indoors. Quite why third-rate replicas of the Eaton Centre are needed in countries with temperate climates is a mystery that archeologists of the future will have to wrestle with as they explore the ruins of these air-conditioned behemoths. The Eaton Centre, however, is a handsome building inside and clearly based on Joseph Paxton's hugely influential Crystal Palace of 1851.

HILLINGDON CIVIC CENTRE

RMJM, 1979 LONDON, ENGLAND

Very rum. A concatenation of bricks and tiles that is somehow meant to represent the friendly face of local government in one of London's western-most suburbs. The upshot is a confused giant of a building that is not quite sure whether it wants to be friendly or not. With its defensive walls and even what looks like a moat, Hillingdon Civic Centre (or what used to be called a town hall or council offices) seems to want to keep its public at bay. Or is it meant to be the Englishman's Castle? Or were the architects trying somehow to knit as many semi-detached suburban houses together to give the appearance of one big and jolly house that everyone would recognize as belonging to an area dominated by avenue after close after cul-de-sac of tweedy brick houses? The answer lies somewhere in the folksy world of what was often referred to as English "Neovernacular" design. In fact, there was plenty that was "neo" in the design of this peculiar building. Behind that tidal wave of orange brick and folksy pitched roofs, there lurks a largely open-plan interior based very much on Herman Herzberger's Centraal Beheer insurance offices in Apeldoorn (p.254).

RMJM (Robert Matthew Johnson-Marshall and Partners) was a prolific architectural practice capable of designing in any number of styles, although inclined, as here, to be tweedy.

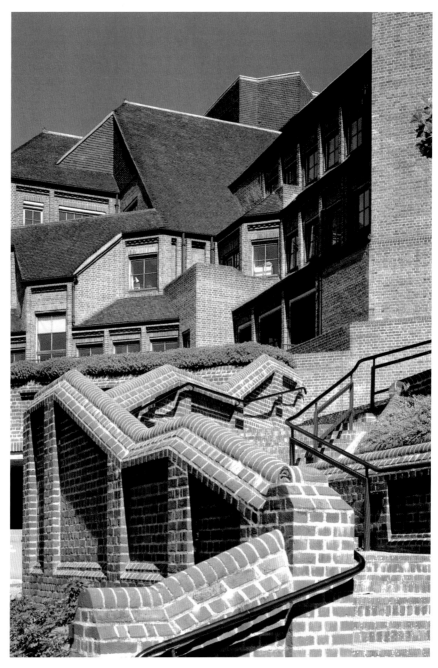

ST MARK'S ROAD HOUSING

JEREMY AND FENELLA DIXON, 1979 MAIDA VALE, LONDON, ENGLAND

From the time of the "oil crisis" of 1973 and the shocking collapse of Britain's economy under the Tory premiership of Edward Heath in the "winter of discontent" (1973–4), the design and construction of high-rise housing and giant prefabricated concrete estates were all but ended. In fact, over the next 25 years, Britain was lucky to see any new public housing of any scale, quality or ambition. Small-scale schemes, however, made a quiet return, as a reaction against "high-rise horrors", as an economic necessity and as architects themselves turned away from the inward-looking estate and, quite literally, came back onto the street. This modest, yet delightful, row of houses in west London showed

how it was again possible to design intimate, small-scale homes that had a real character and presence and if gentle were not twee. The architects, Jeremy and Fenella Dixon, had a talent for getting this subtle balance just right. With their endearing mixture of Dutch and pure London details, these houses add to the architectural mix of the street they animate without being loud or showy even though here are hints of impending Postmodernism in their fashionably "eclectic" façades.

Jeremy Dixon went on to develop the idea further with houses in the same area that drew imaginatively on historical precedent without recourse to pastiche.

ZENTRALSPARKASSE

GÜNTHER DOMENIG, 1980 VIENNA, AUSTRIA

When was banking ever funny? Perhaps this bank is meant to make you laugh; perhaps its prognathous jaws – just look at that entrance – are a reminder of how the bank manager can chew your head off when you go too far into the red. Maybe Günther Domenig (born 1934) simply wanted to strike a pose in the polite and rather dull Favoriten, one of Vienna's central shopping streets. Whatever, this is one of those potty buildings that children adore and which has inevitably become something of a tourist attraction in a city that has too many of these already. On the surface – and only on the surface – Vienna is such a genteel city; no wonder spirited architects have wished to shake it up a little. Adolf Loos must have turned in his grave when this crazy confection opened in 1980. The nuttiness does not end with the scrunched-up metal façade. Inside and up the stairs of the six-storey building, pipes and ducts appear to worm their way out of bending and twisting walls as if auditioning for parts in Terry Gilliam's film *Brazil*. A gruesome concrete hand reaches out from one wall as if Roman Polanski had been asked to help with the decoration. Although batty, the bank is finished with a typically Viennese attention to detail which somehow redeems its decorative excess.

TEATRO DEL MONDO

ALDO ROSSI, 1980 VENICE, ITALY

This beautiful and ethereal tower was built for the 1980 Venice Biennale and, sadly, broken up long ago. The wooden tower (an iron frame covered with planks) was mounted on a raft and towed along the waterways of Venice where it could be seen weaving its way past the city's magnificent and wobbly monuments before being anchored alongside the Customs' House on the Dorsoduro in the shadow of the great dome of Il Salute and across the Grand Canal from St Mark's Square.

The tower was a romantic gesture to one of the world's most romantic cities by an architect always described as a Rationalist. Aldo Rossi (1931–97) may well have been a "Rat", but his was a romantic, aesthetic rationalism, owing more to say the haunting townscape paintings of de Chirico than to the scientific rationalism of many contemporary German and US architects. Rossi, born and educated in Milan, was an important theorist. He had worked for the journals *Casabella* and *Il Contemporeano* before designing buildings, and in 1966 he published his manifesto *L'Architettura della Città*. His architecture and his cities were, for the most part, mournful creations, silent monuments, funereal and empty. In certain contexts – the San Cataldo cemetery, Milan (p.330) – this had its place; in others, such as the social housing he designed in the guise of a seemingly infinite and icy arcade in Milan's Gallaratese 2 suburb, it seemed downright spooky. The Teatro del Mondo was the delightful exception.

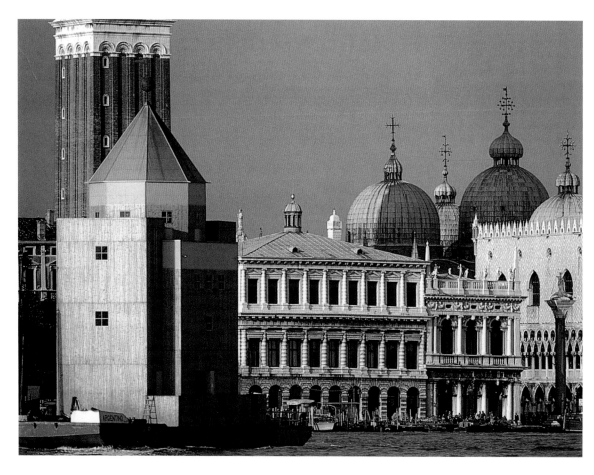

GARDEN GROVE CHURCH

PHILIP JOHNSON AND JOHN BURGEE, 1980 LOS ANGELES, CALIFORNIA, USA

Only in America could you find a building quite like this. Commissioned by a wealthy preacher, the "Crystal Cathedral" is a vast, technologically sophisticated and utterly banal expression of the power of bible-bashing and cult Christian sects. Truly vast – 125 by 60 by 49 metres (410 x 196 x 160 ft) high – Johnson and Burgee's cathedral is based on a plan in the shape of an elongated four-pronged star. From this a technically brilliant, white-coated steel structure rises up at dramatic angles to reach a peak high above the preacher's podium. This frame is then clad entirely in reflective glass: the interior of the building remains as mysterious as God until you enter. Inside, up to 3,000 people can sit in white-marbled splendour. As this is Los Angeles, the car park is as big as the church.

By this stage of his long career, Philip Johnson had experimented with just about every style going. The Crystal Cathedral was a diversion into a kind of Hollywood Hi-Tech, but it was certainly no dead end for the century's most determined eclectic. A few years later, his headquarters for the Pittsburgh Plate Glass corporation was designed as a kind of Barry and Pugin Westminster extravaganza, the whole prickly conceit faced in acres of glass. And as the architect might have said, "You ain't seen nothing yet."

THE ATLANTIS

ARQUITECTONICA, 1982 MIAMI, FLORIDA, USA

Funny what a little sunshine will do. Take one straight up and down 18-storey apartment block. Add bright primary colours, a few zany details and bathe in bright Florida sunshine. What do you get? The Atlantis, a well-known and much liked building that in most other places in the world and without a few key magic touches would simply be a big, bland downtown block of no special interest. Designed by Bernardo Fort-Brescia (born 1950) and Laurinda Spear (born 1951) of Arquitectonica, The Atlantis is a well thought through apartment block that makes the most of the local climate. The north side of the block is faced in reflective glass. The south side is divided into a grid of blue squares, each framing three balconies one above the other on three floors. One of these squares has been hollowed out and replaced by an open air pool shaded by a palm tree, overlooked by a balcony and framed by a bright red spiral stair that climbs the three storeys of the cut out. It is a clever way of bringing a blocky building to life and a feature that, having caught the popular imagination, has been photographed endlessly. Copies of The Atlantis can be found even in China.

AT&T BUILDING

PHILIP JOHNSON AND JOHN BURGEE, 1982 NEW YORK CITY, USA

What a fuss this ugly building caused when it was first unveiled. Was it really so very important? Yes and no. Yes, it was the first big-time, ruthlessly commercial Postmodern office block and so brought mega-buck finance into line with the latest architectural fad. No, because it was a bit of a bore. The AT&T building was simply another stack of offices piled high into the sky, but this time clad in pink granite, topped with a mammoth split-pediment and entered via what looked like a huge Venetian window and a lift lobby adorned with a questionable statue of a gilded and naked youth entitled the "Genius of Electricity". Heaven knows where Philip Johnson's genius was the day he signed off the drawings for this overbearing Chippendale cabinet. The building was meant to be witty, but architectural jokes are never very funny and the fact that they are forced, by the nature of buildings, to do the rounds for a century or even more makes them about as funny as a music hall joke circa 1882. Johnson could be a funny man, but the danger of becoming the profession's full-time comedian is that he was expected to come up with more and more outrageous jokes. By the end of the 1980s, Johnson was clearly bored with what was always going to be a cultural dead end.

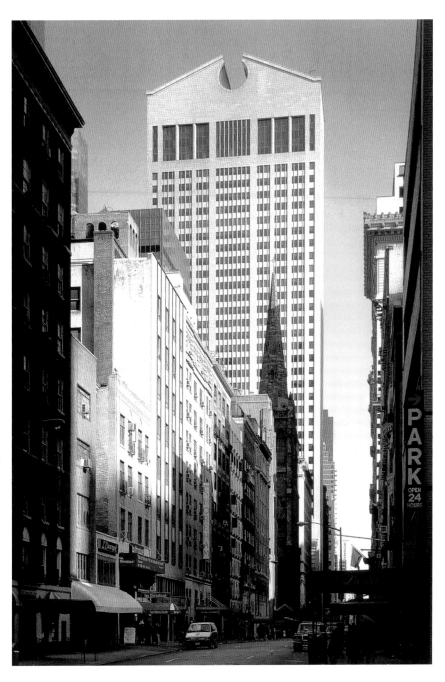

STATE MUSEUM

HANS HOLLEIN, 1982 MÖNCHENGLADBACH, GERMANY

Any architect who munches his way through the bones as well as the flesh of a roast pigeon while dining in the formal splendour of the River Room of London's Savoy Hotel has to be interesting. Hans Hollein (born 1934) is very interesting. Born in Vienna and educated there, at the Illinois Institute of Technology, Chicago and Berkeley, he enjoyed a rightful reputation as one of the few architects truly able to join together the obsessions of artists, architects and designers. Close to many avant-garde artists, he worked closely with Joseph Beuys, among others, on the design of this complex and richly enjoyable German civic museum.

Here, on the sloping garden of what was once a monastery, Hollein built a kind of modern Acropolis, a dense and rather exquisite urban landscape composed of pavilions, steps and piazzas. Together these various elements were the museum, a building of many faces and many parts. The entrance could be reached from one of three directions, all of them oblique, but leading to a pavilion sheathed in white marble and adorned with eye-catching chrome pilasters.

From then on in, Hollein performs a superb balancing act, keeping visitors guessing as to what might be around the next corner – the variety of spaces here is prodigious – while leading them on with veiled hints of what there might be. The variety of finishes, materials, colours too are all as prolific as they are attractive. And the art on show isn't half bad either.

PARLIAMENT BUILDING

GEOFFREY BAWA, 1983 COLOMBO, SRI LANKA

Built on a lake like a traditional palace in the region, the Sri Lankan parliament has a magnificent setting. From afar, with its great roofs, it looks to be a very convincing attempt to create a truly regional architecture, one of the concerns throughout the world at the time of its construction and especially in the countries of the developing world. Close up, however, the building is not quite so exciting nor so romantic. This was not the fault of the architect Geoffrey Bawa (born 1919), a Sri Lankan long known for skill in marrying modern plans to traditional facades, materials and craftsmanship. The building was rushed up by a Japanese contractor forced to use much more concrete and artificial stone than Bawa would have liked. The hectic pace of the project also meant

that the normally flamboyant Bawa was very restricted in the use of decoration: where visitors expect elaborately carved screens and other richly carved details, there are none. The assembly chamber itself is impressive if only for its scale – high and spacious to allow the hot air rising from the benches below to dissipate – and for the tented lightweight steel ceiling, a clever piece of decorative engineering. The chamber sits at the heart of the complex and is guarded by four pavilions in the same style.

The importance of the building, aside from its function, is in its attempt to find a language of design that reflected both local values and modern construction. It seemed a hard thing to do and rarely succeeded.

PUBLIC SERVICES BUILDING

MICHAEL GRAVES, 1983 PORTLAND, OREGON, USA

It lasted just a decade, an extraordinarily short working life for a building that was talked about and published worldwide. The Public Service Building put Portland on the map. Big, bold and colourful, it was in many ways the apotheosis of Postmodern architecture. Essentially, it was just a square, 15-storey office occupying an entire downtown block. What made it different was its very superficiality: four sides of bragadoccio "wallpaper" leaden with heavy-handed "jokes". To be fair, the original design was meant to be a lot more fun, with flamboyant statues, swags and ribbons adorning marble cladding. Cuts in the initial budget did away with the frills and fa-las and the marble was ditched in favour of paint. A host of comic-book Classical pavilions on the roof went too, so the "jokes", with references to Otto Wagner and the Viennese Secession, were rather thin on the façades. Several critics described it as looking more like a biscuit tin than a building, but those who worked here had more important cookies to crumble. They looked out to Portland through tiny square windows arranged to make funny facades rather than to make staff happy. But this was what Postmodernism was about, a rejection of humane, rational values in favour of a few laughs. Michael Graves (born 1934) was Po-Mo's court jester. Once upon a time he was a white Modern, then Postmodern, and then he did much of his work for Disney.

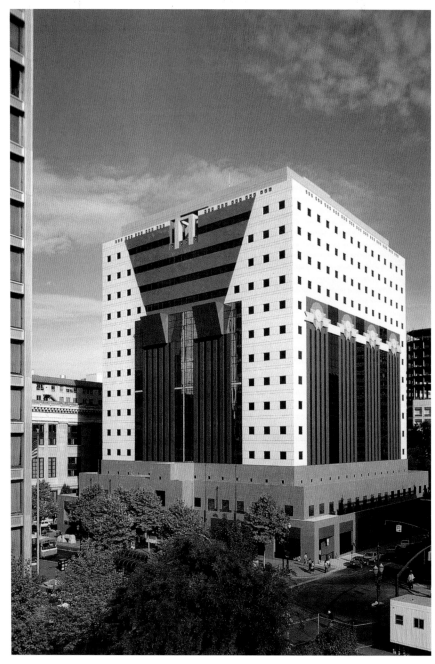

TV-AM BUILDING

TERRY FARRELL, 1983, CAMDEN, LONDON, ENGLAND

Terry Farrell (born 1940) opened up an English vein of Postmodernism, which if a little bloodless when set against the full US monty, was redeemed in part by the thoughtfulness of its planning. TV-am was the first British exercise in Po-Mo. Farrell converted a garage alongside the canal at Camden Lock into a studio and offices for a company long since melted into the airwaves of history. He tacked on a lively façade, bands of brightly coloured neon and designed an entrance hall that represented a journey across the world. The exterior was animated with eye-catching paint and its roofline topped with glass-reinforced plastic egg cups, a play on the idea of TV-am's remit: it was a breakfast-time station. Farrell gave London much of its Postmodern skyline during the 1980s, exporting his style profitably to Hong Kong and other points east in the 1990s. He is respected as an intelligent and subtle urban planner.

SAN JUAN CAPISTRANO PUBLIC LIBRARY

MICHAEL GRAVES, 1983 CALIFORNIA, USA

By the time he designed this "pueblo" public library, Michael Graves was well on his way to becoming one of the principal architects for Disney. Some-where, over the Postmodern rainbow, the wonderful world of Disneyland and EuroDisney beckoned. This was hardly surprising for, having given up on the white Modernism of his early days as one of the New York Five along with Richard Meier (p.346), Graves saw in a cartoon-like style of architecture a way of connecting modern architecture to popular sensibilities. The later work for Disney was both over the rainbow and over the top. Perhaps, though, there was a moment when Graves managed a balance between playfulness and worthwhile architecture.

This colourful library with its Spanish–Mexican influences just about gets away with it. It is more or less in keeping with the prevailing style of this sun-bleached sweep of southern California and has a low-key charm that Graves' major commissions lacked. Even so, the interior is disappointing. The decoration seems to have been applied with a thin brush and the rooms feel more like sets from an exhibition than those you might expect of a public library with its connotations of permanence and learning from the past.

Postmodernism might have given architects the chance to break away from what might have seemed like the puritanical rigours of the Modern Movement, but given what they must have supposed to be freedom, they appeared to have little idea of what to do with it.

VILLA ZAPU

POWELL-TUCK, CONNOR, OREFELT, 1984 NAPA VALLEY, CALIFORNIA, USA

A house for a Modern fairy tale; if ever Tim Burton's fictional character Edward Scissorhands had decided to give up his Gothic roots and go Modern, this would have been his ideal home. In fact it was commissioned by the Swedish wine grower Thomas Lundstrom as both a home and holiday retreat for guests and as an image-building exercise for his Villa Zapu label. He chose his architects well. David Connor (born 1950) and Julian Powell-Tuck (born 1952) were two Royal College of Art graduates who came into architecture via interior design. They designed the famous Punk shops for Malcolm Maclaren and Vivienne Westwood and wild flats for two of the members of the flamboyant glam-punk band

Adam and the Ants. Gunnar Orefelt (born 1953), a Swedish architect joined the practice, bringing with him a more rigorous approach to the as well as adventurous clients such as Lundstrom.

Villa Zapu is built of timber throughout. It comprises a thin, arrow-like house with a tall, detached guest tower separated from the main house by a long swimming pool. Although the villa is a little tricksy, it comes together as a convincing composition and is one of the very houses of its kind – an expression of the fashion-into-punk-into-graphics-into-architecture movement that made London such a hotbed of young creative talent from the mid-1980s.

SAN CATALDO CEMETERY

ALDO ROSSI AND GIANNI BRAGHIERI, 1984 MODENA, ITALY

A long time in the making, the San Cataldo Cemetery dates from the beginning of the 1970s. It is significant that at this time Rossi had been close to death after a car accident. Perhaps his thoughts on death were refined as a result. Certainly, this is one of the most memorable cemeteries to have been built in modern times, a city of death that moves the visitor to silence. Rossi was to die in a second smash-up in 1997.

The cemetery is a representation of an entire city, but a silent city and one that expresses both the absolute nature of human death and the immortality of the architecture that frames human life. For Rossi, whose buildings were never less than funereal, this was his finest moment. Without the

uncertainties of irrational human life to subvert his architecture, he was able to build a city of memory and dreams in which the streets and buildings are inhabited only by the ghosts of our imaginations. They can be anything we want them to be. A superb sequence of hypnotic monuments etched with deep shadows and set along unyielding axes, the cemetery is built up from Rossi's elemental and mythical "house". "In my house designs", he wrote, "I refer to the basic types of living [or dying] which the architecture of the city has formed through a long process. On the basis of this analogy, every corridor is a street, every court a city square, and a building reproduces the places of the city". At San Cataldo, death has rarely had such a thoughtful and rational dominion.

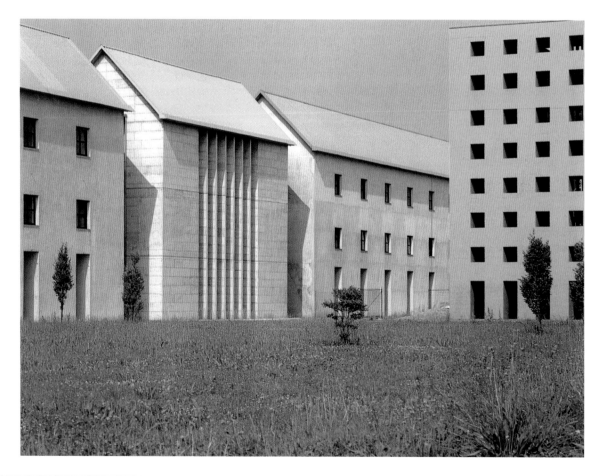

NEUE STAATSGALERIE

JAMES STIRLING AND MICHAEL WILFORD, 1984 STUTTGART, GERMANY

Stuttgart's Neue Staatsgalerie is one of the few convincing major buildings realized in a self-consciously Postmodern manner. It is a compelling fusion of Neoclassical and Modern Movement architecture, interrupted by High-Tech wizardry, comic book details, bizarre colours and pedestrian links that connect the building to various parts of Stuttgart and root it to the city. James Stirling (1926–92) was a bombastic and original architect who drew on the vocabulary of twentieth-century architecture as if it was a game. In this sense he was the successor of Sir Edwin Lutyens, another consummate gamesman. And, like Lutyens, Stirling's style evolved. His move into a new Classicism in the 1980s was bold and original; his concern, as this gallery shows, was with integrating colourful monuments into the existing fabric of cities rather than with imposing striking designs on them, as so many architects have tended to do throughout the century.

NATIONAL COMMERCIAL BANK

SKIDMORE, OWINGS AND MERRILL, 1984 JEDDAH, SAUDI ARABIA

Gordon Bunshaft (1909–90) was, for many years, one of Skidmore, Owings and Merrill's top architects. Here in Jeddah he demonstrated how a modern corporate headquarters could be made to work successfully in the Middle East in both functional and symbolic terms. The offices are set back at an angle within sheer containing walls that have a powerful emblematic presence from any distance while performing the essential role of keeping the heat of the sun under control and shielding windows from glare. The triangular tier of offices can be seen rising through the great rectangular openings cut out of the walls. The openings act as wind funnels and help to cool a form of office accommodation that would make little sense in this climate if designed along the lines of, say, Skidmore, Owings and Merrill's very own Lever Building in New York. The monumentality of the building makes sense given the lack of place here. What is the architect to do, particularly if the client is set on making its presence felt? By offering monumentality in a sea of earlier banality, Bunshaft gave character and order to what was in danger, like so many cities in this region, of becoming a non-place. Even then a city of striking commercial monuments, no matter how thoughtful or refined, would still be a rather alienating place.

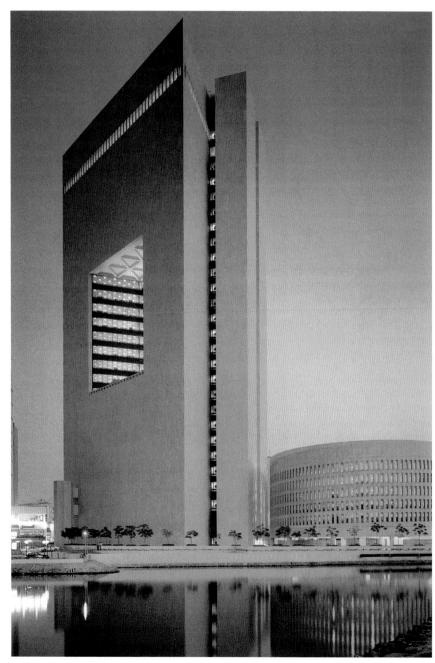

CALIFORNIA AEROSPACE MUSEUM

FRANK GEHRY, 1984 LOS ANGELES, USA

Prankster, funster, jester. Frank Gehry plays the Fool to Architecture's aged Lear and gets it right and wrong in what looks like equal measures. Gehry (born 1929) has spent many years pulling conventional architecture apart and putting it back together again in crazy planes and angles. One of the craziest planes of all is the F-104 jet fighter he mounted on one of the zig-zag walls of the California Aerospace Museum. This building, rushed up in time for the 1984 Los Angeles Olympics, comprises an odd conglomeration of galleries piled up in front of an older and conventional building. This simple yet striking motif imbues the building with real energy and makes it unforgettable.

Gehry's mission, rather like Gaudí's before him, appears to have been to rip up the rules of architecture and replace them with the limits of his own imagination. The first inkling of what he might do unfettered was the manner in which he rebuilt his own house in Santa Monica (1978). A simple and rather dreary home was exploded, with wire, corrugated fencing and timber extrusions into a sort of adult playpen or climbing frame. It was just the beginning. With each new project Gehry stretches his clients and audience that bit further. However crazy, Gehry is always a class act.

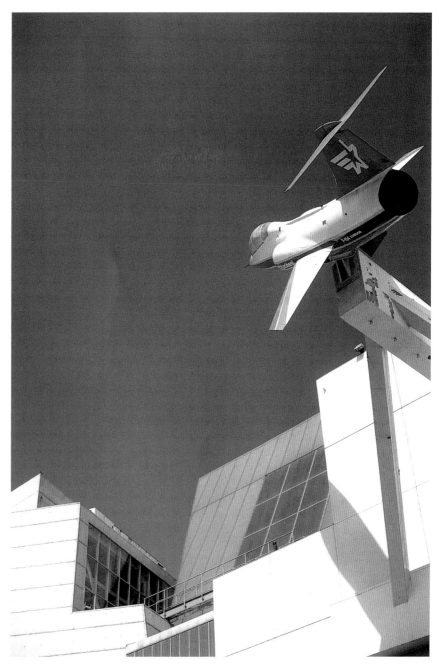

SAINSBURY WING

VENTURI, SCOTT-BROWN, 1987 NATIONAL GALLERY, LONDON, ENGLAND

This Postmodern-Classical trifle was the sorry end of a dismal saga in British cultural politics. The National Gallery wanted to build an extension to house its magnificent collection of early Italian paintings and to free up space in its existing Regency building. A developer offered to build a nice gallery sitting on top of lettable offices. He got a long way down the line – this was Margaret Thatcher's money-mad Britain – before a competition was announced for a serious design. It was won by Ahrends Burton Koralek, whose design was described by the Prince of Wales as being like a carbuncle on the face of an old friend and scuppered. Enter Sainsburys, the billionaire grocers, Robert

Venturi and a limp-wristed building that tries to be clever and fails dismally until the galleries where the paintings steal the show. You can hang a Bellini Madonna in a garden shed, however, and its ineffable beauty would still shine through.

The Sainsbury Wing is entered separately from the main gallery. The way up to the galleries is obtuse – an ugly stair sheathed in office-style glazing and determinedly off axis. The front is ugly, the back – and this is meant to be funny – resembles the rear end of a London cinema or theatre: in other words, ugly. Was the once iconoclastic Robert Venturi tamed by the cautious British establishment? Or was it just a bad heir day?

VITRA MUSEUM

FRANK GEHRY, 1988 WEIL-AM-RHEIN, GERMANY

Under the spirited direction of Ralph Fehlbaum, Vitra became one of the most adventurous manufacturers of Modern furniture. Over the years, the Fehlbaum family had collected a vast number of chairs, all the classics and many of the imponderables or otherwise unsittables. Where to put them? Fehlbaum commissioned Frank Gehry to design a museum in the grounds of the Vitra factory. It was a wise choice. Gehry came up with a design that managed at one and the same time to be pure and clean, white, bright and crazy. Walls and light towers shot, cartoon-fashion, every which way. But it was also beautifully built and the plan behind those provocative façades was neatly ordered. Inside, the drama comes from the swoop of the roofs and the chairs themselves, which are mounted for the most part on simple white geometric pedestals and lit, as far as possible, by the sun. Not only was the building a delight, but it was evidence to the effect that a zany-looking building might yet be rational, and that strongly sculpted architecture would draw the crowds, assuming you wanted them.

Gehry was to be asked to do this again and again over the next decade, culminating in his voluptuous Guggenheim Museum in Bilbao (p.347). His façades might seem gimmicky, yet Gehry's plans are there to remind the sceptical that, despite the bombast, everything is in order.

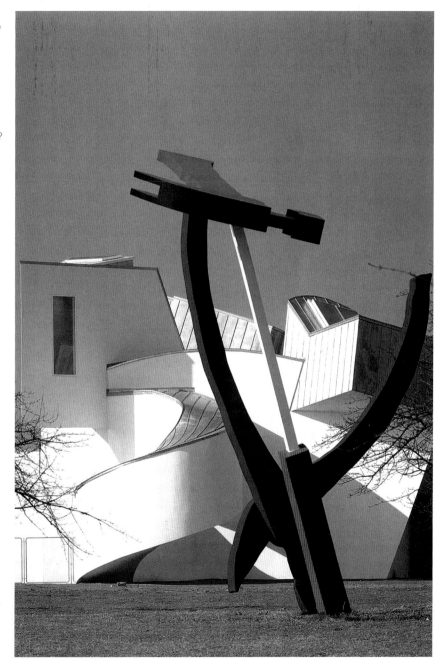

BROADGATE CENTRE

SKIDMORE, OWINGS AND MERRILL, ARUP ASSOCIATES, ET AL, 1988 CITY OF LONDON, ENGLAND

A strange – for London that is – yet successful chunk of urban planning. Muscular, broad-shouldered and well fleshed, like a boxer in a shiny, double-breasted suit, Broadgate is a spacious pile of flashy, deep-plan office blocks, gathered around some fine and popular new public squares. Nice piazzas, shame about the architecture. The problem with the buildings – their unmitigated bulk – is the reason they exist. In the mid-1980s, the City of London stock market was deregulated and, as if out of the blue, the City needed dealing rooms by the score. Existing offices were too old and skinny to handle these: enter the deep-plan office. At Broadgate, these behemoths were dressed in marble, granite, slate and stone, adorned with brass, bronze and some seriously good sculpture. But, they were Ugly Sisters whatever artists and architects could do to disguise their size. The spaces in between, however, were very welcome: squares to sit in, steps to sit on, an ice-skating rink in winter, bars and cafés galore. All these, plus instant access to Liverpool Street station, one of London's most important junction boxes. The City "crashed" before Broadgate was completed and no developer was brave or foolhardy enough to try anything quite like it again in central London.

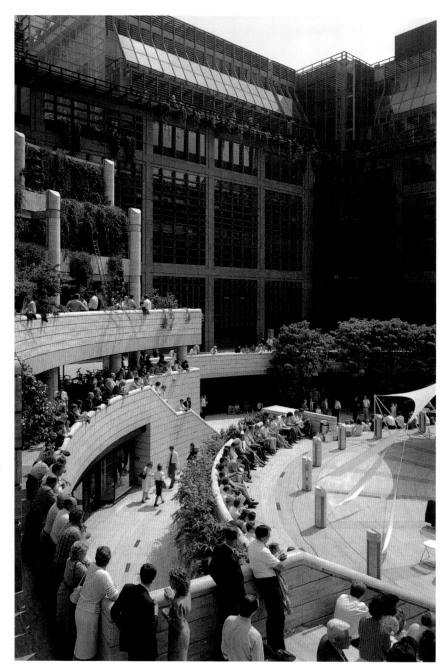

NOE BUILDING

BRANSON COATES ARCHITECTURE, 1988 TOKYO, JAPAN

Nigel Coates (born 1949) taught for a decade at the Architectural Association, London, before commissions for restaurants, bars, cafés and nightclubs arrived from Japan. It was a remarkable moment: an architect who never expected to build was an overnight star in Tokyo. The Noe Building – Noah's Ark, but filled with human beings eating, drinking and clubbing – was Coates's first free-standing building. It was both funny and provocative.

Coates' concerns had long been with what he called "narrative architecture", buildings and the spaces between them that in themselves told, retold and celebrated the stories of city life. This meant a busy architecture full of incident and detail and one that could be by turns funny, spiky, cool and even erotic. Coates did pack much of this sort of detail into his Tokyo interiors and the Noe Building, but it would take another decade before he was taken seriously enough to be entrusted with a large building in Britain. When it came – the Museum of Popular Music in Sheffield (p.350) – Coates found himself a major figure encouraged by the Labour government of Tony Blair. Coates is also professor of architecture and design at the Royal College of Art and a leading figure in a move to link architecture not just to other to other arts, but to contemporary music and fashion too.

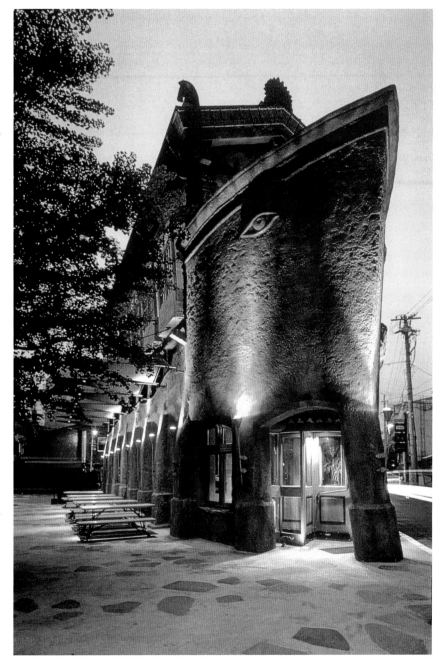

PUMPING STATION

JOHN OUTRAM, 1988 DOCKLANDS, LONDON, ENGLAND

A one-time RAF pilot, John Outram (born 1934) has become one of the most exotic British talents in the last two decades of the century. A Postmodernist, perhaps, he created an architecture very much his own, richly decorated and full of abstruse and colourful meaning. Not that the observer needs to know what Outram means; it is enough to enjoy the energetic and unabashed way in which he took a civic utility like this pumping station on the River Thames and turned it into an architectural occasion, to know that he is on the side of the angels and not just another bandwagon Postmodernist.

The pumping station is a simple box full of powerful and inscrutable machinery. Outram decorated this box with elements drawn from ancient cultures and turned it into a story, should you be able to decipher it, of river gods and goodness knows what else. It quickly became a favourite landmark of tourists chugging up and down the river and taking in the sights on their way from Westminster or Tower Bridge to Greenwich.

Some years earlier, Outram had worked the same colourful magic with some very prosaic industrial warehouses at two locations in west London. It was fun to see architecture buffs creeping into what for them must have been terrifying factory yards bristling with jeering workers to peep at the latest in picturesque English architecture.

ROOFTOP OFFICE

COOP HIMMELBLAU, 1989 VIENNA, AUSTRIA

Wolf D. Prix (born 1942) and Helmut Swiczinsky (born 1944) are a couple of live-wire Viennese architects who like to appear dark and sinister. The Red Angel drinking hole they designed at the beginning of the 1980s in Vienna was wonderfully menacing. So, too, this lawyers' office in the roof of a nineteenth-century city block. The elaborate rooflight looks as if it has landed on the roof like some mechanical bat. The architects themselves have likened it to a bolt of lightning. Whatever, it is an impressive device and one that does that rare thing – makes a roof interesting. This was something that remarkably few architects have done in the twentieth century, as if the arrival of the flat roof marked the

end of architectural invention above the cornice line. The great exceptions have been Gaudí – the roofscape of the Casa Milà (p.75) is one of the hidden wonders of twentieth-century architecture and decoration – architects such as Gehry or Böhm, for whom the roof is indistinguishable from the walls, and Coop Himmelblau in this small, yet widely published project. The offices beneath it do not disappoint although they are not as quirky as this celebrated rooflight. The way the roof opens up as if to bite or swallow the mechanical bat (or to discharge this bolt of lightning) is as delightful as it is the stuff of nightmares. Prix and Swiczinsky moved on to international projects in the 1990s.

PYRAMID

I. M. PEI, 1989 LOUVRE, PARIS, FRANCE

Such was the controversy generated over the announcement of plans to erect a glass pyramid in the main courtyard of the Louvre that a fight broke out within these hallowed portals in 1984 between police and protesters. From the vantage point of the end of the century it seems hard to know what the fuss was about. Just as Parisians hated the idea of the Eiffel Tower when it was first built, so they took against the idea of the pyramid. They soon got to like it. It was no slavish copy of an Egyptian pyramid, but a very impressive glass reinterpretation of the ancient model. Flanked by two baby glass pyramids and vigorous fountains, the ensemble is as striking as it is memorable and, with no doubt, it enhances the bulbous and richly decadent architecture of the famous museum.

The pyramid was designed by the skilful Chinese-American architect Leoh Ming Pei (born 1917), designer of the East Wing extension of the National Gallery of Art in Washington (1978), a bold and massive abstract composition. The glass pyramid, one of President Mitterand's *grand projets*, was just the tip of an architectural iceberg: Pei's crystalline pavilion was the entrance pavilion that led down to a spacious and refined new lobby, in which visitors were able to orientate themselves before setting out in quest of the Mona Lisa or Venus de Milo. This successful and, ultimately popular, scheme was greatly extended in 1992.

PARC DE LA VILLETTE

BERNARD TSCHUMI, ET AL, 1989 PARIS, FRANCE

This "Deconstructivist" park was one of the (incomplete) architectural surprises of the 1989 bicentennial celebrations of the French Revolution. Neither blatantly monumental nor symbolic, it was laid out over six years and designed to be a delight and nothing else – *folie de grandeur* perhaps, but a folly nevertheless. Ultimately the park, planted on the site of the former central Paris abattoirs, was to have been overlain with a grid of no fewer than 42 brightly coloured follies, each an enjoyably useless Deconstructivist design by Bernard Tschumi (born 1944) with intellectual input from the hip Deconstructivist philosopher, Jacques Derrida. The follies were, for the most part, painted bright red and slowly, slowly became wrapped around with trees, grass, plants and people. Visitors came here in gradually increasing numbers to see the new science museums and outsized films in the IMAX cinema housed, secretly to the uninitiated, in the compelling "Geode", a giant mirror-finish ball, by Fainsilber. The follies were meant to frame a rich programme of events, yet, year by year, these never quite seemed to materialize, although one folly now serves as a restaurant, another as a café and a third as a viewing platform. The follies are arranged in a rigorous mathematical sequence and are a rare example of modern architecture without any real or predetermined function.

JUDGE INSTITUTE

JOHN OUTRAM, 1993 CAMBRIDGE, ENGLAND

The Judge Institute was a management college designed to train a generation of young British people to manage rather than manufacture. As Britain turned from an industrial to a service economy in the 1980s and aped the United States in business manners, language and culture, so its architectural landscape began to change from one of essential plainness to an increasingly flamboyant and swaggering transatlantic style, based on the florid language of Postmodernism. Perhaps, then, it made perfect sense to house a service economy management course in one of the most florid buildings of its generation. John Outram's temple to budding business executives was an extraordinarily rich conceit, a kind of overbaked Roman basilica stirred into a heady shopping mall stew and spiced with more than piquant decoration. The result was indigestible from any point of view, although the building was carefully thought out in terms of use of space, the organization of its services and its use of energy.

Outram was a pioneer of the British "High Tech" school from the 1950s. The temptation to become ever more decorative, however, seemed only to undermine his essential seriousness of purpose. This was the Postmodern, post-industrial, service economy era and every company and college wanted a distinctive brand. This is what the Judge Institute got.

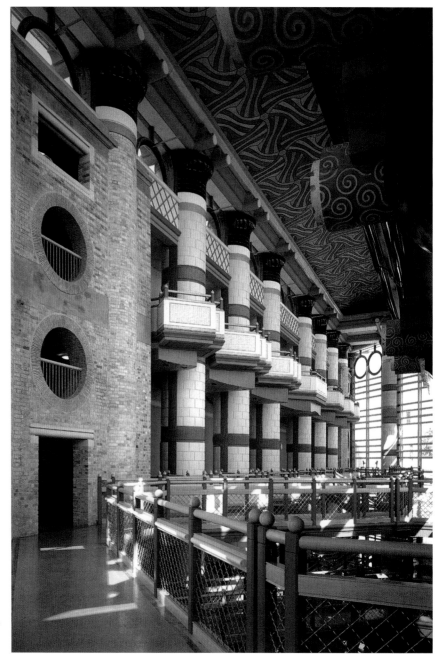

SUPREME COURT

RAM KARMI, 1993 JERUSALEM, ISRAEL

The result of an international
competition, Ram Karmi's
Supreme Court is an
important moment in the long
attempt in the last quarter of
the century to reconcile past
and present in architecture.

Its muscular forms are
taken from a romantic view
of ancient Israeli architecture,
from fortresses, from the
architectural legacy of British
and Israeli architects working
together in what was then
Palestine in the 1920s and
1930s and in a modern
design that takes fully into
account not just history and
symbolism, but climate too.

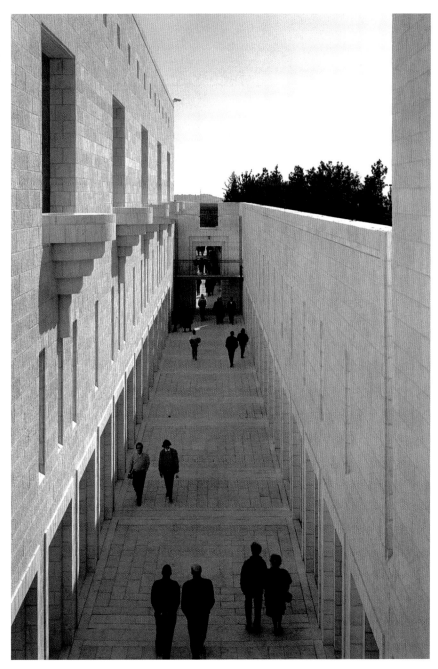

BIBLIOTHÈQUE NATIONALE

DOMINIQUE PERRAULT, 1995 PARIS, FRANCE

Known locally as the BGV (*Bibliothèque à Grande Vitesse*), this massive national library was commissioned, designed and built within five years. If that was an extraordinary achievement, the building itself is questionable and in several ways downright perverse. Perrault (born 1953) arranged the building, located on the banks of the Seine, in the form of four giant open books, made – or so it seems – almost entirely from glass and rising from a great stepped podium. The centre of the podium was hollowed out into a garden courtyard around which the reading rooms were cloistered. The giant books, one at each corner of the podium, were the bookstacks. On paper this was an enjoyable conceit: the stock of national learning was there for everyone to see. The

problem was also obvious for everyone to see: the precious books were exposed to sunlight. So the book towers were lined top to toe with wooden louvres to protect their cargo. This was an odd way of doing things, designing a building as a problem and then spending considerable energy solving the problem. The design of the Library was also criticized for the lavish use of rare and endangered hardwoods in many of its public parts. Nevertheless, Parisians have long been famous for moaning about brave new buildings and then taking them to their hearts. At the end of the 1990s there are signs that Perrault's perverse design is winning converts. It has a great sense of occasion and drama and is an enjoyable and flirty meeting place.

PETRONAS TOWERS

CESAR PELLI, 1997 KUALA LUMPUR, MALAYSIA

The "tiger" economies of Southeast Asia began to lose their claws at the very end of the twentieth century, but for the best part of two decades they terrified the old industrial west as they took to manufacturing like a crispy duck to pancakes and their GDPs (gross domestic product, a standard measure of national wealth) soared. The architectural corollary of this unprecedented economic growth was, at it had been in Chicago in the late nineteenth century, the skyscraper. Southeast Asian nations competed with one another to build the tallest towers. It was hard to say where it would all end, but the tallest to be completed by the century's end were the twin Petronas Towers located in the centre of the Malaysian capital's "Golden Triangle". Such is the importance of the towers to national prestige that a golf course – held in near veneration in this part of the world had to be torn up to make way for them.

Designed by Cesar Pelli (born 1926), the 88-storey, 451-metre (1,480-ft) towers are joined at the waist by a bridge. They have the appearance of a salt and pepper condiment set, although the profile of the towers is based (very loosely) on those of local Buddhist temples. They might be kitsch, but it would be hard to argue that the early skyscrapers of New York and Chicago were really any different.

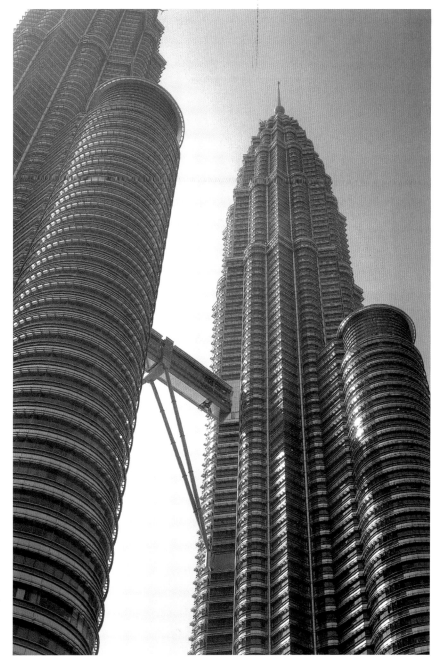

GETTY CENTER

RICHARD MEIER, 1997 LOS ANGELES, CALIFORNIA, USA

A late twentieth-century Acropolis, the Getty Center sits on top of a hill high above the suburban sprawl of Los Angeles as if dispensing art, culture and learning to all around. Remote, chaste and refined, this city within a city is a remarkable achievement. A white tram takes visitors up the hill from a giant car park to a plaza from which they can wander all day long from one handsome pavilion to the next, take in peerless views of the city, its mountainous backdrop and the Pacific Ocean, catch the sun's rays from the Center's many terraces, bask in its glorious gardens, eat in its cafés and restaurants and even take in some art before making the descent back down to the crowded freeways and air-conditioned shopping malls below.

The Getty Center, which cost a cool one billion dollars, is a monument to the wealth and oil exploitation of the Getty family. Here, art and conservation work carried out in Getty's name around the world redeems the spirit of rampant US capitalism. Or something like that. The Center comprises a galaxy of beautifully constructed galleries, studios, workshops, lecture theatres and other public functions in chaste pavilions made of concrete and clad in travertine by Richard Meier. It is very impressive, very detached and an enchantingly surreal place to spend a day.

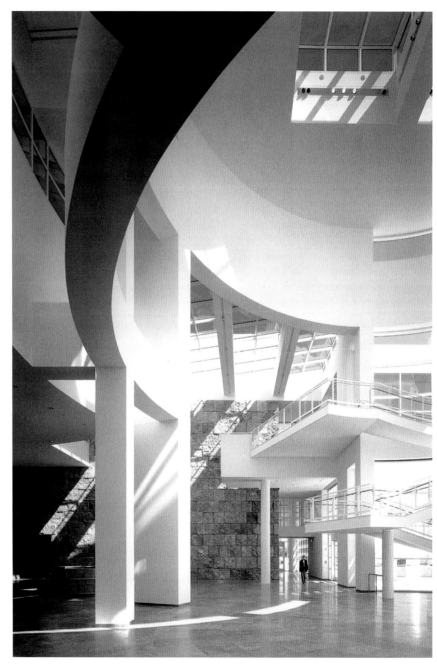

GUGGENHEIM MUSEUM

FRANK GEHRY, 1997 BILBAO, SPAIN

One of the most talked about buildings in years, this Basque outpost of the Solomon R. Guggenheim Collection transformed Bilbao's image. Until then this ancient city with its unique language was associated with the ETA (the Basque separatist movement) and violence, its busy port and not much more. From late 1997 it became the focus of weekend breaks. And what people came to see was Gehry's madcap museum. ETA did its best to blow up King Juan Carlos when he came to open the building; a bomb was discovered in a tub of flowers which, had it exploded, would have destroyed Jeff Koon's *Puppy* sculpture that stands guard over the

museum, the King and at least some of the sensational titanium cladding that distinguishes this acclaimed building. The bombing would have been a mistake, because Bilbao and the Basque country have won more sympathy through the museum than through years of guns and hatred.

The building comprises a central gallery, a on several levels with offshoots that include an *enfillade* of classical galleries for the display of intimate artworks, and an elongated gallery for big Pop sculptures, including Richard Serra's *Snake*, three tall sheets of steel winding more than 30 metres (100-ft) along the gallery. Crazy, but wonderful.

NO1 POULTRY

JAMES STIRLING AND MICHAEL WILFORD, 1997 CITY OF LONDON, ENGLAND

The son of a successful London property developer, Peter Palumbo had a dream to commission Ludwig Mies van der Rohe to design an office tower in the City of London. This would replace a pile of pretty, if petty, Victorian offices and shops opposite the Mansion House, official home of the Lord Mayor of London. Palumbo Jr flew to Chicago to visit Mies in 1959. It took another 30 years for Palumbo, thwarted at every turn, not to build one of the very last designs by Mies – it was much like the Seagram Building (p.223). After two public enquiries and despite a team of experts on his side, Palumbo was forced to give up. Instead, he commissioned a polar opposite by Stirling and Wilford, a wilful Postmodern oil-tanker of a building that appeared to be heading on a collision course with the Mansion House. Hardly subtle, this ship of the developer's line took many years to build; it comprises offices, shops, bars and restaurants, a roof garden and an entrance to Bank Underground station. Big, brightly coloured, perhaps it is meant to be witty, but Po-Mo jokes had never worn well assuming they were ever funny. Palumbo, however, was unabashed and seemingly oblivious to criticism. A collector of buildings in many different styles he owns, among others, Mies van der Rohe's Farnsworth House (p.206) and Le Corbusier's Maisons Jaoul (p.218).

JEWISH MUSEUM

DANIEL LIBESKIND, 1999 BERLIN, GERMANY

A lightning bolt zig-zagging beside the old Berlin Museum, the Jewish Museum is one of the most powerful and extraordinary buildings of the twentieth century. Its plan is rooted around a central void that connects the many galleries in this zinc-clad building. The void expresses the absence of the 250,000 Jews who lived in Berlin at the beginning of Hitler's Third Reich: those who were able abandoned the city they loved; those who stayed were slaughtered. Yet, although this atonal building has all the power of Schoenberg's unfinished opera *Aron and Moses* – a work that Libeskind (born 1946), a trained musician, turned to over and again during the design of the museum – this is not a memorial to the Holocaust. Rather, it is a

reflection and a celebration of a people, a way of life and a culture that was quite literally taken out of the city and murdered.

The nearby S-Bahn links Wansee at one end of the line (the Wansee conference of 1942 set a seal on the Final Solution) and Orianenberg at the other, where the headquarters from which Heinrich Himmler ran his concentration camps with such infamous zeal are now local council offices.

The ghosts of Berlin have yet to be exorcized fully. Libeskind's brooding museum, with no entrance that you can see from the street, is the architecture of memory writ as large and as powerful as it has ever been.

MUSEUM OF POPULAR MUSIC

BRANSON COATES ARCHITECTURE, 1999 SHEFFIELD, ENGLAND

Teenagers and pop music were mid-century phenomena. By the end of the century they had a long history and many of the early pop idols had passed into the great gig in the sky and the first teenagers were grandparents. Perhaps they would be zimmering their way up to Sheffield in 1999 to recapture the shakin' and shimmerin' days of their youth at the rather pedantically named

Museum of Popular Music. This is designed in the guise of four steel drums, symbolizing the driving beat that accompanies virtually all pop music and paying homage to the city of Sheffield still, despite Britain's

feverish attempt in the 1980s and 1990s to abandon every last bit of its heavy industry – with trade unions and working-class radicalism meeting the same fate – a centre of steel making.

The plan is a satisifying one in that it allows visitors to walk straight to the heart of the building and to orientate themselves before deciding on what they wanted to see rather than trekking aimlessly through galleries in a stupor which has been all too often the fate of gallery-goers in the late twentieth century. The architects were able to build a miniature inflatable prototype of the museum (1998), which was erected in Horse Guards Parade in London and housed "powerhouse::uk", a government-sponsored exhibition of British design creativity and a symbol of New Labour's "Cool Britannia".

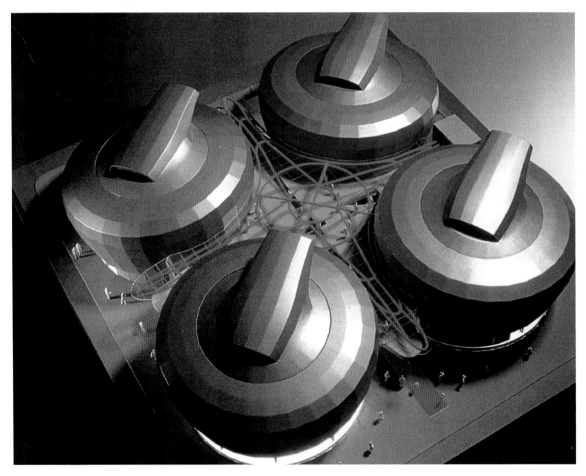

THE SPIRAL

DANIEL LIBESKIND, 2001 VICTORIA AND ALBERT MUSEUM, LONDON, ENGLAND

In Stanley Kubrick's epic *2001: A Space Odyssey*, the near future was presented as one in which humans attempted to stamp a rational design on the universe. This was expressed in their clothes, furniture, spaceships, computers and conversation. Yet, despite their best attempts, they were undermined by the forces of unreason, chaos and interference by ineffable forces from somewhere on high. Architects throughout the twentieth century fought a battle between the rational and the irrational, between romance and reason, order and disorder. Who could say who won? In fact there were no winners. In London as a new century approaches, Daniel Libeskind's spiralling design for new galleries at the Victoria and Albert Museum represented the tussle between these opposite forces. It was as if his proposed building was twisting and turning between the forces of order and chaos or being pulled askew by the magnetic attractions of polar opposites. The building was to have packed a lot of varied spaces into a confined courtyard. The galleries were to have spiralled up, adding to the eccentric and colourful South Kensington skyline. The Spiral was to have been clad in terracotta tiles arranged in complex fractal patterns by Cecil Balmond, mathematician and structural engineer, giving it a crystalline and enduring appearance. Due to uncertain funding, the project was cancelled.

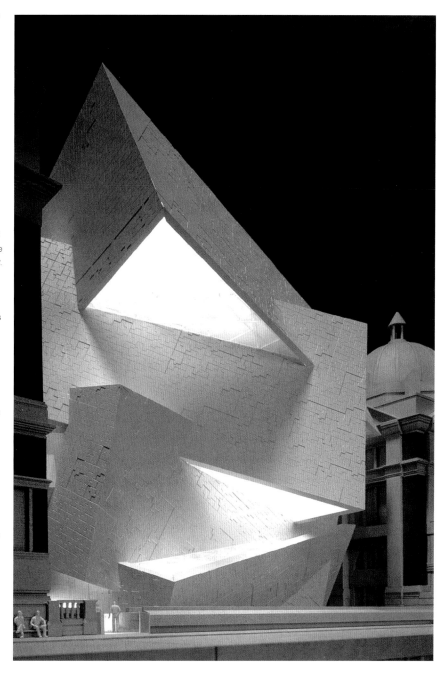

CATHEDRAL OF OUR LADY OF ANGELS

RAFAEL MONEO, 2001 LOS ANGELES, USA

Los Angeles may be known as the city of angels, but they have never had the roosting place they deserve. Although founded by the zealously Catholic Spanish, the place has never boasted a cathedral to match the surprising strength of its religious community. Surprising, that is, to the casual visitor expecting amorality on an epic scale.

The city's new cathedral rises alongside Highway 101. It is a muscular yet numinous building, which promises to be as much a home to God and Angeleno Catholics as a key component in the cultural, spiritual and commercial resurrection of downtown LA, alongside the Museum of Contemporary Art by Arata Izosaki, and Frank Gehry's Disney Concert Hall (p.453). This being LA, the cathedral sits on top of a 600-bay car park. On much the same scale as St

Patrick's, New York, it rises like a cliff face 45 metres (150 ft) above a palm, pool and pergola-fringed plaza. A detached campanile alongside, topped with a 10-metre (30-ft) cross, houses a carillon of 18 bells. Concrete walls are a warm, rich sandstone-like colour. The plan is based on a stylized cross, but as the building reaches its rooftops, it assumes the form of a pair of giant abstract angel's wings. A beautifully day-lit ambulatory runs around three sides of the 2,500-seat, 41-metre- (125-ft-) high, 109-metre- (333-ft-) long nave. This covered walkway is interrupted by a chain of irregularly planned, top-lit side-chapels. The nave boasts 2,500 square metres (27,000 square ft) of windows. It features a full-immersion font, a timber roof, a mighty organ, gospel choirs and masses said in 38 languages.

SAID BUSINESS SCHOOL

DIXON JONES, 2001 OXFORD, ENGLAND

Oxford is, famously, a city of dreaming spires. But a ziggurat? This is the stepped, copper-clad tower of the Said Business School, designed by Jeremy Dixon and Ed Jones. It is based, says Jones, on the tower of Nicholas Hawksmoor's St George's Church, Bloomsbury, which, in turn, is derived from the legendary Temple of Halikarnassos, in modern-day Turkey, and one of the Seven Wonders of the World. The connection between Oxford and the Middle East is not forced. The Said Business School has been funded, controversially, by the billionaire Syrian arms brokers Wafic Rida Said.

Architecturally, however, the college is a place very much at peace with itself. It is entered through a peristyle that feels much bigger, if not plusher than that of historic Oxford colleges.

It has about it a Miesian austerity: simple, yet richly textured, all smooth concrete, polished French limestone and leather seats. Beyond is a calm cloistered garden with formal rows of pruned trees and timeless metal chairs dotted beneath them. Beyond the garden rises an amphitheatre for outdoor lectures. Handsome things, the indoor lecture theatres leading off the cloister are quite unlike the yawn -inducing spaces known to most university students. The crowning glory of the college, though, is less its colourful ziggurat, a chimney of sorts, than its great barrel-vaulted library. Here, though, the students have eyes only for their computer screens – there are precious few books. This is, despite its underlying references to the ancient Middle East, a decidedly modern place.

HOTEL INNTEL

WAM ARCHITECTS 2010 ZAAMDAM, NETHERLANDS

What on earth, or in Holland, is this? It looks like a pileup of traditional Dutch houses in bright greens and blues, their pediments, gables, windows and roofs pulling and pushing in each and every direction. This glorious conceit is the Hotel Inntel Zaandam, a madcap fairytale of a building. At first, it looks like a trick, a conjuring act, as if some maverick architect had run off to join the circus, and learned how to balance one building on top of another, possibly while riding a bike. It's a happily oddball addition to the skyline of Zaandam, capital of the Zaanstad region, close to Amsterdam. Wilfried van Winden, its architect, says that the design is based on that of traditional Zaanstaad houses. These, though, included humble

workers' cottages as well as a grand house belonging to a local notary. Although Dutch architecture is normally associated with restraint and decorum, there is a tradition of exuberance (Het Schip, p28) that Van Winden has encouraged in his teaching and buildings. The key idea behind the design was to offer hotel guests an individual "home from home" rather than an anonymous box; here, every one of the 160 rooms has its own character. It certainly makes guests smile, and, inevitably, it has become a tourist attraction in its own right. The hotel is now surrounded by new streets lined with neo-traditional houses and other buildings so that it feels less freaky than it did when it first opened.

ONE NEW CHANGE

JEAN NOUVEL 2010 CITY OF LONDON

Known as the "Stealth Building" because its profile apparently reflects the design of a radar-cheating American "Stealth Bomber", One New Change is an enormous, dun-coloured shopping mall and office block landed to the immediate east of St Paul's Cathedral. Set down on an edge-of-town site, such a monster might have worked; here, though, it looked as if some bruised old pugilist had punched and swaggered into the City challenging anyone to try and stop him. This seemed a shame, because Jean Nouvel can be an architect of great sensitivity, having designed such translucent and filigree city-centre buildings as the Fondation Cartier (p.288) in Paris. Squeezing such a big building as One New Change into the City of London has been a bit like pouring a heavyweight boxer into a City boy's suit. And, rather like a bespoke three-piece, while the exterior of the Nouvel building is essentially formal, its cruise-ship-shiny, shop-lined interior is as flash as a loud silk lining.The big idea is that the building appears to be a single block of material with passageways or "streets" carved through it, so that it feels like at least four separate, yet connected, buildings, turning around a central atrium. These "streets" are lined with shops and cafés, and have sloping walls. The biggest of them leads from the heart of One New Change to St Paul's Cathedral, framing studied views of Wren's enduring monument. As a shopping venue, though, it was almost bound to be a big success.

ROBOTIC

MACHINES FOR LIVING IN

The nineteenth century saw the development of new types of building and structure designed by engineers. While architects fought battles of style – should they dress the frames of their masterpieces in Gothic copes, Classical togas or be terribly daring and try both together? Engineers, and a few wide-eyed architects it must be said, explored the possibilities of new materials and structures. As they finally got to grips with these at the turn of the century, the vast majority of architects felt they had to dress them up. It seemed impossible to them that such structures were more beautiful naked. Yet very often they were. Up until, and even beyond, World War One, this batty division between what was architecture and thus Art (no matter how hideous) and what was engineering and thus Science (and often extremely beautiful) struggled lamely on. And then the dam burst. Airship hangars (p.360), factories (pp.359, 361, 363, 378, 391) and even coastal defences (p.370) proved to be works of high art in their own right even if a world apart from the Classical orders and all forms of decoration. Ultimately, the tables were turned and architects began to design in an engineering style themselves. By the late 1970s and in the hands of Richard Rogers, Renzo Piano and Norman Foster, this had become an art form in its own right. The style, for it was one, was nick-named Hi Tech, although the intriguing thing about it was that the best of these buildings, far from being naked engineering structures, were highly finished artefacts that required an extraordinary amount of sophisticated craftsmanship to complete. They were celebrations of structural engineering as seen through the eyes of architects, and in a sense their highly polished and refined exhibitions of steelwork, pipes and ducts were as much a form of decoration as Classical columns and swags of plaster fruit.

These were ostentatious buildings and designed, perhaps, to prove that an architecture that owed nothing to convention could be very glamorous indeed. Richard Rogers' Lloyds Building (p.393) was every bit as refined and custom-designed as Josef Hoffman's Palais Stoclet (p.26).

There were, however, at least two other strands of Robotic buildings. First, there were those that were first and foremost machines and not for normal or regular human habitation. These include the various communications towers and centres shown in this section as well as the former Financial Times printing press in London's Docklands by Nicholas Grimshaw (p.394) and the beautiful satellite receiving station at Affleur, Austria, designed by Gustav Peichl (p.389). Such impressive structures could hardly help impressing themselves on the sensibilities of architects who came to prominence in the age of mass communication and sophisticated technology. Second, there is a long tradition of brutally functional yet attractive buildings designed to cover as much space or to reach as high into the sky as possible without any attempt to make light of the fact. These include the John Hancock Tower in Chicago (p.383) and the outsized geodesic dome Buckminster Fuller built for the Union Tank Car Company in Baton Rouge, Louisiana (p.373).

The most satisfying of these machine-like buildings, however, are either the most pure, or those that fuse the talents of engineers and architects seamlessly. Look at the airship hangar at Orly (p.360) or the aircraft hangar at Orbetello (p.368). Perfection. Or else consider the magnificent new airports at Kansai (p.400) and Hong Kong (p.403). These are machines for flying from and have an openness and honesty about them that architects working in other Modern traditions found difficult to achieve.

FULLER BUILDING

DANIEL BURNHAM, 1902 NEW YORK CITY, USA

Known from its beginning as the "Flat Iron" because of its distinctive footprint, the 20-storey Fuller Building is an early masterpiece of downtown high-rise design. Burnham made the most of a potentially awkward street corner site to create a building with a highly distinctive and memorable profile. It marked the emergence of the true "skyscraper": all the available technology needed to reach for the sky was now available. Elisha Otis provided the passenger elevator as early as 1857; the great Chicago fires of 1871 and 1874 encouraged the development of iron and steel frames for buildings; foundations were developed that would take the weight of these secular towers of Babel; and techniques for cladding iron and steel frames with brick and stone panels had become practical and reliable. Within five years of the completion of the Fuller Building, New York "skyscrapers" had topped 152 metres (500 ft) and the sky was truly the limit.

Climbing high above Manhattan, the Fuller Building followed the principles enshrined in Louis Sullivan's famous essay "The Tall Office Building Artistically Considered" (1896), in which the ideal office building was composed on the lines of the façade of an ideal Palladian house or a Classical column, with a base containing shops and lobby, a middle section containing any number of office floors and a top floor in the guise of an attic storey.

FIAT FACTORY

GIACOMO MATTÉ-TRUCCO, 1923 TURIN, ITALY

"We affirm", wrote the poet Filippo Tommaso Marinetti in his Futurist Manifesto, "that the world's magnificence has been enriched by a new beauty: the beauty of speed." That was in 1909 when cars were not exactly fast and just six years after the Wright brothers had proved that powered flight was possible (at 20 kph/12 mph). In 1920, Giaccomo Matté-Trucco (1869–1934) began work on the construction of the new Fiat Factory at Lingotto, not far from the centre of Turin. It was, as any building could be at the time, a symbol of Futurist ideals. Dedicated to the speedy and efficient production of cars, it boasted a parabolic test track on its elongated roof. Images of Fiat cars speeding around the top of this imposing factory have long been used to capture an

era in which the machine was king (or dictator) and speed his mistress. Even so, the factory is a concrete heavyweight and, test-track aside, is fairly far removed from Futurist ideals which looked not just to speed, but to a fundamental lightness of structure and being.

The vast complex no longer makes cars. It has since become, very gradually, a major exhibition complex and cultural centre, remodelled sympathetically by Renzo Piano. As an image of the brave new machine world opening up to architects, engineers and designers after the brutal experimentation of World War One, it remains forever that famous concrete race-track buzzing like an angry wasp above a city drawn into the future.

AIRSHIP HANGARS

EUGÈNE FREYSSINET, 1923 ORLY, PARIS, FRANCE

These imposing structures were destroyed by Allied bombing in 1944. The memory they have left in the minds of architects and engineers has been indestructible. Eugène Freyssinet (1879–1962) was not just a great engineer but one of the first poets of concrete. A pioneer of pre-stressed concrete and a designer of great intuition, he used this material to create bridges, a locomotive depot at Bagneux (1929), a dam at Beni-Bahdel, Algeria, (1940) and other structures of elegance and profound grace.

The airship hangars at Orly are 175 metres (574 ft) long, 91 metres (300 ft) wide and 60 metres (200 ft) high. They are constructed from parabolic arches, the concrete as thin as 9 cm (3½ in) where possible. Sadly, we can only gaze longingly at photographs of these twin structures and imagine how magnificent they must have been. Freyssinet showed that gigantic modern structures need not be monstrous. The titanic scale of these monuments to the age of the airship would have become apparent only as one approached their mighty concrete portals. The genius of Freyssinet's design was as much in the profile of the arches as in the fact that the wall spaces in between could be extensively glazed; these were not concrete caverns, but concrete cathedrals. Their superb design also demonstrates how even the largest buildings can be free from all decoration and yet ornament the landscape they stand in. I long to have seen them both from the ground and circling overhead.

FORD GLASS FACTORY

ALBERT KAHN, 1924 DEARBORN, MICHIGAN, USA

Albert Kahn (1869–1942) was the founding father of the modern factory. Born in Germany, he emigrated to the United States as a child and was brought up in Detroit. After designing hospitals and housing blocks, Kahn found his niche in factory design for the motor industry, beginning with Packard and moving on to Ford and Chrysler. The planning of the massive Rouge River glass factory for Ford was absolutely rigorous. Inside the confines of this long structure, glass for late Model-Ts and new Model-As was cooled, cut and polished on conveyor belts that ran 24-hours a day. Heat was vented from angled openings in the largely glass roof. The factory was given a strong presence by the row of four chimneys – industrial Doric – provided for the furnaces.

A visiting delegation from the USSR was so impressed with the neatness, logic and efficiency of the plant that they offered Kahn the job of designing a tractor factory in Stalingrad (1930). In his four year stint in the Stalin's Soviet Union, Kahn was responsible for the design of no fewer than 521 factories.

Back in the America, Kahn's office accounted for about 20 per cent of all new American factories by the outbreak of World War Two. Kahn's last project was the Glenn L. Martin bomber factory in Omaha, Nebraska (1943). Kahn's contribution to industry was to rationalize and bring together under one impressive roof the disparate workings of giant twentieth-century factories.

DYMAXION HOUSE

BUCKMINSTER FULLER, 1927

Buckminster Fuller (1895–1983) was an intellectual jack-in-the-box, a brilliant US inventor with the gift of the gab; anyone who ever sat through a Fuller lecture wondered where on earth those four or even five or six hours went. His one great obsession was to create lightweight structures and to achieve the greatest technical performance with the least expenditure of energy and materials. In this, he could certainly be said to have been well ahead of his times.

Fuller's first project was the Dymaxion House ("Dynamic plus maximum efficiency") prototype of 1927. This was a literal interpretation of Le Corbusier's dictum that a house was a machine for living in. Its lightweight structure comprised six triangular rooms suspended from a central structural core that also housed the main services (kitchen, bathroom, plumbing etc). With a diameter of 15 metres (49 ft) and a height of 12 metres (29 ft), the house weighed just 2,227 kg (4,900 lb) and could be dismantled and transported with the greatest of ease. The trouble is that no one really wanted to live in a machine like this, and in any case the traditional North American balloon-framed timber house was also easy and cheap to build and could be moved from one site to another too. The Wichita House he built in 1946 was a more sympathetic development of the Dymaxion House, although it still looked more like a Martian spaceship than an American home.

VAN NELLE TOBACCO FACTORY

MART STAM, JOHANNES ANDREAS BRINCKMAN, ET AL, 1930 ROTTERDAM, THE NETHERLANDS

This graceful factory was largely the work of the Mart Stam (1899–1987) who spent two years in the office of Brinckman (1902–49) in the mid-1920s. Martinus Adrianus Stam was from early on a dedicated socialist; having worked with Hans Poelzig and Max Taut in Germany in the early 1920s, he went to the fledgling Soviet Union where he worked with the revolutionary Soviet architect El Lissitzky (Eliezer Markovich, 1890–1941) in Moscow before transforming the Van Nelle project into one of the iconic designs of the early Modern Movement.

The factory was housed in one handsome extensively glazed block with a cafeteria perched on its roof like an airport control tower. An ancillary three-storey block curving away from the factory housed offices, a library and a café for white-collar workers. Aside from being much lighter and airier than most contemporary factories, the all-embracing design kept the site free of clutter and makeshift buildings. It was much visited by factory owners and architects from around the world and became a model for the look as well as the physical organization of the modern industrial plant. Stam went on to teach at the Bauhaus in Dessau, while Brinckman began working on the Bergpolder housing block, Rotterdam (1934), one of the very first residential buildings to stand on stilts.

CHRYSLER BUILDING

WILLIAM VAN ALEN, 1930 NEW YORK CITY, USA

Possibly the best loved high-rise building in the world, the Chrysler Building is a masterpiece of engineering skill and Art Deco showmanship. Designed by William van Alen (1883–1954) to be the tallest building in the world (320 metres/1,048 ft), it held this record for just a year before the Empire State Building (381 metres /1,250 ft) on New York's Fifth Avenue broke it. Even so, the Chrysler Building is generally considered to be the prettier of the two. The architect Rem Koolhaas has famously illustrated the rival Manhattan skyscrapers as a pair of lovers in bed together enjoying a post-coital rest: he depicted the Empire State Building as male, the Chrysler Building as female. The technology to build this high (in steel) was tried and tested by the late 1920s, yet the Chrysler Building stretched the capabilities of the US construction industry to literally new heights. The chief attraction of the building, however, lies largely in its flamboyant stainless steel decoration; the lantern or "crown" that caps the tower is exquisite. The skyscraper was commissioned by the Chrysler Corporation, which explains the name and the many automotive references in the building's extensive decoration, but Chrysler was never to occupy the building. Van Alen himself was accused of various financial improprieties during the construction and rather disappeared off the architectural map after 1930.

EMPIRE STATE BUILDING

SHREVE, LAMB AND HARMON, 1931 NEW YORK CITY, USA

Phenomenon, icon, movie star, magnet for low-flying World War Two bomber and tourist attraction, the Empire State Building has been one of the world's most famous buildings since it opened just in time to meet the real impact of the Wall Street Crash of 1929. It is not a building much discussed in architectural histories as it is seen as an over-the-top example of Art Deco styling wrapped around a stock steel frame. This is unfair. Aside from being the world's tallest building for more than 40 years, the Empire State Building acts as a magnificent fulcrum on the Manhattan skyline.

Its appearance is elegant and its cladding of limestone and granite, decorated with a minimum of Art Deco flourishes, is stylish rather than flashy. In urban terms the 380 metre (1,250 ft) tower – 450 metre (1,472 ft) if you count the communications tower added to the roof in later years – performs its role well. From the sidewalk nothing more than the eight-storey base can be seen: the tower is set back and can be seen only from a distance. The base is cut through with a noble arcade that includes useful shops, services and cafés. The Empire State is a very public building. Since 1931, about 120 million visitors have made their way up to its viewing galleries. The architects were Richmond H. Shreve (1877–1946), William Lamb (1883–1952) and Arthur Loomis Harmon (1878–1958).

GIOVANNI BERTA STADIUM

PIER LUIGI NERVI, 1932 FLORENCE, ITALY

Extended and slightly spoilt in recent years Pier Luigi Nervi's (1891–1979) communal stadium at Florence was this great engineer's first triumph. The design is simple – an oval of concrete stairs and 35,000 seats with one section covered by a concrete shell grandstand that has the appearance of a giant pair of jaws. The design owes as much to precedents set in ancient Rome as it does to a new, plastic use of reinforced concrete.

Nervi was born at Sondrio, Lombardy and studied engineering at Bologna University. He set up his own firm in 1920. He ranks with Freyssinet (p.360) and Maillart as an engineer who was also an artist, a designer who could turn logical calculations into a form of poetry realized in modern materials. In his many writings, Nervi insisted that the process of creating form was the same for engineers and architects as it was for artists. It depended as much on intuition as it did on logic and mathematics. His first built project was a cinema in Naples in 1927; within a decade he had become one of the world's most impressive and expressive structural engineers. He summed up his wide-ranging thoughts on the subject in a number of important books, among them *The Art and Science of Construction* (1945), *The Architectonic Language* (1950) and *New Constructions* (1963).

EMPIRE TOWER

THOMAS TAIT AND LAUNCELOT ROSS, 1938 GLASGOW, SCOTLAND

Tait whacked this Russian-inspired Constructivist tower up to its full height of 76 metres (250 ft) in just nine weeks. Not bad considering it featured a fully operational restaurant as well as a viewing gallery. And, by night, the tower was lit up. The tower could be seen from up to 130 km (80 miles) away from the hills surrounding Glasgow. The occasion for its unheralded design was the Empire Exhibition of 1938. The tower was the structural anchor of the show that was held at a time when Glasgow, now a city better known for its nightclubs and fashionable bars, was the home of British engineering and shipbuilding at its very best. Great liners and railway locomotives were launched from its shipyards and rolled out from its workshops. Tait's tower was an impressive example of what Glasgow could do when pressed for time. The speed of construction was made possible by Tait's choice of steel angles, rivetted together and clad in the corrugated steel that Glasgow manufactured in vast quantities for export around the world. The net effect was remarkable: here at last, in Glasgow of all places, a Soviet Constructivist tower had been erected and in record time. Sadly, the tower was demolished soon after the exhibition. A sitting duck for Lutfwaffe bombers, it would have been a miracle if it had seen out World War Two as Glasgow as was badly hit.

AIRCRAFT HANGAR

PIERO LUIGI NERVI, 1940 ORBETELLO, TUSCANY, ITALY

The Italian fascist dictator, Mussolini, once said "I am a reactionary and a revolutionary according to circumstance". Nowhere was this statement more true than in the architectural policies encouraged and pursued by Il Duce from the 1920s until his fall in 1943 when the German army seized Italy before losing it to the Allies.

Right until the end, Piero Luigi Nervi was designing and building a sequence of a dozen or so magnificent and revolutionary aircraft hangars in pre-cast concrete. Here was proof – sad in a way – that sabre-rattling and war itself can stimulate some of the most inventive and beautiful design and engineering. The hangar at Orbetello (destroyed) was perhaps the finest of Nervi's sequence. Here a cat's

cradle of a roof – a latticework of prestressed concrete members, or bones – is supported on six, delicately curving concrete buttresses. The roof measured no less than 102 metres (336 ft) by 36.5 metres (120 ft) and was covered with asbestos-cement sheets. The effect was one of cathedral-like Gothic beauty, belying the savage purpose of the machines of war gathered under this peerless vault. Nervi, unlike many engineers, never denied that he was seeking beauty in his designs: his quest for filigree and lightweight concrete structures was as much to delight the eye as it was to push forward the boundaries of structural engineering. For Nervi, the quest of the artist, architect and the engineer was one and the same.

WOLF'S LAIR

TODT ORGANIZATION, 1940 KATSZYN, POLAND

Adolf Hitler railed against the decadence of Modern architecture, yet for most of World War Two the Führer ran his blitzkrieg campaigns from the bowels of some of the most radical concrete structures yet built. Deep in Poland's Mazurian Forest, the Todt organization (named after the engineer who built Hitler's autobahns) built the Wolfsshanze (Wolf's Lair), 27 acres of bombastic concrete buildings and bunkers. This is where Colonel von Stauffenberg failed to assasinate Hitler in 1944 and where the Führer walked his pet German Shepherd, Blondi, before morning briefings. The complex included a casino and sauna, fortified houses for Hitler, Goering and other heads of staff, together with officers' quarters and barracks for no fewer than 3,000 personnel. Hitler's own gargantuan bunkers looked disturbingly like the architecture of the so-called Brutalists of the 1950s.

The SS wired the buildings up so as to self-destruct in the event of the Wolf's Lair being overrun by the Red Army. Eventually the Soviets arrived and the complex was blown up; yet, such was the quality of Todt's reinforced concrete that it was all but impossible to destroy the Wolf's Lair. At the end of the twentieth century it survives as a monument to Hitler's flawed ambitions and as proof of the great strength and enduring qualities of concrete construction.

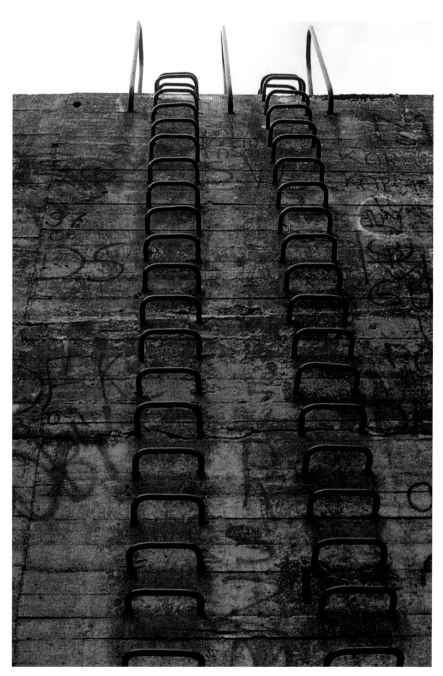

COASTAL DEFENCES

TODT ORGANIZATION, 1944 FRANCE

In preparation for the Allied invasion of Europe, the German army called on the Todt Organization, headed by Albert Speer (p.53) after the death of Fritz Todt, to build a defensive wall of gun emplacements from Calais to Bordeaux. In the event, the Allies landed further north and largely escaped the wrath of Todt's fortresses. What is remarkable about these twentieth-century castles is that they are obviously architectural in spirit. Far from being purely utilitarian they were designed with much the same enthusiasm and with as much aesthetic consideration as Michelangelo gave to his designs for the defence of sixteenth-century Florence. The

fortresses clearly owed much to German Expressionism: they were both anthropormphic and aggressive at the same time. Few military works this side of the castles the English built to subdue the Welsh have such a savage power combined with a chilling sculptural beauty. Because of their Nazi associations, the coastal defences fell into decline, yet they have remained haunting tourist destinations. They seem to prefigure the work of British Brutalist architects of the 1950s who set about creating art galleries, schools, shopping complexes and even a New Town (Cumbernauld, Scotland) in the guise of Nazi gun emplacements.

DOME OF DISCOVERY

RALPH TUBBS, 1951 LONDON, ENGLAND

The Festival of Britain was a brave attempt to raise the expectations of a public that had been heavily bombed during World War Two and which, until 1954, had to shop for food and other basic supplies with ration books. It took place a century on from the Great Exhibition of 1851 that had been held in the unprecedented and superb Crystal Palace erected in London's Hyde Park by the gardener Joseph Paxton. In the event the five-month festival of 1951 was an enjoyable spectacular, although many observers thought it gimcrack and a bit too much like a sixth-form school chemistry set for comfort. The most exciting of the structures built for the Festival was the Dome of Discovery designed by Ralph Tubbs (1912–96). At the time it was

the largest domed building in the world, with a maximum height of 28 metres (93 ft). Inside, stairs and a long escalator led up to three platforms under the imposing web-like construction of the steel roof. On display were the technological wonders of the immediate postwar era.

The Dome was demolished soon after the Festival closed on the express orders of Sir Winston Churchill, the wartime leader, who at the end of 1951 was voted back into office as Prime Minister of a Conservative government after six years of socialist government. To Churchill the Dome represented the spirit of socialism. Posthumously, it was to influence the design of Richard Rogers' Millennium Dome at Greenwich (p.407).

SKYLON

PHILIP POWELL AND HIDALGO MOYA, 1951 LONDON, ENGLAND

Two years after graduating from the Architectural Association, London, Philip Powell (born 1921) and Hidalgo Moya (1920–94) won a competition for the design of Churchill Gardens (1946–52), a development of local authority flats fronting the River Thames and facing Sir Giles Gilbert Scott's famous Battersea Power Station. It was a brave attempt to humanize public housing on a large scale. Their next major project could hardly have been more different: the design of the Skylon, an elegant masted structure that was to become the symbol of the 1951 Festival of Britain. In an era of austerity, the Skylon was a welcome escape from the matter-of-fact architectural concerns of the day. It stood like a giant insect from the depths of space – this was the age when flying saucers and science-fiction films were all the rage – or else a decorative missile about to be sprung into space from the launch pad of its delicate base. The Skylon stood in front of the Dome of Discovery (p.371) and its ethereal verticality was designed to act in point-counterpoint to the scale and materiality of the Dome, much as Sir Christopher Wren had set the spire of St Martin's Church, Ludgate against the immensity of the dome of his St Paul's Cathedral. The Skylon, like the Dome, was destroyed by Churchill (as in Churchill Gardens); various plans to rebuild it have come to nothing.

REPAIR SHOP

BUCKMINSTER FULLER, 1958 BATON ROUGE, LOUISIANA, USA

A building that must have looked as if had come from Outer Space in the heyday of American B-movie science fiction. There was nothing B-grade, though, about the railway wagon repair shop Buckminster Fuller designed for the Union Tank Car Co. When completed, it was the largest circular building in the world, with a diameter of 117 metres (354 ft) and a height that was the equivalent of a ten-storey office block.

Fuller had been working for decades on the form of construction that allowed this dome to be so big, so light and so easy to erect and maintain. He called this type of dome structure "geodesic". It was based on series of metal or plastic octahedrons or tetrahedrons that allowed the builder to enclose vast spaces economically:

the geodesic dome meant the provision of the greatest possible volume of enclosed space in relation to the surface area of the enclosing form. Which wasn't just clever: in Fuller's hand the idea had its own beauty. The wagon repair shop is made up of steel sections. If it looks a bit like a gigantic igloo from a distance, this is because the paintshop extends out of the main body of the dome in a 35-metre (117-ft) long tunnel using the same structural components. Fuller's system of construction is often said to be a logical development of the lightweight, prefabricated methods the gardener Joseph Paxton used in the design of the Crystal Palace (1851). Its finest flowering was Fuller's US Pavilion at Expo '67, Montreal.

FACULTY OF ENGINEERING

JAMES STIRLING AND JAMES GOWAN, 1963 LEICESTER, ENGLAND

A triumphant trumpet-blast of a building that put British architecture back on the international map after a period in the creative doldrums. It was also the last work designed jointly by James Stirling (1924–92) and James Gowan (born 1923). The two had teamed up in London in 1953, going on to produce a succession of inspired and uncompromising Modern designs culminating in the Leicester Engineering building. Rising boldly over playing fields, the tower, clad in hard orange brick tiles, dominates a run of dramatically profiled workshops. Its design is outlandish, drawn from the naval architecture Stirling knew well as a child in Glasgow where his father was a naval engineer; from the Constructivist monuments (unbuilt) of the early days of the Russian Revolution, and from the works of Mies van der Rohe. The building was a brilliant collage of ideas and images drawn from across the previous half-century. It was certainly brave. So was Stirling, who as a young lieutenant in the paratroopers dropped behind enemy lines on D-Day only to be gunned down by a Tiger Tank, or so he claimed, designed by Ferdinand Porsche (1875–1952). The building demanded a high degree of maintenance and windows of the tower were unsympathetically replaced in the 1980s. Stirling's life and work was cut short by a routine operation that went tragically wrong.

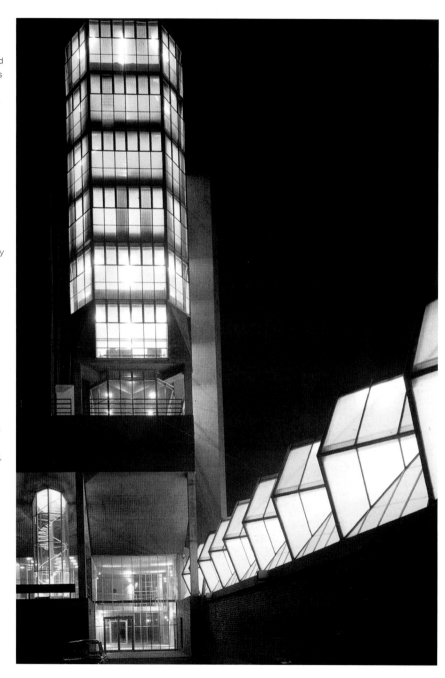

OLYMPIC SPORTS HALLS

KENZO TANGE, 1964 YOYOGI, TOKYO, JAPAN

One of Tange's crowning achievements, the two sports halls erected for the 1964 Tokyo Olympics were an awe-inspiring international spectacle at a time when – foolish things – Europeans and North Americans were still sneering at the low design input of Japanese cars, motorbikes and consumer goods. The Olympic Games and these magnificent tented structures lifted the Japanese game plan onto a new level altogether. Both buildings boasted vast, concave cantilevered roofs that swooped in great ellipses around the masts from which they were tautly suspended. The result was a pair of buildings with an organic quality – like great sea-shells – despite their bravura use of the very latest developments in structural engineering. Inside, the halls did not disappoint.

Their dramatic structures were boldly expressed and their fly-away roofs must have seemed astonishing to spectators in 1964. By this time in his career, Tange was questioning more and more the validity of the notion of "functionalism". And, like Le Corbusier before him, he came to the conclusion that the way architects had understood and used the word was destructive. "Beauty", he said, "is the only functionalism." In other words, an architect's duty – his function – was to create beauty and not soulless boxes that were functional in the sense only that their doors opened and their lavatories flushed. The Olympic sports halls were more than ample proof that even the largest-scale Modern architecture could be inspiring, beautiful and, yes, functional.

POST OFFICE TOWER

ERIC BEDFORD, ET AL, 1964 LONDON, ENGLAND

The Post Office Tower symbolized the "white hot technological revolution" the Labour government (1964–70), led by Harold Wilson, promised the people of Britain. Where Germany, Japan and Italy were all modernizing rapidly from the mid-1950s, Britain, by and large, continued to enjoy an after-lunch nap and was still very much living in the 1930s at the beginning of the 1960s. The Post Office, soaring more than 180 metres (600 ft) into the London smog, beamed microwaves across the North and South Downs and the Chiltern Hills rising above the London basin, taking television and radio broadcasts and countless telephone calls with them. The pencil-thin concrete tower, which rose from an eight-storey base, was clad in steel and glass to make it look more polite than it would have been in naked concrete. Although it looks as if there are offices rising the length of the tower, this is just an illusion. However, because the Post Office was keen to show off its leap into the white, hot future, Eric Bedford and his team at the Ministry of Work designed public viewing galleries and a revolving restaurant at the top of the tower. Though hugely popular, these were sadly closed to the public after an IRA bomb shattered them in 1971. They have never reopened, although the restaurant is now a hospitality suite for the management of British Telecommunications.

NORTHERN AVIARY

LORD SNOWDON, CEDRIC PRICE AND FRANK NEWBY, 1965 REGENT'S PARK ZOO, LONDON, ENGLAND

What looks to be an outsized cat's cradle overlooking Regent's Canal turns out to be an ethereal structure alive with birds both exotic and homely. Sparrows, pigeons and other winged cockney urchins fly into this near-invisible structure to spend a day with more colourful relatives who wouldn't last very long outside the likeable confines of this giant birdcage. A rectangular base with pools is spanned by a zig-zag concrete bridge (for human visitors) and these are covered by a mesh of anodized aluminium supported by tension cables attached to four tetrahederal frames. The birds nest wherever they can and have room to spread their wings and fly. For these facts alone, Snowdon (born 1930), Price (born 1934 and Newby (born 1932) deserve a special mention in zoological as well as architectural despatches. The London Zoological Society had long championed intelligent design, from as far back as the 1830s when Decimus Burton (1800–81) built the handsome brick Camel and Giraffe Houses, and a century later with Berthold Lubetkin's Penguin Pool (p.191). Until the construction of this aviary birds were confined to iron cages in which they were unable to fly. The soft structure of this radical birdcage allows the birds to fly, ensuring that if they crash into the walls they will not hurt themselves.

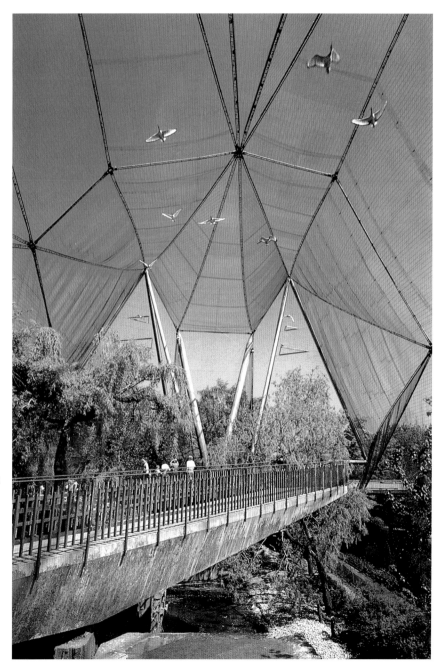

RELIANCE CONTROLS FACTORY

TEAM 4, 1965 SWINDON, WILTSHIRE, ENGLAND

This cool, clean, clinical industrial machine – no more and no less than a finely detailed steel envelope containing the maximum possible amount of clear, brightly lit, neutral space – is one of the first important designs of Norman Foster (born 1935) and Richard Rogers (born 1933) together with their first wives Wendy (1938–89) and Su (born 1940).

Foster, born and trained in Manchester, teamed up with Rogers, who had trained in London, while a postgraduate student at Yale University. They returned to London and set up in practice together, working on a number of projects that took as their starting point the building as a smooth-skinned shed or elegant machine with materials and details drawn from the very

latest palettes and portfolios . Their work was quickly labelled "Hi-Tech", a tag that was to stick. Both architects went on on to become major players on the international stage in the 1980s, having made their name with buildings that were glamorous and sophisticated yet cheap, easy and quick to build.

Many light industrial buildings and the architecture of Britain's first US-style business parks had something of the look of the Reliance Controls factory about them. Swindon, once famous for the Great Western Railway locomotive works (the town grew up around the railway), was to become the heart of Britain's "Silicon Valley" as the computer industry and its Hi-Tech headquarters surfed this way.

VEHICLE ASSEMBLY BUILDING

MAX URBAHN ASSOCIATES AND ROBERTS & SCHAEFER COMPANY, 1966 CAPE KENNEDY, FLORIDA, USA

A twentieth-century pyramid of sorts, standing in relation to the NASA settlement at Cape Kennedy much as the Egyptian pyramids must have once to Memphis, the Vehicle Assembly Building (VAB) was, at the time of its construction, the largest building in the world. It needed to be: this is where the giant *Saturn* rockets were pieced together which, in July 1969, were to lift the *Apollo 11* mission on its way to the very first Lunar landing. As tall as cathedrals, the rockets were a development of the *V2* rockets, designed by the precocious young Nazi scientist, Werner von Braun. Designed by Max Urbahn (1912–95), the architect-planner and engineers Roberts and Schaefer, the steel-framed monster made no overt concessions to style, yet had a monumental magnificence of all its own and a notably Classical layout. To give some sense of its herculean scale, the main doors are 150 metres (500 ft) high and 20 metres (70 ft) wide. The building was designed to house four *Saturn V* rockets, which were moved in and out of the VAB on mobile launch-pads. The VAB was an important monument in humankind's quest for the stars, just as the Egyptian pyramids had been some 4,000 years earlier: the big difference was that rocket fuel, computers and a wing and a prayer had replaced the power of prayer alone.

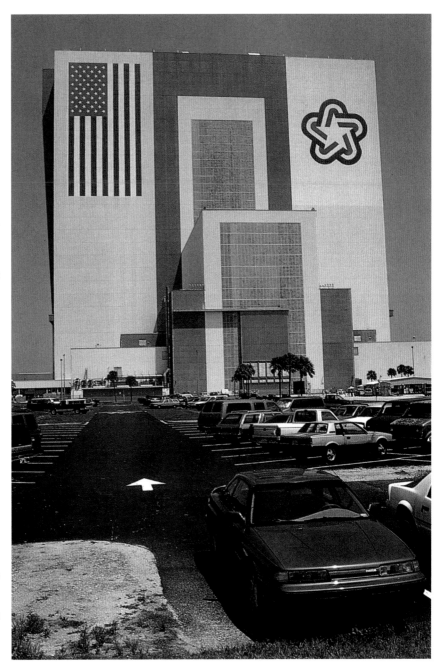

YAMANASHI PRESS AND BROADCASTING CENTRE

KENZO TANGE, 1967 KOFU, JAPAN

Although it has never been completed and never will be – the open-ended nature of this powerful building is also the essence of its form – Tange's hugely impressive communications centre feels somehow right. Set against a backdrop of hills and mountains it has the quality of a medieval castle, lacking only the turned-up gable ends and the intricate, filigree decoration of ancient and ritualistic Japanese architecture: it could easily be the home of a brotherhood of modern Samurai. The massiveness of the structure is implied by the 16 hollow concrete tubes that support the deep-plan floors (housing television studios, a newspaper printing plant and a radio broadcasting station) and carry the services needed to

run this modern fortress. The conceit of the structure is that it can be extended almost indefinitely. The conceit of the architecture is that is has no end, no beginning, no façade and is all but indeterminate. And yet, for all this, it has an imposing presence and is one of the greatest buildings in modern Japan. It also represented Kenzo Tange, then in his early fifties, at the height of his powers. As he competed for more and more international projects, so his special magic appeared to be undone: that magic had been his bringing Modernism to Japan as it reinvented itself after World War Two and developing a recognizably Modern Japanese language of design.

TELEVISION TOWER

D. BURDIN, L. BATALOV AND N. NIKITIN, 1967 OSTANKINO, MOSCOW, RUSSIA

Moscow's television tower rockets 533-metres (1750-ft) towards the Moon. It is a thrilling and dizzying structure that, beneath its aerial, contains panoramic viewing platforms and a three-storey restaurant. There are also eleven floors of mechanical plant and technical gubbins galore. The superb tower rises from a multi-storey podium made up of four floors of television studios topped with a multi-storey office block. Not surprisingly the base of the tower is immense and the sky-piercing structure is a blatantly heroic example of what concrete can do. It is also a symbol of the way in which the former Soviet Union devoted huge resources to scientific enterprises both as a way of trying to raise living standards and to show the capitalist world that Communism really did work. The Soviets were the first to put a satellite into orbit around the Earth and Yuri Gagarin was the first man in space. For a while it looked as if the USSR really was overcoming what many observers saw as inherent structural weaknesses in its economy and its society. In the end they proved to be right. Even so, hopeful symbols like the television tower at Ostankino remain to show what the Soviet Union wanted to be: a triumphalist, one party state with lashings of highly-visible high technology.

ELGIN ESTATE

GREATER LONDON COUNCIL ARCHITECT'S DEPARTMENT, 1968 MAIDA HILL, LONDON, ENGLAND

Imagine seeing a television set being hurtled from the twenty-second floor of a plastic-clad tower block. Imagine watching the Fire Brigade putting out a savage blaze on the eighteenth floor of its twin and being told that this was just a routine "chip-pan blaze". Built with such confidence in new technology, the twin plastic towers of the Elgin Estate were soon to become a "sink" for the most disadvantaged of west London families. Local authority architects believed they were doing their best not only to solve London's perennial housing shortage, but also to create a new type of city home for the age of instant technology. The result was a pair of towers that looked too much like refrigerators and washing-machines for comfort. They were quick to build, taking just ten months, yet speed was certainly no guarantee of decent homes. There was no pleasure to be had from not being able to open a window beyond a minimal angle (save when you tore it out so you could heave the television overboard). This was the sort of sad housing block that conservationists, who once had eyes only for Georgian terraces and Victorian churches, wanted to preserve at the end of the century. Dear things, they had obviously never had to live in or near the Elgin Estate. The blocks were finally pulled down in the 1990s and replaced by low-rise homes.

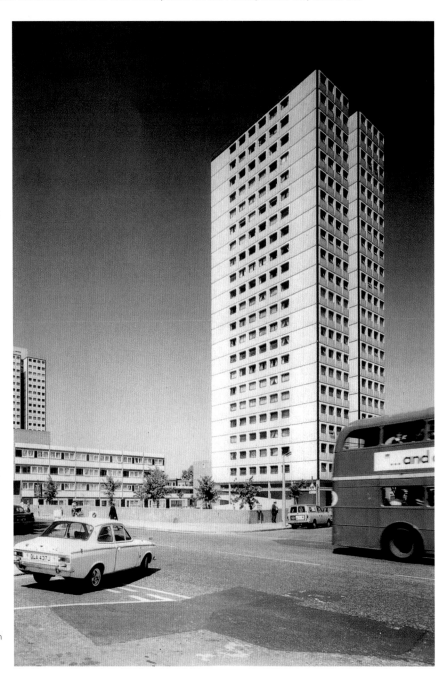

JOHN HANCOCK CENTER

SKIDMORE, OWINGS AND MERRILL, 1970 CHICAGO, ILLINOIS, USA

As the skyscraper became ever taller and more complex, so the engineer came to play an ever-increasing role in its design as well as its construction. Although nominally designed by a team led by Skidmore, Owings and Merrill's Bruce Graham (born 1925), the hugely impressive John Hancock Center – a black hole appearing to suck all available light into its dark immensity – owed its dramatic exposed structure, and thus its entire character, to the brilliant engineer Fazlur Khan. Khan developed a way of cross-bracing a skyscraper with steel beams on the outside of the building: this method can be seen in the huge X-braces that criss-cross their way up this Chicago behemoth.

The net result was office floors free from the interruption of structural columns. This was a revolution in building design over which property developers must have wept with delight: from now on, the net-to-gross ratio of office space to building structure was all in favour of the renter. Fortunately, the John Hancock Center is not just a sky-high filing cabinet for office workers. Inside what appear to be countless floors – there are exactly 100 – are 670 apartments as well as to shops, restaurants and garages. The roof, about 300 metres (1,000 ft) above the sidewalks, is topped by antennae that have always looked rather disturbingly like missiles. Not a building to be messed with.

NAKAGIN CAPSULE TOWER

KISHO KUROKAWA, 1972 TOKYO, JAPAN

What looks like a large scientist's model of a molecular structure turns out to be a cheap, overnight hostel for workers in the Ginza district of Tokyo. The tower is made up of 140 prefabricated "living capsules", each looking like a washing machine and slotted into a concrete climbing frame in a complex and lively manner. This is the sort of architecture that can be made in basic Lego sets and, like Lego bricks, its construction is simple but very clever. Living space is always at a premium in Tokyo, which is why the "living capsule" made sense here, but the tower was also a vivid expression of ideas that had been floating around the globe concerned with the the creation of instant cities. The idea that "living capsules" could be added when needed was appealing at a time when technology became available to realize the dream.

Kisho Kurokawa (born 1934) set up his own office in Tokyo in 1961 having worked with Kenzo Tange. He was much influenced by the science-fiction-like housing at the time and the "living capsule" idea was one that caught the imagination of the media worldwide. How could anyone live in such small spaces for even one night? Only the Japanese could do so. Of course, this wasn't true. Within 15 years of the building of the Nakagin Tower, Europeans were checking into hotels built alongside motorways along the same principles, but without the ingenious architecture.

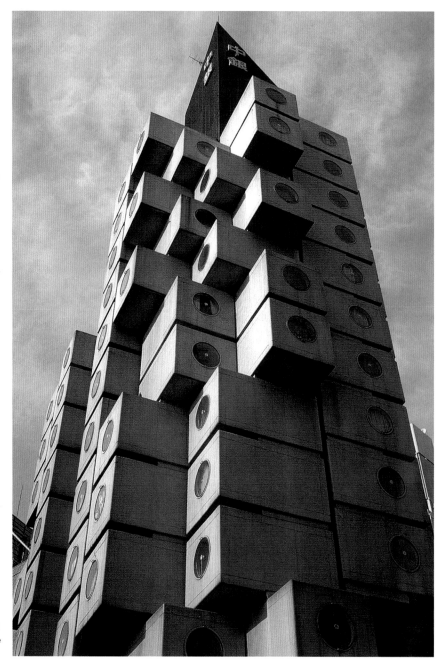

HOPKINS HOUSE

MICHAEL HOPKINS, 1975 HAMPSTEAD, LONDON, ENGLAND

A one-time partner of Norman Foster, Michael Hopkins was a keen exponent of Hi-Tech design before he changed course some time in the 1980s and began to pursue a tweedy architecture that appealed to conservation bodies, planners and government agencies without the slightest whiff of controversy. Before he developed this diplomatic style, his buildings were noted for their industrial strength and rigour and for a particularly clean and satisfying use of factory components. In this sense, his own home in a beautiful leafy street near Hampstead Heath went one step further than even the Eames had done in the 1940s (p.204). Those brought up in the house remember its noisiness

and lack of privacy, and probably it made better sense as a summer pavilion than as an all-year family house. Even so, it was a brave attempt to strip the family house of its protective façade and to display it warts and all. Not that you find anything so unpleasant in an English architect's house. They are nearly always neat and trim, reflecting the very suburban values they appear to want to escape.

Hopkins went on to design a fine Hi-Tech factory for the Greene King brewery in Bury St Edmunds, Suffolk, and the inspired research laboratories for Schlumberger on a greenfield site outside Cambridge (p.390) before he had what appeared to be a change of heart and style.

SONY TOWER

KISHO KUROKAWA, 1976 OSAKA, JAPAN

A forerunner of Lloyds of London (p.393) and the Pompidou Centre (p.388), the Sony Tower deserves to better known outside Japan. What Kurokawa built here was a 72-metre (235-ft) tower off which were slung steel-clad toilet capsules and up which ran lifts inside a largely transparent tube. The floors in which Sony displayed its latest electronic goodies were entirely free of columns or other spatial intrusions. The building is rather like a spaceman who clips oxygen tanks and other life support systems to his Hi-Tech suit. Or the tower can be seen as a kind of exo-skeleton. Whatever, it is one of the triumphs of the "Metabolist" movement of which

the young Kurokawa was a leading light.

If the Metabolists had a clear-cut programme, it had much to do with bridging the gap between private and public space. Traditionally in Japan, every building was separated from the next, if only by the width of a hand. The private realm was defiantly distanced from the public. Kurokawa's reaction to this idea (it was not always quite so true in practice, not, at least in the twentieth century), was to make his connections loud and clear: plugged-in, slotted together in a powerful display of the possibilities and strange poetry offered by new materials and technology.

SAINSBURY CENTRE

FOSTER ASSOCIATES, 1977 UNIVERSITY OF EAST ANGLIA, NORWICH, NORFOLK, ENGLAND

One of the handsomest sheds in Christendom – or anywhere else in the world – the Sainsbury Centre for Visual Arts is an exquisite aircraft hangar in spirit conjured by Norman Foster's magic into one of the most glamorous of all art galleries. Commissioned by wealthy grocers, the Sainsbury Centre is a part of the University of East Anglia and fine art students get

to study in its shimmering interior. The design is simple. A white steel truss is sheathed in what were once silver and are now white panels, and all the services needed to run the building are tucked in between these two elements. At either end, the structure is glazed from floor to ceiling. And that's about it. However, this simple description of an essentially simple building tells only half the story: not only does this shed sparkle on the outside, but its interior is quite breathtaking and remains so even after several visits. Inside this art hangar is all but one great space, superbly lit and animated with beautiful tribal sculptures and other exotic works of art. A gallery floor contains lecture rooms and offices.

An extension dating from the early 1990s, also designed by Foster, has been dug underground at one end of the building. Here, the patron's paintings are held in a store that is a curious cross between a Hi-Tech bank vault and a pharaoh's tomb in the Valley of the Kings. The Sainsbury Centre is also a machine for teaching in: both a gallery and an academic institution.

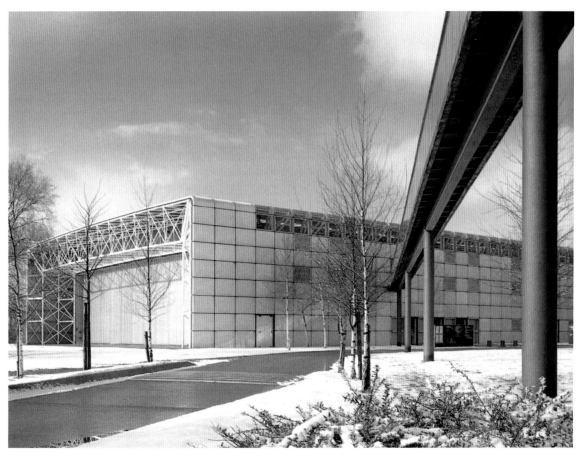

POMPIDOU CENTRE

RENZO PIANO AND RICHARD ROGERS, 1977 PARIS, FRANCE

Bombastic. Iconoclastic. Bowellist (it wears its insides on the outside). Think of any more or less suitable term you can to pin down this explosion of a building and you will still be struggling to make sense of it. The Centre Georges Pompidou is one of the most exciting, wilful, eccentric and popular of all twentieth-century buildings. Most remarkable of all, it was commissioned by a right-wing French president and designed by a gang of rather left-wing architects and engineers led by the ebullient and charming Renzo Piano (born 1937) and Richard Rogers.

The team did not expect to win the international competition; it entered at the very last moment in 1970 when the design was very much a loose concept. With a great

deal of help from Peter Rice up went this vast assembly of brightly coloured pipes and ducts and tubes. The result is not quite as wilful as it seems. What you are looking is a vast art centre designed so that it has the maximum amount of uninterrupted floor area. Even the lifts and famous escalators – rising in glass tubes up the side of the building – are on the outside. The result is a busy machine on the outside, an adult climbing frame, with what might have been calm spaces for the contemplation of art inside. No such luck. The building became a tourist attraction and one that has rivalled the Eiffel Tower in popularity. It has always been crowded, and by the late 1990s was exhausted. It was closed to be refurbished in time for the Millennium.

GROUND SIGNAL STATION

GUSTAV PEICHL, 1980 AFLENZ, AUSTRIA

Gustav Peichl (born 1928) has a particular genius for creating sculptural, artful buildings from scientific functions and public utilities that are normally framed in dreary, all too functional sheds. Peichl's aesthetic has been very much his own. Radio stations in Graz and Eisenstadt, Austria, a phosphate treatment plant in Berlin and this ground signal station at Aflenz, Austria, are wonderful designs rooted in a kind of late twentieth-century Baroque, and yet distinctly Modern too. No Postmodern irony here, just one man's highly individual eye at work on buildings that deserve to be celebrated rather than hidden. Peichl's decorative vocabulary – shiny pipes, portholes, gantries, gangways, ladders – is clearly drawn

from ships, and his buildings sail, fully rigged, as if through designed landscapes.

The ground signal station is the most restrained of his gleaming architectural machines. It had to be. Scientists found that the best place for the satellite signal receiver was in the middle of a nature reserve. As a result, Peichl dug his buildings into the ground. The result is deeply satisfying, with offices, receiving station and laboratories grouped around two interconnecting circular courtyards. In summer, these are surrounded with lush grass and meadow flowers; in winter, they are capped with snow. The quality of finishes here lives up to the beauty of the surrounding landscape.

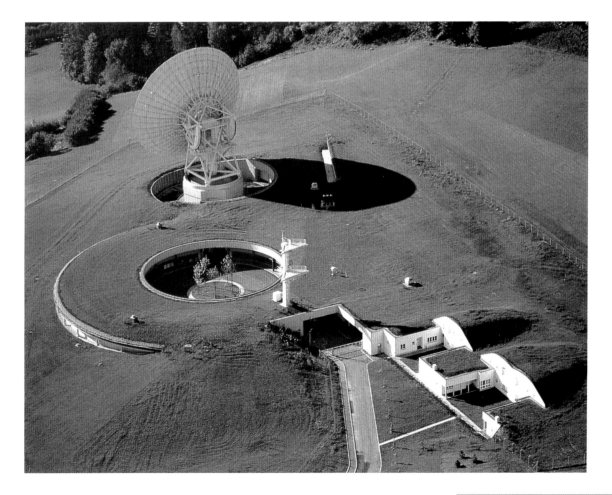

SCHLUMBERGER RESEARCH LABORATORIES

MICHAEL HOPKINS, 1981 CAMBRIDGE, ENGLAND

This is Hopkins' finest effort, a building that is exciting, yet gentle and animates a flat stretch of countryside on the Bedford Plain at Madingly, just beyond Cambridge. It has lost some of its lustre over the years, yet the basic idea was excellent. Instead of a solid and intrusive technical building, Hopkins came up with what, from a distance, looks like the tents of either a travelling circus or else a Hi-Tech Bedouin caravan. Beautifully lit at dusk, the three tents are held up by a concatenation of tall steel masts and tensile cables. The laboratories are housed in extensively glazed, steel-framed structures below.

Hopkins was one of many architects to have become intrigued by the possibilities of fabric roofs at the beginning of the 1980s and was to use them to subtle effect in, among other designs, the much admired Mound Stand at Lord's Cricket Ground, London (p.280). Fabrics were available that were lasting, weatherproof and strong. They played a valuable role in softening the over-mechanical Hi-Tech style that British architects excelled at, but which was always in danger of becoming a cliché. Schlumberger proved to be an energetic patron committed to investment in some of the most sane architecture of the 1980s, notably its new centrein Paris and the Menil Collection in Houston, Texas (p.277), both by Renzo Piano, master of the "Soft Tech" approach explored here by Hopkins.

INMOS RESEARCH CENTRE

RICHARD ROGERS PARTNERSHIP, 1982 GWENT, SOUTH WALES

High unemployment and cheap labour have been staples of life in South Wales for most of the twentieth century. At least two attempts involving some of Britain's most radical architects have been made to inject new jobs and creativity into the area. The first was the Brynmawr rubber factory (p.209) by the Architects Co-Partnership shortly after World War Two; the second was another government-backed scheme, the INMOS factory and silicon-chip research centre designed by the Richard Rogers Partnership.

Standing like some exotic insect in the Welsh countryside, the Rogers' building is magnificent, and quickly caught the attention of advertising agencies as well as architecture critics. Its construction really did appear to herald a new era for this profoundly depressed region, famous for its lack of decent modern design. The building is simple, yet held together by a gloriously complex system of masts. The masts held cables that supported an extensive roof on either side of a central service corridor. All servicing for the building was mounted above the corridor and within the brightly coloured frames of the masts. This bravura show of structural wizardry was as satisfying to gaze at as-a fully rigged sailing ship. It was almost fetishistic in its obsessive detailing and all the more enjoyable for being so.

HAJ AIR TERMINAL

SKIDMORE, OWINGS AND MERRILL, 1982 JEDDAH, SAUDI ARABIA

Each year millions of Muslim pilgrims descend on Jeddah on their way across the desert to nearby Mecca. Until this superb air terminal opened in 1983 they suffered the indignity of simply being too many people confined into inadequate buildings. SOM's design solution was as simple as it was inspired. The new terminal, designated exclusively for pilgrim traffic at the King Abdul Aziz airport, Jeddah, was built in the guise of a massive Arabic tent, albeit using modern materials – steel masts and Hi-Tech fabric. The simplicity of the structure meant that it could be extended almost indefinitely

if and when the pilgrim traffic grew. The design performed two important functions, the first practical, the second symbolic. In practical terms, the high-tented ceilings dissipated both the sense of claustrophobia endemic in many airport lounges and the hot desert air. In symbolic terms, the tents were not only a sophisticated nod to Arabic culture but a new-found way of Western technology shaking hands with that culture and making real friends. Until the arrival of the Haj Terminal in Jeddah, architects from the US and Europe (and anywhere else for that matter) had done precious little to engage with local culture and history; far too many of the buildings that sprouted from Saudi and other oil-rich Arab cities looked suspiciously like rejects from the drawing boards of architects who had put a need or lust for fees above the callings of their art. The Haj Terminal was a pilgrimage for architects too.

LLOYD'S BUILDING

RICHARD ROGERS, 1986 CITY OF LONDON, ENGLAND

Kapow! What can anyone say? The Lloyd's Building is one of the great buildings of the latter part of the century. Much maligned and misunderstood, not least by the pin-striped chaps and shoulder-padded chapesses who moved in here to make and lose huge piles of money at the height of Margaret Thatcher's elected dictatorship, the Lloyd's Building has become as much a part of the City of London as St Paul's Cathedral. If you can imagine the big building stripped of all those cranes, pipes, ladders, tubes, it proves surprisingly simple soul. Tiers of offices are stepped up to a maximum of 12 storeys and breached and saddled by a lofty atrium placed over the enormous Lloyd's "Room" where anything up to 10,000 pink-faced "suits" will be getting excited and doing things with money that the rest of us will never understand. What must be the biggest "room" in the world is penetrated by silent-running escalators that offer a thrilling, if vertiginous, ride. If you find these frightening, keep away from the lifts. Glass-fronted, floored and ceilinged, these race up and down the outside of the building, offering mind-searing views over the City, and are most fun to ride in snow, hail and driving rain or by night. The building's services are on the outside, which is why it is rather like one of those gruesome anatomical drawings in which the flesh is peeled from cadavers to reveal the organs within.

FINANCIAL TIMES PRINTWORKS

NICHOLAS GRIMSHAW, 1988 DOCKLANDS, LONDON, ENGLAND

The *Financial Times* commissioned this sleek printing plant, but sold it on again almost before the presses were warm. This was not a criticism of Grimshaw's confident Docklands landmark, but a sign of how fickle and fast-changing the newspaper industry had become: today's building, yesterday's headline. In fact it was noteworthy that any London-based newspaper was printing in the capital after the Fleet Street diaspora of the mid-1980s prompted new forms of electronic publishing. Yet, for a while at least, the "pink 'un", as the FT was known for the colour of its paper, was printed in the East End and in great style. Grimshaw's building was really little more than a very smart tin box fronted with one of the most adventurous windows yet made. The biggest available

sheets of glass were supported by a finely-wrought web of modern steel tracery that enabled the whole of the big printing press to be seen in one sweep of the eyes. The sight of the newspaper being printed at night was, for that short while, one of the least known but finest spectacles in London. The pink paper could be watched as it coursed at great speed around the vast web, the building lit up in a way that made sure you could best enjoy the action.

Grimshaw (born 1940) worked long and hard on the details of his buildings, so much so that he even put them on show in regular travelling exhibitions. For an architect fascinated by engineering, it was important to be able to work up his own details where and whenever possible. In one sense, these details are Grimshaw's architecture.

CANARY WHARF TOWER

CESAR PELLI, 1991 DOCKLANDS, LONDON, ENGLAND

Canary Wharf Tower was for a brief while Europe's tallest building. Clad in sun-catching stainless steel, 245 metres (800 ft) and 50 floors high, it dominates views of London at almost every turn of the head and can be seen up to 32 kilometres (20 miles) away from the principal approach roads from all points east into central London. The tower, designed by Cesar Pelli (born 1926), is the focal point of Canary Wharf, a titanic development of offices, shops, hotels and apartments in the old London docks. Every building in this unlikely slice of Chicago-shipped-to-London in the late 1980s by the Canadian developer Reichmann was built on a megalomaniacal scale and in a heavy-handed Postmodern style. The enigmatic tower is perhaps the only building here with any real presence. It has become well known as the offices for several national newspapers including the *Independent*, *Daily Telegraph* and *Daily Mirror*. In all other respects it is conventional and even old fashioned. A giant lift lobby gives access to racks of dreary offices, enlivened here and there by some of the sparkier tenants (Live TV boasts a floor decorated by David Connor). Few of those working here get to enjoy the spectacular views which make the whole reason to he here – cheap rents aside – spurious.

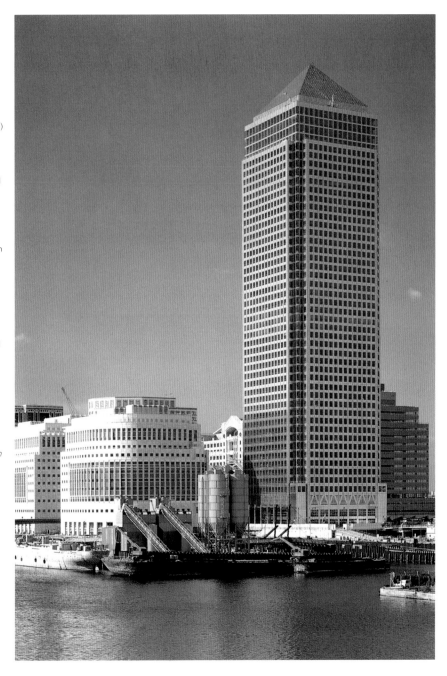

BARCELONA INTERNATIONAL AIRPORT

TALLER DE ARQUITECTURA, 1992 BARCELONA, SPAIN

The death of the dictator General Franco not only restored the monarchy to Spain but brought new found prosperity to the country and a great deal of autonomy and democracy to regions such as Andalucia and Catalonia, of which Barcelona – an anti-Franco city always – is the fiercely independent capital. The 1990s added more major events to Spain's resurrection: Expo '92 at Seville and, in the same year, the Olympic Games in Barcelona. The Olympics prompted far more than major investment in Barcelona, they prompted the city to rebuild itself on a heroic scale. This heroism began at the international gate to the city, the airport.

The new terminal, by Ricardo Bofill's Taller de Arquitectura, was a grandiloquent work. It boasted one of the longest internal axes ever seen and had a hard, almost militaristic logic that appeared somewhat at odds with Barcelona's new-found freedoms and rising prosperity. Franco would have loved it. In fact the new terminal was surprising in other ways too. First, it was a stylistic turn-about for the Taller, which had for more than a decade made its name with its own brand of prefabricated Neo-Classical design: now, the Taller had gone International Modern, with undertones of the monumental Fascist architecture of the 1930s. Second, unlike Rafael Moneo's airport at Seville, which echoed regional architectural identities, Barcelona airport was defiantly "neutral", reflecting the city's role as a major port, its architecture was of the world.

WATERLOO INTERNATIONAL TERMINAL

NICHOLAS GRIMSHAW, 1993 LONDON, ENGLAND

A new gateway to continental Europe from London, Waterloo International has been highly acclaimed. Not only is it determinedly modern, but it also harks back, without any stifling feeling of nostalgia, to the great train sheds of Victorian Britain, notably that of York station with which it shares a gently curving roof. The great glazed roof, held up by a lattice work of blue steel, curves around the exceptionally long platforms and reduces both in height and width as it stretches away from the concourse. The result is a station that appears to squeeze the Eurostar trains from its southern end like toothpaste from a tube. Interestingly, Grimshaw's original proposal envisaged the terminal – it was called "terminal"

rather than "station" because, at the time, Britain's railways, on the verge of being flogged to private enterprise, were keen to pretend they were airlines – as a very regular rectangle. It was the railway engineers and local planners who insisted it follow the established curve of the tracks as they snaked out of Waterloo. Grimshaw rose magnificently to the challenge. The one sadness here is that the beautiful roof is largely wasted on the passengers, who are required to hang around in the lounges beneath the train shed and so only catch glimpses of the roof as they hurry to find their seats. The bulk of the terminal is hidden below, but well lit and thoughtfully planned.

SATOLAS TGV STATION

SANTIAGO CALATRAVA, 1993 LYON, FRANCE

Calatrava (born 1951) is an engineer, architect and designer who brought a new excitement to bridges and railway stations in the 1990s. His forms are organic, challenging and often very beautiful. This station, built to link Lyon airport with the expanding French high-speed rail network, is one of his most bombastic designs and is as unforgettable as it is satisfying for passengers to use. The site, some way from Lyon itself, was anonymous and empty, an emptiness that appeared at the time of the station's construction to stretch away for as far as the eye could see away from the airport. This encouraged the Spanish engineer to create a monument that would be unmissable by travellers, by

rail, road or air: the station is very much on view from the windows of planes landing at Satolas airport. The great, bird-like arch – a wing in flight, a beak, a talon – reminiscent of the work of Eero Saarinen (p.104), forms the concourse that gives on either side and under impressive concrete portals to the long platforms below. The sense of occasion engendered here as the shark-nosed TGVs slide menacingly into and out of the station is something rail travel had been lacking for very many years. This station may seem a little over-the-top, yet its role is to make rail travel exciting and desirable and to make its presence felt in the subtopian landscape of the airport.

COMMUNICATIONS TOWER

NORMAN FOSTER, 1994 BARCELONA, SPAIN

A truly thrilling structure that brought architects and engineers together at their best. Foster's design was engineered by Ove Arup and Partners, who from the 1930s had been the handmaidens of modern British architecture and, thankfully, are still an enormous and inventive international outfit. If a city is to be dominated by a communications mast – and communications technology is an obsession of the 1990s – then that mast ought to be worth looking at. This one is. As tall as the Eiffel Tower, the Barcelona tower was erected on very different principles. Instead of the main body of the structure carrying its own weight, this is taken up by long cables that hold the slim, central mast of the tower in place. It looks like a daring balancing act, and it is. High up, the mast boasts a 14-storey structure containing all manner of technical and electronic gubbins as well as offices. This was constructed off site and on the ground, assembled as one piece and hoisted in eight hours from the ground to its lofty nest where it was bolted into place. It was an extraordinary feat and made the construction of the mast that much easier and safer than it would have been if it had been built in the sky. Foster's design was highly successful in turning a need into a thing of beauty and excitement.

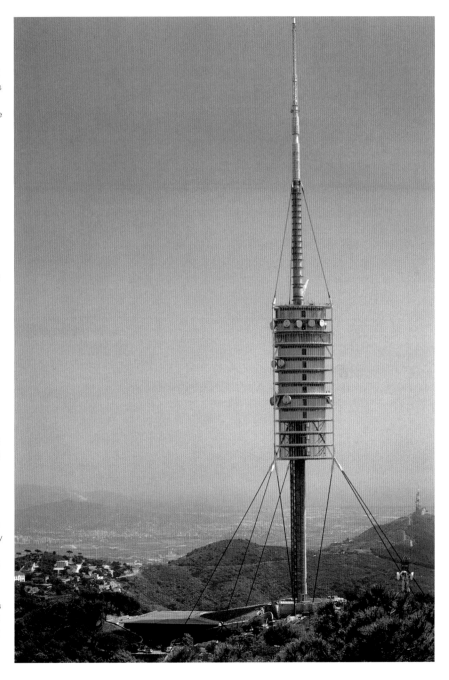

KANSAI INTERNATIONAL AIRPORT

RENZO PIANO–BUILDING WORKSHOP, 1995 OSAKA BAY, JAPAN

You can believe men can fly when you witness a Jumbo Jet take to the sky, but are you ready to give credence to the idea of an international airport floating on water? This is more or less what Kansai Airport does. This giant terminal stands like an elegant, gigantic insect on a purpose-built, man-made island in the Bay of Osaka. Japanese authorities were neither willing to expend valuable coastal land on the construction of a new international airport, nor willing to accept the noise that would follow in its wake. The result is a mind boggling feat of civil engineering upon which Renzo Piano (born 1937), has designed one of the world's finest air terminals. Aside from its fluid, soft, organic form, the terminal is a crystal clear device that allows passengers to move very easily from bus, train or taxi from the mainland to their aircraft; the process is seamless and the aircraft are always in view. Despite its vast size, the building allows people to feel rooted and comfortable inside as the scale of interior spaces is varied and designed to create intimacy from enormity.

Renzo Piano trained as an engineer before becoming an architect, which at least helps to explain the aesthetic of his rational, yet romantic, designs in which engineering forms are never allowed to run wild and for appearance's sake alone as they do in the work of so many so-called High-Tech architects.

AMERICAN AIR FORCE MUSEUM

NORMAN FOSTER, 1997 DUXFORD, CAMBRIDGESHIRE, ENGLAND

Norman Foster was the perfect choice for this shrine to US warplanes. A keen pilot, his buildings have long drawn from the imagery and technology of aircraft. Here though he allowed the warbirds on display full rein. They are the stars and theirs is the design and detailing people who come to this outpost of the Imperial War Museum want to see.

The building takes a back seat, framing the aircraft in a subtle wash of daylight and allowing people to walk around them from both the ground and on high, using a ramp that curves up and around the exhibits. The impressive concrete roof wraps around this ramp – the entrance to the museum is at its apex – and then curves like a shell high above the

aircraft, some of which hang from its vaults, to end in a vast window that allows visitors to look out to Duxford's runway, often the scene of historic warplanes taking off and landing. The roof digs down into a grass mound away from the runway. The intention here was to make Foster's concrete hangar as unobtrusive as possible – it is overlooked by houses presumably lived in by people who dislike historic aircraft, which seems a little odd – and to insulate the structure. The building is really little more than a glorified hangar, but this is its strength, and if it is just a hangar, then it is the handsomest of them all. Foster's genius was to transform plain designs into the stuff of memorable poetry.

COMMERZBANK

NORMAN FOSTER, 1997 FRANKFURT, GERMANY

The tallest building in Europe at the century's end, the Commerzbank is far more subtle than the runner-up, Canary Wharf Tower (p.395) in London. The problem with very tall office buildings is that they have tended to be little more than elongated filing cabinets. Workers shoot up in swish lifts only to be presented with another identical floor. Those who have to make do with desks – or "workstations" as they became known from the 1970s – are not even allowed to enjoy the views. Foster attempted to solve this in Frankfurt by designing the Commerzbank as a spiral of offices climbing up a central shaft. This arrangement allowed for four-storey atria, facing in different directions, to rise with the height of the building. The result is a skyscraper with a powerful and humane logic driving both the way it looks and the way it works. This is in sharp contrast to the towers shooting into the sky at the same time in southeast Asia which have little or no internal character.

Foster attempted a further development of the idea of the skyscraper as hanging garden in the design of a "Millennium Tower" for the City of London (1996). It was to have risen from the site of the old Baltic Exchange, which was destroyed by a massive bomb planted by the IRA in 1993. It would have been welcome, as a symbol of confidence, but planning permission was refused.

CHEP LAP KOK AIRPORT

NORMAN FOSTER, 1998 HONG KONG, CHINA

A breathtaking achievement, Chep Lap Kok Airport is the world's largest of its breed and the largest construction project of its era. And it is destined to grow even bigger. Just six years before, the site had been a range of hills rising out of the sea off the South China coast. These 100-metre (300-ft) peaks were flattened in the process of the creation of an artificial island measuring 6 kms (4 miles) by 3.5 kms (2 miles). Everything needed to build the airport was delivered by boat and at the peak of construction the workforce totalled 21,000. It was planned to be the world's busiest airport, acting as an immense junction box for travellers passing through or flying to southeast Asia. The terminal building, shaped like a giant aircraft, is stupendously big

– 1.27 km (½ mile) long – yet its lightweight structure and clarity – a development of Foster's earlier air terminal at Stansted in Essex – makes it remarkably relaxed and easy to use. Passengers are never confused as to where to go to catch their plane nor are they diverted as they were in so many contemporary airports, and notably in Britain, through labyrinths of duty-free and other shops. Nevertheless the Hong Kong Sky Mall is the largest shopping area of any airport. Over all this Foster placed a lightweight steel roof in the form of a sequence of shallow vaults supported by the building's exposed concrete structure. Along with Kansai (p.400), Chep Lap Kok has raised the standard of airport design at end of the century immeasurably.

PRESS PAVILION

FUTURE SYSTEMS, 1998 LORD'S CRICKET GROUND, LONDON, ENGLAND

The world's first monocoque building, the Press Pavilion at Lord's Cricket Ground was assembled off-site in a boat-builder's yard, transported in sections, lifted up onto concrete supports and bolted into place. It was designed in this way to minimize disruption to the game and completed during two winter recesses. In the first year the support columns, incorporating lifts, stairs and services, were erected while the main body of the building was being assembled elsewhere. In the second year, the pavilion was placed on its pedestal.

The pavilion is an egg-like structure sheathed in aluminium panels and designed to be as light as possible to offer the press uninterrupted views of the famous pitch. It includes a restaurant and bar and is remarkable for its compact nature, its lightness of being, its sophistication and quiet nature. Future Systems, Jan Kaplicky (born 1938) and Amanda Levette (born 1955), is a practice dedicated to forward-looking architecture and came into its own in the 1990s. The time was right because an audience had developed that, tired of Postmodern tricks and keen on the New, were looking out for modern design that was fresh, intelligent and easy to warm to. Perhaps to their own surprise Future Systems fitted the bill.

STADE DE FRANCE

MICHEL MACARY, AYMERIC ZUBLENA, MICHEL REGEMBAL, CLAUDE CONSTANTINI, 1998 PARIS, FRANCE

Eighteen teams of architects and builders battled it out in the course of 1994 to win the important commission to design what was intended to be the most impressive sports stadium in the world. Its real debut was the 1998 World Cup football competition. The winning architectural team, who beat Jean Nouvel to the post, set to work in 1995. The 80,000-seat stadium was designed not simply as a sports venue, but as the focal point of a major urban regeneration scheme in an old industrial quarter of St Denis. As such it was always meant to be beautiful, which it certainly is.

The distinguishing feature of this distant ancestor of the Colosseum is its elliptical roof, a kind of halo, surrounding the stadium 43 metres (140 ft) above ground level. This lights up at night and can be seen glowing softly at the heart of St Denis from many viewpoints and over a considerable distance.

By the late 1990s, sports buildings had again become great works of civic art and engineering they had been both in ancient Rome and at the zenith of the Modern Movement.

GARDEN OF EDEN

NICHOLAS GRIMSHAW, 2000, ST AUSTELL, CORNWALL, ENGLAND

Very much in keeping with the spirit of the times, this complex "biosphere" is a brave attempt to recreate the environments and flora and fauna of key global microclimates. Sheathed in huge, undulating greenhouses designed by Nicholas Grimshaw – who thus forged a spiritual link with his hero, the Victorian gardener and designer of the Crystal Palace, Joseph Paxton – the Eden project is also a way of reclaiming abandoned quarries in Cornwall and bringing employment and purpose back to this far-flung English county that may have been a paradise for holiday makers throughout the century but is less idyllic for local people. The project is an appropriate one with which end the century – and to mark the new one – as it brings together so many of the concerns that emerged between 1900 and 2000 to exercise the minds of architects: the relationships between architecture and nature, architect and engineer, new construction and conservation. It is also an indication of how a future architecture might nurture and protect what remains of threatened eco-systems.

Eden addresses the thorny issue of how to design a popular public attraction with a purpose beyond pure entertainment, framed by an architecture that broadens the mind rather than taking refuge in the comforts of nursery images and old-fashioned comforts.

MILLENNIUM DOME

RICHARD ROGERS PARTNERSHIP, 2000 LONDON, ENGLAND

A building that is officially beyond criticism, the Millennium Dome is a monument to government "spin" or media manipulation. Although it has no specific purpose, this staggeringly expensive theme-park – costing the equivalent of the Getty Center (p.346) or at least a dozen Gehry Guggenheims (p.347) – was designed to be admired, or else the New Labour "peoples' government" would make its displeasure known and in no uncertain terms. There was to be no opposition to this, the most ambitious dome designed since Albert Speer's Grossehalle (p.82) planned sixty years before. The lightweight structure evokes the design of both

Ralph Tubb's Dome of Discovery (p.371) at the Festival of Britain of 1951 and Powell and Moya's Skylon (p.372) at the same event. It has a certain elegance and many observers in Britain and abroad think it would best serve its stated purpose as a focal point of Millennium celebrations if it could have remained empty. As Stephen Bayley, the design director of the project in its early days, said after he was fired referring to the government's claim that the Eiffel Tower and the Festival of Britain had been unpopular with critics when they were under construction, "then the philistines were on the outside; this time, I'm afraid, they're on the inside."

TGV STATION

JEAN-MARIE DUTILLEUL/AREP, 2001 AIX-EN-PROVENCE, FRANCE

The French national railway's new TGV-Med service is one of those engineering marvels worth experiencing for its own sake. The line is not just superfast but offers a new wave of fine railway architecture at Avignon, Valence and Aix-en-Provence, designed under the direction of Jean-Marie Duthilleul of AREP, the station development arm of SNCF. All three stations give maximum impact to the Roger Tallon-designed TGV trains that serve them, and which never fail to impress. These first went into service in 1981, and since then the TGV network has carried more than 800 million passengers without loss of life. TGVs now serve 200 destinations, including forays into Switzerland and Italy, and account for 65 per cent of SNCF's main-line passenger traffic.

Aix-en-Provence station owes more than a little to Renzo Piano's design for Kansai international airport (p.400). The elongated air-foil roof, supported by a forest of tall columns, and the sheer generosity of space below it will be familiar to anyone who has experienced the Genoese architect's aero-industry masterpiece. The difference is that with its extensive use of timber and its vaulted concourse ceiling, the French station feels, if not natural, then more homely than the Japanese airport. The station works particularly well because the composition, platforms, concourse and car park have been treated as all of a piece. This clarity of design is a treat at a time when much of the new architecture intended to serve as gateways to European cities keen to present themselves afresh is becoming over the top.

GLASS FACTORY

GUNTHER HENN, 2001 DRESDEN, GERMANY

Volkswagen's Glaeserne Manufaktur (glass factory) is an industrial revelation – a revolution even – as far from the car plants of Detroit and Dagenham as it is possible to imagine. Even more remarkable is the fact that this futuristic German motown blossoms in a new park in Dresden's Strasburger Platz. Here, for the first time since Giacomo Matte-Trucco's charismatic Fiat car plant in Turin (p.359) is a large factory designed to enhance a European city centre. The Glaeserne Manufaktur is proof that twenty-first-century industry can be a part of our cities and something to celebrate.

It looks, at first glance, like a combination of factory and art gallery. This makes sense, for this is where rare buyers of the luxury VW Phaeton – teutonic rolling sculpture– come,

not just to collect their massive cars, but to see them being built. These are assembled in airy, timber-floored halls that feel like a cross between the galleries of Tate Modern and the Guggenheim, Bilbao. Finished cars are stored in a 15-storey glazed drum overlooking the parks, domes and Soviet-style housing blocks of the city. Materials and components are delivered by freight-only trams. The aim has been clear: the integration of the factory with the spirit of the reinvigorated Saxon capital, and the creation of what must be the world's first truly civilized car plant. The result is a powerful building, full of theatrical interest, yet wholly resolved. In this sense it is Baroque, twenty-first-century century Baroque, and so a natural player on the Dresden city stage.

NATIONAL SPACE CENTRE

NICHOLAS GRIMSHAW AND PARTNERS, 2001 LEICESTER, ENGLAND

Red-brick Leicester is not exactly the kind of city where you would expect to find buildings even hinting at the gleaming white imagery of Stanley Kubrick's epoch-making film, *2001: A Space Odyssey* (1968). In fact, when the tower of the new National Lottery-fuelled National Space Centre hoves into view above the banks of the River Soar, it is reminiscent of some giant, comic book-style prop from a 1950s sci-fi film. It is, though, a particular delight, a live space centre, connected via the University of Leicester to real space exploration.

The centre's tower, clad in what looks like a translucent version of the Puffa jacket, or boiler-cladding, shrouds a brace of spindly space rockets. The material is ETFE, a self-cleaning polymer, resistant to damage or discoloration from ultraviolet light. So in 20 years' time, this eye-catching and revolutionary tower should, hopefully, look much as it does now. And if some guttersnipe decides to take a crack at the tower's inflatable skin with an air-rifle, the pellets will merely sink into the pillows, then pop back out again as the material regains its shape. From the top of the tower it's possible to see the project as a whole. Below, the buildings radiate out from the centre point of the dome of its Buckminster Fuller-inspired space theatre, moving in a spiral out through the landscaped grounds and car park – and then, if you use your imagination, beyond the flatlands of Leicester and into infinity.

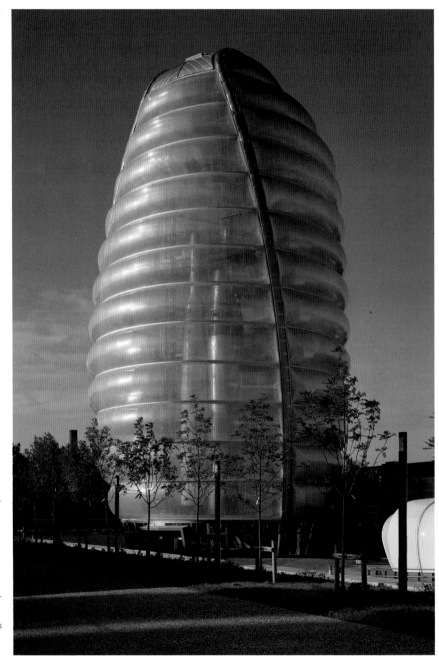

ESO HOTEL

AUER AND WEBER, 2002 CERRO PARANAL, CHILE

By the end of the twentieth century the night sky as seen from Earth had become so polluted with artificial light, much of it from buildings, that scientific observatories needed to be sited in increasingly remote locations. The latest outpost of ESO, the European Southern Observatory, is on top of a wind-blasted 2,600-metre (8,530-ft) peak, 120 kilometres (75 miles) south of Antafagusta in the Atacama Desert. Here, through its VLT (Very Large Telescope), earthbound astronomers have the finest view of the stars this side of the gods. They have something else, too – a place to stay in comfort at the foot of the peak. This is the Eso hotel, designed by Munich-based architects Auer and Weber, and engineered, in the most testing conditions, by Mayr

and Ludescher. This, though, is not a public hotel. A shame, perhaps, because it promises true luxury: five stars – pah! – this one has a million. Beautifully designed, set sensitively and silently into the landscape like some ultra-modern monastery, the coolly geometric building is chaste, almost austere. Its entrance is buried at the end of a ramp leading down from the desert. Its bedrooms, gathered around a covered courtyard, are like monks' cells, 108 of them lined and stacked up in a soldierly row. Its concrete walls – made with a mix of red oxide – are the same colour as the Martian desert beyond its slit-like windows. Here contemporary architecture, landscape, science and the shining heavens are truly in harmony.

SELFRIDGES DEPARTMENT STORE

FUTURE SYSTEMS, 2003 BIRMINGHAM, ENGLAND

Brent Cross shopping centre in north London opened in 1976. It was an ambitious, yet super-bland, modern cathedral celebrating an English retail renaissance in an age in which shopping would now be our saviour. Parish churches that had served the religious needs of local communities faithfully for 1,000 years would pass into the care of the Redundant Churches Fund, formed that same year. Birmingham's 26-acre Bull Ring, which reopened after reconstruction in 2003, is something else again: a holy city of retail. It contains 146 shops, but by far the most striking is Selfridges, a vast and colourful cliff of a building, a computer-age geological outcrop as distinctive and eye-catching as the white cliffs of Dover. Four storeys high, and wrapped in a sinuous, seamless outer skin decorated with 15,000 spun aluminium discs painted blue, like some XXXL-size dress by Paco Rabanne, Selfridges is an audacious achievement by Future Systems. If it has something of a Pop-era frock about it, its design also reflects something of both the sea and of outer space. Seen from almost any nook and corner viewpoint in central Birmingham, this unexpected building – unclassifiable in neat, art-historical terms – is all but guaranteed to raise a smile. An ersatz urban cliff, a giant sea anenome, a friendly, blob-like alien, the mother of all magic mushrooms, this is the department store as unalloyed architectural entertainment. The interior is the stuff of Vincent Korda's 1936 film *Things to Come* brought up to date.

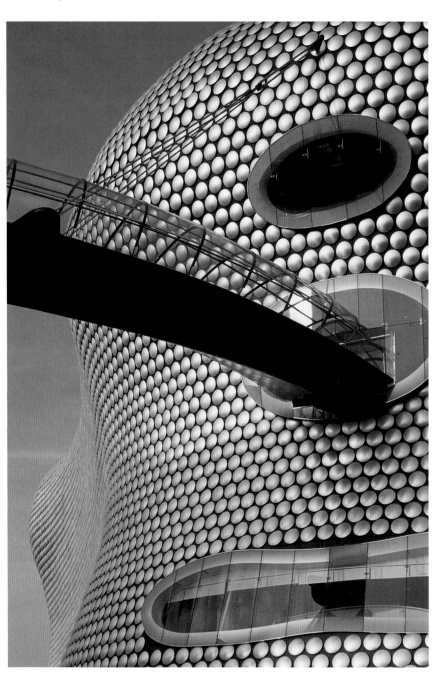

ROLLS-ROYCE ASSEMBLY PLANT

NICHOLAS GRIMSHAW AND PARTNERS, 2004 GOODWOOD, ENGLAND

In 1981, when Rolls-Royce was still in British ownership, Martin Wiener published a compelling essay, *English Culture and the Decline of the Industrial Spirit*. He argued that the British, while making fortunes from the Industrial Revolution, had never really been keen on industry itself. As soon as they got rich, they opted for the life of the country squire. If they made a fortune, they reinvented themselves as a kind of uber-aristocracy, building country houses far bigger than any mere duke's.

Today, that most aristocratic of British cars, the Rolls-Royce, is a German-owned product assembled in a factory hidden in the grounds of glorious Goodwood, seat of the Duke of Richmond. Surrounded by 400,000 young trees, it is all but invisible. A model of clear, light and elegant design, the factory would be a welcome sight above ground elsewhere. Even so, the assembly line is clearly visible to well-heeled visitors and, overall, the factory impresses with an appropriate and consistent display of rock-solid quality: York stone floors here, severe Fritz Hansen furniture there, smoothly polished concrete columns, pools of daylight. The turfed main roof is bedecked with meadow plants and wild flowers, while rainwater, drained from the roofs, is channelled into an artificial lake and then back into the low-energy factory for a variety of uses. Grimshaw's factory is a turning point not just in British manufacturing, but in the way we experience the countryside: this can be productive and enjoyable, industrious and romantic, at one and the same time.

SKI-LIFT

BEARTH AND DEPLAZES, 2004 AROSA, SWITZERLAND

The glowing entrance of this large and handsome Swiss ski-lift station is particularly welcoming to those making their way down from the peaks at sunset. It can be seen, like some gentle beacon, from high up in the mountains. Close up it looks good, too, although in season the subtle zig-zag profile of its roof and walls are covered in snow, so that all that can be seen of it is the amber glow of the light within. The angular entrance is framed with translucent polycarbonate sheeting that adds to the luminescence. From even quite close up, these sheets look like layers of glowing ice.

This is one of many fine new ski-related structures designed by architects throughout Switzerland. What makes it, and others like it, special is that it is designed to blend almost entirely with the landscape while maintaining its integrity as a work of contemporary architecture. It is also highly functional, yet undoubtedly stylish. The excellence of much new Swiss mountain architecture derives, in part, from the training of many young architects who value their highly practical knowledge of engineering, landscape and craftsmanship. Valentin Bearth (born 1957) worked for the brilliant Swiss craftsman-architect Peter Zumthor (p. 123) before setting up his own studio in 1988, while one of his partners Daniel Landner (born 1959) trained as a plasterer before becoming an architect. The ski-station at Arosa might look ethereal from a distance, yet its steel frame is strong enough to support emergency helicopters.

ALLIANZ MUNICH STADIUM

HERZOG DE MEURON, 2005 MUNICH, GERMANY

Come on you Reds. I mean, you Blues. Or is it the Whites? At the new Allianz Munich Stadium, it can be red, white or blue, or any combination of all three, for this chameleon-like building is able to change the colour of its inflated skin. Dreamed up by the football-crazy Swiss architects Herzog and de Meuron, the stadium is home to two local teams; Bayern Munich, the Reds, and TVS Munich 1860, the Blues. The Whites are the German national team.

Like most new football grounds, the arena is plonked down on one of those nowhere places besides a motorway intersection a long way out of town. A discontented setting is made glorious, however, by the games the new building plays. During the day, its bubble-wrap skin appears silvery-grey; at dusk the light show begins and the building comes dazzlingly alive. From the outside only, of course: inside, the 66,000-seat stadium is austere, a thing of colourless concrete, stern grey paint and grey, no-nonsense plastic seats. This lustreless palette is quite deliberate; nothing inside the arena must distract from the beautiful game. Players and crowd are cocooned inside the architectural equivalent of a giant bubble, or, to be more exact, 2,816 inflatable ETFE-foil cushions, made from an extremely lightweight and highly translucent fluorocarbon-based polymer. Collectively, these are very strong – able to withstand a 1.6-metre (5.25-ft) fall of snow. They are supported on a frame made up of 96 radial steel cantilevered trusses, each 50 metres (164 ft) long.

LIGHT HOUSE

GIANNI BOTSFORD, 2005 LONDON, ENGLAND

Can you imagine light translated into three solid dimensions and then shaped into the guise of a modern house? To put the question another way, can you imagine a house formed almost entirely from a rigorous study of daylight? This is what Gianni Botsford did for the design of a remarkable new family house at the back of a west London mews.

Like light itself, this extensive town house is all but invisible. Although constructed of solid concrete, along with steel, aluminium and a great number of sheets of glass, it is hidden behind a dense meshed-steel wall; for the casual passer-by, there is absolutely nothing worth seeing. Behind the screen, though, Botsford's house of light is a thing of architectural sorcery. Lit almost entirely from a great glass roof and a number of courtyards, some glazed, others open to the sky, this unexpected and quietly revolutionary structure was designed using a process the architect had been researching and developing over several years. By commissioning a new house that gives absolutely nothing away, and therefore causes no possible offence to planners, Botsford's clients have ended up with a home that perfectly suits their particular set of preferences while taking the city house into new territory. It takes it into ancient territories, too; hiding behind a high wall, grouped around courtyards and with its ultra-modern spaces connected by sliding screens, the house refers, tangentially, to the city haunts of well-to-do ancient Romans and to Edo-era Japanese homes.

ROOFTECTURE-S HOUSE

ENDO SHUHEI, 2005 KOBE, JAPAN

Japanese architects are well known for building highly imaginative, and sometimes rather mad, houses in very unlikely urban settings. One architect designed a house for his mother in the early 1980s as a "theatre of cruelty". Impossible to understand? Undoubtedly. Yet it is perfectly clear why such houses tax the attention of Japan's brightest architects: in this land of mountains and earthquakes there is precious little space to build. Land is thus very expensive and every last possible location counts.

Added to this is the fact that for a number of cultural reasons, many Japanese people prefer to live in detached houses even if the gap between them and their neighbours is a matter of a few centimetres. Endo Shuhei (born 1960), principal of

Paramodern Architecture, has built this challenging and rather exciting family house on a tiny diagonal sliver of land alongside the main line railway just outside Kobe. Trains here do not exactly trundle past; they can rocket by at anything up to 280 kph (174 mph), so the house necessarily presents a strong, solidly concrete acoustic wall to one side. Inside, space opens up in unexpected ways; for all its proximity to an exceptionally busy railway line it is peaceful, bright and open-handed. You might expect it to be much more of a solid box than it is, yet Shuhei's diligent research into structure, acoustics and vibration has led to a remarkably open design. It points the way for architects and their clients, worldwide faced with the seemingly intractable problem of ever increasing land costs.

ST PANCRAS INTERNATIONAL

ALASTAIR LANSLEY, 2007 LONDON, ENGLAND

Perhaps the most stunning building of the Gothic Revival, the Grade I listed Midland Grand Hotel in London, designed by Sir George Gilbert Scott, is about to be brought back to life after a long, dark slumber. From 2007, Eurostar trains will run into St Pancras via the new 300-kph (186-mph) North Kent high-speed rail link – the first major new British railway in a century – and travellers from Paris, Brussels and beyond will arrive in twenty-first-century London through this gloriously theatrical Victorian adventure.

The platforms of William Barlow's renovated 1860s' train-shed have been extended under a lightweight, functional steel and glass roof. Eurostar trains will take centre stage, with Midland main-line and suburban trains on either side.

Barlow's roof will be restored to its original condition, its great iron trusses painted sky blue. The undercroft of the station will serve as the new Eurostar departure hall. At once ultra-modern and old-fashioned, St Pancras should delight both those with a passion for the past and those for whom only the very latest in design, engineering and architecture will do. Quality is promised at every turn: the station will be a place of hard surfaces, with timber and slate or granite floors instead of the stinking carpets of the sort found in British airports and at Waterloo International. The sheer generosity of space here – the heights of ceilings, the breadths of passageways – will be unfamiliar to anyone used to cramped British railway stations and airport lounges.

TERMINAL 3, BEIJING INTERNATIONAL AIRPORT

FOSTER AND PARTNERS, 2007 BEIJING, CHINA

"It's the largest covered structure ever built," said Norman Foster in 2006. "There are 40,000 workers on site, working eight-hour shifts around the clock. Construction began on April 6, 2004, and will be complete on December 31, 2007, well in time for the 2008 Beijing Olympics." The roof of this vast, dragon-like structure covers a space 3.25 kilometres (2 miles) long by 785 metres (858 yards) wide. It is so long that a train will connect various parts of the terminal, along with 175 escalators, 173 lifts and 437 travolators. By 2020, it is estimated, 55 million people will pass through its portals each year.

"To get an idea of the scale," says Foster, "imagine Heathrow terminals 1, 2, 3, 4 and 5 together under one roof and then add an extra 17 per cent of floor space. It's so big that in certain lights you can't see one end of building from the other." Foster has every last detail of this colossus at his fingertips. He loves aircraft; he loves flying. Since his National Service days with the RAF, he has loved the architecture of aircraft hangars, and ways in which the heavyweight art of architecture might learn from the latest lightweight technologies and materials. His Sainsbury Centre for the Visual Arts in Norwich, completed in 1978, is the most exquisite hangar yet built. Ever since, Foster's architecture has reached for the sky – and so have his ambition and workload. By any standards, and whether or not you agree with the staggering expansion of air travel, Beijing Airport is simply stratospheric stuff.

BMW WELT

COOPHIMMELB(L)AU 2007 MUNICH, GERMANY

A great metal cloud of a building, BMW Welt rises alongside the 3-series car factory, together with the Bavarian carmaker's distinctive 1970s headquarters, its company museum and, across the road, the wave-like roof of the 1972 Olympic Stadium. This cinematic building is where 45,000 BMW buyers a year venture to collect their new cars and to while away their special day in the steely arms of the mighty Bayerische Motoren Werke AG. Here, the faithful are happily immersed in a baptism of corporate beneficence and culture in this cathedral to public relations, a shrine ablaze with the company's slogan: *Freude am Fahren* (joy in driving). To woo new buyers, or to keep old ones loyal, BMW believes it must stamp its brand into their hearts, minds and souls. BMW Welt is nothing more,

and nothing less, than an architectural branding iron. The building itself takes the form of a swirling, double-coned vortex of steel spinning out of the ground and apparently supporting the billowing 3,000-tonne steel roof, which is in fact held up by 11 slanting, tapering, concrete columns. Beneath the roof is a vast, sun-blanched gathering place, or "forum", set around with visitor "experiences" and computer games, and, most importantly, a vast deck covered in 20 smoothly operating, car-sized turntables. Here, consumerism is raised to a kind of sacred ritual in a building that, in its own modern way, matches the ambition of the highly theatrical and technically brilliant baroque and rococo abbeys rising from the Bavarian landscape.

WALKING HOUSE

N55 ARCHITECTS 2008 WORLDWIDE

What if a house could get up and walk? What fun. You might live anywhere if you could find the land to settle on. The idea is as old as the caravan, and yet the dream of a robotic walking house continues to excite the imagination of architects. This one – a 3.5-metre (12-ft) diameter hexagon of black steel tube, 3.5-metres (12-ft) long – can walk, although rather slowly. Its top speed is 0.1 mph (0.16 km/ph), but then any faster would spill your tea. Six electrically powered, lunar-module-like legs with bright yellow pads, or feet, enable the house to go walkabout. Designed by the Copenhagen artists' collective N55, Walking House is an essentially romantic idea lovingly realized using new, environmentally friendly technology. The inspiration for the design was the Romany travellers' traditional way of

life, roaming the country, and across borders, by caravan, but brought up to date: Walking House has no need for horses and reins or diesel engines, gearboxes and wheels to make it go. While standing still, it generates power through solar cells and small windmills and when fully charged it gets up and walks.

The NASA-style prototype has been designed for four people, although the members of N55's Walking House team – Ion Sorvin, Oivind Alexander Slaatto and Sam Kronick – point out that its structure can be extended, while if stacked together, a group of Walking Houses could form temporary villages. The prototype features polycarbonate windows, built-in furniture, including sleeping platforms, a composting lavatory and a wood-burning stove.

BURJ KHALIFA

SOM 2010 DUBAI

The world's tallest building opened shortly before the economy of Dubai imploded. Many saw this mind-boggling building as a tower too far, sheer *folie de grandeur*, or a twenty-first-century Tower of Babel. There should certainly be no question as to the exceptional quality, and daring, of the engineering achievement. Here is a tower so tall that the microclimate around its pinnacle is notably different from that around its base. Initially known as the Burj Dubai, the 828-metre (2,717-ft) tower was built to celebrate Dubai's seemingly unstoppable and stratospheric economic rise. It was also meant to be a tourist attraction: if you think the Empire State Building is exciting, then what about this? It was also a matter of pride to local sheikhs that the Arab world

again boasted the tallest building in the world, a prize (of sorts) it had lost to the West in the fourteenth century when the spire of Lincoln Cathedral, England, surpassed the summit of the Great Pyramid of Cheops, Egypt. The architects and engineers – SOM in both cases – have a heady and impressive track record in the design and construction of very tall buildings. Adrian Smith (lead architect) and Bill Baker (structural engineer) were an ideal team to realize this structural phenomenon. Ingeniously, the structure was rooted in considerations of both sheer practicality and in patterns found in traditional Islamic architecture. The tower does indeed spiral upward, losing mass as it soars upward, making it a distant relation of the Tower of Babel.

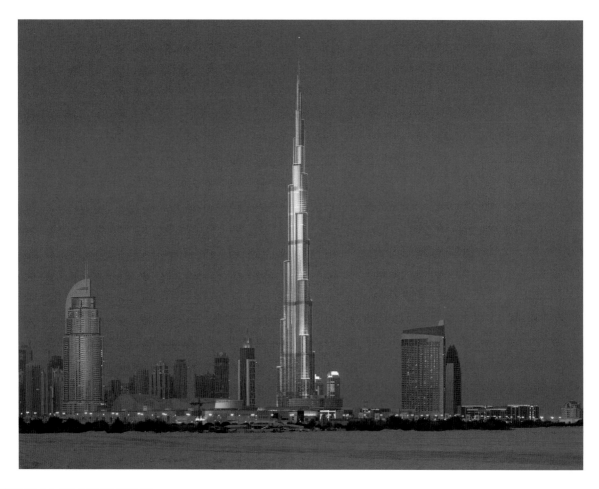

BLOB VB3

DMVA ARCHITECTS 2010 MECHELEN, BELGIUM

This hard-boiled egg of a building is the brainchild of dmvA architects who were looking for ways to get around building codes while trying to design and build a house extension. The result is this clever and likable 20-metre (66-ft) square movable pod. It is a bit like a caravan, but few caravans – this side of the famous American Airstream – have ever been so determinedly novel and modern. A polyester-sheathed, plywood-framed structure provides uninterrupted, top-lit space inside. Cupboards, beds, kitchen equipment and any other fixtures and fittings are installed in niches in the walls. The narrow end houses a bathroom. The nose can be opened to allow the easy installation of whatever anyone who chooses to live this way might need. It also serves as a canopy, useful if when planning

to eat or work outside. Increasingly, homeowners in crowded and highly regulated parts of the world are looking for house extensions that do not need conventional planning permission. Although there are number of traditional timber designs available for this purpose – and, of course, you can always make your own – there are precious few contemporary designs. Architects have been experimenting with "living pods" like Blob VB3 since the 1960s, notably Archigram (p.439) and Future Systems (pp.300, 404, 412). Few people seem to pick them up on it, and the traditional "shepherd's hut" or knock-together, timber-framed out building continues to take precedence. Still, here is one uncompromisingly modern design, and it might just make you smile.

CITIES

SHAPING THE HUMAN ZOO

The twentieth-century city grew and grew and grew. This brought with it enormous problems of health, transport and crime, of housing, energy and pollution. These concerns were there at the start of the century and just got bigger all the while. Architects and planners addressed these issues with a bewildering variety of schemes, many left on the drawing board (thank God) and many others built. Few of these were anything like successful. The problem of the city is one that refuses to go away: when it thrives it expands and threatens to veer out of control. A healthy city from the point of view of finance and jobs is often chaotic. The most dynamic of all, such as Hong Kong, Shenzen and Tokyo, late in the century, saw buildings pulled down even before they were completed as land values rose and a more profitable projects were hatched. And yet it is this economically healthy chaos that has disturbed the tidy minds of architects and planners who have in their mind's eye ordered streets lined with handsome, unchanging buildings.

The best answer progressive architects and designers could come up with in the early years of the century was to make a break from old cities and lay out brand new cities in the heart of the countryside. The Garden City (p.426) was an English invention, but it was soon exported around the world. At heart it was suburban in outlook, envisaging the laying out of small urban settlements that lacked the vibrancy and creative energy of, say, London and Paris, Berlin and Vienna, Chicago and New York.

The garden city idea maintained its grip throughout the century, manifesting itself as far afield as Canberra and New Delhi. Rival ideas included those driven by Le Corbusier who believed that the country could be brought into the heart of the city if traditional streets were razed and high rise apartment and office blocks could take their place standing on stilts above verdant parkland.

Few city authorities, however, felt able to put such iconoclastic plans into action. They did happen, though, but not for the best after European and Japanese cities were blitzed during the course of World War Two. Here, at last, was the chance Modern Movement architects and planners had to put their ideas into practice. Away with old-fashioned streets and square, rows of eighteenth-century houses and roadways too narrow for the car. The car was the future. It was given priority at all costs. Pedestrians would have to avoid it by walking along concrete gangways in the sky. Their homes would be in the clouds too, but built down to low budgets and imbued with none of the grace let alone the gardens and generously lit rooms proposed by Le Corbusier. The pattern was repeated worldwide. It was very sad. Hitler had given architects the chance to damage their cities more effectively than the combined efforts of his Luftwaffe, rockets and tanks. If this sounds unfair, then ask those who had to live in them.

This destruction of the traditional city led soon enough to an increasingly intense global study of how to weave its fabric back together again, of how to find ways of coping with the car, of redeveloping at a pace and on a scale that people could keep up with and make sense of. It was a slow and exhausting process and there was no sign that it would let up as long as people chose to live in cities and as long as cities continued to be the engine of social wealth and the heart of art and culture.

At the beginning of the twenty-first century the fastest growing cities are in Southeast Asia – especially in China; yet while the Chinese spawn cities with precious little regard to environmental concerns, Europeans and Americans struggle to contain the excesses of urban growth. The imbalance between these two approaches can only become further out of kilter in coming years.

LETCHWORTH GARDEN CITY

RAYMOND UNWIN, ET AL, 1903 HERTFORDSHIRE, ENGLAND

Letchworth was the first Garden City and the source of much fun for critics and cartoonists at the time. "Visitors are requested not to tease the citizens," was one notice that appeared in a cartoon doing just that. Why? Because the citizens of Letchworth must have seemed an odd bunch at the time. The first Garden

City, an idealistic fusion of town and country set apart from the modern, industrial world in rural Hertfordshire was initially a haven for all sorts of arty-crafty cranks and eccentrics. In the new roughcast Voysey-style cottages with their limewashed walls, oak furniture and tapestries lived an unprecedented generation of hatless, gloveless

Theosophists, socialists and vegetarians. The men wore smocks and sandals and espoused such quixotic causes as Esperanto. Day trippers from London came to laugh at them. Letchworth was truly a human zoo. Planned by Raymond Unwin (p.22), it was a direct result of a close reading of two powerful books by the polemicist and planner Ebeneezer Howard (1850–1928) *Tomorrow: A Peaceful Path to Real Reform* (1898) and *Garden Cities of Tomorrow* (1902). Letchworth was constituted in 1903, its team of eminent architecture consultants including Richard Norman Shaw (1831–1912), W. R. Lethaby (1857–1931) and Halsey Ricardo (1854–1928). Unwin's plan for the heart of the new city was based on Wren's 1666 plan for the City of London, but, like the original never got off the ground. Cosy with its Arts and Crafts cottages and Neo-Georgian civic buildings, Letchworth was nicely built, thoughtful and, after the novelty wore off, rather dull. However, at the end of the century British planners have responded anew to Letchworth as they seek ways of building millions of new homes.

PLAN VOISIN

LE CORBUSIER, 1922 PARIS, FRANCE

This is the plan that, in so many ways, helped to give the Modern Movement a bad name. One look at this early plan by Le Corbusier to knock down a vast chunk of Paris north of the Seine and to replace it with a high-rise concrete apartment blocks towering into the sky was enough to confirm the worst suspicions of those who thought Modern architects little more than crazed megalomaniacs with a mission to destroy historic cities. Le Corbusier loved Paris. It seems very unlikely that even if he had been given the power to do so that he would have put the Voisin Plan into action. It more an idea of how Modern citizens might live in the future. The idea is crystal clear, dogmatic and a reproach to the Garden City and Garden Suburb movement that had taken root in England and which was spreading its mimsy gospel across Europe. Corbusier believed that the country could be brought into the heart of cities in the form of urban parkland and that densely occupied, but light and airy, apartment blocks would rise above them. This way it was possible for citizens to live densely while enjoying fresh air, sunlight and good health the city of the Industrial Revolution had denied them. The city would be zoned, so that only the professional classes would live in this Modern splendour. What about the workers? They would live further out, connected by road and rail links. The Plan Voisin was clearly not meant to the harbinger of the high-rise working class estates of thirty and forty years on.

BERLIN

ALBERT SPEER, 1937 GERMANY

Albert Speer's North–South axis plan for the new Berlin, or Germania, that was to be built after Germany's victory at the end of World War Two, was truly the stuff of nightmares. Thankfully, and for many other more important reasons, Hitler's Nazi war machine was stuffed by the Allies and Speer was imprisoned for 25 years. When he was released from Spandau Prison on the edge of Berlin in 1966, he was driven to the airport along part of what would have been this, the mightiest street ever conceived. In a flash of inspiration, Speer saw "what I had been blind to for years ... our plan [his and Hitler's] completely lacked a sense of proportion."

He wasn't kidding. The scale was hard to believe. The grand processional avenue began at the Grossehalle (p.53), passed under a victory arch twice the size of the Arc

de Triomphe – its architect was Hitler himself – and then passed ranks of engorged Neoclassical monuments. These would have included palaces for Goring and Hitler, an SS high command complex that looked like the Shell Centre built on London's South Bank in the 1950s seen through a magnifying glass, a monument to Mussolini as big as Bernini's arcade in front of St Peter's Rome and a university capped with a skyscraping tower. In between there were to have been muscular hotels, enormous cinemas and many boring ministry buildings. Speer had made a study of Daniel Burnham's 1909 plan for Chicago as well as Lutyens's plan for New Delhi, but the effect in Berlin was very much his own. Very little of Germania was built and very little of it survives today.

MILTON KEYNES

MILTON KEYNES DEVELOPMENT CORPORATION, 1962 BUCKINGHAMSHIRE, ENGLAND

Milton Keynes was new kind of Garden City, modelled in part on the free form of Los Angeles and in part on an older English tradition. It was the first city be to heavily marketed. An advertising campaign extolling the virtues of a new city where there were far more trees than people ran for many years. The city slowly came to life and at the end of the century it has the feeling of a well-ordered suburb on a very large scale. However, it also has the feeling of having no real centre except for the railway station which ferries its citizens backwards and forwards to London to work some 70 km (45 miles) to the south. Otherwise there is an elongated shopping mall and a square of routine Modern offices and shops leading off from this along fairly featureless avenues. Houses, designed mostly

in a modern "vernacular" style – lots of bricks, stained timber and pitched roofs – are loosely arranged in clumps a good way from the shops and station. A car is very much a necessity for many people living here and the city was designed around it. To an outsider the sheer number of roundabouts guiding traffic from one anonymous area to another can be baffling. It is easy to get lost as there is no sense of place or of a centre to head to as visitors do to historic or more conventionally planned cities. The saving grace is the design of nearly all roads as avenues.

By the last decade of the twentieth century these had matured and are very beautiful for most of the year. They also add to the deeply ingrained suburban character of this city as a marketing dream.

LUXEMBOURG PLAN

LEON KRIER, 1976 LUXEMBOURG

Leon Krier (born 1946) is an iconoclastic figure who launches into offensives against contemporary architecture and town planning and then retreats again as if to re-arm for the next assault. Born in Luxembourg, he worked with James Stirling in the 1970s, a decade in which Stirling built little but was much influenced by Krier's vision of born again Classical cities and architecture. In Krier's skilful hands such designs were tremendously seductive.

This scheme for his native Luxembourg is typical of Krier's romantic vision and fine draughtsmanship. The fundamental idea is the restructuring of the city centre so that it becomes a home and a workplace. The density of occupation is thus much greater than in most modern cities: Krier believed that cities worked best when no-one was more than twenty minutes' walk from their place of work. Better still, they

should live over the shop. This was essentially a medieval idea and indeed Krier's clarion cry was really for a return to a past world, a kind of Neoclassical Arts and Crafts paradise, if such a thing could ever make sense. Nostalgia coursed through his designs – bi-planes buzz through the skies, Bugattis and other exotic cars of the 1920s and 1930s roll along the grand boulevards below. The buildings themselves are piled up as if on top of one another in the manner of medieval Italian hill towns. Many feature towers. The net result is an urban dreamscape detached from the contemporary world.

Krier's attempts to get his plans off the ground seemed always doomed to failure. He tried to replan Spitalfields in London and Poundbury (p.68). The former came to nothing, the latter was watered down to the point of offence.

SHENZHEN

VARIOUS, FROM 1975 CHINA

Shenzhen is a phenomenon, the sudden and startling realization of the conversion of China from communism to capitalism. When China decided to beat the West at its own game after the death of Mao Zedong in 1976 it did so with an energy that confounded observers who imagined the country to be trapped in some parallel universe that would never see the degree of economic growth needed to feed, educate and nurture its billion plus population. As late as the early 1970s, Shenzhen was a seaside fishing village but within a single generation, local people went from being villagers, living the kind of life they might have done at almost any time over the previous two thousand years, to supermarket-shopping, golf-crazy modern citizens. Young Chinese architects were roped into the Shenzhen "special economic zone" to help churn out tall buildings at a rate of knots. To witness them designing skyscrapers sitting at kitchen tables in tiny flats with the help of a lap-top computer was not just a bizarre sight; it was evidence of just how much the architect's role had changed in the course of the century. Shenzhen is only one small piece of an urban jigsaw being pieced together around the Pearl River Delta. Ultimately it will be one giant conurbation spreading up from Hong Kong through Shenzhen to Guangzhou and down the other side of the Pearl River to Zhuhai and Macau.

IIT CAMPUS PROJECT

REM KOOLHAAS–OMA, 2000 ILLINOIS, USA

It is always a brave if chancey, move to re-address the work of an architect considered to be one of the all time "greats"; yet this is what Rem Koolhaas, the Dutch architect did when he announced a new masterplan for the campus of the Illinois Institute of Technology in 1998. The character of the campus had been established by Mies van der Rohe (p.217), during his tenure there as a teacher. To Mies the institute owes the ethereal yet commanding Crown Hall.

Koolhaas's scheme is very different to that of Mies. Where Mies went for a purist, Modern Movement reinterpretation of the idea of an ideal Greek city, Koolhaas's plan represents a very different line of thought: here is a university campus at the end of the twentieth century, designed with the complexity of a new world of apparently endless choice in mind.

For Koolhaas and the Office of Metropolitan Architecture (OMA), the modern city was a thing of vibrancy, narrative and endless connections and possibilities, a place of uncertainty, choice and casual encounter. So here there are to be no absolutes, neither in terms of paths through the campus nor in the design of new buildings. The idea that a building or the plan of a campus or even a city, should be a little like the internet – choose where you want to go, what you want to find from an almost infinite network of paths and sources – is still radical at the end of the century. Can the city and architecture survive without certainty? That is the question Koolhaas, among other architects, has posed; it is not an easy one to answer much less face up to.

MILLENNIUM VILLAGE

RALPH ERSKINE, ET AL, 2000 GREENWICH, LONDON

Ralph Erskine was 84 when he unveiled this competition-winning plan for the Millennium Village at Greenwich in 1998. The proposal was for a "green" or "ecologically sustainable" urban development - mostly housing - to be built on reclaimed industrial land on the North Greenwich peninsula. This previously uninhabited area of London braves the icy cold winds that scythe across East Anglia from Siberia and the Arctic, and stands in the shadow of the Millennium Dome designed by the Richard Rogers Partnership.

Erskine's proposal for a mix of 12-storey towers with low-rise flats and houses sheltering from the wind behind them along curved avenues was built in truncated form. These homes, however, remain the best of a very poor assortment of developers' tat built since 2000 in an area stretching east from Greenwich along both banks of the Thames and dubbed "The Thames Gateway". Erskine's homes were designed so that they could expand or contract as families grew or shrank. In theory, demountable internal walls mean that a growing family could stretch across more than one home. In reality, sky-high London property prices have made this an impossibility. On the plus side, the homes are more energy efficient than the vast majority of London housing. The upshot is a fresh take on the English garden suburb shipped into an old industrial urban area. Thoughtful, well-intended and well-mannered, this is a twenty-first century slice of Hampstead Garden Suburb without the drama of Lutyens. The Millennium Village has never been completed.

FUTURES

BRAVE NEW WORLDS

This area is a huge subject and one that has exercised the minds of architects around the globe and down through the last century. What will the future be like and how could they have helped to shape it? Of course there are those who have wanted to hinder it, to slow change down or even to reverse it. This was true of certain Arts and Crafts, Classical and Organic architects. Whatever they believed or wanted, however, the world span taking a dazed and confused society and an increasingly eclectic architecture with it.

In the early days of the twentieth century and up until World War Two, many Europeans and Americans, and increasingly people from all over the world, were enthralled by the notion of progress. The world could become a better place if only airplanes could fly higher and break the sound barrier, if cars and trains could race along at ever greater speed along guided expressways and tracks, if buildings could be taller, sleeker and kitted out with more and more gadgetry. And then we would fly into space, served increasingly by intelligent machines, robots at first, then computers and ultimately a combination of the two.

Speed, energy, progress. These words were at the heart of the twentieth-century journey into the future. Just look at how excited the Italian Futurists were by them at the time of World War One. It is not difficult to understand why they longed for change. The world they inhabited was stifling, corrupt and probably as sick as they imagined it to be. World War One tore it apart. Now progress was possible, and although the global economy was wobbly, and even disastrous, all the way between 1918 and 1939, progress seemed to be a reality. The fast planes and trains and cars really did arrive as did Modern architecture. World War Two, however, rocked the notion of human progress.

If the Germans could really do what they did to the Jews and if all the other atrocities were taken into account together with the physical destruction of cities, then who could ever believe again that the twentieth century was the century of progress and that a golden age lay not so very far off in some technological future?

This section shows a few of the dreams that have inspired architects or been drawn by them at various times in the course of the last hundred years. The images are taken from films as well as architects' own projects because the twentieth century was the century of the mass-produced and globally circulated image. From now on all people with access to cinemas and then television and, in the 1990s, the Internet received and consumed the same images. This did not necessarily mean that one day in the future all architecture would be the same, because people in different parts of the world have different ways of looking at it. It did raise, however, the possibility that one day architecture might die and be replaced by simple containers on which people could, with the aid of new technology, project whatever image they wanted. There would be no more style wars: all styles could have a place. Equally, this deluge of images and gamut of technology might well encourage a reaction against all too visible high technology, and certainly there are signs by 1999 that more and more people want their homes to be beautiful, simple and yes Modern escapes from the sheer busyness of the world. They might not want to run away from it altogether as thinking people with a bit of money behind them did at the beginning of the century, but would learn how to separate the world of Architecture – Le Corbusier's masterly, correct and magnificent play of light on surfaces – from that of the Building.

AIRPORT/RAILWAY STATION FANTASY

ANTONIO SANT'ELIA, 1913

Antonio Sant'Elia (1888–1916)
burst onto the architectural stage
in 1914 with a display of heroic,
imaginative schemes for a radical
city of the future. The venue
was the first Nuove Tendenze
exhibition in Milan. Two years later,
Sant'Elia, who had volunteered to
fight in the Italian army, lay dead
somewhere near Monfalcone. His
influence, however, simply grew
and grew, affecting generations
of forward-looking architects
from Matté-Trucco, architect
of the Fiat Factory (p.359) one
of the few Futurist monuments
built, to Richard Rogers in the
1970s and 1980s with buildings
such as the Lloyd's Building in
London (p.393). Sant'Elia studied
in the school of architecture at
Como, the Accademia di Brera,
Milan and the Scuola di Belle
Arti in Bologna, graduating in
1912 and with four years to
live. He teamed up with the
iconoclastic Futurist movement
of poets, writers and artists
founded by the charismatic
Filippo Tommaso Marinetti,
who championed the cause of
unbridled speed and technology.
He worked feverishly on the
creation of an imaginary "Città
Nuova" (future city), which
included designs such as this
one for a combined airport
and railway station. Every
line in the drawing suggests
energy and speed driven by an
overpowering and imperative
technologia. The ideas were
taken up by Fritz Lang and
translated onto celluloid in
Metropolis (1926). Sant'Elia's
memorial to the war dead was
the one structure he designed
that was built – posthumously.

THE CABINET OF DR CALIGARI

ROBERT WIENE, 1919

To spend too much effort trying to make head or tail of this surreal film would be a mistake. Best to sit back and enjoy the way it looks. It is famous for the topsy-turvy world it created, full of crazy angles and strange lighting. The sets seemed to borrow something from the radical design movements afoot in the newly born Soviet Union and from the German Expressionists. They also presage, and had some influence on, both the short-lived Punk approach to architecture witnessed in Britain around 1980 and the work of the Deconstructivists of a decade later.

The film is a bizarre mixture of horror and early science fiction about a mad doctor who gets what look like the walking dead to do his strange business.

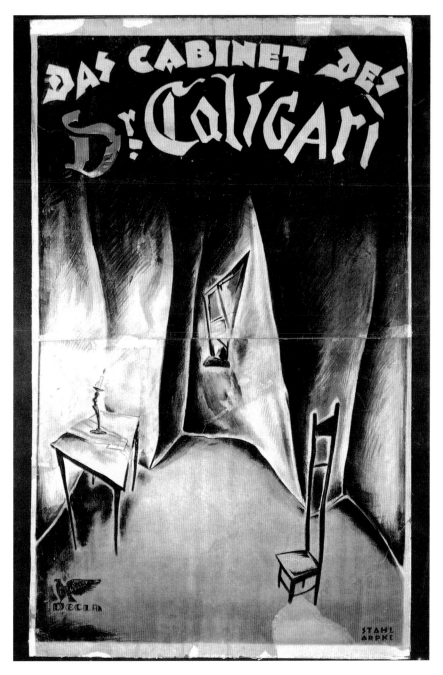

METROPOLIS

FRITZ LANG, 1926

This imposing and ultimately ineffable film boasted some of the finest sets in the history of cinema. *Metropolis* was a part-futuristic, part-Gothic-horror evocation of a titanic and malevolent city of the twenty-first century in which human beings are slaves to a half-crazed mechanized society. The city is brilliantly realized and owes much to the pinnacled skylines of Chicago and New York. Lang, however, interpreted the city of the future as a kind of representation of heaven and hell: the world high above the city lived in by its rulers was ultra Modern, while that of the slave workers was a steaming, subterranean nether-world dominated by vast machines.

Every beautifully made and intelligent film that followed in the wake of *Metropolis* and that tried to evoke the city of the future tended to have more than a little of the look and atmosphere of the film about it: *Things to Come* (1936) and *Bladerunner* (1982) are perhaps best known. The latter, directed by Ridley Scott, is in part a homage to Fritz Lang's masterpiece and brilliantly creates a fantasy world in which the city of the future is an unhealthy fusion of *Metropolis*, Los Angeles, and a kind of crazy high-rise southeast Asian city, in part Hong Kong in part Guangzhou. It is all too close to the truth to make comfortable viewing; Lang, however, had got there first a half century earlier.

WALKING CITY

RON HERRON, 1964

Ron Herron (1930–91) was one of the members of Archigram, the Beatles of Pop architecture, who made an international name for themselves with a succession of funny and brilliant cartoon architectural storyboards in the mid and late 1960s. One of the most delightful was Herron's "Walking City". Here was the city as a megastructure on the move. Plugged into water, local services were available and it could wander off wherever its free-spirited citizens wanted it to go. "Walking City" moved on giant legs, and it was fun to see the drawings in animated form and to watch this urban behemoth strut across the landscape.

The team – Peter Cook (born 1936), Dennis Crompton (born 1935), David Greene (born 1937), Warren Chalk (born 1927),

Michael Webb (born 1937) and Herron, met while working on a project to redesign London's Euston station in 1960. They published a magazine, *Archigram*, from the next year and put together a first exhibition of their designs at the ICA (Institute of Contemporary Art), London, in 1963. Their ideas were championed internationally by the influential critic Reyner Banham, and eventually they even got to put some of their wacky ideas into practice, notably the Archigram Capsule at Expo '70 in Osaka.

Ron Herron went on to form his own design practice in London. The interior of the Imagination headquarters, London, (p.284) was the best thing he did.

PLUG-IN CITY

PETER COOK, 1966

Peter Cook's Plug-in City was one of the best things to come out of Archigram. It was a dream of a future megopolis in which hedonism blended happily with ultramodern technology. At first glance, Cook's urban utopia looks very much like the Pompidou Centre (p.388) by Renzo Piano and Richard Rogers (1977) or Norman Foster's unbuilt design for a new civic centre and transport interchange at Hammersmith in west London (1979). This shouldn't be surprising as Rogers and Foster were both influenced by Archigram and Rogers, in particular, was excited by the notion of a liberating technology that would help people to enjoy themselves in city centres rather than threaten them in a "Big Brotherish" or *Metropolis* manner.

Plug-in City was topped with cranes to show that it was in a state of constant flux: if someone wanted to move their living capsule or pleasure pod, or whatever, they could. Cook's architectural ideas were premised on the idea of people having a good time but within the context of a new and highly responsive architecture. Plug-in City was influential, but it will have to remain on paper until cities are built in space and a clip-on, plug-in way of building communities will make sense. After Archigram, Cook designed many fantasy projects, yet few, if any, had the vital impact of Plug-in City.

CARDIFF OPERA HOUSE

ZAHA HADID, 1995 CARDIFF, WALES

Unbuilt for all the wrong reasons, the Cardiff Bay Opera House is one of the finest unrealized projects of the 1990s. Its fate was a small tragedy for Wales, a country that has never been famous for the quality of its architecture and which seemed determined to behave in a small-minded way over this superb design. The idea was that a new opera house would become the cultural hub of the reclamation and urbanization of Cardiff Bay that forms the seaside hem of this city in South Wales. An international competition was held drawing many of the world's finest architects. It was won by Zaha Hadid (born 1951), an outspoken and fiercely distinguished Iraqi-born architect who had the disadvantage of being a woman, an Iraqi (the West had been at war only two years before the

competition with the Iraqi dictator Saddam Hussein) and at the very edge of the avant-garde. Shafted by narrow-minded local business interests and crusty chaps at the Millennium Commission (a national body set up to spend Lottery money), Hadid's masterpiece vanished yet remained unforgotten.

Hadid's style, often best represented in her striking paintings, is a fusion of the obsessions of Russian Constructivists, modern Deconstrucitvists and her own powerful aesthetic of dynamic, acutely angled forms. In 1998 she won a competition to design a new museum of contemporary art in Cincinnati, Ohio and was, at long last, able to prove that her architecture had what it took to re-energize the image of a city.

ICONIC

THE "BILBAO FACTOR"

Something happened to architecture in the 1990s. Refinements in computer-aided design, in new materials and in the desire of cities worldwide to market or "brand" themselves as if they were giant shops or consumer goods encouraged a spate of ambitious new buildings that screamed "Look at me!" louder than ever before. The fairy godmother of these often overly grand designs was undoubtedly the Guggenheim Museum, Bilbao designed by Frank Gehry. Sensational, provocative and all but unprecedented, it made mayors and city managers throughout the world want a dose of what they quickly learned to call the "Bilbao Factor". The building itself was widely described as "iconic", a label which was soon applied to any new building that clearly wanted to make an exhibition of itself.

Whether this was good, or not, for architecture and cities generally, is open to question. "Iconic" design was, at its best, a bit like epic cinema and, at its worst, the architectural equivalent of a "reality" television show. It filled the pages of newspapers, supplements and magazines; even the most philistine features editors would be squealing for an "iconic" building to splash across their pages. The purpose, planning and content of such buildings were by and large irrelevant: what mattered is that they were eye-boggling, childrens' toys on a vast scale that everyone and anyone could get excited about. By 2005, it was enough for an architect to produce a madcap design – the crazier and more puerile the better – to win the front page of the most sober broadsheet newspaper. No one cared if the building was real or not, or if it was simply a flight of public relations-driven imagination. All that mattered was the "iconic" image.

Architecture had clearly gone the way of Marshall McLuhan (1911–80), the great Canadian thinker whose famous book

The Medium is the Massage (1967) evoked a near future when "what" we said would be of little importance compared to "how" we chose to say it. This was the coming world of mass and glib communication, a world that would, in a sense, turn the old Modernist maxim "form follows function" upside down and inside out. Who cared, by 2005, whether or not clones of the Gehry's Guggenheim were purposefully functional or not; what mattered most was their "iconic" value.

New computer technology, meanwhile, allowed architects to shape buildings on screen and then to stretch, distort, twist and turn them to their eye's content. And the latest construction technology could, by the 1990s, make the most provocative buildings real. So, a building could be anything you wanted it to look like, from an office in the guise of Marge Simpson's hair-do (Marge was a hugely popular American cartoon character), proposed by the British architect Will Alsop for a gullible northern English twin in search of a "makeover", to Norman Foster's highly resolved and dramatic "Gherkin", an office tower in the City of London that looked more like a giant pine, or space rocket, than a pickled relish.

The "iconic" building, whether in the guise of a new concert hall, art gallery, museum or office block, appeared to be a powerful reaction to an earlier obsession with contextualism, the idea that new buildings should respond intelligently and sensitively to their surroundings. Iconic design aimed at the polar opposite, encouraging a rush of melodramatic new buildings that appeared to be as much at home in their surrounding as a mountain gorilla in a frock and full make-up would be in the Petit Trianon at Versailles. Occasionally, of course, some of these let-it-rock buildings were truly exciting.

CHAPEL OF SANTA MARIA DEGLI ANGELI

MARIO BOTTA, 1998 MONTE TAMARO, TICINO, SWITZERLAND

This extraordinary chapel on Monte Tamaro was built for the owner of the mountain's cable-car company, in memory of his late wife. It was designed by Mario Botta, the last of the architects to have worked straight from college with Le Corbusier. The stone-clad structure extends as if infinitely along a belvedere into the mountains beyond. Walking alone here, as the cold highland air thins into an ethereal whiteness, one can readily imagine coming face-to-face with God himself. If you are tempted to believe that modern architecture is unable to achieve the sacred qualities of medieval cathedrals, take the train to Rivera and the cable-car up Monte Tamaro. Botta's chapel may just change your mind, and your point of view; for the view here, at 1,500 metres (5,000 ft), is truly divine.

The chapel is reached by a long stone-clad bridge that flies over the entrance and on, seemingly, into the mountains beyond. It has the appearance, already, of having been here forever. The chapel itself is a dark, numinous space, its black cement-plastered walls lit ethereally by indirect daylight through low windows that point down to the valley far below. The artworks, by Enzo Cucchi, are designed, in part, to dissolve into white light in certain conditions at various times of day. The whole construction is a kind of labyrinth, encouraging visitors to walk slowly and to reflect calmly even though they are just a few metres away from the cable-car station and the thrill of fast, downhill ski-runs.

LONDON EYE

DAVID MARKS AND JULIA BARFIELD, 1999 LONDON, ENGLAND

This enormous hi-tech Ferris wheel quickly became one of the most popular tourist sights in London. More than this, it changed or affected countless views of the city centre. Naturally, it was controversial. Would it ruin views? Was it plain daft to build a giant version of what was essentially a nineteenth-century fairground gizmo directly across the Thames from Barry & Pugin's world-famous Palace of Westminster? The answer to these and other questions came within a year of the opening of the 137-metre (450-ft) diameter wheel: from the start pretty much everyone loved it.

Its design was filigree, like some enormous, yet very beautiful bicycle wheel. It made views along many dreary old streets exciting, and it was fun to ride on and to see London laid out, especially as the sun went down and the city lights switched on, like some near infinite magic carpet spread far and wide below. Remarkably, for all the official huffing and puffing about how exciting the new millennium and its architecture would be, this was the only wholly brand new structure of any significance built to celebrate London in the year 2000. The world's biggest Ferris, or "observation", wheel, weighs in at 1,625 tonnes, and is held up by 6 kilometres (3.75 miles) of steel cables. Components were supplied from across Europe. Because of its size, the whole caboodle was assembled over the River Thames and then hoisted up, with some difficulty, into position; this operation was a remarkable public spectacle. Although officially a temporary structure, it is likely to stay.

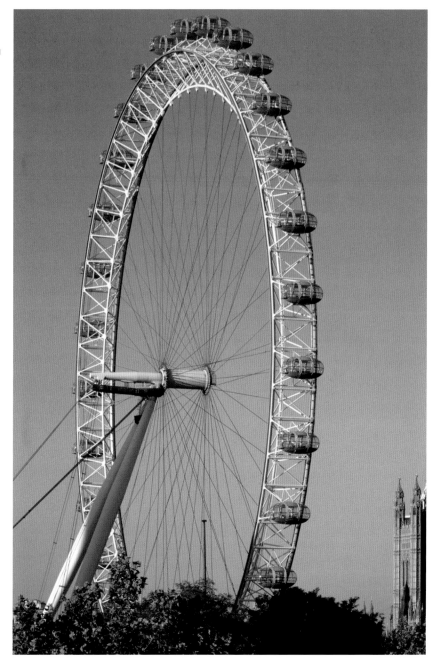

BLUEWATER SHOPPING CITY

ERIC KUHNE, 2001 DARTFORD, ENGLAND

It is possible that one day, in the not-too-distant future, we will all live in one more or less continuous built-up settlement, where shopping malls flow seamlessly and hermetically into railway stations, car parks, airports, hotels, schools and housing, and ultimately into what remains of the countryside itself. If this happens, 99 per cent of the world's population will feel as if it had died and gone to heaven. The remaining one per cent will be voluntarily repatriated to its choice of small, medium or large country – Malawi, Bolivia or Russia east of the Urals – where there are plenty of wide-open spaces, bracing air and wildlife, but few, if any, shopping malls, executive homes or skinny lattes. Far-fetched? Not far enough.

The most convincing model for this twenty-first-century way of life, and death, is Bluewater, a giant and flamboyant shopping mall rising from an old chalk quarry, and the hub of a new shopping city arising around it. Here 7,250 homes are being appended to Kuhne's mall for worshippers of the gods Nike, Prada and Gucci, a city with no cathedral or temple beyond the naves and domes of the mall itself, and with no ultimate purpose beyond stupefying consumption. Kuhne talks of creating a haven of health centres, schools, leisure and community buildings, libraries, crèches, parks, lakes and wildlife refuges. Yet all these things can exist within the framework of existing towns and cities. Bluewater, however, is the model of a future most people will be more than happy to live with.

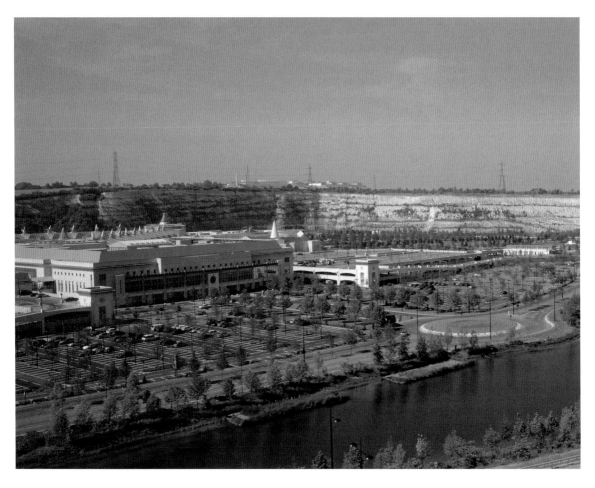

PADRE PIO CHURCH

RENZO PIANO BUILDING WORKSHOP, 2002 SAN GIOVANNI ROTONDO, ITALY

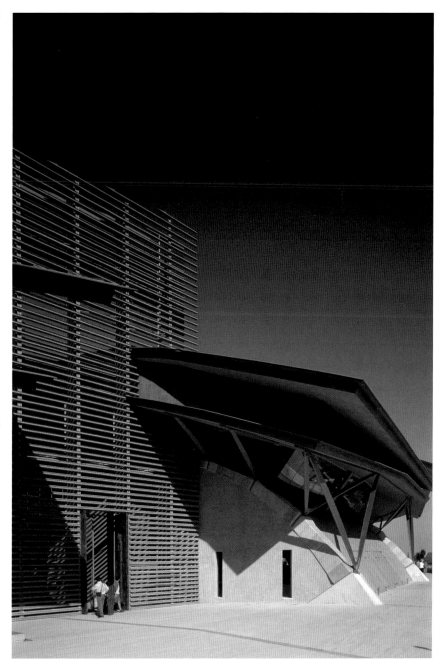

The massive new basilica of San Giovanni Rotondo is the centre of the global cult of Padre Pio, the legendary Capuchin friar canonized by Pope John Paul II in 2002. Padre Pio (Francesco Forgio, 1887–1968), the subject of at least 600 biographies, allegedly bore the stigmata, the five bleeding wounds that marked Christ's body as he hung on the cross at Calvary. Investigated twice by the Vatican for alleged fraud and sexual misconduct, and banned from saying Mass in public at one later point, he was reinstated with honour. Allied pilots during the Second World War claim to have seen the face of the saintly friar appearing in the clouds, beseeching them not to bomb San Giovanni Rotondo. The village survived.

The main span of Piano's low-lying church's shallow central dome, designed to enfold congregations of 6,000, is, at over 50 metres (164 ft), possibly the longest supporting arch ever built out of stone. "This is not an attempt to get into the record books," says Piano. "It is simply a desire to find out what can be done with stone today, almost 1,000 years after the Gothic cathedrals were built." Architecturally and spatially, the new church is a very long way from Padre Pio's cell in the nearby Convent of the Capuchin Friars. So small it can only hold two people, this is furnished with no more than a bed, a crucifix, a chest for linen, a bedside table, a writing table, two chairs and a small bookshelf. The public is not admitted.

SERPENTINE GALLERY PAVILION

TOYO ITO, CECIL BALMOND, 2002 LONDON, ENGLAND

Ito has been the designer of some of the world's most magical and refined buildings, mysterious marriages between the solid and the transparent, the substantial and the ethereal, the sensual and the coolly technological. A master of lighting effects, he created a modern masterpiece with his Tower of Winds (1986), near the central railway station in Yokohama, Japan. By day, this tall, circular sheath of aluminium serves as a ventilation shaft for an underground shopping mall; by night, atmospheric changes and the sounds of the city transform it into a mesmerizing light show, a kind of architectural firework. It is truly beautiful.

Teamed up with Cecil Balmond, the inventive Arup mathematician and engineer, he produced a truly magical summer pavilion in Kensington Gardens, London, for the Serpentine Gallery. A happy exercise in asymmetry and wily maths, this steel-framed structural enigma was an attempt to blur the boundaries between walls, floor and ceiling, and between interior, exterior and parkland setting. Here Ito played a game, with Balmond providing the mathematical and logical framework, in which solid and light elements were balanced on an architectural knife-edge. Balmond says that, notionally at any rate, the roof, walls, windows and doorways were a sequence of geometrically generated planes that "appear to be infinitely in motion". This was a non-linear architecture, "resulting from a design process where structure and surface amalgamate". Whatever it was, the result was delightful and hugely popular, and showed a glimpse of what a new architecture in the process of being invented might be.

YOKAHAMA PORT TERMINAL

FOREIGN OFFICE ARCHITECTS, 2002 YOKAHAMA, JAPAN

One of the most intelligent and beautiful mass-transit buildings of recent years, this is a spirited meeting of complex geometry, flowing space and refined building craft. It doubles up as a seaside transport terminal and a hard-surfaced public park; it is a generously planned place of welcome and farewell. And yet, despite its inventive architecture and heroic scale, it is an unpretentious design and almost serene.

The terminal was designed by the London-based husband-and-wife team, Spanish-born Alejandro Zaera-Polo and Farshid Moussavi, from Iran, and was engineered by Cecil Balmond of Arup. Although subtle, the Port Terminal has a special drama of its own, although this is not immediately evident. In fact, when ships tie up here, they tower over the

structure, and disembarking passengers appear to be looking down on nothing more, or less, than a particularly well made and elegant modern pier, all serpentine steel handrails and seaside adventure. Yet beneath this public promenade is a magnificent arrivals and departures hall, its roof a kind of computer-generated, twenty-first-century Gothic vault. The wonderful drama of the space is kept in tight check by the restricted palette of materials and colours used throughout this very large building. It all feels of a piece, interior and exterior flowing seamlessly into each other. Ship shape. The idea of creating city buildings that become an extension of the urban landscape is not new, but here it has been executed in convincing and exemplary fashion.

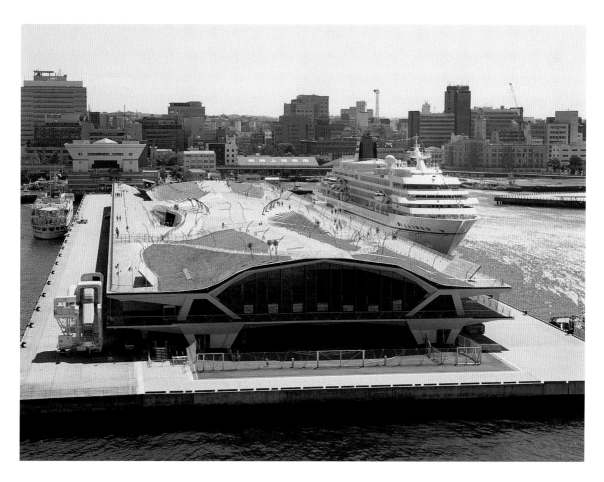

PARLIAMENTARY LIBRARY

RAJ REWAL, 2002 NEW DELHI, INDIA

This thoughtful seat of learning lies in the regal shadow of Herbert Baker's circular imperial parliament building, set in a campus of munificently planned and beautifully executed government buildings designed by Baker and Edwin Lutyens from 1911. It remains one of the great set pieces of world architecture, as if the exquisite grouping of Baroque palaces at Greenwich by Jones, Webb, Wren and Hawksmoor had been transplanted from under the grey London cloudscape to the blazing skies of north-west India; the chirrup of sparrows replaced by the electric scream of peacocks.

The first major addition to the old imperial capital since independence, the library is a big building. Parliament, however, insisted that it must relate harmoniously to the great colonnaded drum of Baker's building, so only its domed roof rises above the massive neo-classical plinth behind it. Rewal's trick has been to shape a building that is at once discreet and animated, the animation reserved for the roof and the generous interiors, the discretion expressed in the building's low profile. The building is much bigger than it appears to be: only two floors rise above ground, while a hidden pair – readily accessible book-stacks – sink below its superstructure. This leads to some magic moments inside the building, especially when the Scholars' Library reveals itself in all its four-storey splendour. With its landscaped gardens merging into the building, its turfed roofs and a gentle symbolism Hindus and Jains will recognize, this is a subtle and special building.

CENTRE FOR MATHEMATICAL STUDIES

EDWARD CULLINAN, 2003 CAMBRIDGE, ENGLAND

In seven lush suburban acres of Cambridge, seven eye-catching pavilions form Cambridge University's Centre for Mathematical Studies. Seven years in the making, here are seven pillars of architectural and academic wisdom. Instead of responding to this suburban site with twee and tweedy, fey and bricky buildings, as so often happens on the fringe of English country towns, Cullinan's team conjured an exuberant, almost exotic skyline from ecologically sound and truly intelligent design.

In the wrong hands, such apparent waywardness could easily spell a giddy, postmodern-style architectural confection, or mess. Yet this gently exuberant university development is nothing of the sort. The profile of this joyous gaggle of buildings will probably make you smile gently, in the way, perhaps, that the work of England's most expressive Arts

and Crafts architects would have done here a century ago. The Centre represents a marriage between two university departments: applied mathematics & theoretical physics and pure mathematics & mathematical statistics. These, in turn, comprise 25 mathematics groups and require 340 separate offices. The solution, keeping all parties happy, was these seven pavilions gathered around a central, partially sunken building containing restaurant, communal meeting space and lecture theatres. The inner four pavilions clustered around this focal building form a new university courtyard. The Centre for Mathematical Studies is a happy resolution of an equation made up of squares and straight lines, curves and circles, civil architecture and wilful suburbia. It has a feet-on-the-ground, head-in-the-clouds quality that matches and mirrors the exact yet ever questing world of mathematics itself.

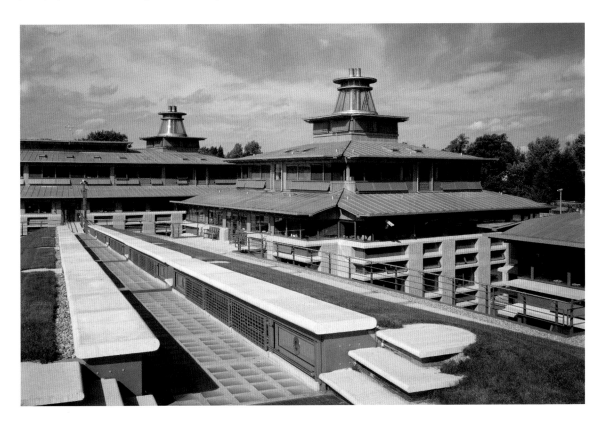

30 ST MARY AXE

FOSTER AND PARTNERS, 2003 CITY OF LONDON, ENGLAND

Popularly nicknamed "the Gherkin", this striking office tower soars above what had been the wreckage of the former Baltic Exchange, an Edwardian building badly damaged by an IRA bomb in 1992. Far from resembling a pickled relish, the circular tower evokes the outline of one of the great dirigible airships of the 1930s, or one of Wernher von Braun's early space rockets.

Tethered firmly to the ground, this sleek and sensational "towering innuendo", commissioned and owned by financial services group Swiss Re, is home to some 4,000 office workers and far more than just another cynical filing cabinet in the sky. The building's circular form generates considerably less wind at street level than conventional right-angled towers. The circular form also provides for a generous public plaza at its base. The real environmental achievement here, however, is felt behind the building's outer skin of 7,500 windows. Spiralling up between outer and inner skins is a sequence of six-floor atriums. These admit daylight deep into the plan, offer views up and down through the building and suck fresh air up the height of the 180-metre (590-ft) tower. The glazed crown or nose cone of the tower boasts a restaurant, and, above it, a spectacular bar gained by a spiral stair or glass lift. It looks very much like a Ken Adam film set, the lair of some 1960s James Bond villain with designs to take over the world. Sadly, it and its master-of-the-universe views are for Swiss Re employees and their guests only.

WALT DISNEY CONCERT HALL

FRANK GEHRY AND PARTNERS, 2003 LOS ANGELES, USA

"It's strange that Walt Disney and Frank Gehry never worked together; they might have. If Dad had lived ten years longer, I know their paths would have crossed." Together with her late mother Lillian, Diane Disney Miller was one of the driving forces behind the gloriously cartoon-like Walt Disney Concert Hall, which might be seen as Walt Disney's Fantasia in three eye-boggling dimensions. It was designed before, yet completed after, Gehry's Guggenhein, Bilbao. "In some ways," said Gehry, "the delay worked out well for us; getting the Guggenheim done was like a training ground for LA. We got to know how best to build it." Which was just as well.

This is a richly complex building, a thing of compound curves, stainless steel fronds, leaves and petals, wrapped over and around a customized steel frame. It is the product of some 30,000 computer drawings and highly skilled construction. Gehry likes to compare it to a huge flower blooming in a gigantic garden: "Lillian Disney loved flowers and gardens. I don't think she understood the form of the building. She liked to bring me pictures of little brick cottages with thatched roofs and little ducky ponds and hoped that I'd incorporate these in my designs. I promised I'd build her a garden." The stainless steel Disney Concert Hall, with its light-filled main auditorium seating 2,265, is a rose of sorts, blooming in its own strange bed, while, inside, the building unfolds like the most exotic lily.

ONE CENTAUR STREET

DRMM, 2003 LONDON, ENGLAND

Shoehorned between railway tracks outside Waterloo station, eighteenth-century cottages and 1950s housing estates, One Centaur Street rises four storeys from a former scrapyard. It is a prototype for intelligent and elegant city housing that could happily be repeated, and profitably so. The solid concrete block is clad in a form of contemporary clapboard. What might be taken for old railway sleepers bolted along the walls turn out to be dark, concrete sections animating all four sides of the building. Set close together at its base, these grow wider apart as the building pops its head above the railway viaduct, causing the block to lighten as it rises. This clever, yet restrained, use of materials continues throughout the building.

De Rijke and his partners, Philip Marsh and Sadie Morgan, have created their own vocabulary of materials, playing intelligently with unusual woods and tiles offset by finely finished concrete, glass and industrial components. The design is a fusion of the European horizontal apartment and the English vertical terraced house. In practice, this means that each of the light and thoughtfully planned flats is arranged on several levels connected by a contemporary take on the traditional, narrow London staircase. The effect is of living in a small, sunlit house inside an apartment block. The block, seen as a single entity from the outside, is rather like a Rubik cube inside. Residents share a garden made of concrete and old timber railway sleepers lined with honeysuckle, Willow Herb – a railway plant, Busy Lizzie and London Pride.

STUDIO WEIL

STUDIO LIBESKIND, 2003 PORT D'ANDRATX, MALLORCA

Ambiguous. Barbara Weil and Daniel Libeskind used this word when discussing Studio Weil, the first domestic project by the Polish-American architect of the striking Jewish Museum in Berlin. Their use of the word, fashionable with many architects at the time, was not, however, loose. For it is not clear whether this building, overlooking the sea at Port d'Andratx, Mallorca, is a studio or a home. It is probably both, although whether Weil will ever live here full-time is another matter. The romantic and traditional single-storey home where she had lived and worked as a sculptor for the past 35 years, lies across the road from Libeskind's dazzling-white provocation.

The Libeskind design is as far removed from most people's dreams of what a house should be as it is possible to get.

Monumental yet introspective, its echoing, bare concrete acoustic is otherworldly. Here, there is no sun deck and, except for a glimpse at the very top of a long, exterior stair, no view of the sea. Mallorcan houses usually abound with balconies and windows framing views of mountains, beaches and boats. Studio Weil does the opposite. Libeskind describes it as "landscape as house and house as artistic landscape", and Weil says it is a "space for contemplation, domestic reverie and presentation of artworks". Studio Weil is, in fact, a brave and remarkable structure and a fascinating example of creative synergy between two artists who, unknowingly, had shared something like a common approach to visual form long before Libeskind became news.

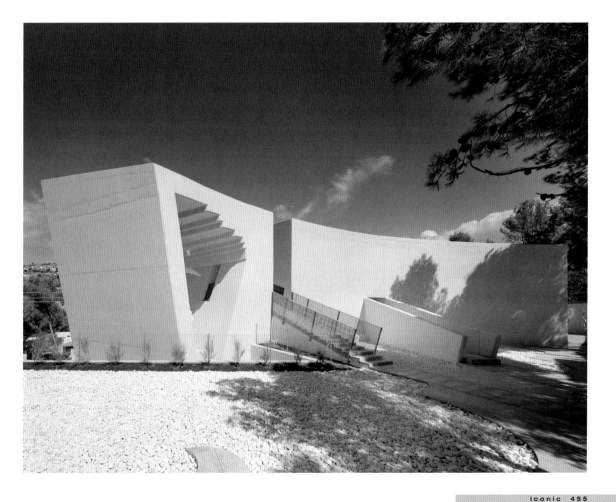

DE YOUNG MUSEUM

HERZOG & DE MEURON, 2005 SAN FRANCISCO, USA

Now you see it, now you don't. Within a decade of the opening of this new Californian art museum, the 3,600 copper panels that clad its walls will have turned green and the massive, meandering building will have all but disappeared into the rich foliage surrounding it. This is a delightful conceit, although the building's predecessors both disappeared for good, one in the earthquake that devastated San Francisco in 1906, the other in the earthquake that shook it badly in 1989. It is curious, perhaps, that soon enough this museum, set in Golden Gate Park some way from the city centre, will appear like the ruins of some ancient Mayan city peeking up over the suburban jungle. Perhaps it is a comment on the fragility of

architectural endeavour. Perhaps it is just a bit of fun.

The copper walls, embossed with patterns sourced from local foliage, shroud the extensive, low-lying galleries of a museum with a rather curious collection of not so very distinguished art drawn from the States and around the world. The building is very much the event here rather than the collections on show. The architects have designed it as a kind of enclosed and sinuous walk through the park with no obvious grand formal spaces to locate the visitor; the courtyard around which the galleries are gathered performs that task. The other defining moment is the oddly twisted lookout tower, which is, in fact, the education department's roost. From the top you can see the city.

BMW CENTRAL BUILDING

ZAHA HADID, PATRIK SCHUMACHER, 2005 LEIPZIG, GERMANY

Car manufacturers, once so radical, gave up the ghost for several decades when it came to designing imaginative buildings. Then came Volkswagen with its glass factory in Dresden (p.409) and BMW with this equally extraordinary building at its 3-series manufacturing plant on the outskirts of Leipzig. Zaha Hadid was commissioned by the Bavarian manufacturer in 2002. As BMW would have expected, Hadid did her best to turn the conventional car factory upside down and inside out. Her building serves as the junction box, or compression chamber as she calls it, between manufacturing and administration at Leipzig. It is, in fact, the centrepiece of four buildings, the other three designed by BMW's in-house architects and engineers. Inside the sweeping and impressive Hadid building, blue- and white-collar workers share space; the floors they co-habit are staggered along and across the architectural equivalent of overlapping tectonic plates. In this way, the entire building and all its many overlapping functions and workers can be viewed from any one point inside. Visitors, too, are encouraged, so that the production plant becomes a public spectacle rather than something grubby hidden away out of sight on the edge of town. The cars themselves, in an unfinished state, cross the space on their way between production sheds along a cage-like conveyor belt passing above employees. This serves to animate the administrative offices and, importantly, to remind everyone at Leipzig that they are involved not just in paperwork but the production of cars.

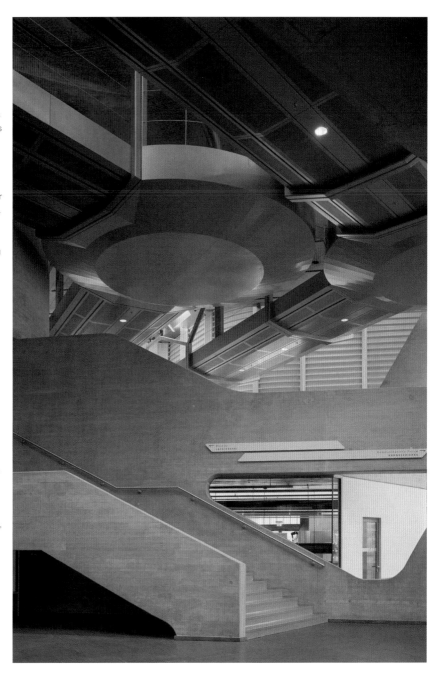

CASA DA MUSICA

REM KOOLHAAS/OMA, CECIL BALMOND, 2005 PORTO, PORTUGAL

Memorably described by one Dutch critic as a "hasty meteorite attack on Porto", the Casa da Musica is a wilfully powerful design that challenges its host city to a kind of cultural duel. A vast solid, its edges cut like some gigantic and crazy diamond, this new House of Music is the epitome of what was known as "iconic" architecture in the first decade of the twentieth century, a monumental building shouting loudly and hyper-fashionably for attention.

Even so, the Casa da Musica is an immensely sophisticated structure, and beguiling in parts. Its monumental, meteorite-like form proves to be a shell hiding an extremely complex interior, decorated in a dazzling display of rich materials. One side of the apparently all-so-solid structure is cut away, revealing the concert hall, which overlooks the old city centre. The auditorium is set high in this precise white concrete meteorite and reached by a procession of stairways and interior spaces every bit as Baroque, and as bonkers, as those found in Garnier's chocolate-box of an opera house in nineteenth-century Paris. Here, though, instead of Garnier's more or less horizontal procession through a magnificently madcap building, Koolhaas offers a vertical climb up through the narrow slit of the public entrance. Up go visitors into a bizarre and entertaining world of polished aluminium walls, walls covered with traditional Portuguese blue-and-white tiles depicting religious themes, walls of gold leaf and plywood. It is, ultimately, great fun, a meteorite with a sense of occasion and humour, if not exactly good civic manners.

FIGGE MUSEUM

DAVID CHIPPERFIELD, 2005 DAVENPORT, IOWA, USA

This luminous building was the result of a brave aesthetic decision. When the trustees of the former city-owned Davenport Museum of Art, now the privately run Figge Art Museum, decided to build anew on the banks of the Mississippi, they decided not to go for some fashionable "iconic" architectural gew-gaw. Instead they sought, in Thomas Figge's own words, "a timeless and classic" design. Given that the museum was also intended to breathe fresh life into downtown Davenport, this might have seemed a tall order. Surely everyone wanted novelty in the first decade of the new century; and, surely Frank Gehry had pointed the way with his stunning and internationally popular Guggenheim Museum on the old dockside in Bilbao? Instead, the Figge chose this

tautly drawn design by David Chipperfield, an architect whose work has, increasingly, more than a measure of Mies van der Rohe's classically-inspired purism and rigour about it, and even a dose of the older Prussian classicism that, in turn, inspired Mies. The result is a graceful, crystal-clear building that raises the cultural stakes in the Iowa city several-fold. This is especially impressive given the fact that the collections here – regional American, Haitian, Mexican and European art – are not an obvious draw, or at least not in terms of wooing large new audiences. With its handsome public spaces, chic restaurant overlooking the river, its art studios, auditorium and two floors of temporary exhibition space, the new museum is a popular as well as critical success.

PHAENO SCIENCE CENTRE

ZAHA HADID, 2005 WOLFSBURG, GERMANY

So many monumental new buildings of the first years of the twenty-first century were described as "spaceships" of one kind or another that the metaphor, if that is what it was, began to wear gossamer thin. But, here, indeed, was the mother of all architectural spaceships, the gloriously exciting and almost otherworldly science centre in the heart of Wolfsburg, the city devoted, from its foundation by Adolf Hitler in 1938, to the manufacture of Volkswagen cars. Now the centre of Wolfsburg is both a factory and a hugely popular car-based theme park. Rising ethereally, despite its robust concrete construction, alongside the town's railway station, the science centre acts as a connecting device between the residential and manufacturing halves of Wolfsburg. The building is raised

up on a massive, sci-fi Gothic vaulted concrete undercroft, which will one day find a function. Above, Hadid has created an enormous exhibition hall, one that slopes and slip-slides away in every direction and dimension. This sensational internalized architectural landscape is the mysterious and dazzling heart of the building.

This is Hadid's architecture as she has long struggled to make it, a world very much of her own imagination and yet one solidly realized in concrete and steel, materials that she has stretched to obey her strong will. Whatever "interactive" toys are installed here over time to keep the hundreds of thousands of visitors rallying here happy, the building will long be the most exciting thing to see in Wolfsburg.

WELSH ASSEMBLY

RICHARD ROGERS PARTNERSHIP, 2005 CARDIFF, WALES

Was it worth the wait, the debate, the hate and the money? The one architectural piece of the jigsaw that had been long missing from the regenerated Cardiff Bay was the new Welsh Assembly building. For many years the building remained nothing more than a big hole in the ground because of political storms in pint glasses in Cardiff pubs, mean-mindedness and general bitchery.

Finally completed in 2005, this is a fine design executed with clarity, grace and ingenuity. Rising on three levels from a great stepped slate plinth leading up from the water's edge, embracing the buildings and public spaces around it, and reaching through its crystal-clear interiors, the building is at once ultra-modern and classical. With persuasive intelligence, the architects have shaped a strictly contemporary, low-energy building with echoes of the ancient Greek agora, or marketplace, and of a Greek temple, a modern Acropolis overlooking a bay that bobs with leisure boats. Its adventurous roof, punctuated by the great funnel of the debating chamber, is a necessary release for the inevitable volume of hot air generated below. It is held up by stick-thin steel columns, and the whole structure serves as an umbrella, or parasol, protecting the public spaces, committee rooms and assembly chamber clustered beneath it. The building is as transparent as possible, evoking the notion of open government. The public can walk up the great slate plinth, into and around the building, and look down on members of the elegantly cosseted Assembly in full rhetorical flight.

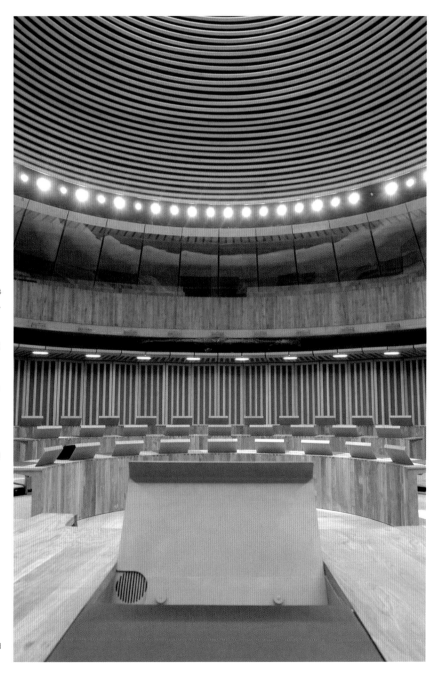

ZENTRUM PAUL KLEE

RENZO PIANO BUILDING WORKSHOP, 2005 BERN, SWITZERLAND

Here is what appears to be a simple sketch willed, by immense skill and honed artistry, into elegant new architecture. Graphic, expressive, subtle, the Zentrum Paul Klee is sited on the agricultural edge of Bern and is skirted by a motorway. As well as housing a huge collection of the artist's works, it contains a temporary exhibition gallery, an auditorium for music, drama and talks, art rooms for children, a centre for research and a high and airy glazed internal walkway connecting all parts of the building. The apparent simplicity of the structure, etching three steel and glass "hills", as Piano describes them, into the Swiss landscape belies the complexity of the building. What started out as a permanent home for a collection of 4,000 paintings and drawings by Paul Klee (1879–1940), a local artist of international renown, became a centre for creating art as well as displaying it.

Each of the three "hills" covering the now extensive galleries and rooms, is a different size and shape. The first "hill", the largest, covers the entrance lobby, a covered "forum", a 400-seat auditorium and art rooms for schoolchildren. The middle "hill", slightly smaller than the first, contains the permanent Klee collection and the temporary exhibitions gallery. The third, smaller again, shelters the research centre and administrative offices. All three "hills" disappear into the cornfields, poppies, meadows and forest above and behind the centre, so that the building is truly a part of the landscape it adorns.

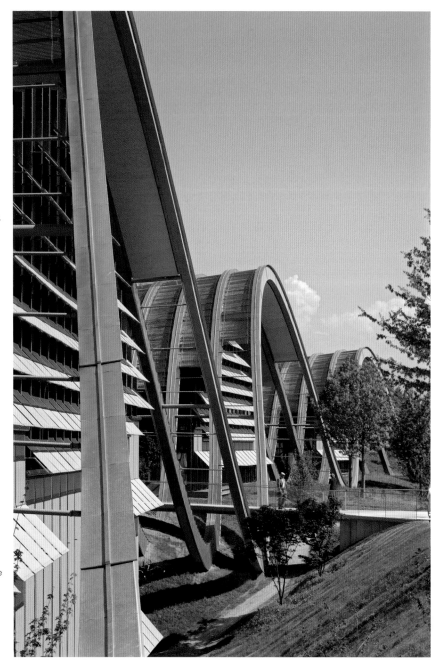

LEWIS GLUCKSMAN GALLERY

O'DONNEL AND TUOMEY, 2005 CORK, IRELAND

The Lewis Glucksman Gallery climbs up among the trees of the university grounds at Cork in a sequence of dramatically cantilevered twists and turns, enough to keep you guessing, but not so many as to be eccentric. In fact, this handsome gallery was designed this way to keep the floor plan as tightly knit as possible, and to allow the three floors of galleries to face out with a variety of views across trees, a winding river and the white-faced Gothic quad of the original university buildings. Not a single tree standing in the Victorian garden has been so much as pollarded to make way for the newcomer; it weaves between them. In this sense, the Glucksman Gallery feels as if it was intended to be here.

Galleries fan out from a high internal courtyard. On the fourth floor, a terrace opens like a ship's deck, leading us from curated artifice into manicured nature. The floors of the building, part timber clad, part galvanized steel, part rough oak, have something of the look of wooden boats stacked up in a boatyard. Cork is a city on water and boats are a part of its life. Tuomey has said that one of the most beautiful things he has ever seen was the National Museum of Ireland's display of a Viking ship in Dublin's Kildare Place. The ship was raised on stilts at an angle among the trees like some "celestial vessel straining over a stone terrain". This building has much of that feeling.

EU COURT OF JUSTICE

DOMINIQUE PERRAULT 2008 LUXEMBOURG

Gold is not a colour normally associated with courts of law. Dominique Perrault, Parisian architect of the newly reconstructed European Court of Justice in Luxembourg begs to disagree. After all, this is not, he argued, a criminal court. "It's not a place concerned with prisons and punishments. It's to do with relations between European countries, with constitutional concerns." When the sun catches the base of the court's eyecatching twin towers, they light up like a pair of giant candles. Located on top of the Kirchberg plateau, separated from Luxembourg City by a deep ravine, the court was until recently a rather soulless place. Perrault has succeeded in introducing an unexpected playfulness. When it was announced that EU membership would increase to 27 countries, Perrault

was commissioned to wrap a new building around the existing complex. His brief was to ensure that every one of its 2,000 staff, formerly spread across a huge campus, was housed under one roof. Beneath that roof is a shimmering, golden palace. The main courtroom sets the scene with a net-like ceiling straight out of *One Thousand and One Nights*. The smaller courtrooms, while less dramatic than the main chamber, are timber-lined and warmly finished. These are encircled by a new two-storey corridor or internal street of crisp, modern spaces – lobbies, cafés, libraries and judges' chambers. Daylight filters through the building, while the artificial light is playful and imaginative. The overall impression is of an earnest giant who, despite himself, wants to dress up and play.

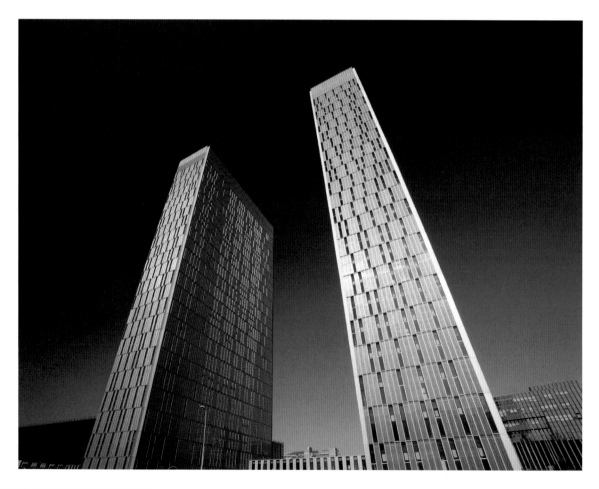

KINGS PLACE

DIXON JONES 2008 KING'S CROSS, LONDON

Kings Place in London, home of the Guardian Media Group, is a building in a number of unexpected movements. It is at once a commercial office block, a media HQ, home to two art galleries and a wholly unexpected 450-seat concert hall. Indeed, the emotional heart and architectural pivot of the building is not its bright and airy central atrium, flanked with cafés and bars, but this music box below it. Where else in Britain will you find a commercial building given over as much to the arts as to business and rents? The façade is a theatrical glass curtain rippling along the length of the building opening into a stage-like atrium. The glass curtain was made in Venice and, as you walk through the building, you find yourself faced with a canal basin and, if not gondolas, then a flotilla of London barges. The idea of Kings Place is very much that of its developer, Peter Millican, who just happens to have a passion for art and music. The 450-seat concert hall is truly remarkable, one of the most handsome and intriguing new venues in central London. A shoebox auditorium, it is by necessity sealed and windowless to keep the relentless roar of traffic at bay. Lined throughout in veneer garnered from a single, 500-year-old Black Forest oak, it has all the elegance and grandeur of a Greek temple. Above, in bright, open-plan offices, and perhaps a little less musically, journalists and others toil away.

BIRD'S NEST

HERZOG AND DE MEURON 2008 BEIJING, CHINA

Known as the "Bird's Nest" for obvious reasons when you see it, here is an epic adventure in the serving up of steel and concrete. An eye-catching design even from a distance, the stadium is a mind-bogglingly complex artefact close up, and it is just as dizzying on the inside. The Chinese named it the Bird's Nest as soon as its creators – Swiss architects Herzog & de Meuron, working with Arup and the China Architectural Design and Research Group – unveiled their design in 2003. It measures 320 metres by 297 metres (1,050ft by 974-ft), and is 69 metres (226-ft) high. Its steel frame, 41,875 tonnes in all, loops, swoops and swirls over and around the great, red, concrete 91,000-seat arena. What had seemed to be a solid structure from a distance

proves to be a filigree Chinese puzzle close up. Jacques Herzog has described this 12-metre-deep (39-ft) frame as "an architectural forest", its beams, stairs, frames and other steel elements standing in for trees and branches, and providing an awe-inspiring transitional space between the exterior and the interior, where the arena awaits. The latter, a great, red bowl of concrete, proves to be almost circular, so everyone is equally close to the running-jumping-vaulting action. Above the tiers of plastic seats and giant clocks, the roof is a simple membrane designed to keep out sun and storm – the 2008 Olympics took place in August, when Beijing was sweltering – and to act as a foil to that intricate, bird's nest of a steel skeleton.

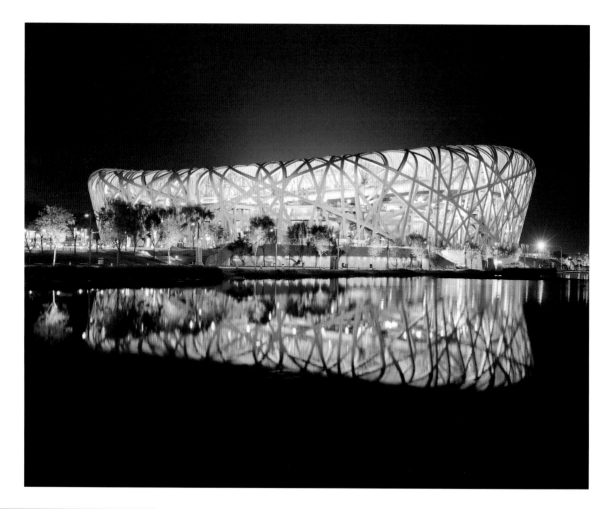

ACADEMY OF SCIENCES

RENZO PIANO BUILDING WORKSHOP 2008 SAN FRANCISCO, USA

An elegant, simple diagram of a building, the Academy of Sciences has been designed to respect the height line of the trees surrounding it, to respect the world of Nature around it. And, so its vast programme – a planetarium, several slices of rainforest, a colony of seabirds, giant reptiles, classrooms, bats, 18 million pickled animal specimens, chameleons, temporary exhibition spaces, geckos, auditorium, frogs, cafeteria, lungfish, and millions of visitors – meet and work together below one vast, low and respectful roof. Here, all is lightness and transparency. The steel columns that support the enchanting green roof – and its 1.7 million plants – are so thin, they must be held in tension by long wire cables. These not only permit the interior of the

museum to be as bright and as free from structural intrusion as possible, but, in the event of an earthquake, they should allow the building to sway safely like a ship weathering a storm at sea. The museum's clear glazed walls reveal some of the attractions inside, notably the two great spheres of its planetarium and artificial rainforest. From the outside, you can see straight through the building into the park from almost any angle. "You can say that the building is made of shadows," says Renzo Piano. "Being inside is like being under a tree in summer. The green roof is like foliage wrapping itself over branches." And Pacific breezes flitting through the interior ensure you never feel trapped inside an institutional building.

CCTV

REM KOOLHAAS/OMA 2008 BEIJING, CHINA

This vast and almost overarchingly ambitious monument to the power of television rises like some steel colossus above acres of new building development in Beijing. Designed with the visionary engineer, Cecil Balmond and his team at Arup, the new headquarters of China Central Television (CCTV) is a truly enigmatic project. It offers broadcast facilities and studios that can only make programme makers in other countries gasp; and, yet, the whole enterprise, with its 16 broadcast channels, is tightly controlled by the state's propaganda department. With its radical and daring steel structure, the building seems to be the expression of a free-spirited enterprise, and yet it couldn't be more different. Even so, CCTV acts as a giant new gateway to the new Beijing, the switched-on and dynamic new China. The CCTV tower is nothing if not ambitious. It boasts 44 floors. It is 234 metres (768ft) high and designed in the shape of a 3D Chinese character (locals say "boxer shorts"). Its steel structure forms a continuous spatial loop climbing up and around the central, open core of the building. It had to be built in two sections that were joined together; the process of its construction was a public performance in its own right. Inside this complex structural web, there is a "media village" (more like a city actually), complete with places to eat and play, and a sensational public viewing gallery. It is a rollercoaster of radical ideas yet remains closed to foreign devils, although times may change.

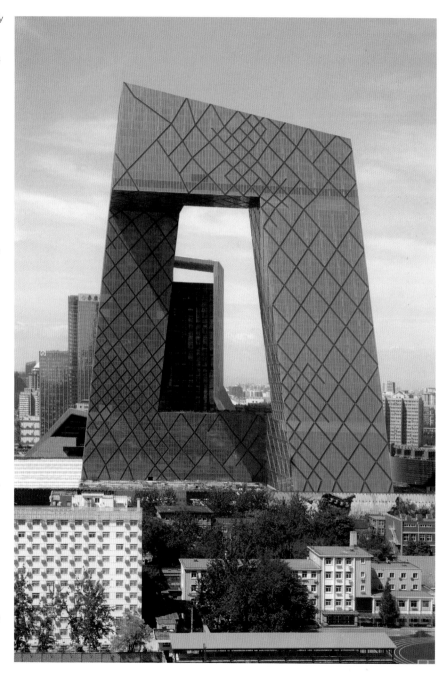

LIEGE-GUILLEMINS STATION

SANTIAGO CALATRAVA 2009 LIEGE, BELGIUM

This gleaming station, commissioned by the Belgian state railway, is easily one of the world's finest. Its ethereal, transparent, filigree architecture suggests openness, a dissolving of boundaries, infinite horizons, speed, grace and ease: everything that train travel should be. Its seemingly delicate yet immensely strong structure is evidently the work of engineers with an appreciation of spiders' webs, not to mention the Forth Bridge and the Eiffel Tower. The way its canopies seem to ski down from the heights is masterly, suggesting a designer in love with the idea of trains, stations and their rhythmical to- and -fro. The design is the idea of one man, Santiago Calatrava, engineer and architect. Here, five long platforms are sheltered, in their middle stretches, by a lofty, transparent bird's cage of

a roof. Made of 39 steel arches, it is 200 metres (656ft) long, 35 metres (115ft) high, and open (whenever practical) to the elements. There is no single grand façade: this symmetrical building offers equal value to all viewpoints. As Calatrava says, "We completely reinvented the façade. Or, better, we said, 'There is no longer a façade.'" Instead, there are only large openings announced by the gleaming metallic canopies that overhang them. Glass brickwork between the tracks and platforms illuminates a huge, grotto-like undercroft. This is, quite simply, a beautiful building. To stand under that great white steel shell is to feel the architecture soaring with all the majesty and daring of a gothic cathedral, bound up with notions of speed, of hurtling towards the future.

AQUA TOWER

STUDIO GANG 2009 CHICAGO, USA

Rising up in a dance of ever-changing concrete forms, the Aqua Tower has something of the look of a multi-layered Lake Michigan rock formation, soaring above downtown Chicago. This landmark design has broken out of the city-wide straitjacket of right angles and smooth surfaces as if Gaudi had taken up skyscraper design, or a spinning ballerina had morphed into a building. The 250-metre (819-ft) residential tower is also the tallest building yet designed with a woman in charge. Skyscrapers are traditionally seen as an expression of overbearing male libido, a sort of mine's-taller-than-yours competition. So, even today, it is a surprise to find a woman building so swaggeringly high. Gang, who wanted to be an engineer before she decided on architecture, grew up in a small town near Chicago. She says she thinks of the city as a mountain range rising up from the flat Illinois plains that flank Lake Michigan. "When we got the commission, we were partly thinking of building a mountain. But, being steeped in engineering, I also saw the project as a work of urban infrastructure. The tower is a machine plugged into the city – working for people – as well as being a kind of peak, or rock formation." Behind its weaving balconies, this 82-storey residential and hotel tower is a largely conventional building. Conventional in plan, that is, yet unexpected in terms of form; it is laced through with the latest amenities and luxuries and, from the sidewalk, forms a surprisingly natural part of the cityscape.

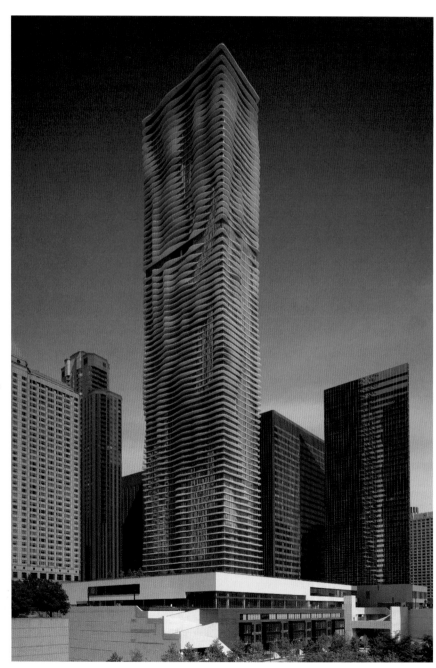

ACROPOLIS MUSEUM

BERNARD TSCHUMI 2007 ATHENS, GREECE

Tschumi's new museum dedicated to the celebration of Greek antiquity, and home to some 4,000 ancient artefacts has the almost impossible job of engaging with the nearby Parthenon, the sublime 5th-century BC temple dedicated to the goddess Athena. Tschumi's building, however, has also had to be impressive enough to help the Greek government in its lengthy quest to bring the Elgin Marbles – the frieze from the Parthenon – back here from the British Museum in London. The result is a calm and noble building entirely free of decoration. It does, though, play a number of clever structural games. The glass-floored entrance lobby, for example, straddles the excavation site so that, as you enter the museum, you see below you the outlines of shops, alleys, houses, baths and workshops dating back to 600 AD. You can also make out the irregular forest of concrete columns the new museum stands on, the antithesis of the beautifully rhythmic spacing of the Parthenon's Doric columns. Each is placed to avoid touching the ancient fabric below. In times of tremor, the columns will dip and sway, enough, hopefully, to save the building from collapse. Up a great ramp, the first floor reveals a vast, sunlit and many-columned chamber for the display of Greek sculpture. Crowning the museum is a great glazed box skewed to face north to the Acropolis. The views are picture-perfect, except for the missing Elgin Marbles that are, one day, meant to be on display in this Parthenon-sized room. One day.

GREEN POINT STADIUM

GMP ARCHITEKTEN 2010 CAPE TOWN, SOUTH AFRICA

This stunning white apparition rises like a porcelain bowl from a podium set in restored parkland, between the breakers of the Atlantic and the commanding backdrop of Lion's Rock, Devil's Peak and Table Mountain. Is there a stadium anywhere in the world with a more sublime setting? Fifteen storeys high with curving walls, the 68,000-seat "Diva of Cape Town" is sheathed in a translucent fabric mesh, made from woven fibreglass coated with Teflon. This sounds coldly technical, yet during the course of the day the building's filigree skin glows blue at noon, rose in the late afternoon and red at sunset. On stormy days, it can appear silver, grey or even pewter. By night, and with its 360 internal lamps switched on, the skin becomes all but

transparent, revealing the undulating swoops of the stadium's three tiers of seats, its airy public concourses, and something of its quietly thrilling structure. Its design and engineering is as crisp and as pristine as a Braun radio by Dieter Rams, or a Silver Arrow Mercedes-Benz racing car. The thinking is that all the necessary colour was to be provided by players, crowds and the human drama enacted in this exquisite sports machine. Occupying a site the size of six city blocks, the stadium is enormous, with a delicacy and grace that belies its bulk. The big question for buildings like this is what happens to them after the attention-grabbing global events they were designed for, on such a scale, have gone?

SHANGHAI EXPO PAVILION

THOMAS HEATHERWICK 2010 SHANGHAI, CHINA

The British Pavilion at the Shanghai Expo 2010 was certainly a prickly affair. In fact, Thomas Heatherwick's mesmerising structure boasted no fewer than 60,000 perspex prickles, looking as if they were bursting from its core. The design was meant to represent a giant dandelion at the point where its seeds are about to fly off. Each of the prickles contained a seed from the Kew Gardens Millenniun Seed Bank in Wakehurst, West Sussex. The plan was for the prickles and their seeds to be donated to schools across China when the £35billion expo closed its gates at the end of the year. And, so, in a special and peculiar way, the pavilion was recycled in a spirit of gentle goodwill. The prickles, though, had a second role.

Being transparent, or translucent, each was used to bring daylight inside the cube. So, after queuing for many hours, what visitors saw was nothing – there were no displays – except for a delightful play of curiously filtered sunlight that made enticing patterns on walls, floor and ceiling. While this did not impress visitors in search of British goods to see, and even buy, it was an officially sanctioned display of the pure imagination and, thus, a very rare thing indeed at such a trade show. And, without doubt, it also gave architects and interior designers ideas of how a room or building might be lit in new and special ways. Whether this was enough for the crowds in Shanghai was another matter.

MAXXI

ZAHA HADID 2009 ROME, ITALY

The drawings for this undeniably exciting art gallery for the twenty-first-century – XXI are the Roman numerals for 21 – looked like a cross between a surreal motorway inter-section overlain with a gigantic and fiendishly complex wiring diagram. The end result is an architectural adventure that divided critics. There were those who thrilled to this mind-stretching, and structurally dynamic gallery and those who thought the architecture was altogether too dominant. How would art find its proper place in such powerful and provocative architecture? But, the truth was that the gallery had been founded, quite deliberately, with no permanent collection and the on the premise that no one knew quite what the art of the new century would bring; the building, then, was a kind of magnet, drawing attention to both itself and to what might happen or be seen inside it. There are moments here where walls become floors and even threaten to become ceilings, diving and curving like bobsleigh tracks. Hadid said she wanted the building's concrete curves to "unwind like a ribbon in space". From the outside, though, the building is remarkably modest, insinuating itself almost politely in an old military barracks square in the Flaminio district of Rome. The architect's firepower has been reserved for the interior, at once futuristic and yet also Baroque, the dramatic, sculptural style created and nurtured in Rome in the seventeenth century. Stairways weave their way theatrically through the building, vanishing mysteriously into its far recesses. The sense of drama is palpable.

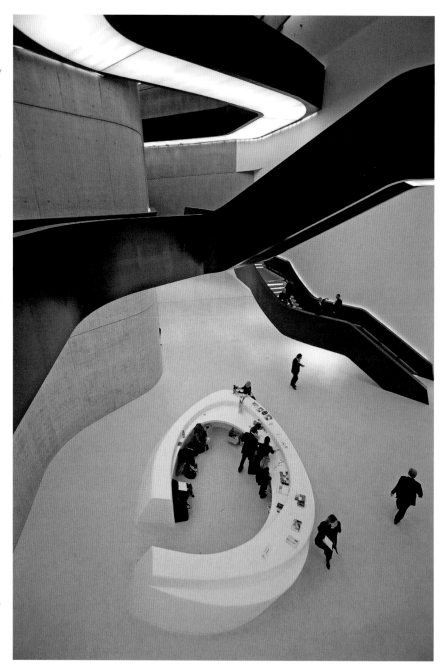

LONDON BRIDGE TOWER

RENZO PIANO BUILDING WORKSHOP, 2012 LONDON, ENGLAND

When completed, this sky-high "Shard of Glass" will be the tallest building in the European Union. In global terms, however, it will rank close to the bottom of the top 50, such is the rush to build as high as possible as developing economies flex their new found financial muscle and political prowess. The tower will rise above London Bridge station across the River Thames from the City of London. It will dominate views of the City and central London from most viewpoints. At 310 metres (1,017 ft) high, it will boast 72 floors given over to shops, flats, offices, a hotel and a public viewing gallery. The tower, a concrete-and-steel structure sheathed from top to toe in glass has been developed by Irvine Sellar, best known before his association with Renzo Piano for his Carnaby Street shop selling flared trousers and floral-patterned shirts in the late 1960s. Renzo Piano says his design was inspired by the spires of the London skyline painted by the Venetian artist, Canaletto, and by the sailing masts that were such a notable feature of the River Thames centuries ago. But, whereas the spires of Canaletto's London rose in the service of God, the "Shard" is a paeon in praise of Mammon. And, yet, as the god of the City of London has probably always been Mammon – London was founded by the Romans first and foremost as a trading city – perhaps Renzo Piano's epic tower belongs here as much as any church spire.

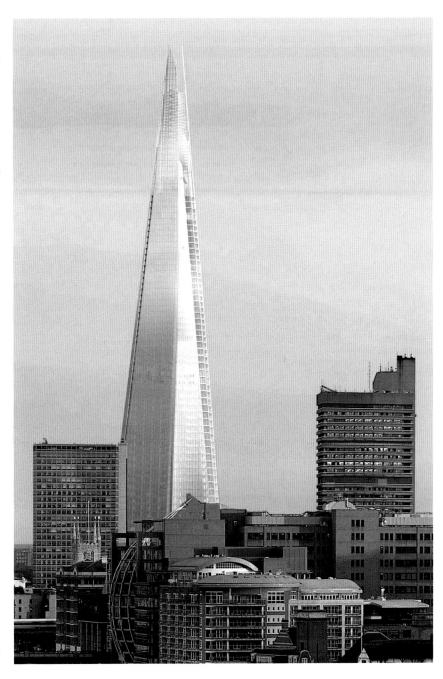

INDEX

PICTURE CREDITS

The publishers would like to thank the following sources for their kind permission to reproduce the pictures in this book:

Alvar Aalto Museum: /M.Holma: 188; /M.Kapanen: 211
Alamy: /AfriPics.com: 472; /Construction Photography: 465; /Falkensteinfoto: 464; /Chris Laurens: 305; /MARKA: 471; /View Pictures Ltd: 133; /Rod Williams: 355
AKG London: 5tr, 34, 50, 53, 54, 85, 87, 428, 437; /Hilbich: 108
Arcaid: /Alex Bartel: 52, 71, 79, 111; /Richard Bryant: 4br, 5bl, 6, 8, 9, 18, 27, 28, 74, 76, 80, 102, 106, 194, 246, 259, 260, 272, 274, 275, 276, 277, 280, 281, 283, 285, 289, 291, 293, 295, 296, 317, 325, 327, 331, 335, 338, 341, 343, 345, 348, 349, 374, 386, 393, 394, 395, 396, 399, 401; /Stephen Buzas: 110; /David Churchill: 65, 122, 192; /Niall Clutton: 334; /Peter Cook: 284; /Stephane Couturier, Archipress: 340; /Nick Dawe: 182, 193; /Colin Dixon: 278; /Malcolm Dixon: 101t; /Barry Edwards: 248; /Richard Einzig: 247, 266; /Mark Fiennes: 25bl, 44, 90, 198, 309, 318; /Scott Francis: 172, 365; /Scott Francis/Esto: 196; /Derek Gale: 25r, 162, 238, 291, 388, 390; /Chris Gascoigne: 191; /Dennis Gilbert: 145, 237, 344; /Martine Hamilton Knight: 135; /Michael Halberstadt: 186; /Steve Hall/Hedrich Blessing: 470; /Martine Hamilton Knight: 187, 342; /Martin Jones: 235; /Ian Lambot: 402; /Lucinda Lambton: 11, 15; /John Edward Linden: 4tr, 4bl, 33, 43, 73, 288, 346, 397, 400; /Joe Low: 68; /Bill Maris: 205; /Peter Mauss/Esto: 323; /James Neal: 83; /Robert O'Dea: 72r; /Paul Raftery: 2, 3, 75, 101b, 146, 346, 398; /Ezra Stoller/Esto: 104, 203, 214, 223, 251, 265, 273, 383; /Natalie Tepper: 177, 208, 242, 333; /Richard Waite: 59, 190, 329, 336
Architectural Review: 163
24H Architecture: 131
Artur Architekurbilder Agentur: /Roland Halbe: 411, 457
Architectural Association: 225, 363; /Archigram: 5br, 439, 440; /Valerie Bennett: 30, 152; /Stephan Buerger: 220; /Alan Chandler: 157, 161; /G.Clarke: 210; /Peter Cook: 24, 324; /Sandra Denicke: 175; /Taylor Galyean: 313; /Gardner/Halls: 95, 180; /John T Hansell: 213; /Seki Hirano: 112; /Peter Jeffree: 197; /Philip Keirle: 77; /Rik Nijs: 93; /Andrew Mincyin: 321; /S.Mintz: 96; /Michael Pattrick: 212; /Tim Street-Porter: 105; /David Smith: 268; /D.Tinero: 226; /Bob Vickery: 254; /Dennis Wheatley: 267, 376; /Tony Weller: 391; /Nathan Wilcock: 158; /Peter Willis: 252; /F.R.Yerbury: 168, 174
Arup: /Roland Reinhardy: 124
ASAP: /Bastin & Evrard: 13, 84
Bearth & Deplazes Architekten AG: 414
Behnisch & Partner: 279
Bennetts Associates Architects: /Peter Cook: 290
Bildarchiv Preussischer Kulterbesitz: 78, 82, 113, 153, 176

Maria Ida Biggi: 320
De Bijenkorf bv: 183
Helene Binet: 287, 301, 420, 460
Jan Bitter Fotografie: 455
Peter Blundell Jones: 86, 167
Ricardo Bofill/Taller de Arquitectura: 62, 63
Mario Botta Architetto: /Enrico Cano: 444
Branson Coates: 337, 350
Archivio Storico Breda: 98
British Cement Association: 366
William P. Bruder Architect: 118
Buckminster Fuller: 362, 373
Carson Pirie & Scott: 147
Castelvecchio Museum: /Maurizio Brenzoni: 233
Catedra Gaudi Barcelona: 81
Central Milton Keynes Shopping Management Company Ltd: 429
Martin Charles: 41, 45, 56, 155, 181
Chicago Historical Society: 217; /Hedrich-Blessing: 207, 243
City of Newcastle upon Tyne Council: 264
Prunella Clough/Irongate Studios: 173
Coop Himmelblau: /Gerald Zugmann: 5tl, 339
Corbis Images: /Paul Almasy: 238, 250; /Peter Aprahamian: 185; /Dave Bartruff: 107; /Bettmann: 38, 358; /James PBlair: 57; /Stephanie Colasanti: 311; /Alessandro Di Meo/epa: 474; /John Dakers/Eye Ubiquitous: 384; /epa: 475; /Macduff Everton: 29, 431; /Eye Ubiquitous: 227; /Rufus F.Folkks: 443; /David Forman/Eye Ubiquitous: 103; /Lynn Goldsmith:199; /Tim Griffith/Arcaid: 422; /Paul Hardy: 452; /Robert Holmes: 244; /Angelo Hornak: 231; /Jeremy Horner: 35; /Hulton-Deutsch Collection: 51; /Harold A. Jahn/Viennaslide Photoagency: 20; /Andrea Jemolo: 170; /Robert Landau: 352; /James Leynse: 303; /Franz-Marc Frei: 409, 420; /Michael St.Maur Sheil: 425/Kelly-Mooney Photography: 312; /Charles & Josette Lenars: 314; /Philippa Lewis/Edifice: 256; /Peter Macdiarmid/Reuters: 298; /Dennis Marsico: 258; /Kevin R. Morris: 55; /Michael Nicholson: 171; /Kai Pfaffenbach/Reuters: 415; /Proehl Studios: 467; /Christian Richters/VIEW: 137; /Paul Thompson/Eye Ubiquitous: 114; /UPI: 36; /Richard Waite/Arcaid: 448; /Patrick Ward: 322; /Nik Wheeler: 316; /Michael S.Yamashita: 58, 297
Maria Elisa Costa: 201
Country Life Picture Library: 16, 19, 47
Cuban Embassy: 106
James Davies Travel Photography: 115
Michael Denancé: 462
DMVA Architects. www.dmva-architecten.be: 423
The Earth Centre: 300
Empics: /AP/Paulo Duarte: 458
English Partnerships: 433
Aldo Van Eyck: 228
Eye Ubiquitous: /Frank Leather: 61; /P Thompson: 307 Fiat UK Ltd: 359
First Garden City Heritage Museum, Letchworth: 426t

Fondation Maeght: /Claude Gaspari: 236
From the Collections of Henry Ford Museum & Greenfield Village: 361
Foreign Office Architects: /Satoru Mishima: 449
Foster & Partners: 299, 378, 403; /Nigel Young: 419
Fundación Alejandro de la Sota: 215
Future Systems: 404
Roberto Gabriele: 49
Getty Images: 138; /AFP: 142, 354, 469; /Allsport/D Rogers: 405; /Hulton Archive: 371, 372; /Rudi Sebastian: 141;
J. Glancey: 37, 40, 42, 66, 369, 426b
Glasgow School of Art Collection, endpapers
Ronald Grant Archive: 357
Michael Graves Architects: 326, 328
Nicholas Grimshaw & Partners: 406
W.G. Habel: 88
Zaha Hadid: 441
Robert Harding Picture Library: 22, 26, 60, 241, 377, 364, 379
Hartill Art Associates: 159, 166, 268
Zvi Hecker: 234
Hedrich Blessing: 206
Adriano Heitmann Fotografo: 255
Eduard Hueber: 263
Timothy Hursley: 120
Van Heyningen & Haward Architects: /MGI: 127
The Image Bank: 1, 94, 116, 245, 308
Kenzo Tange Associates: /Yasuhiro Ishimoto: 219; /Osamu Murai: 375, 380
Kida Katsuhisa: 121
Luuk Kramer Fotografie:132
Leon Krier: 430
Lucien Kroll: 262
Akademie Der Kunste: 184
Sir Denys Lasdun: 230
Geleta Laszlo: 119
Daniele De Lonti: 330
Duccio Malagamba Fotografía de Arquitectura SL: 130, 304, 456
Makona Architectural Studio: 119, 125
London Metropolitan Archives: 382
Office for Metropolitan Architecture: 432
Millennium Jason Shenai: 109; /Richard Glover: 298, 385
Museo Nationale de Arte Romano, Merida: 64
Silvia Zenobio Nascimento: 200
National Film Archive: 438
Michael Nicholson: 4tl, 21
Novosti (London): 381
Frank Den Oudsten: 154
PA News: /Andrew Stuart: 407
Panos Pictures: /Daniel O'Leary: 221
Gustav Peichl: 373
Photolibrary: /Inigo Bujedo Aguirre/View Pictures: 473; /Eastphoto: 468; /Paul Felix: 143; /Craig Holmes/Loop Images: 297; /Christian Kober: 466; /Rudi Sebastian: 134; /Rob Taylor/Loop Images: 136
Gio Ponti Photo Archives: 212
Carlo Pozzoni: 195

Jean Christophe Pratt: 218
Press Association Images: /Chris Radburn/PA Archive: 421
Private Collection: 261
Andrew Putler: 351
RCHME: /Peter Behrens: 188
Rag Rewal Architects: 450
RIBA: 12, 14, 17, 31, 46, 48, 89, 97, 148, 149, 150, 151, 165, 169, 179, 209, 239, 319, 360, 367, 368, 386, 427, 436
Christian Richter: 459
The Royal Collection©2005, Her Majesty Queen Elizabeth II: 69
Yutaka Saito: 100
Science Photo Library: /NASA: 435
Scotland In Focus: /A.G. Firth: 92
Shokokusha Co: 229
Julius Shulman: 99, 164, 194, 202, 204, 222
Henry Pierre Schultz Fotografie: 123
Claudio Silvestrin: 294
John Simpson & Partners: 67
SITE: 315
Skidmore, Owings & Merrill LLP: 392; / Wolfgang Hoyt: 332
Jose de la Sota: 232
South African High Commission: 39
Spherovision: 418
Margherita Spiluttini: 178
Tim Street-Porter: 7, 156, 216, 249
Sutherland Hussey Architects: /Peter Mackinven: 126
Hisao Suzuki Fotografo: 257
Tempere Tourist Office: 23
Curtis Trent: 253
TRH Pictures: 370
Tadao Ando Architects & Associates: 117, 270, 282, 286
Ticino Turismo: 271
Marco Verona: 91
View Pictures: /Michael Betts: 412; /Dennis Gilbert: 353, 448, 463; /Richard Glover: 302; /Roland Halbe/Artur: 128; /Nick Hufton: 446; /Hufton & Crow: 453; Peter Mackinven: 451; /John Maclean: 445; /Raf Makda: 454; /Christian Michel: 408; /Paul Raftery: 447; /Christian Richters: 139; /Edmund Summer: 129, 140, 413, 417; /Nathan Willock: 410
Roger-Viollet: 160
Welsh Assembly Government: /Alex Skibinski: 461
Westminster Cathedral, The Administrator : 72bl

Special thanks to Lynne Bryant, James Neal and Lucy Waitt at Arcaid; Deborah Fioravanti and everyone who kindly supplied images for this book. Every effort has been made to acknowledge correctly and contact the source and copyright holder of each picture, and Carlton Books Limited apologizes for any unintentional errors or omissions which will be corrected in future editions of this book.